CITYSCAPES OF NEW ORLEANS

CITYSCAPES OF NEW ORLEANS

RICHARD CAMPANELLA

LOUISIANA STATE UNIVERSITY PRESS
BATON ROUGE

Published by Louisiana State University Press
Copyright © 2017 by Louisiana State University Press
All rights reserved
Manufactured in the United States of America
First printing

DESIGNER: Michelle A. Neustrom
TYPEFACES: Whitman, text; Adagio, display
PRINTER AND BINDER: Sheridan Books, Inc.

LIBRARY OF CONGRESS CATALOGING-IN-PUBLICATION DATA

Names: Campanella, Richard, author.
Title: Cityscapes of New Orleans / Richard Campanella.
Description: Baton Rouge : Louisiana State University Press, [2017] | Includes bibliographical
    references.
Identifiers: LCCN 2017008826| ISBN 978-0-8071-6833-2 (cloth : alk. paper) | ISBN 978-0-
    8071-6834-9 (pdf) | ISBN 978-0-8071-6835-6 (epub)
Subjects: LCSH: New Orleans (La.)—History. | New Orleans (La.)—Description and travel. |
    Neighborhoods—Louisiana—New Orleans—History. | Architecture—Louisiana—
    New Orleans—History. | New Orleans (La.)—Geography.
Classification: LCC F379.N557 C239 2017 | DDC 976.3/35—dc23
LC record available at https://lccn.loc.gov/2017008826

For Marina and Jason

All human landscape has cultural meaning—
no matter how ordinary. . . .
All our cultural warts and blemishes are there,
and our glories too.

    —PEIRCE F. LEWIS, "Axioms of the Landscape," 1976

CONTENTS

CONTENTS

URBAN GEOGRAPHIES

REGIONAL GEOGRAPHIES

DISASTER AND RECOVERY

CONTENTS

PREFACE

"The cultural landscape," wrote geographer Carl O. Sauer in 1925, "is fashioned out of a natural landscape by a cultural group. Culture is the agent, the natural area is the medium, the cultural landscape is the result." A cityscape, then, is the urban corollary of a cultural landscape, the *tout ensemble* of all that constitutes a city: its underlying natural landscape, its biota and water, its built environment fashioned by various human agents and their social settlement patterns, its infrastructure and idiosyncrasies. A cityscape is the unique visible signature of the multifarious expressions of urban geography.

As each generation inscribes its projects and priorities into urban space, it renders spatial circumstances to which succeeding generations may conform—or transform. The results build up anew all around us, but rarely do they completely erase their antecedents. A trained eye can thus "read" a cityscape and, with the help of archival documents and other sources, extract from it stories about our past, which in turn help explain the present and guide the future.

Reading cityscapes lets you see a whole different world. It brings the past to life, and makes the banal extraordinary. An off-plumb driveway on Royal Street— what could be more mundane?—suddenly couldn't be more interesting once you understand it traces precisely the geometry of an old French colonial fort. That confusingly juxtaposed street grid in the Seventh Ward becomes enchanting when you realize it reflects plantation lines surveyed in 1720. That long-ago deluge in 1849 might seem irrelevant until you understand policies enacted in its aftermath helped paved the way for the complete transformation of the deltaic plain—and New Orleans's future flood risk.

Once you "see" these stories in the cityscape, you can't help but want to share them, and that's why I compiled this book. *Cityscapes of New Orleans* is a collection of analytical essays on the spatial dimensions of the Crescent City, a metropolis whose very sobriquet exudes geography. It has one primary goal, and that is spatial explanation—elucidating the *why* behind the *where*. It explains the morphology of the metropolis, including street grids, parcel lines, and municipal systems;

the character and distribution of its peoples, neighborhoods, cultures, and economies; the origins of its architecture and fate of its prominent buildings; the challenges of its urban environment and trauma of its disasters; and the complex relationship it maintains with the rest of the nation and world.

New Orleans has intrigued me since my early childhood (sight unseen, growing up in Brooklyn, New York), and has engrossed and perplexed me for the twenty-plus years I've been studying it. That interest has produced nine prior books and hundreds of articles, some of which appear in this volume in the form of essays (sans the apparatus of footnotes and references, which may be found in my academic work). The essays, though grouped thematically, are self-standing and may be read in any sequence, as this book pretends to be neither a traditional chronology nor a comprehensive history of the city. Rather, it is a reader intended for those who know and love the city; a certain base knowledge of the metropolis is presumed but not crucial. The essays are adaptations of my contributions to three publications over the past six years, and are presented here with their permission: NOLA.com/ *The Times-Picayune,* where I have a monthly "Cityscapes" column; *Preservation in Print,* to which I contribute monthly articles; and *Louisiana Cultural Vistas,* the quarterly publication of the Louisiana Endowment of the Humanities, where I have a column named "Geographer's Space."

I am indebted to a number of individuals and institutions in the making of *Cityscapes of New Orleans.* First and foremost, I thank my wife Marina Campanella and son Jason Campanella for their love and support. I gratefully acknowledge the Tulane University School of Architecture and Dean Kenneth Schwartz for the academic position which enables me to conduct this research, and to the New Orleans Center for the Gulf South, directed by Rebecca Snedeker, where I am a Monroe Fellow.

Deep gratitude goes to Susan Langenhennig, editor of the InsideOut section of NOLA.com/*The Times-Picayune,* who cold-called me in 2013 with an invitation to be a contributing writer for New Orleans's oldest and largest newspaper. Susan and I agreed to name the column "Cityscapes," which has since become a popular monthly feature, and is paired with a WWNO radio interview of me by journalist Eve Troeh. This volume would not have happened without Susan and her editing and production skills making "Cityscapes" possible. I also thank former editor-in-chief of NOLA.com/*The Times-Picayune* Jim Amoss for his support and permission to include the essays in this volume, and extend my appreciation to current editor and vice-president of content Mark Lorando and president of NOLA Media Group Tim Williamson as well.

Similarly, I am indebted to Danielle Del Sol and the late Mary Fitzpatrick of the Preservation Resource Center, editors of *Preservation in Print*, who extended a similar invitation to me in 2012, and to the staff of the Louisiana Endowment for the Humanities, including Brian Boyles and Miranda Restovic as well as former editors David Johnson and Michael Sartisky, for my "Geographer's Space" column in *Louisiana Cultural Vistas*. I have been writing for all three periodicals ever since, and it has been a rewarding experience. Additional thanks go to editors Nancy Levinson of *Places Journal*, Errol Laborde of *New Orleans Magazine*, and Joel Kotkin of *New Geography*, all of whom have published articles of mine and granted permission for their inclusion in this volume.

I also wish to thank the staff at Louisiana State University Press, namely Director MaryKatherine Callaway, Executive Editor Rand Dotson, and Senior Editor Catherine L. Kadair, as well as freelance editor Stan Ivester.

And of course, I am most indebted to the city and people of New Orleans, who fashioned these splendid cityscapes and have kept me busy ever since.

PEOPLE, PATTERNS, AND PLACE

A GLORIOUS MESS
A Perceptual History of New Orleans Neighborhoods

We allow for a certain level of ambiguity when we speak of geographical regions. References to "the South," "the West," and "the Midwest," for example, come with the understanding that these regions, unlike states, have no precise or official borders. We call the subregions therein the "Deep South," "Rockies," and "Great Plains," assured that listeners share our mental maps, even if they might outline and label them differently.

It's an enriching ambiguity, one that is historically, geographically, and culturally accurate *on account* of its imprecision, rather than despite it. (Accuracy and precision are not synonymous.) Regions are largely perceptual, and therefore imprecise, and while many do embody clear geophysical or cultural distinctions—the Sonoran Desert or the Acadian Triangle, for example—their morphologies are nonetheless subject to the vicissitudes of human discernment, and limn discordant shapes. Ask ten Americans to delineate "the South," for instance, and you'll get ten different maps, some including Missouri, others slicing Texas in half, still others emphatically lopping off the Florida peninsula. None are precise, yet all are accurate. It's a fascinating, glorious mess.

So too New Orleans neighborhoods—until recently. For two centuries, neighborhood identity emerged from bottom-up awareness rather than top-down proclamation, and mental maps of the city formed soft, loose patterns that transformed over time. Modern city planning has endeavored to "harden" these distinctions in the interest of municipal order—at the expense, I contend, of local cultural expressiveness.

But more on that later. First, let us recount how New Orleanians recognized neighborhoods in times past. It's not my intent here to present a standard developmental history of New Orleans; rather, I hope to capture the evolution of residents' spatial perceptions.

Neighborhood Perception by Bourg and Faubourg

We'll start with New Orleans's original neighborhood, today's French Quarter, which Adrien de Pauger laid out in 1722. Pauger's plat certainly looks like a rigid *bourg* absent of any ambiguity, and in terms of the street layout, it was. But as a cityscape, early New Orleans had organic edges. Rear blocks remained forested in the early years, and most of the actual settlement clustered around the *place d'armes* and the Mississippi River. The urban fringes were barely distinguishable from the wilderness beyond the fortifications—which themselves were rather desultory, until a century later, when new blocks replaced them. Modern New Orleanians see those additions, today's 100 and 1300 blocks, to be "in" the French Quarter. Yet they were not in the original *bourg*, nor were any of the blocks riverside of what is now Decatur Street, which lay mostly in the river in the 1700s. To add more elasticity to our seemingly rigid grid, the 100 blocks today are outside the jurisdiction of the Vieux Carré Commission, the city agency charged with protecting the historic district, yet inside the state-legislated French Quarter Management District. Riverside areas and the 1300 blocks, meanwhile, fall within both jurisdictions. There was a time in the 1950s when parts of Royal and North Rampart were excluded from commission jurisdiction, only later to be reinstated. So where exactly is New Orleans's first neighborhood, this epitome of spatial order? And what shall we call it—the Vieux Carré? French Quarter? The Quarter? "Da quarters"? The one neighborhood that comes the closest to having clear boundaries and an official name has, in fact, neither.

Starting in 1788, New Orleanians developed a new neighborhood nomenclature: *faux bourg*, or faubourg—literally, "false town," which Spanish authorities translated as *suburbia*. The first inner suburb, Suburbio Santa Maria (Faubourg Ste. Marie, or St. Mary) was laid out immediately after the Good Friday Fire of 1788 to give the city new living space in what is now the Central Business District, or CBD. Seventeen years passed before another faubourg would form—and then they exploded, after Americanization in 1803.

Faubourg development occurred as a free-market response to New Orleans's burgeoning population and its need for living space, which gave owners of adjacent plantations an opportunity to make more money through urbanization than agriculture. One by one the planters subdivided their parcels, starting with the Faubourg Marigny in 1805. Within the next five years, streets would be laid out (in chronological order by their initial platting) in faubourgs named Delord, Duplantier, La Course, L'Annunciation, Plaisance, St. John, Tremé, Saulet (Solet), and des Religieuses—today's upper CBD, Lower Garden District, Tremé, and Bayou St. John.

It took many more years for these lots to be fully developed; many were used for working farms or pleasure gardens, or simply remained vacant. But as new houses slowly came into place, new faubourgs appeared downriver—Washington, Daunois, Montegut, Clouet, Montreuil, Cariby, and deLesseps, in today's Bywater,

1807–40s—as well as upriver and toward Bayou St. John, with the faubourgs Lafayette, Nouvelle Marigny and Franklin, Livaudais, Carrollton, Bouligny, Hurstville, Delassize, Greenville, Friburg, Bloomingdale, Hagan, Avart, St. Joseph, Rickerville, Burtheville, and Delachaise. By the Civil War, most of the crescent had been gridded with streets, and faubourgs predominated in the lexicon of place.

Neighborhood Perception by Physical and Human Geography

New Orleanians two hundred years ago used various other spatial references. Topography and shipping drew most human activity toward the Mississippi; ergo, areas closer to the river came to be perceived as the town's "front" while areas farther away, and topographically lower, came to be known as the "back-of-town," a phrase still heard today. Potable water needs and maritime activity imparted significance to the flow direction of the river, and New Orleanians internalized that "up"/"down" vector in their spatial orientation. Everyone knows that "upriver"/ "downriver," or "uptown"/"downtown," are the local equivalents of "west" and "east," but few may know that, before there was uptown and downtown (Americanisms imported from Manhattan), there was the upper and lower *banlieue*, the French term widely used to refer to the city's outskirts in the early 1800s. A carriage ride from the Old City to the upper banlieue would get you to the "Chapitoulas Coast," meaning the deepwater bend in the Mississippi around the present-day Orleans/Jefferson parish line. That indigenous word lent itself to the road accessing that area, a "T" having been added for the benefit of francophone tongues. This is today's Tchoupitoulas Street.

Keep going "up" and you'd reach Cannes Brule ("Burnt Cane"), which referred to the present-day Old Town Kenner area. Continue upriver and you'd be on what Abraham Lincoln called Louisiana's "Sugar Coast," what we now call the River Road region.

The lowlands behind the city were known as "the woods," "the swamp," "the backswamp," *la ciprière,* or, if marshy rather than forested, *prairies tremblantes,* for the way the mucky gumbo shifted and consolidated. The swamps were transected by topographic ridges followed by important roads; the one that wended westward got named for its numerous little farms and dairies—*metairie*—whereas the eastern ridge, which boasted a number of estates outside of New Orleans proper, gained the name of a comparable estate outside Paris—"Chantilly," our Gentilly.

As that ridge continued to the eastern marshes, where for reasons unknown it gained the name Chef Menteur ("Big Liar"), its scrubby tide-washed vegetation

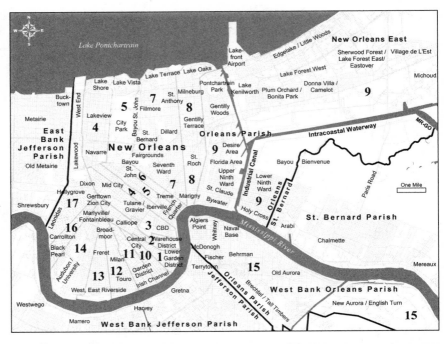

Official city neighborhoods and wards (numbers) of New Orleans, plus communities in adjacent parishes. *Map by Richard Campanella.*

earned it the French name Petit Bois—today's Little Woods neighborhood. Later, when railroads rimmed what is now New Orleans East, nomenclature derived from train stations, many of which were adjoined by tiny enclaves of fishermen, hunters, gardeners, and orchard-growers—places with names like Seabrook, Citrus, Edge Lake, South Point, Lee, Micheaud (Michoud), an outpost called Chef Menteur by Fort Macomb, and a deep channel (Rigolets) by Fort Pike. Half these names persist in the lexicon today, though not necessarily at the same spots— testimony to the fluidity and caprice of place identity.

Ethnic settlement patterns deeply informed antebellum neighborhood perceptions. The francophone Creole population generally resided in the lower half of the metropolis, namely the French Quarter, Bayou Road toward Bayou St. John, faubourgs Tremé and Marigny and those of the lower banlieue. The incoming anglophone American population generally preferred the Faubourg St. Mary (dubbed the "American sector" or "American quarter") and the faubourgs of the upper banlieue. Throughout both banlieues as well as the back-of-town settled large numbers of immigrants, mostly Irish and German, so much so that upper riverfront areas came to be known as the "Irish Channel" while areas downriver were nicknamed "Little Saxony" and "Soxahaus." All three, however, could have swapped monikers, on account of their thorough ethnic intermixing. Smaller numbers of newcomers from myriad other states and nations also co-resided, such that there was no one hegemonic culture—but instead two predominating ones, Creole and Anglo.

Neighborhood Perception by Municipalities, Municipal Districts, Wards, and Ethnic Enclaves

Creole and Anglo rivalry led to neighborhood enmity and ultimately to economic and political discord. Either reconciliation or violence could have won the day; instead, a rather ungainly spatial solution was devised, and in 1836 New Orleans divided itself into three semiautonomous "municipalities," each with its own governmental apparatus ostensibly united under a single mayor and general council. For the next sixteen years, "neighborhoods" in New Orleans meant municipalities—even as faubourgs, banlieues, and sundry other spatial allusions flew about.

Because Canal Street generally separated Anglo and Creole residences, that corridor became the logical dividing line for the two new municipalities in which each ethnicity dominated. The mostly francophone Creole area from Canal to Esplanade was labeled the First Municipality, and the mostly anglophone American area from Canal to Felicity (New Orleans's upper limit at the time) became the Second Municipality. Because Esplanade divided the Creole roughly evenly, that prominent thoroughfare became the line between the First and Third municipalities. Farthest from the urban core, the Third Municipality found itself on the losing end of most local maneuverings. Wags dubbed it "The Poor Third," "The Dirty Third," and, at its sardonic best, "The Glorious Third."

The grossly inefficient municipality system was abandoned in 1852, after which another wave of spatialization ensued. It entailed the renaming of the old First Municipality as the Second Municipal District and the Second Municipality as the First Municipal District, while the Third remained the Third. It also added a Fourth Municipal District by annexing the former Faubourg Lafayette, hitherto a separate city in Jefferson Parish, now today's Garden District and Irish Channel.

The 1852 reunification also devised a new ward system, which survives today as a premier modern spatial reference—but, alas, not the only one. Because Felicity Street had previously marked the Jefferson/Orleans parish line, the new wards were enumerated starting from Felicity (the First Ward) and continuing downriver to the St. Bernard Parish line. Each ward extended from the front of town to the backswamp. To equalize populations, the high-density French Quarter was sliced into the narrowest wards—the Fourth, Fifth, and Sixth—while lower-density faubourgs were sized broader. The lowermost banlieue was so vacant that a single mega-ward, the Ninth, enveloped the entire expanse, which explains why Bywater and the wild marshes of the Rigolets share the same ward today. City fathers then swung around above Felicity and sliced newly annexed Lafayette into wards 10 and 11. The enumeration continued upriver as more Jefferson Parish communities merged with New Orleans: Jefferson City became wards 12, 13, and 14 (aka the Sixth Municipal District) in 1870, shortly after Algiers on the West Bank (often called the "right bank" by mariners) was annexed as Ward 15—or the Fifth Municipal District. Upriver expansion concluded when New Orleans annexed Carrollton in 1874, which became wards 16 and 17—aka the Seventh Municipal District. As development later spread toward the lake into today's Lakeview and Gentilly, the circa-1852 spatial divisions emanating from the curvaceous river were extended rather awkwardly to converge against the smooth lakeshore.

The modern-day map of New Orleans's municipal districts and wards, unchanged since the 1880s, thus reflects the city's piecemeal growth since 1852. In a capricious way, some units, such as the Seventh Ward and Ninth Ward, found their way into the modern neighborhood vernacular, while others did so among some people, or during certain times, or not at all.

If districts and wards didn't work, residents used an extemporized vocabulary of pathways, nodes, and landmarks to reference space. "Magazine Street" or "Esplanade," for example, might be used not just to refer to those arteries but for the swath of blocks paralleling them. Public markets like the Poydras or St. Mary, churches like St. Teresa's or "the Italian Church," business clusters such as "the cotton district" or "the sugar landing," and salient features like "the Old Shot Tower" or "the Fairgrounds" formed a spatial language as universally understood as it was inexactly delineated. Ethnic enclaves were also used: there was "the Jewish neighborhood" along Dryades Street, and "the Greek neighborhood" around North Dorgenois—which others thought of as "the Creole area" or, alternately, as the Sixth and Seventh wards. There was "Chinatown" around Tulane and South Rampart, which some folks called the "Third Ward" and others, including Louis Armstrong, called the "back o' town." And there was Little Palermo, the mostly Sicilian parts of the Fifth and Sixth wards, which could just as well be called the lower French Quarter—also home to a Filipino enclave and a fair number of aging francophones. As for Vieux Carré, that term had died out with the French language, but was revived in the 1910s by the nascent tourism industry and preservation movement.

Well into the twentieth century, neighborhood identity in New Orleans remained flexible and nebulous. To be sure, some areas did self-identify clearly and consistently in ways we would recognize today; people spoke regularly of "Carrollton," "Algiers," or "the Garden District," and fought over land use and nuisances— though not as much as today, because property value did not constitute as large a portion of household equity. But there were far fewer neighborhood associations and almost no agreement, indeed hardly any debate, about exact neighborhood limits and names.

The Hardening of Neighborhood Identity

This began to change with the advent of professional planning in the 1920s. American cities had become ever more complex and contentious by the new century, and homeowners vexed over the potential impact of an unwanted neighbor on property values. Rather than leaving the fate of cities to market forces and reactionary ordinances, a new generation of urban planners began to proactively manage urban growth and pre-zone potentially antagonistic land uses (not to mention residential occupancy by peoples of different races and lower classes) to minimize conflict, maximize property values, and increase real estate taxes. They brought science to the task, in the form of data analysis, which required precise lines and official names on maps. You cannot count how many people live in Gentilly, for example, unless you demarcate a certain space and declare it unequivocally to be Gentilly.

The first full attempt at planner-driven neighborhood delineation appeared in the 1929 *Handbook to Comprehensive Zone Law*. Its compilers borrowed lines devised by the U.S. Census Bureau as part of its nationwide experiment to aggregate population data at finer levels than the wards previously used. These early "census tracts" were adopted by the City Planning and Zoning Commission, which called them "districts" and used them for cartographic and planning purposes starting in the 1930s. The Census Bureau in Washington, meanwhile, officially adopted census tracts for the 1940 Census, making those semi-arbitrary puzzle pieces increasingly useful for local planners.

Hardly, however, did they reach the masses, and residents of mid-century

New Orleans continued to spatialize their city in their own vernacular ways. As evidence, consider Pontchartrain Beach's "Neighborhood Night" beauty contests of the late 1940s and early 1950s. The racially segregated amusement park's management designated special nights for a cross-section of white middle-class neighborhoods throughout the metro area, using the sobriquets Gentilly, Freret Street, Magazine Street, Carrollton, Broadmoor, Metairie, Bywater, and Westside—that is, Algiers and Gretna. The nomenclature denotes the influence of historical tradition, subdivision names, principal arteries and their merchant associations' names, and even telephone exchanges (BYwater).

Beauty contests can endure spatial imprecision; bureaucracy cannot. The next major official effort to harden New Orleans neighborhoods came during the 1960s–70s, when initiatives traceable to President Lyndon B. Johnson's Model Cities Program manifested themselves in the 1974 Housing and Community Development Act. Foreseeing a need to target Community Development Block Grant funds slated to be allocated by the Development Act, the U.S. Department of Housing and Urban Development partnered with Mayor Moon Landrieu's Office of Policy Planning (OPP) and the New Orleans–based Curtis and Davis Architects to delineate and name citywide "planning areas." Toward this end, OPP pollster Allen Rosenzweig surveyed residents on issues of quality-of-life and needs, as well as "the name they used to describe the neighborhood where they lived," as Rosenzweig recounted in a recent email to me. He and his colleagues in City Hall passed the results to Curtis and Davis, which proceeded to delineate and name 73 "planning areas" from the survey responses. Some areas, like Carrollton and Algiers, formed consensuses and handily won selection as official names, as did modern tract-housing subdivisions like Pontchartrain Park and Plum Orchard, which had been branded since inception. But many older and less-famous areas had a plurality of folk monikers, in which case the team either revived historical names or christened their own. "Black Pearl," for example, was coined by the chief OPP planner, Marion Greenup, and/or Curtis and Davis planning team member Pat Watt in recognition of a hitherto-unnamed uptown riverfront area's predominantly African American population through which ran a street named Pearl. (Some now call that neighborhood Uptown Triangle.) Areas that simply defied nomenclature were named arbitrarily: the blocks bounded by La Salle, Napoleon, Magazine, and Jefferson, for example, were officially called "Uptown," which is a little like renaming Wyoming "The West." It was surrounded by neighborhoods declared to be "Milan," "Touro," "West Riverside," "Audubon/University," and "Freret"—likely news to most of their residents.

The new neighborhood map appeared in Curtis and Davis's widely distributed *New Orleans Housing and Neighborhood Preservation Study* of 1974. The OPP, however, hesitated to accept the map because it "found that data could not be collected in the neighborhood units proposed by Curtis and Davis" due to their nonalignment with U.S. Census Bureau tracts. So the OPP and the City Planning Commission in 1975 redefined Curtis and Davis's 73 units, based, according to city documents, on "historical definition, natural barriers, major arteries, and socio-economic homogeneity." What resulted were 87 modified neighborhoods. When another citizen survey was added to the mix in 1977 and the process repeated, over a hundred neighborhoods resulted. According to a 1981 *DAU Report*, "a compromise set of 70 neighborhoods was derived . . . by taking the 'best set' [from previous versions] and moving boundaries to the closest census tract lines" of the 1980 Census. Those latest modifications rendered, among other things, a neighborhood dubbed Country Club/Dixon ("North Hollygrove") being separated from "Lakewood South," and the conflation and/or distinction of various housing projects with adjacent areas. OPP planner Darlene Walk, who is credited with many of the neighborhood boundaries, crunched raw census data and produced scores of demographic pamphlets organized by the new neighborhood shapes and names, thus concretizing them. Her *Neighborhood Profiles* publications, valuable synopses of human geography from an era when data were difficult to tabulate and distribute, are the ancestors of the Web-based compendia we have at our fingertips today.

A perusal of city planning documents from the 1970s to 1980s shows a progression of neighborhood iterations, from as few as 62 to as many as 104 units, their boundaries and names shifting in an irreconcilable dance between ad-hoc localism and rigid officialdom. Eventually the number settled to the 73 we have today, coincidentally the same total Curtis and Davis enumerated forty years ago. Each one is a carefully drawn polygon with straight lines and measured angles, with zero ambiguity, just as a scientist would want. As if to illustrate the empiricist's conviction that neighborhoods are the products of hard numerical data rather than soft human perception, one map in a 1982 OPP report was titled "Major Neighborhood Boundary Changes *Caused by* 1980 Census Tract Definitions" (emphasis added), a revelation that might give pause to a modern-day cultural advocate who might have presumed official neighborhood units to be organic in their provenance and indisputable in their veracity.

This era also saw the rise of the preservation movement, which in its quest to draw attention to impending demolitions and heavy-handed development, endeavored to rebrand decaying old neighborhoods. "Few people ever heard of the Lower Garden District," wrote one *Times-Picayune* reporter in 1974, "until somebody said they were going to build a bridge there." When that proposed span was contemplated instead for Press Street, it became clear that "a lot of people who live in New Orleans have no concept of where Press Street is, and a lot more people have never heard of 'Bywater.'" After architectural historians adopted "Lower Garden District" (a term coined extemporaneously by preservationist Samuel Wilson Jr. while giving a walking tour of the area in the early 1960s) as the title of the first volume of the *New Orleans Architecture* series, the public came to value anew that Coliseum Square area. Later volumes had a similar effect on the "American Sector," "The Creole Faubourgs," and "Faubourg Tremé and the Bayou Road." Now eight volumes strong, that influential series has helped revive historical faubourg names, some of which have found their way onto the official map—to the delight of real estate agents, who benefited from the subsequent rise of property values. Here and elsewhere, historic renovation and gentrification walk hand-in-hand with neighborhood name changes, and social advocates for those who find themselves at the wrong end of the transformations have come to view neighborhood rebranding as a sinister harbinger of rising rents and possible displacement.

Another favorite preservationist tool is the historic district. "National register districts" from the U.S. Department of the Interior influence neighborhood perceptions in part because the Preservation Resource Center features them prominently in their maps and literature. Each usage reifies spatial perceptions of architectural value and historicity, even though the national register district lines rarely coincide with those of the 73 OPP/Curtis and Davis neighborhoods—or, for that matter, with local historic districts, which are overseen by the Historic District Landmarks Commission. Neighborhoods, no matter how we demarcate them, simply defy accord.

"The 73" nonetheless gained momentum with the growth of Geographic Information Systems (GIS) computer mapping software in the 1990s. GIS files of official neighborhoods from the City Planning Commission carried with them an ordained sense of legitimacy which won over many insiders and nearly all outsiders, among them journalists and researchers. This was particularly the case immediately after Hurricane Katrina, when legions of confused newcomers seeking spatial clarity in the unfathomable city found them in the 73, and embraced them unquestioningly. Recovery planners went further and aggregated them into 13 new "planning districts" for the Unified New Orleans Plan, which are still used by the City Planning Commission today. Needless to say, neither the 73 nor the planning districts accord with municipal districts, wards, precincts, national historic register districts, local historical districts, police districts, or city council districts—which, by the way, were redrawn after the 2010 U.S. Census.

The 73 now circulate in GIS files downloaded freely over the Internet, and have been ingested into countless projects and theses and adopted by media, academia, and nonprofits. As for the public, newcomers love them; old-timers, not so much. "As a child of the '50s and '60s," wrote a perplexed Yvonne Hiller to a local newspaper, "all I ever heard about was uptown, downtown, Kenner, Metairie, and 'out by the lake.' Now I hear about Bywater, Carrollton, Gert town, etc." The 73 are here to stay, though they may well be modified again. And, frankly, they do a decent job of enabling analysts to aggregate and report large amounts of raw data in a readable fashion.

Official Neighborhoods: Some Problems

So what's the problem?

The problem is we read too much reality into "The 73." They originated from a technical need on the part of planners. But we've come to view them as cultural-geographical gospel, even as most New Orleanians would be at a loss to identify half of them, much less trace their outlines.

By privileging for the power of official maps, we've come to view neighborhoods not as the richly tenuous perceptual spaces emergent from the bottom up, but as doctrine ordained from the top down. We've over-empowered what are, for the most part, arbitrary polygons traceable originally to federal offices, and tossed out our own local awareness as ill-informed and erroneous.

Reading too much into the 73 perpetuates the notion that cities are the products of the authorities who manage them, and that space and place are best left to the professionals to inscribe with character. It accommodates the dubious philosophy that those at the top control society's narrative. It's the same dogma that, in other contexts, leads to the wearying insistence that there is only one correct way to pronounce "New Orleans," only one definition of "Creole," and only one valid telling of the city's history.

Official neighborhoods, arbitrary as they are, are nonetheless consequential because they drive statistical aggregations of everything from population to crime rates, real estate values, and recovery metrics. They produce their own reality, and I myself recognize that they are necessary. The statistical tables published by the Greater New Orleans Community Data Center, the reporting of local media,

13

and my own geo-statistical number-crunching all require that unsightly patches be stitched over beautiful urban fabric. Through the process of reification—that is, the concretization of an abstraction—official neighborhoods influence policy, politics, and resource allocation, as well as the formation of neighborhood associations, with their notoriously uneven levels of civic clout. Officially defined neighborhoods are a necessary evil, an important delusion, a fake reality. They should be viewed as useful cartographic and statistical tools—and no more.

Because they are defined by their perimeters, official delineations also perpetuate the problematic premise that neighborhoods have strong peripheries and weak cores. In fact, the opposite is the case, both nationally and locally. Nearly all Americans, for example, would agree that the State of Illinois and Grand Teton National Park are in the heart of the regions we call the Midwest and the Rockies, respectively. And nearly every New Orleanian would agree that Coliseum Square forms the core of the Lower Garden District, and that the Canal/Carrollton intersection forms the core of Mid-City. But hardly anyone agrees on the peripheries of all four of these spaces. So be it! Let your neighborhood perception extend outwardly from a universally recognized core, and bleed gradually into adjacent areas. Similarly, official delineations often use grand avenues and boulevards to divide neighborhoods. In fact, they unite them, in the same way that the Mississippi, Ohio, and Missouri rivers unify their respective valleys. We once understood this, and described entire neighborhoods by their transecting arteries. Think how different Bywater would be today if we considered St. Claude Avenue to be its unifying linear axis rather than its divisive edge.

Such enriching ambiguity, while imprecise, accurately reflects how urban residents truly sense their surroundings—and we have three hundred years of evidence that it's usually a glorious mess.

"A WAR OF RACES"
New Orleans's Messy Municipality Era, 1836–1852

One hundred eighty years ago, New Orleans embarked on its most peculiar experiment in city management. It would last for sixteen years and leave behind influences still evident today.

On March 8, 1836, the state legislature amended New Orleans's original 1805 charter by dividing the city "into three separate sections, each with distinct municipal powers." The First Municipality would include the French Quarter and Faubourg Tremé, the Second Municipality would run from Canal Street to the upper city limit of Felicity Street, and the Third Municipality spanned from Esplanade down to the present-day St. Bernard Parish line.

The three municipalities were then sectioned into wards, each of which elected a number of aldermen based on its population size. These Councils of Aldermen controlled all municipality affairs, from taxes and finance to infrastructure, education, sanitation, and other services. The three Councils of Aldermen would meet annually in the Cabildo on May 1 to form the General Council, which answered to a single mayor. Together, they legislated citywide matters such as business licensing, port management, policing, and incarceration. Debts were distributed among the three municipalities according to their ability to raise revenue.

It all seemed to make sense on paper, and some compared it benignly to the relationship between states and the federal government. But in reality, the system was egregiously divisive in both its effects and its root cause: an ethnic rivalry ongoing since the Louisiana Purchase in 1803.

On the one side was an uneasy alliance between French-speaking Creoles (New Orleans natives) and "foreign French" (immigrants from France, refugees from Haiti, and other francophones not from Louisiana) as well as people from the Mediterranean, Caribbean, and Latin America. This loose coalition, unified by their Catholic faith and a generally Latin culture, formed the majority and thus dominated local political and cultural life in the early 1800s. In the vernacular of the era, they were known as "the Creoles," else "the French," "the Gauls," and sometimes "the Latins."

On the other side were English-speaking, mostly Protestant transplants of Anglo-American ethnicity who arrived after the Louisiana Purchase. Ambitious in their pursuit of business opportunities, "the Americans" enjoyed commercial dominance and shored up their political power through liaisons with German and Irish immigrants.

The Creole/American rivalry underscored nearly all aspects of city life, and either side constantly found fault with the other. "There is, as everyone knows," reported visiting philosopher Harriet Martineau in the 1830s, "a mutual jealousy between the French and American. . . . The French complain that the Americans will not speak French [and] will not meet their neighbors even half way, [while]

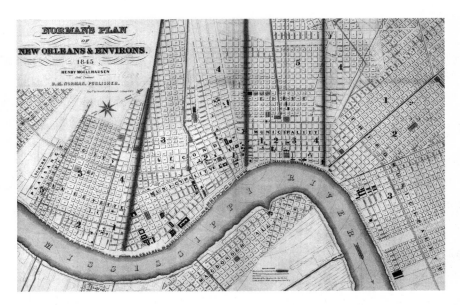

The New Orleans area during the city's disputatious "municipality era," 1836–1852. From left to right: Jefferson Parish's City of Lafayette and Second, First, and Third municipalities of New Orleans. Numbers indicate wards within each jurisdiction. *Norman's Plan of New Orleans & Environs, courtesy Library of Congress.*

the Americans ridicule the toilet practices of the French ladies; their liberal use of rouge and pearl powder."

Exacerbating the tension were parallel hostilities between enslaved people and slaveholders, and between free people of color and whites. Members of these and other demographic groups also found themselves positioned along the Creole/American, native/newcomer cultural spectrum.

How did this schism end up in the municipal split of 1836? The answer lies in the tendency of people to live among their own, forming ethnic neighborhoods. Americans predominated in the recently developed upper faubourgs (present-day CBD, Lower Garden District, Irish Channel, Garden District, and Central City), whereas Creoles prevailed in the older neighborhoods of the French Quarter and the lower banlieue, namely Tremé and the Bayou Road, and Marigny down to present-day Bywater.

This residential agglomeration raised the possibility that partitioning New Orleans along the lines of its ethnic geography might resolve the political problem of its ethnic infighting. Why work out your differences when you can just get a divorce and divide up the property?

In the historical memory, it's usually the Americans who get the blame for the 1836 split, and for good reason. What's less remembered is that both Americans and Creoles had long pined for such a division. In 1826, for example, City Council members of both ethnicities called for what one journalist deemed the "dismemberment" of New Orleans, cleaving the city down the middle of Canal Street. A subsequent bill circulated for "converting the whole [of New Orleans] into two cities, to be called the Upper and Lower City," according to council records, "arising from the opposing influence of American . . . and French interests." When American elements finally got their way in 1836, it was probably to the relief of many Creoles as well: each group would finally control its own domain. Good riddance.

And at first it appeared to work. Big new hotels and banks opened; waterworks and gas works were installed in both the First and Second municipalities, while the Second opened its ("New") Basin Canal to compete with the First Municipality's Carondelet ("Old Basin") Canal.

But the Panic of 1837 set finances afoul both locally and nationwide, and soon tripartite government would cause more problems than it resolved. It increased bureaucracy, engendered confusion, and wasted resources, in that everything had to be done in triplicate. It pitted the municipalities against each other as residents came to perceive a zero-sum game, where one's gain came at the other's expense.

Worse, ethnic rancor intensified, as did inequity, because the larger and more powerful First and Second municipalities left little for the Third Municipality below Esplanade, an area known wistfully as the "the Dirty Third" and "the Poor Third." In one 1849 editorial, the Third's newspaper *Daily Orleanian* spelled out what was on most Creoles' minds: "Had the Legislature sought, by the most careful efforts, to create a war of races, to make distinction between Creole and American, they could not have chosen a better means . . . than the present division operates."

The system also landed the city deeply in debt, which lowered its credit rating and thwarted its ability to float bonds for much-needed improvements such as railroads. Something had to be done. So motivated, the state legislature on February 23, 1852, finally repealed the 1836 act and reconsolidated the municipalities back into one city.

Significantly, in a separate act on the same day, it annexed Jefferson Parish's City of Lafayette—today's Irish Channel, Garden District, and Central City, between Felicity and Toledano—into New Orleans, bringing along with it all its Anglo-American, German, and Irish voters. The annexation helped make the Americans and their allies, whose numbers had been increasing all along courtesy of inmigration, the numerical majority in the reconsolidated city. Increasingly they would win elections, adding to their growing power in politics and culture even as they dominated in the economic realm.

After 1852, English would be heard more often in the streets of New Orleans, American architectural tastes such as Greek Revival and Italianate began to appear more frequently, and English common law would make inroads into the state's Roman-influenced civil code. Urbanization expanded faster in the upriver (American) direction, which attracted even more investment to that side of town, while the lower faubourgs and their working-class populations grew more modestly.

New Orleans was Americanizing, and old Creole culture was waning. The 1836–52 municipality era was not the cause of this epic metamorphosis, but it was its key transitional stage.

Relics of the strange era remain with us today. The term "neutral ground" arose in the 1830s as hyperbole for the adversaries of the First and Second municipalities living on either side of Canal Street and its extra-wide median. By the 1860s, folks began to apply that term to other street medians. Today the colloquialism is used by everyone citywide—and by no one else anywhere in the nation. Another vestige is our present-day system of municipal districts, the first three of which align precisely with the old municipalities, while the boundaries of the Fourth reflect those of old Lafayette at the time of its annexation.

Up until just a few years ago, each municipal district had its own elected tax assessor, a redundant system highly reminiscent of the old municipalities. And like its antecedent, that unconventional system was practically unique in the nation.

The year 1852 saw the launching of our present-day ward lines and numbers as well as the revision of the city's confusing house-address system, which was again updated to our current method in 1894. The municipality era also lives on in two of our most cherished historic buildings. The Cabildo, built in 1799 in the Creole-favored Spanish Colonial style and located in the heart of the Creoles' neighborhood, served as City Hall until the end of the municipality era. When power shifted uptown, so too did City Hall. The new building, today's Gallier Hall, embodied the Greek Revival fashion favored by Anglo-Americans, and was pointedly positioned in the heart of the American sector.

To this day, city government remains entirely above Canal Street, and one can find far more mansions and old money in the upper half of the city than in the lower faubourgs, where a Mediterranean and Caribbean ambience persists.

"NEUTRAL GROUND"
From the Political Geography of Imperialism
to the Streets of New Orleans

"Neutral ground," that only-in-New-Orleans term for street medians, intrigues newcomers as much as locals enjoy explaining it. The story usually goes something like George Washington Cable told it in 1885: Canal Street's "tree-bordered 'neutral ground,'" he wrote in *The Creoles of Louisiana*, "was 'neutral' when it divided between the French quarter and the American at a time when their 'municipality' governments were distinct from each other." The term stuck and got applied to medians throughout the city.

I do not question this explanation; it is reasonably accurate. But there are opportunities to flesh out the origins and chronology of this unique local idiom.

"Neutral Ground" as a proper noun and a toponym entered the Louisiana lexicon in 1806, before Canal Street even existed, as part of a military resolution to a lingering imperial disagreement in present-day southwestern Louisiana. That discord arose during the prior century, when Spanish colonials in Mexico viewed the land between the Sabine and Calcasieu rivers as the easternmost frontier of New Spain, while French authorities in the Mississippi Valley saw it as the westernmost reaches of their Louisiana.

Neither colonial power made too much of this irresolution; there was no gold or silver at stake, and both governments had priorities elsewhere. But they did keep an eye on each other. When the French established Natchitoches near the Red River in 1714, for example, the Spanish responded a few years later by pointedly erecting their fort just to the west. For decades to come, this region, known as Los Adaes, formed an unusual cultural interstice where isolated Spanish, French, African, and indigenous peoples interacted in a power vacuum, a space without a hegemon.

The inter-imperial tension became moot when, in 1762, France, foreseeing defeat in the French and Indian War, ceded Louisiana to the Spanish to keep it out of the hands of the English. Now Natchitoches and Los Adaes answered to the same king.

Fast forward four decades, and the boundary problem returned. The Spanish by this time had retroceded Louisiana (1800) to the French, who sold it three years later to the United States. But because the disputed region had never really been officially resolved, ownership of the "Sabine strip" remained unclear. Now it was the Spanish and the Americans who stared down each other over piney woods and prairie.

Enter at this point Spanish lieutenant colonel Simón de Herrera and American general James Wilkinson, who in 1806 hammered out an agreement in which neither would send forces into the area between the Sabine River and Arroyo Hondo, the Spanish name for the Calcasieu River. They called this area "Neutral Ground," and despite its inexactitude, the accord succeeded in keeping the peace. Wrote historian J. Villasana Haggard in 1945, "the Neutral Ground was recognized as a well-known area lying between two sovereign nations but under the authority of neither."

"Neutral Ground" thus entered the Louisiana discourse as a proper noun, capitalized and officially defined. It affected the state's boundaries when Louisiana joined the Union in 1812, and when, in 1819, Spain agreed to relinquish the Neutral Ground to the United States, thus creating our current Texas/Louisiana border. The term appeared in territorial and state papers during the 1810s–20s, and presumably circulated in conversations in and around the state capital of New Orleans. Even after its administrative resolution, the former Neutral Ground made news as a lawless region with more than its share of rogues and ruffians. Some called it the Sabine Free State.

While "Neutral Ground" as an official political geography disappeared from the Louisiana map, "neutral ground" nonetheless continued to resonate as a concept and a common noun. It seems to have particularly reverberated with anglophones in postcolonial Louisiana: these were, after all, English words in a francophone society, and newly arrived Anglo-Americans constantly found themselves living between and amongst rival factions they did not understand, but knew they had to coexist with. The expression formed a useful trope for negotiating the contested spaces in Creole New Orleans as it underwent the oftentimes-painful process of syncretizing with American culture. The moniker's mildly sardonic hyperbole—it's not like Creoles and Americans were actually preparing for violent conflict, although sometimes it felt that way—imparted a jaunty, in-the-know tone which made the term all the more appealing.

In 1836, when Creole-American ethnic rivalry came to a head, authorities reached into the tool bag of political geography for a solution: redrawing jurisdictional lines to subdivide New Orleans into three semiautonomous municipalities, each with its own council, police, services, schools, and port, united under one mayor and a general council.

The 171-foot-wide Canal Street "neutral ground." The term, likely borrowed from a circa-1806 military agreement made along the Texas/Louisiana border, first took hold amid the rivalrous ethnic geography of antebellum New Orleans. *Early 1940s photograph from author's NOPSI/Entergy collection.*

The drawing of municipality lines entailed an overlaying of ethnic geography upon urban geography. The Creole-dominated French Quarter and Faubourg Tremé would become the First Municipality, and would be divided from the poorer Creole and immigrant lower faubourgs (Third Municipality) by prominent Esplanade Avenue. Heading upriver, the First Municipality would be separated from the Anglo-dominated Second Municipality by 171-foot-wide Canal Street.

A system designed to ameliorate intra-urban antagonism, however, ended up only reifying it. Municipalities competed for scarce resources, and costly municipal services all had to be triplicated. Most of the rivalry played out between the densely populated First (mostly Creole) and Second (mostly Anglo) municipalities, on either side of Canal Street and its spacious median.

One rainy morning in January 1837, a new newspaper hit the streets of New Orleans. It was named the *Picayune,* and it was published in English by Anglo-Americans from an office on the Anglo side of Canal Street. Apparently those rains continued all winter, rendering Canal Street one muddy mess—enough for the *Picayune* to gripe about the problem repeatedly. On March 11, 1837, it wrote,

"The Neutral Ground"—This fair portion of our beautiful city is becoming daily . . . an object of deep interest. A large number of emigrants from the neighborhood marshes have settled on this territory. We suppose they intend laying it off into lots, and giving it the name of *Frog Town.* . . . Canal street—it is to be called by the above name in the future.

This is among the first clear published uses of "neutral ground" to refer to Canal Street's median, and while a direct link to the circa-1806 usage might be difficult to make, it stands to reason that locals would reach into their local vocabulary and, with tongue in cheek and a fair dose of irony, pull out a familiar term which accommodated a comparable local situation. Note that the anonymous writer put the term in quotes, implying it was familiar enough to go unexplained, yet new enough to warrant conscientious punctuation. Verbal vernacular usually precedes printed appearances, so it is likely folks in New Orleans were making reference to Canal Street's neutral ground for a number of years prior to its 1837 appearance in the *Picayune.*

Similar uses appeared throughout 1837 and 1838, usually under the same dateline of "The Neutral Ground." A May 21, 1839, editorial mentioned the municipalities it separated: "'The 'Neutral Ground.'—We intend giving the First and Second Municipalities . . . a regular dose [regarding] the abuses in Canal street." Stated an April 21, 1840, article in the same vein, "The boundary war and the improvement of the neutral ground in Canal street occupy a large space in the public mind." This time, the term appeared without quotation marks, which by the 1850s became standard. (Why was Canal's neutral ground such a mess? Possibly because two adversarial municipalities shared jurisdiction of it, which would have shifted responsibility to the general council—the very governing body rendered ineffective by the inane municipality system. It was finally abandoned in 1852.)

"Neutral ground" by the late antebellum age was widely used to describe Canal Street's median, and soon began to spread to other arteries. "The alley which runs between the St. Louis Cathedral and the old Court House buildings may be regarded as neutral ground," joked the *Picayune* in 1852, "where saints and sinners may assemble without injury to the character of either." A nostalgic 1864

Picayune article written during the federal occupation described "the centre grass plat [of] Esplanade street" as the "neutral ground" between the old First and Third municipalities. An 1865 article in the same paper cited a lawsuit on the "right to locate a fruit stand on the neutral ground of Poydras street." The *New Orleans Times*, 1867: "through the neutral ground of Claiborne." The *Picayune*, 1870: "the neutral ground of St. Charles"; 1875: "neutral ground of Rampart"; 1892: "the neutral ground of Carrollton," and so on.

Long after the original Neutral Ground on the Franco-Spanish-American frontier disappeared from the Louisiana map, and long after New Orleans's municipality system ended and its Creole/Anglo rivalry gave way to hybridization, "neutral ground" persisted in the New Orleans vernacular. It's as strong as ever today, and unlike some other local shibboleths, such as *banquette, red gravy,* and *making groceries,* this one is spoken daily, without self-awareness, by just about every New Orleanian—and by no one anywhere else.

Except, that is, for residents of rural southwestern Louisiana, who commemorate the unusual heritage of what some call the "neutral strip" with the Sabine Free State Festival, held each November in Florien.

CITYSCAPES OF THE NEW ORLEANS SLAVE TRADE

Social memory benefits from an associated structural framework—that is, a place or object that reflects and evokes a certain history. As we treasure mementos to commemorate times past and loved ones lost, our societies collectively save old buildings, erect monuments, name and rename streets, designate hallowed grounds, and protect historical cityscapes so that citizens may synchronize their narratives of who they are as a people, where they came from, and where they should be going.

As a city with a complex, glorious, colorful, and tragic past—and a modern-day economy based on marketing it—New Orleans proliferates in structurally based social memory. It uses the French Quarter, for example, to recount antebellum Creole society. It points to the Garden District to recall wealthy nineteenth-century Anglo society, and (more recently) upholds Tremé to commemorate free people of color and African American contributions. It welcomed a museum complex built in part to salute the city's key role in World War II, something that had previously gone completely unrecognized. Preservation is intrinsic to this arrangement; without it, we would forget, or fail to convince newcomers, of these narratives. Note, for example, how the demolition of the South Rampart Street commercial corridor, Louis Armstrong's neighborhood, and Storyville has impaired the social memory of jazz. (Tourists regularly come away disappointed when they learn that the "birthplace of jazz" is more municipal slogan than visitable place.) Out of sight, out of mind—and conversely, in sight, in mind. Hence the power of preservation.

New Orleans's role in the slave trade illustrates that power by providing a case study of its absence. To be sure, the modern city teems in the handiwork of enslaved labor: hundreds of antebellum structures, including prominent public edifices, stand in silent testimony to the toil of hired-out slaves, as do the numerous slant-roof rear quarters that housed enslaved domestics. Structural relics of slave *trading*, however, are a different story.

After the prohibition of international slave trading in 1808, New Orleans's port formed a premier node in the shift of the commerce to domestic movements of "surplus" slaves, exported from the tired soils of upper South tobacco farms and imported to the lower South with its insatiable demand for sugarcane and cotton labor. Well over 750,000 people were forcibly shipped southward during the antebellum era, a flow so significant historian Ira Berlin called it a "Second Middle Passage."

Marched overland or shipped coastwise or downriver, they arrived at New Orleans and would find themselves amid a cityscape replete with the machinations and spaces of the slave trade. Its high visibility—in the form of shipping, escorting, jailing, preparing, marketing, presenting, auctioning, and purchasing of people—captured the attention of countless visitors, some of whom scribed their observations in travelogues and articles about the "peculiar institution." Those written by Europeans or northerners (the lion's share) usually expressed compassion for the slave, dismay at the institution, and outright loathing for the trader. Southern sympathizers, ever fond of pointing out paternalistic master-slave relations and anecdotes of slave contentedness, either remained silent on the grim spectacle of the auction block, or scapegoated the trader so as to exonerate the master and institution. Other witnesses came away seared, among them a young Abraham Lincoln, who guided a flatboat to New Orleans in 1828 and 1831 and, for the first and only time in his life, saw large-scale southern plantation vassalage and big-city slave trading up close and personal. What he witnessed in the streets of New Orleans would inform his personal development and later affect the channels of American history. What follows is a gaze at the cityscapes (that is, the visible urban elements) of the New Orleans slave trade in the era of Lincoln's visits, the high antebellum decades of the 1820s–30s.

Despite the grotesque spectacle of the slave trade, city leaders in both the public and the private sectors made little attempt to hide or disguise it. The commerce entailed numerous professions, from shippers, brokers, and traders to lawyers, auctioneers, pen-keepers, notaries, and others who earned incomes in the change-of-ownership process. New players entered the market constantly, and proclaimed their openings with collegial solemnity. "Newman & Mortimer," read one such announcement in 1828, "have formed a partnership [of] Brokers, offer[ing] their services to their friends and public [in the] buying and selling of real property, slaves and all kinds of produce." Nearly all New Orleans's professional firms, banks, and insurance companies had their hands in the slave trade to one degree or another.

Most slave transactions took place in two types of spaces: private pens run by dealers, brokers, or traders, who bought and displayed numerous slaves and sold them to walk-in customers; and public auctions, where auctioneers coordinated transactions between current and prospective masters in large assemblages. Auctions were held in prominent places, open to all free classes, and advertised widely. Because of their open access and scheduled nature, public auctions attracted much more attention from visitors than the private one-on-one retail transactions occurring at the pens.

Auctions generally occurred in "coffee houses," a loan translation of *maison de café,* which meant, in France, an establishment that served coffee in the morning and alcohol later. In nineteenth-century New Orleans, coffeehouses were traditional saloons with a rather sophisticated if garish atmosphere, catering to men of the establishment class. Their commercial functions earned them the name "exchange," which implied a full-service business-networking center: places where white men could convene, discuss, negotiate, socialize, recreate, gamble, dine, drink, and lodge. Among the first in the American era, the Exchange Coffee House on Conti Street (1806), grew so popular as a saloon that it attracted commercial activities such as the auctioning of ships, houses, land, and, inevitably, slaves. It soon found itself competing with a new operation erected in 1810–11 at the corner of Chartres and St. Louis streets. Originally called Tremoulet's Commercial (or New Exchange) Coffee House, this business became Maspero's

Intersection of St. Louis and Chartres streets in the French Quarter, one of the busiest slave-auctioning locales in antebellum New Orleans. *Photograph by Richard Campanella.*

Exchange in 1814, Elkin's Exchange after Pierre Maspero's death in 1822, and by 1826, Hewlett's Exchange, named for new owner John Hewlett. The two-story, 55-by-62-foot edifice boasted behind its gaudy Venetian screens a 19-foot-high ceiling, four twelve-lamp glass chandeliers, framed maps and oil paintings (described by one northerner as "licentious"), wood and marble finishing, and an enormous bar with French glassware. Like many New Orleans coffeehouses, the upper floor contained billiards and gambling tables. Throughout the mid-antebellum years, Hewlett's Exchange buzzed with trilingual auctioning activity, in which everything from ships to houses to land to sugar kettles to people legally changed hands. The city's seven auctioneers worked the block on a rotating schedule, every day except Sunday, oftentimes while maintaining other jobs elsewhere. Joseph Le Carpentier handled Mondays, Wednesdays, and Saturdays; Toussaint Mossy (president of the New Orleans Architect Company) worked Tuesdays and Fridays; H. J. Domingon, George Boyd, and Joseph Baudue got Tuesdays, Thursdays, and Saturdays; and the busy Isaac McCoy and François Dutillet worked six days a week. At the time of Lincoln's visit, Hewlett's Exchange was the New

Orleans business community's single most important public meeting site for networking, news gathering, and wheeling-dealing.

Slave auctioning would later add two illustrious new venues to the New Orleans cityscape. In 1837 the magnificent St. Charles Exchange opened in the Faubourg St. Mary, followed the next year by the imposing City Exchange on St. Louis Street in the Old City (for which Hewlett's Exchange and adjacent structures were demolished). Both edifices, occupying entire city blocks, rising over four stories, and topped with landmark domes, ranked among the nation's most splendid hotels. Both became famous, and infamous, for their auction blocks.

Not all slave owners subjected their human property to the slave pens and auction houses. Some masters, particularly residents of the city proper, opted to handle sales themselves by inviting prospective buyers to their homes; urban domestic slaves often changed hands in this manner. For-sale-by-owner ads appeared in local newspapers at a rate of one or two per day: "For Sale—A NEGRO WOMAN 18 years of age: guaranteed against the diseases and vices proscribed by law . . . speaks English and French—understands cooking either in the French or English stile [sic], something of a washer, and a good nurse." Prospective buyers of this teenager were directed to visit master J. Montamat at his house on Elysian Fields Avenue. Another announcement, posted during Lincoln's 1828 visit, advertised "a young and likely Negro fellow [and] several others of both sexes, for sale by the subscriber [David C. McClure] at No. 116, Bienville street." One of McClure's slaves later escaped, prompting the perturbed master to post a ten-dollar reward for thirty-three-year-old "John . . . very stout built, black complected, [with] rather a frown on his countenance."

Comparative measurements of the nation's urban slave marketplaces are difficult to ascertain because each city documented trafficking in differing ways. Yet nearly all qualified observers, in both historical times and today, agree that New Orleans's slave-trading enterprise trumped that of all other American cities for most of the antebellum era, usually by a wide margin. The reason stemmed from the same economic-geographical factors driving New Orleans's overall commercial rigor: the metropolis was perfectly positioned as a transshipment point along the watery intercourse between the slave-supply regions of the upper South and the labor-demanding plantations of the lower Mississippi Valley. As the largest city in the South, serving the nation's highest regional concentration of millionaire planters, New Orleans also exploited thousands of slaves for its own needs, and eagerly developed the physical, financial, and administrative infrastructure to handle their profitable buying and selling.

27

The size of that commerce may be estimated through varied sources. Evidence from the 1840s indicates that two hundred to three hundred local professionals dealt directly in the city's slave trade, handling at least a few thousand sales per year. Journal accounts provide estimates of the ever-rotating population of the city's slaveholding pens. Wrote one visitor, "There were about 1000 slaves for sale at New Orleans while I was there" in March 1830. "I cannot say as to the number of negroes in the [New Orleans] market," wrote a trader in 1834, "though am of the opinion there is 12–1500 and upwards, and small lots constantly coming in." Other eyewitnesses estimated three thousand slaves for sale at a particular moment later in the antebellum era, equating to roughly one marketed slave for every five resident slaves in the city.

Official documents provide further insights into the size of New Orleans's slave trade. According to historian Donald Edward Everett, conveyance records of real property transactions (Louisiana's civil law system viewed slaves as real estate, thus requiring title) show that 4,435 slave purchases occurred in the city just in the year 1830. That same cohort was also tracked through the Notarial Archives' collection of Certificates of Good Character, the document required by law from 1829 to 1831 to prevent "undesirable" upper South slaves from entering Louisiana. Economic historians Herman Freudenberger and Jonathan B. Pritchett tabulated 2,289 such slaves arriving into the New Orleans market in 1830. Their findings show that this group came mostly from the Old South states along the Eastern Seaboard. They were disproportionately male by roughly a 60-40 ratio, possibly reflecting the demands of sugarcane cultivation. Over 93 percent ranged from eleven to thirty years old, with healthy young adult males typically selling for around five hundred dollars. Those who embarked at the major export cities of Richmond, Norfolk, and Charleston endured coastwise journeys lasting about three weeks. Those who were marched overland in coffles suffered tortuous experiences that could easily take two months. Whether the slaves were delivered by sea, river, or land, Virginia supplied the largest share (44 percent) to the Deep South, followed by North Carolina (19 percent) and Maryland (15 percent), with other southern states ranging between .02 and 5 percent. The buyers, on the other hand, were mostly from Louisiana (71 percent). Scores of Virginians, Tennesseans, Georgians, and others also bought members of this cohort of 2,289, but it is likely these out-of-state planters had Louisiana ties.

Slave sales were not evenly distributed throughout the year. They rose steadily in late autumn and peaked in January, February, and March as the planting season approached and the business and travel season peaked. Sales declined as temperatures rose and bottomed out with the high heat of the epidemic months of late summer and early fall. Slaves were thus imported and traded here in greater frequency and in wider view precisely as visitors circulated throughout the city in greater numbers. Because slaves typically endured an average of forty days in limbo—that is, after arriving but before being sold—they accumulated in holding pens and camps throughout downtown New Orleans, creating yet another jaw-dropping spectacle for the uninitiated. New Orleans not only boasted the nation's busiest slave market, but its trafficking of human beings, wrote historian Frederic Bancroft, "had a peculiar dash: it rejoiced in its display and prosperity; it felt unashamed, almost proud." A typical newcomer like young Abraham Lincoln, strolling the levee or peeking into an exchange, would have encountered the crass realities of the human chattel business constantly, unavoidably.

Citizens sometimes launched efforts to curtail the flagrancy of the commerce, perhaps because its unsettling appearance played into the hands of abolitionists, but more likely because concentrations of slaves in transit were thought to constitute a public health nuisance. During the time of Lincoln's 1828 visit, a session in City Hall recorded that "several inhabitants of this City" signed a petition "to ask the Council . . . to prevent exposing negroes for sale on the sidewalks." Leery officials wavered on the request, procrastinated, read a report on the matter, and finally rejected it, for fear of tampering with the lucrative industry. The issue came up a few months later, when citizens asked "if it would not be proper to fix places for storing negroes for sale outside the body of the city," fearing risk of an epidemic. Others complained of the odors emanating from the pens, and from the cooking of cheap barrel pork used to feed the captives. Finally, in the year between Lincoln's visits, the City Council passed laws prohibiting public exposition of slaves for sale, as well as their nighttime lodging, in the area bounded by Girod Street, Esplanade Avenue, Levee Street along the riverfront, and Tremé Street behind the city. Even then, the law did little to conceal the spectacle. Protests from slave traders below Esplanade Avenue led the Council to clarify, in 1830, that "all negroe traders may keep and expose for sale their negroes within the whole extent of the limits of the suburb Marigny, all resolutions to the contrary notwithstanding." At least one trader above Esplanade Avenue, where public exposition was supposedly banned, nevertheless openly inaugurated a private slave-trading operation during the time of Lincoln's second visit in 1831. His ad in the New Orleans *Bee* read:

R. Salaun, Broker and Exchange Broker, Royale, between Hospital and Barracks streets, has the honor of informing his friends and the public, that he attends to the sales and purchases of slaves and real estate. Persons, who may feel inclined to leave their slaves with him, for sale, can be assured that no exertion will be neglected to have them disposed of on the best terms and shortest delay. He offers for sale, at present, laundresses and plaiters [braiders], seamstresses, cooks, carpenters, painters and blacksmiths.

In 1835, the law against public exposure of "negroes for sale" was expanded to the entire city, but once again was promptly amended to permit such activity in the faubourgs above Gaiennié Street and anywhere in the Faubourg Marigny, provided the slaves were lodged in brick buildings at least two stories high.

These and later laws show that city officials actively grappled with slave dealing, but mostly out of concern for the health, comfort, profit, and public image of the empowered white caste. Other southern cities did the same for similar reasons: Natchez, for example, passed laws in 1833 relocating its downtown slave pens to the infamous "Forks in the Road" beyond city limits. Rarely did authorities fret over the slaves' trauma or degradation, and never did they question the underlying institution. Lincoln arrived while this debate played out, and if the laws were enforced as they were written, he may have witnessed slave trading in the cityscape to a greater extent during his 1828 visit than in 1831. Had he returned twenty-five years later, he would have seen an even broader and deeper manifestation of the controversial commerce: in the late 1850s, around twenty-five slave depots, yards, pens, or booths dotted the heart of Faubourg St. Mary (present-day Central Business District), with a dozen on Gravier Street, a half-dozen on Baronne, and others on Common and Magazine streets. Another dozen functioned in the Old City, on Exchange Place, St. Louis Street, Esplanade at Chartres, and elsewhere.

A visitor to New Orleans arriving any time prior to the Civil War could not help but witness an entire cityscape of slave trading. Visitors today, however, would be hard-pressed to find any substantial, identified physical evidence remaining; it's all been cleared away by demolition, conflagration, or the ravages of time. Lacking preserved clues in the cityscape of this historical reality enables social memory to falter.

AUTHOR'S NOTE: *An ongoing effort by local historians working with the National Park Service aims to install historic signs at key slave-trading spaces in the city, among them the corner of Chartres and Esplanade in the Faubourg Marigny. Now the site of a 1920s*

Spanish Revival church converted to apartments, this parcel once hosted the largest pens in the lower city, where thousands of people, including Solomon Northup, spent their limbo time between owners. Overseers and traders lived in adjacent houses, some still standing, and a palimpsest of the pen's two-story appendage may be seen etched on the exposed brick wall of 1413 Chartres.

BEFORE STORYVILLE
Vice Districts in Antebellum New Orleans

Say "New Orleans" and "red-light district," and Storyville usually comes to mind—for good reason. Operating from 1898 to 1917, that famous tenderloin district represents the city's best example of a spatially confined and legally defined vice zone, and has been extensively documented by historians and depicted in art.

But it was not the first. For nearly a century prior, the city boasted—or endured—a number of other *sub rosa* spaces that had formed organically, had soft edges, and operated at the margins of both the law and the city. Practically nothing remains structurally of these spaces; indeed, there is hardly any historic memory of them: how many people think of O'Keefe or Girod streets in today's Central Business District as being hotbeds of debauchery?

Abundant as they were, vice spaces in the early nineteenth century generally scattered themselves opportunistically throughout New Orleans. Grogshops and tippling houses, "caravanserai" (flophouses), music and dance halls, gambling dens, and brothels popped up wherever demand and supply shook hands, and that meant most neighborhoods, if not most blocks. Yet spatial concentrations did exist, for the same reasons other industries form clusters and districts: to take advantage of a mutual client pool, for the convenience of supply chains and workers, to lower costs through economies of scale, and to maximize accessibility while minimizing scrutiny.

Police reports, court records, and news articles about illegal sex activity (1846–62), gathered by the late Tulane historian Judith Kelleher Schafer and mapped by this researcher, show that most prostitution and its attendant activities occurred in three principal zones. One was located in the middle-rear edge of town, another in the upper edge, and the third along the lower riverfront. When

31

mapped, these zones trace the periphery, rather than the core, of the antebellum metropolis.

In the First Municipality—that is, the French Quarter and Faubourg Tremé—the vice zone lay around the intersection of Customhouse (renamed Iberville in 1901) and Burgundy streets. Schafer unearthed at least seventy-five illegal sex reports from court records and other sources, many of them involving scores of arrests, with addresses on Customhouse, Burgundy, Dauphine, Conti, Bienville, Basin, Franklin, and adjacent streets. Why here? This area lay behind the Old City—none too elegant, none too pricey, yet conveniently proximate to clients galore in the urban core. Better yet, the nearby Old Basin (Carondelet) Canal dock and its attendant industries drew a steady stream of potential johns. Testifying to this area's repute is the police blotter from a single day in 1853, when fifty-four brothel-keepers were arrested around Customhouse's intersections with Burgundy and Dauphine. Two years later, police detained an additional fifty-three prostitutes in the same area—"nymphs de pavé," the press called them, lamenting that they "were more sinned against than sinning, [their] woe-begone appearance aptly illustrative of their fallen fortunes." Another article described the whores of the Dauphine, Burgundy, and Conti area as "the originators of all kinds of scandal." Potation usually accompanied prostitution, so it is probable that numerous grogshops operated here as well. So prevalent was illicit sex in and around Customhouse Street that a number of doctors and pharmacists specializing in the treatment of sexually transmitted diseases set up their practices here. This vice area would later form the Tango Belt, a competitor of sorts with Storyville and a predecessor of today's Bourbon Street.

In the Second Municipality (today's Warehouse District, Central Business District, Superdome area, and Lower Garden District), a crescent-shaped geography of sin spanned from the rears of Gravier and Perdido streets, up Phillippa (now Roosevelt Way, O'Keefe, and Dryades), and down Girod and Julia to the Mississippi River. Here could be found the back-of-town near Charity Hospital, the turning basin of the New Basin Canal and its leatherneck workforce, the hard-labor projects and industries along the semirural periphery, and above all, the uptown flatboat wharf along the Mississippi River.

From the 1790s to the 1860s, thousands of young western males guided flatboats down from "the upcountry" (hinterland) to the uptown flatboat wharf, whereupon they unloaded their cargo, vended it, dismantled the vessel, and sold the scrap wood. Flush with cash, the boatmen usually treated themselves to a few days or weeks footloose in the big city, liberated from farm toil and nagging kin and free to "see the elephant." (In frontier lexicon, "to see the elephant" meant to witness the utmost and live the experience to the fullest. Popular from the 1840s to around 1900, the expression may trace its origins to traveling carnivals which would hold out their most popular exhibit, a live elephant, as a climax. The phrase later took on darker connotations, meaning death or violence, but in this era, it was usually used salaciously, and young travelers often spoke of "seeing the elephant" in New Orleans's vice districts.)

Venues gratifying the desires of the transient flatboatmen opened immediately along the flatboat wharf (present-day South Peters Street), in part because the lads would often use their docked vessels as rent-free base camps. That custom became a flashpoint for merchants, citizens, and authorities, who saw the riverine encampments as both a physical and a moral nuisance. "The flat-boats permanently moored [on] the levee . . . are the dens of sharpers [cheating gamblers] by day, and robbers and murderers at night," complained the *Bee* in 1835, "yet not the slightest precaution is used." An earlier visitor reported seeing flatboats "used as huckster shops, dwellings [and] pigpens." Others disdained the mile-long "line of gambling-shops" formed by the flatboats on Sundays, not to mention the boatmen themselves, who, by one springtime 1830 account, numbered "5000 or 6000," or 10 percent of the entire city's population. Curious visitors in the early 1800s made a point of seeing the flatboat wharf in the same manner that even the most pious visitors today take a peek at Bourbon Street.

Once boatmen were finally crowbarred out of their floating lairs, they spilled into adjacent streets seeking cheap room and board. The high-rent arteries of the Second Municipality, such as St. Charles, Camp, and Magazine streets, generally eschewed the scruffy vagabonds. Back streets, however, were a different story: these village-like margins were a bit more forgiving, with their enticingly discreet and dimly lit shelters and refuges. To this area gravitated (mostly) young single male transients, with time on their hands, cash in their pockets, and anonymity in their identity. Phillippa Street bore witness to a remarkable concentration of brothels, particularly around Gravier, Perdido, and Girod, and with them were all the affiliated didoes, scams, and crimes.

The most adventurous males debauched in a sketchy purlieu known as "the Swamp." Located a dozen blocks inland from the flatboat wharf, where Julia and Girod petered out into the backswamp, this area absorbed all that civilized New Orleanians ejected: the eerie Girod Street Cemetery (1822), the smelly New Basin Canal (1832), and Charity Hospital and its pestilential aura (1835), not to mention gas works, garbage dumps, shantytowns, prison work yards, and the city stables.

So it comes as no surprise that the boatmen's den of iniquity ended up here as well. Few first-person descriptions of this loathsome honky-tonk survive. An 1828 editorial made reference to "the swamp and grog-shops, in the back parts of town" and bristled at the "tastes of the natives and frequenters of those places," while a more detailed account comes from a reminiscence of the 1820s–30s reported in 1883. "The Swamp," it explained, "was a great rendezvous for the flatboatmen, and here they reigned supreme, the city police never caring to invade those precincts." Today this area would be located between the U.S. Post Office and the Smoothie King Center.

Girod Street, connecting the riverfront flatboat wharves with the New Basin Canal and the nearby Swamp district, hosted a disproportionate share of vice venues and crime. After a particularly gruesome grog-shop killing in 1838, out-of-state newspapers noted that "Girod Street, New Orleans, where the murder took place, is said to be the den of cut-throats, gamblers, and other infamous persons." In an early example of conflating a social problem with its structural environment, the paper "proposed to root them out by tearing down the houses and widening the street." Many locals would have agreed; some called Girod "a sink of pollution" with "scarcely a decent house in the whole street." Even its defenders acknowledged the high numbers of indigent renters and a "laxness shown by the authorities." Into the 1850s, Girod remained in a "shameful condition," and city advocates called for the razing of "all the dirty hovels which have so long disfigured this street, and disgraced the city."

Detailed descriptions of the Girod vice scene come from an 1852 *Picayune* article. "Rows of low tenements . . . leaning against one another, [their] fronts shattered and broken, [with] a few crazy, creaky steps lead[ing] to each door," lined the infamous corridor. Each "tenement generally consists of three apartments, the drinking shop, about four feet deep and eight feet long, a larger or rather deeper room in the rear . . . used for a dining room and kitchen . . . and a loft [used] as common sleeping apartments." Perhaps a "philanthropic stranger" might view the denizens therein as "the honest poor . . . induced to live in these miserable hovels by the low rates of rent; *but the resident of New Orleans knows better . . .* with the recollections of a cracked skull, a bloody proboscis, or darkened optics; and there are some who instinctively grasp their purses when [Girod Street's] famous localities are recalled."

A closer look revealed the activity inside: "There is a red curtain in every window, and drunkenness and vice seem to peep through patched panes. . . . [E]ach of those rickety sheds brings to the owner a monthly payment of $25 or $30 . . .

raised by the sale of poisonous liquors, and by pilfering from the most degraded victims of intemperance. Whiskey is sold in all—an old table, a few dirty glasses, and a bottle [visible in every] open door." The woman of the house—such enterprises were usually run by females, likely madams—"enlarges her business by accommodating boarders and lodgers." Upstairs, strangers paid a dime or a *picayune* for a rude bunk and endured "men in a beastly state of intoxication, with bloody clothes . . . a broken jaw, a stab in the body; while slovenly bloated women hang around them." The "desperate rascal who would rob or murder, [with] police . . . in pursuit," found refuge in the hovels of Girod Street. "This is not a fancy picture," the article concluded.

Notorious as were the Swamp, Girod Street, and the flatboat wharf, they could not hold a candle to the most infamous of New Orleans's antebellum vice spaces, Gallatin Street, now French Market Place. Only two blocks long, Gallatin Street, according to newspapers of the day, was "filled with low groggeries [dive bars], the resort of the worst and most abandoned of both sexes." Journalists characterized with understatement the Gallatin block between Hospital (Gov. Nicholls) and Barracks streets as "the rendezvous of many persons whose characters are not of the most respectable stamp," and reported violence there regularly. The raucous space became a metaphor, such that if one spoke of a woman having a "career on Gallatin Street," or of "the frail daughters of Gallatin Street," everyone knew exactly what that meant. It also earned the rhetorical flares of sarcasm and irony, through such references as "*that classic thoroughfare*," "the numerous and chaste nymphs of *that poetic region*," and "*that quiet, respectable thoroughfare*." References to its thugs were formulated as "the Knights of Gallatin," "the Gallatin street boys," "Gallatin Street Rangers," and "the good . . . and true [men] of Gallatin Street." Its characters and joints became notorious locally, among them "Dutch Pete" Johnson and his California House, and the "houses" or "dens" (brothels all) of Archie Murphy, George Kent, John Swan, Bill Spriggin, William "Scott" Wilson, and Cornelius Keegan. Few New Orleanians would have challenged the journalist who, in inventorying the city's geography of sin in 1855, wrote that "worst among the worse is Gallatin street . . . sons of fraud, treachery and blood meet there the daughters of the night, and with them hold high wassail and unhallowed revelry. There is no redeeming feature to this street of streets."

Nevertheless, more wickedness lay a short distance downriver, around the dogleg-shaped intersection of Elysian Fields Street (now Avenue). Here operated the Sign of the Lion (Lion's Den), the Stadt Amsterdam, the Mobile, the Pontchartrain House, the Whitehall, and Tivoli Gardens. Locals dubbed it Sanctity Row.

Gallatin Street plus Sanctity Row formed the highest concentration of illegal sex, drinking (licensed or otherwise), violence, robberies, pickpockets, and scams in late antebellum New Orleans. Why here? It lay at the periphery of the French or Creole Market, the city's largest municipal emporium, which buzzed with stalls, conveyances, errand runners, day-hires, cheap food, running water, amusements, round-the-clock customers, and cash in every pocket. Such activity attracted loiterers, transients, curiosity seekers, and adventurers to whom bars, brothels, and gambling dens catered. The adjacent streets also rated fairly low socioeconomically; one visitor called this area "the St. Giles of New Orleans . . . where poverty and vice run races with want and passion." It attracted troublemakers with its cheap rents, and lacked the civic clout to keep them out. The nearby U.S. Mint, a smoky industrial operation, further suppressed the cost of living and added to the foot traffic, as did the international shipping wharves at the foot of Esplanade. And on Elysian Fields was the Pontchartrain Railroad Station, which landed visitors from Mobile via Lake Pontchartrain (hence the Mobile and the Pontchartrain House saloons). For many disoriented travelers, this spot formed the back-end gateway to New Orleans, and it had all the right ingredients for a vice district: access, anonymity, low rents, cheap eats, a quick buck, and strangers coming and going at all hours.

Select incidents help paint a picture of Gallatin Street's decadence. One night in 1849, for example, a hapless chap named Chambers got a room in a Gallatin boardinghouse and, predictably, soon found himself "having a chat" with a lady named Miss Bridget. As she cunningly excused herself to get water, a man by the name of Warden suddenly burst in, "asserting [to Chambers] in very strong terms that he was the husband of the lady who had just gone out. As is usual in such cases, a fight ensued." By dawn, Chambers found himself robbed of fifteen dollars, both men found themselves cut and bruised, and Miss Bridget and her accomplice Warden found themselves in the slammer. "This is an old game," admonished the *Picayune,* "and the young gentleman had not paid as dearly as many before him have for seeing the 'elephant.'"

Later that year, three employees of a nearby boardinghouse entered Wilson's Gallatin Street Saloon and, in short order, got into a fight with the barkeeper, who in turn shot one and stabbed another. The wounded comrades returned with "fifteen or twenty [reinforcements, who] commenced an indiscriminant destruction of . . . the bar-room and the upper apartments. They piled up the contents in [Gallatin] street and set fire to the mass." Such large-scale affrays—what the late Tulane historian Judith Schafer characterized as brothel riots—involved alcohol-tinged bad blood between rival establishments, and erupted frequently in the vice districts of antebellum cities. One in 1855 entailed the notorious Archie Murphy and his "Gallatin Street Rangers" invading the brothel of madam Elizabeth Myers on adjacent Barracks Street, "beating her and destroying her furniture." Only recently had the same gang also "riotously destroyed the furniture and fixtures of an oyster saloon" on nearby Levee Street. Today's Bourbon Street pales in comparison to antebellum Gallatin Street.

Laws had been on the books for years targeting "lewd and abandoned women," but they mainly prohibited "occasion[ing] scandal or disturb[ing] the tranquility of the neighborhood" rather than the sex trade itself. Gallatin-style mayhem and the sheer ubiquity and profitability of prostitution, however, impelled city authorities to attempt a legal solution. In March 1857, according to Schafer as well as Louisiana State University historian Alecia Long, the City Council passed an Ordinance Concerning Lewd and Abandoned Women, a sixteen-act, thrice-amended piece of legislation said to be the first of its kind in the United States. Dubbed the Lorette Law after the French slang for prostitutes, the ordinance for the first time restricted the sex trade by taxing prostitutes $100 and brothel keepers $250 annually. Because it applied only to certain areas, the law reworked the geography of prostitution and, by taxing it rather than banning it, routed industry profits into city coffers. The spatial restrictions aimed to make the sex trade invisible: harlots could not occupy one-story buildings or the lower floor of any structure, nor could they "stand upon the sidewalk . . . or at the alley way, door or gate . . . nor sit upon the steps [with] an indecent posture [nor] stroll about the streets of the city indecently attired." The Lorette Law also mandated that white and "free colored" prostitutes not occupy the same house, and banned public women from soliciting johns in cabarets or coffeehouses.

Generally speaking, the Lorette Law had the effect of curtailing prostitution in the front-of-town (the urban core by the Mississippi River) and shunting it outwardly to the rear and lower fringes of the city. Although it remained legal to sell sex so long as it was quiet, unnoticeable, and licensed, the Lorette Law marked the beginning of the end of the old Phillippa/Girod and Gallatin/Elysian Fields vice concentrations, not to mention the scores of dispersed brothels.

However, one old concentration evaded the new delimitations. Because the Lorette Law did not restrict prostitution on the swamp (lake) side of Basin Street between Canal Street and Toulouse, the old Customhouse/Basin/Franklin concentration managed to persist—with great consequence decades later.

The Lorette Law came under legal attack immediately, from public women, brothel keepers, and the landlords who rented to them. One madam, Eliza Costello, refused to pay the $250 fee and ran her case to the Louisiana Supreme Court, which in January 1859 ruled the ordinance unconstitutional on licensing technicalities. Sex workers celebrated with a vulgar victory parade.

Authorities fought back. "For the next forty years," wrote Schafer, "city leaders passed eight new versions of the Lorette Law, all of which attempted unsuccessfully to control, regulate, or just make money on prostitution." Licensing fees and penalties were tweaked variously, but the spatial limits of the law generally remained the same as in 1857. This meant that, by default, the one place in the city where sex workers could ply their trade with no costs, minimal police interference, and maximum proximity to downtown client pools was the Customhouse/ Basin area. Forty years later, that area would form an opportunity for the city to attempt its greatest corralling of vice, one that would cinch New Orleans's enduring reputation for the lascivious and lay the groundwork for today's Bourbon Street. It would become known as Storyville.

As for Gallatin, the city during the Great Depression targeted the seedy old street as part of the New Deal's urban renewal and renovation programs. The French Market figured prominently in those plans, and given Gallatin's forlorn condition—"virtually abandoned by traffic, a loafing place for human derelicts," according to the *Times-Picayune*—a decision was made to raze all buildings on its riverside flank and scrub the area clean of its ancient stigma. In 1935 the city acquired the requisite land and proceeded with demolitions; the next year it renamed Gallatin Street "French Market Place"; and in 1938 it dedicated the new open-air Farmers' Market pavilion, today's French Market Flea Market.

Few of the vendors or visitors there today know of the area's dark history, but this was not the case in the 1930s. Gallatin Street, wrote the *Times-Picayune* in 1938, is "known to modern New Orleans through numerous written accounts as the street where shadowy forms darted in and out, a lane of sinister doing [where] seamen were 'Shanghaied,' smuggled goods were hidden, and men and women were murdered."

UPTOWN SERENDIPITY
How Inaction Created Space for Eden

Understanding the course of history starts with questioning the very notion that it flows neatly in a regular "course." More often, human events lunge unexpectedly in new directions on account of snap decisions, misunderstandings, inclement weather, inexplicable inaction, or sheer serendipity. Such inflection points might make for bad fiction, but they abound in the annals of history, and leave us today pondering questions of "What if ?"

History's caprice both reflects and drives geography. I had a chance to ponder this while preparing for a lecture at the Audubon Nature Institute's inaugural Olmsted Legacy Dinner, in which I described how Audubon Park became the urban Eden we enjoy today. In fact, if history did flow in a regular course, we would not have Audubon Park at all. Nor would we have the campuses of Tulane and Loyola universities, at least not in their current locations.

Let's back up a bit.

During the early 1800s, planters near New Orleans found themselves with an opportunity to make more money by selling their plantations for urban lots rather than continuing in agriculture. One by one they sold, and by the 1840s, nearly all of present-day uptown had been subdivided into streets and parcels, though only sparsely developed with houses.

All, that is, except one. Located five miles upriver from the city and owned in colonial times by the Fontenet family, this plantation, running from the Mississippi River to the backswamp roughly by today's Fontainebleau Drive, passed into the hands of Pierre Foucher in 1792, who expanded it in 1825.

It's unclear whether Pierre Foucher had any designs for his land, but if he were anything like his neighbors, he likely would have hired a surveyor and subdivided it. His death in 1832 passed that option to his son, Louis Frederic Foucher. Louis seemed so inclined as well, having built a race track (located where Uptown Square is today) on an adjacent parcel also owned by the Fouchers, which was indeed later subdivided.

Subdivision became even more likely after 1835, when the New Orleans and Carrollton Rail Road, predecessor of today's streetcar line, began operating on Nayades Street, now St. Charles Avenue. The conveyance made the uptown plantations all the more attractive for residential living. Louis Foucher strove to get a spur line added to the railroad, and extended the old Fontenet oak alley (parts

Audubon Park in uptown New Orleans, with the campuses of Tulane and Loyola universities visible at upper right. *1970s photograph from author's NOPSI/Entergy collection.*

of which still exist) all the way to St. Charles, further suggesting an upcoming suburban subdivision.

But Foucher, a French Creole who never quite Americanized, did not have his heart in the project, nor in returning to agriculture. Rather, he cast his eyes to the Old World and eventually decamped with his family to Paris, where he renamed himself the Marquis de Circé, claimed French citizenship, and all but abandoned his Louisiana property.

Until, that is, he learned that Union troops had wrought damage when they used his land for a field hospital and barracks during the Civil War. His claim for indemnification was actually paid years later, but not before Foucher died in Paris, in 1869, leaving the tract to his widow. Two years later, Madame Foucher sold it to two real estate developers named Bloomer and Southworth. It seemed like a good investment: the area had just been annexed into New Orleans city limits, and denizens of downtown were eager to flee the Old City for the spacious new garden suburbs of uptown. The former Foucher tract was finally about to be urbanized.

But Bloomer and Southworth were more schemers than developers. They devised an elaborate plan in which they lobbied the state to create two new amenities, a park and a state capitol, on either side of St. Charles Avenue. They proceeded to sell the riverside land to the commission charged to create the park, and the lakeside land (now more valuable for its proximity to the upcoming park) to other investors, profiting handsomely in the process.

When the scheme came to light, it outraged corruption-weary citizens and added to the case for the impeachment of Governor Henry Clay Warmoth, effectively ending the state capitol idea. But the scheme did lead to legislation creating the park, and after the City of New Orleans purchased the land for that purpose in 1871, the Foucher tract became Upper City Park.

A decade later, when cotton advocates got Congress to approve a world's fair to stir up trade for New Orleans, they selected Upper City Park as the site for the event. The 1884–85 World's Industrial and Cotton Centennial Exposition, while a financial flop, brought beautiful landscaping and positive attention to the area, and in the years afterwards, the surrounding subdivisions became some of the most attractive residential real estate in town.

The open space lakeside of St. Charles, meanwhile, came to the attention of the Jesuits and the administrators of Tulane University, both of whom were seeking to expand beyond their institutions' cramped downtown quarters. Uptown beckoned, and the old Foucher tract provided the perfect space. Both organizations purchased land there in 1889–91 and proceeded to build beautiful campuses for Tulane and Loyola universities during the 1890s–1910s.

Together with Audubon Park (renamed in 1886), which by this time was undergoing tasteful landscaping by the Olmsted Firm, the twin campuses plus adjacent "residential parks" (private streets) such as Audubon Place added further exclusivity to this area. The universities also created numerous professional jobs and attracted a well-educated and moneyed demographic. Today's Uptown/University neighborhood, one of the most beautiful examples of residential urbanism in the nation, had come together.

And it all happened rather serendipitously, without a city planning commission or zoning ordinances. Consider the what-ifs:

What if the Fouchers had subdivided the family tract, as all their neighbors did?
What if Bloomer and Southworth hadn't come up with their scheme?
What if their scheme had failed to spawn the park?
What if their scheme had succeeded in landing the state capitol?

Uptown under any of these perfectly possible scenarios would be very different today. The academic administrators still would have departed downtown, but my guess is that, without the Foucher tract, they would have established the new

Tulane and Loyola campuses along the Metairie-Gentilly Ridge. Now City Park Avenue and Gentilly Boulevard, this topographic upland was well-drained, had attractive new housing and streetcar access, and lay close enough to the city for convenient access yet far enough that ample space could still be purchased for a reasonable price. (It's for these reasons that land uses with similar exigencies, such as fairgrounds and cemeteries, predominate here, and it's worth noting that three institutions of higher learning—Dillard, Delgado, and the Baptist Theological Seminary—operate here today.)

City Park, meanwhile, would have become the city's one and only major green space, and might have been selected for the 1885 world's fair and later landscaped in an Olmsted fashion. With Tulane and Loyola nearby, this area likely would have attracted wealthy and well-educated families. Uptown, lacking these amenities, might have developed with a more modest housing stock and drawn a more middle-class demographic. Indeed, were it not for the Fouchers' inaction, today's Uptown/University might be more like today's Mid-City/Bayou St. John, and vice versa.

Certainly we'd have a very different urban geography. We'll never know for sure, because history and, by extension, human geography are rarely "meant to be." History twists and lunges into unexpected courses, oftentimes by pure serendipity.

BEFORE TULANE, BEFORE LOYOLA, THERE WAS LELAND UNIVERSITY

Audubon/University ranks today among New Orleans's most affluent neighborhoods. But 150 years ago, it was barely urbanized, only sporadically wealthy, and not even in New Orleans. It fell within Jefferson, adjacent to Carrollton, both of which were cities in Jefferson Parish, and its landscape of recently subdivided plantations comprised mostly isolated houses with gardens amid pastures and orchards. Although the New Orleans and Carrollton Rail Road (today's streetcar line) provided mule-drawn rail access to the urban core, most parcels remained undeveloped and fairly cheap.

Downtown, meanwhile, was getting crowded, and residents and institutions alike, including the predecessors of Tulane and Loyola universities, scanned the cityscape for more spacious alternatives. In 1870, the New York–based Baptist Free Mission Society established another institution of higher learning downtown. Named Leland University in honor of Brooklyn-based benefactors Holbrook and Izanina Leland Chamberlain, the coeducational college aimed to serve students, according to its charter, "irrespective of race, color or previous condition of servitude"—that is, enslavement. In the spirit of Reconstruction, and following in the steps of the Methodists' Straight College (1869, a forerunner of today's Dillard), the Baptists launched Leland University to educate the first generation of emancipated African Americans in curricula that would eventually include Collegiate, Theological, Normal (teaching), and Industrial and Mechanics departments.

Realizing their provisional space in a Baptist church on Tulane Avenue would not suffice, Leland trustees spent twenty thousand dollars for ten acres uptown and, in 1873, moved their campus to bucolic St. Charles Avenue between present-day Newcomb Boulevard and Audubon Street. Known as the Greenville subdivision, this lightly developed area had been annexed into New Orleans only three years earlier, followed by neighboring Carrollton in 1874.

Leland thus became the first university in a neighborhood that would become named for them. But as a charitable institution, Leland was not alone in its move to the outskirts: because the metropolitan periphery offered cheaper land prices yet remained reasonably accessible to the populace, it attracted the establishment of elder homes, almshouses, orphanages, sanatoriums, boarding schools, and other private social-service institutions needing lots of space. By the late 1800s, places like uptown and the Ninth Ward riverfront proliferated with these sort of campus-like entities.

Measuring three hundred feet along the avenue and fourteen hundred feet deep, Leland's campus featured an impressive ninety-thousand-dollar four-story Main Building with a grand gallery topped with a Second Empire roof and tower. The Chamberlain Dormitory, designed by Thomas Sully and built in 1884, sat farther back, separated by a traditional academic quad shaded by live oaks and surrounded by working gardens and landscaping. "No more beautiful or healthful location could be found in New Orleans," wrote the *Weekly Pelican* of Leland, "while its retirement from the crowded city renders it particularly suited to study." By the early 1880s, a hundred students lived the familiar cadence of academic life here: lectures, study, and exams; semesters, ceremonies, and diplomas. The 1885 commencement speaker was famed abolitionist Julia Ward Howe, lyricist of "The Battle Hymn of the Republic."

The year 1885 was a memorable one uptown. The World's Industrial and Cotton Centennial Exposition had drawn international attention to Upper City Park, just steps from Leland's campus, and moneyed families living downriver came to appreciate the area's residential appeal. In subsequent years, land values rose as streetcar access improved and comfortable townhouses were built on parcel after parcel.

Institutions followed: The Jesuits and the administrators of the recently endowed Tulane University acquired adjacent parcels in 1889–91, across from the newly renamed Audubon Park (1886), and proceeded to build the present-day campuses of Loyola and Tulane starting in 1894. That same year, a private "residential park" named Audubon Place was laid out between Tulane and Leland, and promptly became the city's most exclusive address. Lands that had started the 1800s as colonial-era slave plantations were ending the century as a quintessential American streetcar suburb, leafy, wealthy, and white.

Leland University campus (right), fronting St. Charles Avenue on what is now Newcomb Boulevard. *Map detail from 1883 Robinson Atlas, courtesy New Orleans Notarial Archives.*

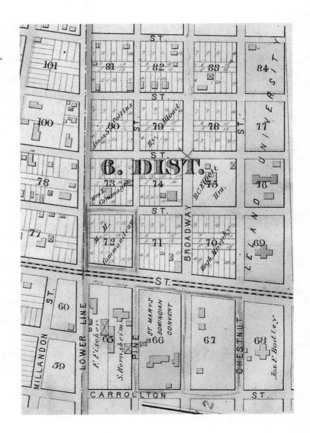

With Tulane newly arrived at one address and Leland at the other, 6600–7000 St. Charles Avenue formed something of a microcosm of these social and urban changes. Likewise, relations between white male Tulanians and black coed Le-landers reflected racial attitudes of the times, not to mention timeless collegiate high jinks. One incident in 1895 serves to illustrate.

The city had just installed wooden passenger platforms along the recently electrified St. Charles streetcar line. Tulanians gained permission to paint their landing green for their school's color, while Lelanders painted theirs light blue—which also happened to be the color claimed by Tulane's sophomore class of 1897.

One night, a group of Tulane sophomores gathered in Audubon Park and, according to the *Picayune*, armed themselves with "pots of coal tar and paint brushes" and proceeded to paint over the blue Leland platform "shiny black" along with "a skull and cross bones [and] an immense '97." Chagrined, Tulane president William Preston Johnston, a former Confederate soldier and son of famed general Albert Sidney Johnston, condemned the ungentlemanly behavior and pressed the culprits to apologize under penalty of suspension. Defiantly, the entire sophomore class endorsed the tar-painting—and got themselves suspended *en masse*. Half would eventually apologize, but the rest refused because the Leland student newspaper had dared label them "vandals and hoodlums." The incident became part of Tulane lore for decades to come, but Lelanders remembered it in a less amusing light. Tulane's school colors today include both green and light blue.

Rivalries and tensions aside, both universities flourished, as did the neighbor-hood. Leland enrollment surpassed one thousand by 1904, and Tulane had over two thousand students by 1908. Audubon Park was undergoing landscaping by the famed Olmsted Firm, and the surrounding residential areas rated among the most desirable in town. Rising real estate values put pressure on the old social-service institutions which had settled here back when land was cheap, and some decided to sell: the Touro-Shakspeare Alms House on Daneel Street, for example, would relocate to rural Algiers to make room for big new homes, while the Asylum for Destitute Orphan Boys at Valence moved to an upriver farm—"another evidence of the gradual tendency to remove such institutions from St. Charles Avenue," the *Picayune* explained, "where at present they are occupying tracts very valuable in-deed as residential sites." In today's parlance, uptown was gentrifying, and Leland found itself sitting on some of the most valuable land in town.

Then came the Great Storm of 1915. First of the modern hurricanes in terms of urban surge flooding, the September gale seemed to save its most tempestuous wrath for landmark buildings. Eleven church steeples toppled citywide, and both

Horticultural Hall in Audubon Park and the old St. Louis Hotel in the French Quarter were so wrecked they were subsequently demolished. Leland's two buildings suffered severe damage as well, enough to necessitate the cancellation of the fall semester, though not so much that they could not be repaired.

Nonetheless, within two weeks of the hurricane, Leland's New York–based trustees responded in a draconian manner. They decided to sell the campus and move the school out of town.

Most people blamed the storm for Leland's demise, but the trustees had been mulling the move for a while and the disaster merely occasioned it. That Tulane University had recently purchased land directly behind Leland for its Sophie New-comb women's college, and had originally eyed Leland's campus for that purpose, gave Leland's trustees all the more cause to sell while the market was hot. "Real estate men regard it as one of the choicest building locations in New Orleans," reported the *Item*, "and it will no doubt sell at fancy prices."

Local black Baptists, many of them Leland alumni, stridently advocated to keep Leland in New Orleans and would continue to do so into the 1930s, although it is unclear whether they explicitly opposed the sale of the St. Charles campus. Trustees nonetheless purchased 212 acres near Alexandria for the new campus, but decided to sell it too because, according to a Leland historical monograph, "whites thought that there would be a conflict between their children and the Black students of Leland."

In 1922, the trustees settled for 160 acres on the former Groom Plantation in Baker, north of Baton Rouge, and reopened Leland College on Groom Road the next year. The new campus was spacious and its buildings attractive, but the student body had shrunk to about three hundred students, probably because it competed with Southern University just a few miles away, while its traditional pool of prospective students lived nearly a hundred miles away. After the American Baptist Home Mission Society discontinued most of its support in the late 1930s, Leland constantly found itself short of funding.

The old campus on St. Charles Avenue, meanwhile, had been purchased in 1916 by industrialist Robert Werk for $175,000, nearly nine times its original cost. The *Item* called it "the largest single adjudication [in New Orleans, and] probably the largest single tract of its nature ever sold for so much money at the auction exchange," and predicted Werk would "clean up $100,000 at least." The development would form the upriver side of Newcomb Boulevard, from St. Charles to Freret, and opulent homes were erected afterwards. The sixteen properties there today have a combined assessed value of well over $15 million.

Leland traced a very different destiny. After struggling financially for decades, the college finally closed in 1960. Its former campus in Baker is now a semirural subdivision surrounded by open fields, not unlike what its original St. Charles Avenue environs looked like 150 years ago.

NEWSPAPER ROW
The Formation and Dispersion of a Media District

The shift to a digital emphasis by New Orleans's longest-running daily newspaper, announced to a shocked readership by the *Times-Picayune* in 2012, precipitated a citywide reflection on the role that print journalism plays in civic life. Significant as it is today, that role was even greater in the nineteenth century, when local newspapers brought to New Orleanians the only consistent source of information about the outside world. Numerous editions in English, French, German, Spanish, and Italian circulated weekly, semiweekly, daily, and twice daily, keeping informed, entertained, and agitated the people of New Orleans and the entire "Southwest," as the *Bee* called the region.

So important were print media in historic New Orleans that industry players spontaneously formed their own dedicated space within the city's economic geography. Firms often cluster spatially to tap the resources, infrastructure, labor pool, services, data, markets, and clients upon which all in the industry depend. "Concerns akin assemble together," observed George W. Engelhardt as he surveyed downtown commercial activity a hundred years ago. Indeed they did: a banking district formed around the intersection of Royal and Conti streets; cotton merchants clustered around Carondelet and Gravier; wholesale grocers operated at Poydras and Tchoupitoulas, sugar and rice traders held court at North Peters and Customhouse (Iberville), theaters thrived around Canal and Baronne, and anything that involved the printed word could be found, from the 1840s to the 1920s, on Newspaper Row: the 300 block of Camp Street plus the adjacent alleys of Natchez, Bank, and Commercial.

Decades earlier, print media initially set up shop seven blocks downriver from that location, in the French Quarter. Francophone professionals of various stripes worked on or near upper Chartres Street, and among them were the city's first generation of newspaper editors and printers. The settlement of anglophones in the upper faubourg of St. Mary, and their subsequent commercial investments in the so-called American sector, would change this pattern. While all seven of New Orleans's editorial and printing offices were located in the French Quarter in 1809, only four of ten remained there in 1838; all others had opened uptown. City directories indicate that, in both relative and absolute numbers, the geographical center of gravity of the New Orleans publishing scene had largely shifted from the Old City to the Faubourg St. Mary by the mid-1840s. What tipped the balance was the arrival of a new player in the industry.

Volume 1, number 1, of the *Picayune* hit the cold, rainy streets of New Orleans on January 25, 1837. Its proprietors worked out of a 12-by-14-foot room at 38 Gravier Street until relocating a few months later to slightly more spacious quarters at 74 Magazine. Before completing its first year, the operation moved once again to 72 Camp Street, where it was the only newspaper operation on that street, although five other papers and journals functioned within a few blocks. Around this spot on Camp Street, New Orleans's most famous newspaper would prosper for more than eighty years.

On February 16, 1850, a conflagration consumed the *Picayune* office and twenty-two adjacent buildings. The smoke cloud, however, had a silver lining: the cleared area allowed the publishers to purchase the lot and construct a custom-made building at 66 Camp to suit its needs. Builders Jamison and McIntosh finished the handsome four-story Greek Revival structure by late 1850, making it the first printing plant erected by a newspaper in the city. There was no mistaking the office of the *Picayune:* a copper eagle hung upon the parapet, an ornate iron-lace verandah lined the second story, and in between was etched into the facade the newspaper's name. Because the depth and common walls of the building restricted natural light, the architects designed a glass sunlight on the roof and painted the interior white for the benefit of the eighty or so employees inside. The building was also fitted with a steam elevator, a dumbwaiter, a network of gas jets, and three Hoe cylinder presses powered by a coal-burning steam engine, all of which were made in New Orleans.

The *Picayune's* commercial success and commanding location drew colleagues and competitors to settle nearby. By 1854, four of the city's fifteen newspapers and periodicals were located on Camp Street, and another seven operated nearby, while only three remained in the Old City, and one in the Faubourg Marigny.

Why Camp Street? Like Chartres in the French Quarter, Camp was as busy as any street in Faubourg St. Mary. The blocks between Gravier and Poydras,

Surviving buildings of Newspaper Row on the 300 block of Camp Street. Former headquarters of the *Picayune* (1850) appears here during its 2016 conversion to apartments; note repainting of newspaper's façade inscription. *Photograph by Richard Campanella.*

where most publishers settled, were centrally located between the new uptown faubourgs and the Old City, while not too close to the bustling riverfront wharves nor the destitute back-of-town. Major banks, hotels, and offices occupied adjacent blocks, as did City Hall, which in 1853 relocated to nearby Lafayette Square. There were no compelling reasons *not* to locate on Camp Street, and plenty of reasons *to* locate there, namely the presence of major players in the industry, starting with the *Picayune* and later the *Times-Democrat, Daily States, City Item, Daily News,* and others. The success of the early-comers to Camp Street, who may have selected the site largely for incidental real estate reasons, lured rivals for the simple survivalist instinct to be in the heart of it all, especially in a competitive information-dependent business like journalism. Once a critical mass formed, support services such as printers and binders also settled in the area, which iterated the trend. Camp Street, however, did not entirely monopolize the industry. While Camp had more newspapers and publishers than any other street for most of the years between the Civil War and World War I, it never had more than 57 percent of all such offices in the city, averaging about 35 percent between 1870 and 1918. Still, those who called Newspaper Row home tended to be the biggest, highest-circulating, and most influential papers.

A visitor walking up Camp in the mid-1880s would have sensed Newspaper Row before seeing it, from the scurry of newsboys and the sounds of their sing-song sales pitch. To his left, on the riverside corner of Canal, he would have noticed the first Camp Street print shop, above which was published the *Louisiana Sugar Bowl and Farm Journal*. After passing the City Hotel, he would encounter a composing and printing shop at 28–30 Camp, indicative of Newspaper Row's ancillary businesses of job (contract) printing for things like business cards, fliers, pamphlets, directories, and books. The corner shop at Gravier and Camp was also occupied by a hand-printing business (type set by hand), while a job-printer shop with a press room ran a few doors down on Gravier. The third and fourth floors of 56 Camp were utilized by a hand printer and bindery, respectively, while all floors of 58 Camp were occupied by one of the city's largest papers, the *Times-Democrat*, an operation running straight back to Bank Place. The *Picayune*, head-quartered prominently at 66 Camp (now 326 Camp), had its offices, composing rooms, and press rooms spread out across all floors plus adjacent buildings. If the windows were open, the clicking of hand-set type may have been audible, until they were replaced in the early 1890s by noisy but efficient Linotype machines. Directly across the street, at the intersection of Commercial Place, were the offices of the *Louisiana Sugar and Rice Report* (61 Camp) and the *Soards' Business Directory of New Orleans*. Back on the river side of the street, the building at 68 Camp was home to the *Mascot*, while the rear of the building at 72 Camp was the cramped office of the *Evening Chronicle*. There may have been a cluster of paperboys gathered across this narrow alley, at the door of the Newsboys' Home, biding time until the latest edition came off the press by rolling dice, racing, or playing ball in Natchez Alley. Insurance offices and banks, which often patronized the print shops, filled the storefronts and upper floors in between. After crossing Natchez Alley—home to the main office of the *City Item*, the *Southwestern Christian Advocate*, lithographers, paper warehouses, and printers—our visitor would pass yet another print shop and the 90 Camp office of the major *Daily States*. Three more publishing-related shops, plus the *Southwestern Presbyterian*, the *Baptist Advocate*, and the *Orion*, occupied portions of buildings in this block before Poydras Street. Above Poydras, the visitor might notice a number of smaller shops—the influential *German Gazette*, the *New Orleans Christian Advocate*, and the *Familien Freund* between 108 and 112 Camp. By the time our visitor made it to Lafayette Square, he would have had plenty of opportunities to pick up some reading material.

Newspaper Row's heyday peaked in 1890–1910, when over twenty of the city's fifty or so publishers operated within two blocks of the Camp/Natchez intersection. The density of journalists in this fiercely competitive business made for a frenetic atmosphere, one that sometimes boiled into brawls and shoot-outs. Mostly, though, the row buildings were filled with diligent reporters, editors, and typesetters intent on meeting deadlines.

The streets around Newspaper Row were the domain of newsboys, most of them orphans, on whom the papers depended for distribution before trucks and vending machines. The number of street urchins was such that, in 1879, the Society of St. Vincent de Paul and the Sisters of Mercy of St. Alphonsus moved their newsboys' home to 20 Bank Place (now 324 Picayune Place), directly behind the *Picayune* office, where the lads were availed the services of a school, dormitory, kitchen, and chapel.

While the industry remained geographically stable, its constituents opened, closed, changed hands, or merged relentlessly. "From the simple operation it had once been, newspaper publication was [becoming] a highly specialized and tremendously costly manufacturing process," wrote Thomas Ewing Dabney in 1944. "Machinery grew larger and more expensive; telegraph tolls increased; the cost of news service rose; paper, ink, and other materials climbed; so did labor." A major merger occurred in 1914, when the *Picayune* consolidated with the *Times-Democrat* (itself the product of an 1881 merger of the *Times* and *Democrat*) and became the *Times-Picayune*. Now owned by the Nicholson Publishing Company rather than the Nicholson family, "the Old Lady of Camp Street" became a corporate entity. With so many papers swallowed up by rivals or hobbled by wartime costs, the number of Camp Street offices dwindled from sixteen to ten. The Newsboys Home on Bank Place closed in 1917, and after World War I, the ever-expanding *Times-Picayune* decided to relocate to a larger building on Lafayette Square near City Hall.

The postwar era saw the demise of a number of old industry clusters in downtown New Orleans, and publishers were no exception. The concurrent demographic diffusion to new lakeside neighborhoods and later to suburban parishes motivated the *Picayune* to relocate once again, in 1968, to a spacious new facility at 3800 Howard Avenue, convenient to new transportation arteries. Following the spatial dispersion of the readership, the *Times-Picayune* established six regional bureaus and commenced publishing spatially specialized supplements, from the

Westwego Picayune to the *Slidell Picayune*, from the *River Parishes Picayune* to the *St. Tammany Picayune*, and from the *Uptown Picayune* to the *Downtown Picayune*. The paper's 2012 shift to three-day-a-week print and delivery schedule is the latest chapter in this story of eternal change, and certainly not the last one.

The era when "concerns akin" benefited by "assembling together" has also since faded. New Orleans's cotton district, sugar and rice district, Chinatown, and the wholesaling district, to name a few, are now all relict cityscapes. Yet spatial clustering still bears fruit for certain lines of work. Consider, for example, the recent success of local entrepreneurs in establishing shared workspaces, oftentimes in the surplus office space left behind when the white-collar oil and gas industry decamped for Houston. Incubation centers such as the Idea Village, New Orleans Exchange, Icehouse, Launch Pad, and the New Orleans BioInnovation Center aim to share fixed-cost assets, reduce risk, network socially, and intellectually cross-pollinate—ingredients for success that all pegged to propinquity. Witness also the impact of overlay districts, a zoning tool designed to encourage certain commercial land uses in a targeted area, which have led to the blossoming of new eateries on Freret Street and the clustering of building-materials recyclers on St. Claude Avenue. Note also the success of the medical district along Tulane Avenue, the government services district around Loyola Avenue, the entertainment districts of Bourbon and Frenchmen streets, the new galleries and performance spaces on St. Claude Avenue, and the rebirth of the theater district—all of which benefit from walkable proximity among competitors.

As for Newspaper Row, we are at least fortunate to retain most of its old buildings. They line the 300 riverside block of Camp, the narrow Picayune Place (formerly Bank Place) behind it, and adjacent Natchez Alley. Only one clue of former occupancy remains visible from the street: the faint palimpsest of THE PICAYUNE etched into the upper facade of 326 Camp. Ironically, despite all the recent turmoil at the *Times-Picayune*, its journalistic activity will soon shift back to its historic location. After decades on Howard Avenue, a site chosen for distribution reasons, the new corporation known as "NOLA.com/*The Times-Picayune*" has since shifted its news-gathering activity to One Canal Place, a few blocks from old Newspaper Row.

CHINATOWN, NEW ORLEANS

New Orleans once had a Chinatown—two, in fact.

To understand how this ethnic enclave originally formed, we have to go back 150 years. The Confederacy had just been defeated, emancipation ensued, and the South's agricultural economy had to be rebuilt from the bottom up, starting with its field labor force. Toward this end, southern planters looked to their peers in the Caribbean, who had responded to emancipation years earlier by importing thousands of East Asian and South Asian laborers whom they called "coolies." The influential New Orleans business journal *De Bow's Review* reported in 1866 that West Indian sugar harvests by South Asians were "much more than in the years of slavery," illustrating how "the advantages of the coolie system" made plantations "highly flourishing" again.

Louisiana planters adopted the idea, and in 1867 dispatched agents to recruit a few hundred Chinese workers out of Cuba. That effort was interrupted by a war on the island, so the agents instead hired 1,600 Chinese out of California, and later China proper, and sent them to lower Louisiana, where they would toil on plantations and build railroads.

Recruitment faced obstacles. The U.S. government, for one, viewed it askance as a surrogate for slavery, and restrictions in Hong Kong and better pay in California made the Louisiana sugar fields a tough sell. Those who took the jobs held out for better pay and conditions, irritating their bosses. By the early 1870s, planters began to look elsewhere for contract labor. The "coolie system" failed in Louisiana, and the Chinese workers migrated to the hope of the city.

It was in 1871 that people of Asian descent became a noticeable presence in the streets of New Orleans. Fou Loy had opened a store on 400 Chartres, which the *Times* described sportingly as "a centre of attraction for hundreds who delight to gaze upon the curious manufactures of China." Yut Sing's curio shop conducted business on Royal, while a Chinese laundry opened on Carondelet. "A year ago we had no Chinese among us," commented the *Bee*, "we now see them everywhere. . . . This looks, indeed, like business." The 1880 U.S. Census recorded 95 Chinese living in New Orleans and 489 in Louisiana; most were young men residing in boardinghouses and apartments, employed in laundering, cooking, and cigar making, a skill likely learned in Cuba.

In 1881, a northern missionary named Lena Saunders began offering classes for local Chinese immigrants. Her effort intrigued leaders of the Canal Street

Presbyterian Church, who in 1882 incorporated Saunders's work into their mission at 215 South Liberty Street. In short time, the Chinese Mission would serve over 200 Chinese and other Asians (the first convert was "Corean"), and in the process made this Third Ward neighborhood—specifically 1100 Tulane Avenue at South Rampart—a hub for the city's Chinese population. By the 1900s, seven Chinese markets, groceries, and merchandise shops filled 1100 Tulane, and an equal number operated nearby.

Despite its small size, New Orleans's Chinatown was the largest in the lower South and was well known locally, perceived by many as an exotic element to the cosmopolitan city. One *Picayune* reporter in 1906 described its Chinese Republican Association building as "suggestive of the mysterious Far East," and its upstairs temple "constructed along the lines of barbaric picturesqueness" and "dedicated to the worship of heathen deities." Chinatown also had merchants' associations, fraternal organizations, clubs, even a cremation society.

Those Chinese who came of age overseas wore traditional garb and spoke their native tongue, while those locally born strove to assimilate. "Kimonos," as the locals called them, and "pigtails" eventually disappeared, but as is often the case in cultural assimilation, food customs proved tenacious. Reported the *Picayune* in 1910, "Most of the Chinese cling to their native dishes, even when they discard Oriental costume. Rice is their staple food [and] fish, birds, and other delicacies are imported from China. They drink tea as Americans do water."

Chinatown was mostly commercial; while some Chinese families lived upstairs or nearby, most resided in or near the neighborhood laundries they operated citywide, and shopped at Chinatown for wholesale and food needs.

New Orleanians of all backgrounds also patronized Chinatown. The Yee Wah Sen Restaurant, according to the *Picayune* in 1911, catered to both the "toughest specimens of the underworld" and "polite society," and served both blacks and whites in segregated seating. Curio shops sold linen, ivory, silk tunics and mandarin coats popular with uptown debutantes, not to mention musical instruments— and narcotics—for nearby Storyville.

Surrounding Chinatown were some of the city's most fascinating neighborhoods. The Fertel family, which would later establish Ruth's Chris Steak House, ran a pawnshop on adjacent South Rampart, a street of racially integrated shopping where Orthodox Jews, Italians, and African Americans owned stores. One block upriver from Chinatown stood the Knights of Pythias Temple (1907), one of the largest black-owned buildings in the nation, and across from present-day Loyola was the ominous Criminal Courthouse (1893), with its medieval-looking

Last historical structure of New Orleans's original Chinatown, 1870s–1930s, corner of South Rampart and Common/Tulane, seen here shortly before its 2003 demolition for a parking lot. *Photograph by Richard Campanella.*

This fading lettering is the last visible sign of New Orleans's second Chinatown, which formed in 1937 on the 500 block of Bourbon Street. *Photograph by Richard Campanella.*

turrets and tower. Louis Armstrong was born nearby in 1901, and would later reminisce how his elders "used to take [us] down in China Town [and] have a Chinese meal for a change. A kind of *special* occasion."

Chinatown remained stable in size because exclusionary immigration laws had restricted the flow of new Asian immigrants to the United States. By the 1920s, the local Chinese American population had become increasingly middle-class, mostly American-born, more mobile, and less dependent on its old enclave. In 1926, the Presbytery moved its Chinese Mission to Mid-City, and in 1937, merchants lost their lease on what had long been the enclave's nucleus, the lower side of 1100 Tulane Avenue. "Chinatown is moving lock, stock, and herb barrel," reported the *Times-Picayune*.

Their destination was 500–600 Bourbon Street, an area where compatriots had previously found success. In 1924, for example, Charles Tung erected the first phase of what would eventually become the five-thousand-customer-strong Oriental Laundry (today's Rick's Cabaret). The French Quarter's rents roughly matched those around the old Chinatown, and Tung's success signaled this block's commercial viability.

By the 1940s, ten Chinese businesses operated around 500 Bourbon, and the new Chinatown became part of French Quarter culture. During World War II, denizens stockpiled illegal pyrotechnics in anticipation of the defeat of the hated Japanese empire. Granted a special police dispensation on V-J Day, two hundred Chinese Americans, according to the *Times-Picayune*, "shot more than $500 worth of firecrackers, turning [500 Bourbon] into a miniature battlefield."

Among Chinatown's top Bourbon businesses was Dan's International Restaurant, the preferred rendezvous of bohemians and power players alike, and by far the most popular Chinese eatery in the city. Another favorite was the Oriental Gift Shop at 641 Bourbon, owned by a woman named Honey Gee. Now ninety-five years old and living in Metairie, Miss Honey, who wrote me a letter of her experiences, recalled one day around 1942 when, as a local man browsed her merchandise, in walked a glamorous woman who appeared to be silent movie star and famed fan dancer Sally Rand—and indeed, she was inspecting Miss Honey's folding fans. "I think that was Sally Rand," whispered the man to Miss Honey as the woman departed. "Do you think?" she responded, and they shared a laugh. The man eventually purchased six Chinese lanterns and "as he was leaving the store, the streetcar named Desire went by." A few years later, that man, Tennessee Williams, gained worldwide fame for his Pulitzer Prize–winning play *A Streetcar Named Desire*. When in the play Blanche DuBois symbolically shades the glare of a naked light bulb with a Chinese paper lantern, she explains she purchased it "at a Chinese shop on Bourbon"—likely a reference to Miss Honey's shop, located just a block and a half from Williams's garret.

Bourbon Street's transformation into a modern entertainment strip paralleled the Chinese merchants' gradual departure for Jefferson Parish. Six remained on Bourbon in 1970, five in 1980, three in 1990, and by 1993, only the On Leong Merchants Association remained. Today, its hand-painted sign at 530½ Bourbon is the only visible trace of either the 1100 Tulane or the 500 Bourbon Chinatowns.

DANCE HALLS, SUPPER CLUBS, AND "NITERIES"
A Night Out in 1930s New Orleans

For suburban youth in metro New Orleans today, an evening on the town might mean hanging out at the food court or the multiplex. For urbanites, it might mean dinner on Magazine and music on Frenchmen, drinks at the Bottom Line, or dancing at the Hong Ngoc Club. Restaurants, bars, music and dance clubs, cinema, and retail spaces make up most modern-day nocturnal amusements. Else, folks stay home and watch television.

That wasn't an option three generations ago. Nocturnal entertainment options in circa-1930 New Orleans were larger in number and broader in range than today, and they reflected every social and urban condition of the era, from Prohibition to segregation to technology and gender relations. It's difficult to assess how New Orleans ranked nationally with regard to nighttime amusements, but it's safe to say that this major American city of nearly a half-million restive, festive souls enjoyed an abundance of options.

Among them was a new concept recently diffused from Paris, the "night club" or "nitery," which in some ways represented the next in lineage after the "concert saloons" of the late 1800s. Both venues brought together entertainment and alcohol (legal or otherwise) in dark, stylized spaces scented with the possibility of sex. Unlike in concert saloons, however, an air of exclusivity circulated among nightclub patrons, construed via fine attire, high prices, membership, a cover charge, a hat-and-coat check, and a velvet-curtain barrier. Restaurant service made nightclubs more of a total-evening experience rather than just a watering hole, and earned them the name "supper clubs" or "dinner clubs." Thematic decor, usually imaginative and sometimes garish, aimed to evoke swankiness or exoticism. Entertainment bookings were eclectic, including comedians, dance acts, contests, and novelty performances, but eschewing anything so vulgar as vaudeville. Patrons danced, as most arrived as couples, quite different from the male-dominated scene of concert saloons.

Nightclubs benefited from, indeed catered to, the liberated lifestyles to which women in the 1920s were laying claim. Whereas women were usually servants, performers, or prostitutes in concert saloons, in nightclubs they were patrons as well, participants in the emerging social trend of "dating," in which young men courted flappers with bobbed hair and cloche hats by treating them for a night on the town. Nightclubs created libidinous but classy and safe private-domain public spaces in which these newly permitted social interactions could take place. Starting in 1925, nightclubs found a home on a street called Bourbon, which over the next two decades would become nationally famous for them.

Additionally, numerous private social clubs, as well as 390 commercial clubs, entertained the thousands of New Orleanians who were dues-paying members. During Prohibition, clubs functioned as private speakeasies, and many if not most also hosted illicit games of chance. Members-only clubs benefited from the illegality of most gambling within Orleans Parish, which pushed the big casinos into neighboring Jefferson and St. Bernard parishes, leaving open a lucrative economic niche within New Orleans proper.

For those who preferred traditional entertainment, awaiting them were sixty-five theaters presenting live performances of one type or another, and fifty-six motion-picture venues including new "chains." Many performance theaters also showed films, and movie houses often staged live acts.

Dance halls were among the most culturally significant social spaces in the 1930s cityscape. A valuable Tulane University thesis written by Elbert Samuel P'Pool in 1930 takes us inside the dance hall scene of this era. There were sixty-three in New Orleans at that time; some were attached to saloons or billiard halls to share clientele; others blurred lines with cabarets or nightclubs. They could be permanent public for-profit enterprises, temporarily rented spaces, or private halls affiliated with churches or organizations. "Open halls" welcomed couples for a cover charge, whereas "closed halls" catered to men without dates who paid a fee to dance with a "hostess" employed by the house. The State of Louisiana passed laws in 1926 to regulate dance halls, imposing closing hours and banning minors, liquor, drunks, loiterers, and disorderly conduct. One of the impetuses

Rainy night on Canal Street, late 1940s. *Photograph from author's NOPSI/Entergy collection.*

for the intervention was the emergence of a popular money-making scheme of dubious legality, in which a young lady employed by the club made herself available for dance or conversation and then beguiled her suitor into treating her to an overpriced drink. For reasons unclear, the ruse came to be known as "B-drinking." So long as a policeman was present, such peccadilloes were overlooked—for a price. B-drinking and bribery, not to mention prostitution, would later become the fortes, and foibles, of post–World War II–era Bourbon Street.

Dance halls spanned the socioeconomic and racial spectrum, and the demographic subsegments of local society generally did not mix inside them. The Gay-Shattuck Law kept whites and blacks segregated wherever alcohol was served, and that was also the case in dance halls. The Pelican at 303 South Rampart and the nearby Astoria Dance Hall catered to better-off African Americans, and prided themselves as dignified and respectable joints—but joints nonetheless, with an entrance policy that required explicit approval of the owner because of the illicit booze inside. A few blocks away on lower Carondelet, the Music Box catered to the white middle class, mostly young local men plus regional visitors. It operated in a well-lit 30-by-70-foot upstairs room which adjoined a billiard hall. For ten cents' admission, a visitor could enjoy a "six-piece Negro Jazz Orchestra," which

sequenced two-minute performances of a waltz, a jazz variation, and finally a cre-
scendo. Want to dance? A dozen hostesses—described by P'Pool as "graceful" and
"cheerful" but "not known for their beauty"—awaited your invitation. The house
charged ten cents per song, from which all the girls were paid a percentage. A refreshment stand brought in a little extra revenue, while a policeman and a matron
kept order from the corner. Apparently order prevailed: P'Pool, who observed the
Music Box one spring night in 1930, saw no evidence of "improper positions or
movements," and judged that it represented "one of the better sort of its type."

Less so was the case for the Alamo Dance Hall on Liberty between Canal and
Iberville, where P'Pool felt decidedly unwelcome, and the Fern and La Vida, on
Iberville between Liberty and Rampart. Adjoined by a slew of sub rosa gambling
dens strung out along Rampart—"with mysterious swinging doors . . . opening
into an unknown rear," these three dance halls were the remnants of the so-called
Tango Belt, a cluster of semilegal joints located around Rampart and Iberville
during and after the mid-1910s decline of Storyville but before the 1930s–40s
rise of Bourbon Street. The crowds here were lower middle class, a bit rougher,
more ethnic (particularly Filipino), and engaged in illegal gambling and drinking.
Beyond that, P'Pool saw "no impropriety," although he did notice that things got
decidedly "fast" when the matron or the police stepped out.

The Tango Belt at this time also had two burlesque theaters, the Dauphine and
the Palace, on Dauphine Street near Iberville. Things were decidedly less proper
here. The dancing was performed not by the patrons but by "twenty women
dressed mostly in their own powdered skins with glittering fringe adornment
about their breasts and hips, [dancing to] salacious music most poorly played. . . .
[R]ude and obscene bodily gestures" flew from both male and female performers,
"sex appeal so crude and overdone," declared P'Pool, "that only the most depraved
could but revolt at the entire performance." And the audience? "Unwashed, un-
pressed, unshaved."

The New Slipper, located a block from the burlesque theaters, had been nearly
as disreputable until it recently reopened under new management following a
bust. This Burgundy Street cabaret now bore more of a semblance to the fancy
nightclubs popping up on Bourbon. Its "six-piece orchestra," led by Albert Brunes
and featuring "all white men, good musicians," sounded like a group that could
have gotten a gig on Bourbon. So too the diva with a "parlor voice," and the hatcheck girl. Unlike the lower-end dance halls, the New Slipper put on sophisticated airs, presented a theme ("The Mystery of Wickedness"), and built a physical
barrier to separate the gritty street from the ritzy interior. Unlike the swankiest

places, however, it obnoxiously pressured visitors to pair up with hostesses, buy illegal drinks, and dance for a twenty-five-cent (rather than ten-cent) fee. "This is the type [of dance hall] that caters to the out of town 'gink' who wants to see some 'night life,'" sniffed P'Pool.

Over on Bourbon Street was Kelley's in the Old Absinthe House—which even in 1930 "boasts its age and purposely keeps a dilapidated appearance outside." At first glance the joint appeared to be closed but for one door ajar, over which stood "a big Negro door man in a sky-blue long-tailed uniform." Couples—some in-the-know, others adventurously curious—would approach the doorman, exchange words, and gain passage. "Everything [inside] was gaudy and dignified, grand and mysterious, furnished in 'tinsel seeming splendor' lined with beaver board." Prices were high and no one complained; tipping was generous because anything "less would have been beneath the dignity of the place." One Mrs. Kelley stayed upstairs in the Old Absinthe House's hidden entresol whenever she was in town; she also ran "a real cabaret" in Panama's Canal Zone and shuttled between the two ports, managing her assets.

Economic stagnation kept the night scene relatively stable in New Orleans throughout the 1930s, although Bourbon Street gained a number of new clubs and bars, as it provided a reasonably priced escape from dismal reality for a small number of visitors. All would change on Bourbon and throughout the amusement industry in New Orleans in the subsequent decade, as tens of thousands of war-plant workers moved into the city, hundreds of thousands of servicemen embarked for combat in Europe and Asia, and millions more took their R&R here from southern military training camps.

Transformations following World War II would, among other things, shift populations outwardly into the suburbs, replace de-jure segregation with the de-facto form, and bring new behavior-changing technologies like television and air conditioning to homes. By century's end, take-out and television came to constitute an evening's entertainment for lots of folks—but not so many that New Orleans today has anything less than one of the most robust nocturnal entertainment economies in the nation, for a city of its size.

ORIGINS OF THE GO-CUP
A Historical Geography of Public Drinking

Testimonies abound regarding the bibulous nature of historic New Orleans. "This place is one of the worst I ever witnessed," wrote an outraged newcomer in 1817 on its gambling and drinking. A kindred spirit rued in 1834 that "cafés and bar-rooms were open" on the Sabbath, and that "rum and gin, Monongahela [rye whiskey], and Tom and Jerry [sweetened hot rum] here live in palaces [with a] whole army of bottles [lining] the shelves." Another man reported in 1847, "the profit is on the liquor," as evidenced by "the immense patronage these establish-ments enjoy[; they] are coining money, [and] monopolize the corners of every square." Wrote French geographer Élisée Réclus six years later, "The city's more than twenty-five hundred taverns are always filled with drinkers. . . . If [a political candidate] doesn't know how to drink a cocktail with style, he will lose popularity and be branded a traitor."

A close read of these and other historical accounts indicates that most alco-hol consumption took place in private spaces within the public domain, such as saloons, taverns, exchanges, concert saloons, grogshops, billiards halls, or "coffee houses." Drinking in the public space appears to have been socially disapproved, and in later years illegal, except during Carnival and other special times. This con-trasts strikingly with current circumstances, in which the sight of people drinking freely in the streets startles first-time visitors as much as it hardly fazes locals.

In fact, legal public-space drinking is a fairly recent phenomenon. Prior to the 1960s, swanky burlesque clubs dominated Bourbon Street, and patrons, including local couples, went to Bourbon to drink inside these stylized places, not to stroll the street drinking outdoors. The action was indoors.

This changed after Jim Garrison became district attorney in 1962. Bourbon Street vice had long been a rallying cry for reformers; Garrison knew it played well among voters, and shined light on it during his campaign. He calculated that burlesque clubs were costly operations with big staffs, and could only turn a hand-some profit if they ran illicit money-making schemes on the side. Knock out those schemes, Garrison figured, the clubs close and Bourbon Street is "cleaned up."

Garrison's vice raids over the next two years achieved all of the above—and then some. Old-line burlesque nightclubs padlocked their doors left and right, and those that survived had to scale down now that they were no longer subsi-dized by extralegal income streams. Many became tawdry strip joints or dive bars,

Bourbon Street on Mardi Gras, 2012. *Photograph by Richard Campanella.*

downscaling to maintain profit margins. It didn't help that patronage in this era was steadily shifting away from well-dressed couples with cash in their pockets, and toward trekking hippies on shoestring budgets. Barkers tried to cajole pedestrians into coming indoors, but had little success. Bourbon Street was in trouble.

Then, sometime in 1967, one unremembered enterprise came up with a better idea. Instead of convincing people outside to buy drinks inside, why not sell inside drinks to people outside? "Window hawking," it was called, and gradually, bars, clubs, and restaurants on Bourbon Street opened tiny outlets in carriageways, alleys, windows, and doorways, from which they sold beer, drinks, hot dogs, corn dogs, and snacks directly to pedestrians. Window-hawking led to "drink-carrying," which fueled widespread ambulatory inebriation in the public space.

Everyone seemed to come out ahead with window hawking—except, that is, for French Quarter residents' quality of life. On the supply side, it enabled owners to tap into the outdoor money stream with a minimum of capital improvements. It put less emphasis on decor, facilities, bathrooms, air conditioning, heating, and other costly overhead. It reduced the need for labor, particularly live entertainment.

On the demand side, window hawking allowed tourists to stroll noncommittally outdoors, amid all the eye-candy and people-watching, while imbibing for a fraction of the cost had they gone indoors. Young people particularly loved buying booze from windows because the hawkers rarely asked for proof of age, knowing their purchases would be all but untraceable. Gift and novelty shops benefited as well because drink-toting pedestrians were more inclined than clubbers to meander inside and buy souvenirs, and the tipsier they were, the more likely they'd make a dumb purchase.

Retailers threw open all their doors, hung T-shirts outside, flooded their shelf space with light, cranked up music to win the attention of passersby, and blasted frigid air into the hot summer night, or warmth into the winter chill, all to blur the line between indoor and outdoor space. Food, debris, Dixie cups, crushed pop-top cans, and broken beer bottles littered the street, attracting vermin and creating a public health hazard. Many of the flashpoints between modern-day Bourbon Street and its residential neighbors today are traceable to this era, late 1960s to mid-1970s, and to this shift in the geography of drinking.

Bourbon's problem came to public attention during Mardi Gras 1969. Afterwards, Mayor Victor "Vic" Schiro formed a committee of prominent club owners to discuss an ordinance on window hawking, which he said "demoralizes our city and cheapens the charm of Bourbon Street." Passed by the City Council, it banned "anyone to sell food or beverages from a window, door, or other aperture facing the street or other public way within the Vieux Carre," and was later modified to prohibit all sales within six feet of the street.

Two years later, the nightly pedestrian mall policy went into effect, and the absence of traffic attracted even more libertines onto Bourbon pavement. More pedestrians upped the economic ante for bartenders to hawk through windows, and they did—by finding loopholes in the ordinance or evading erratic enforcement. When, for example, one well-known entertainer tried opening an outlet in the doorway of her club, as her neighbors had been doing, police busted her capriciously.

But this time, the club fought back by promptly filing a lawsuit. The case fell into the Civil District Court docket of Judge S. Sanford Levy, who in May 1981 ruled the ordinance unconstitutional on account of its vague and imprecise wording. "Does the ordinance prohibit the display of jewelry from windows?" Levy asked. "Does the ordinance disallow a cashier to exchange a crystal chandelier for money within six feet of the doorway of an antique shop on Royal Street?"

The ruling cleared the way for the legal sale of alcohol through apertures for consumption outdoors, forever changing Bourbon Street. Later ordinances mandated plastic go-cups, to prevent injuries from broken glass, and restricted open containers only to the streets of the French Quarter. But because of enforcement disparities—police often looked the other way when Quarter tourists, likely white, toted beers into adjacent neighborhoods but confronted locals, oftentimes black, when they did the same elsewhere—the ordinance was changed in 2001 to allow most alcohol consumption in the public space so long as drinks were in cups and not "opened glass or opened metal containers."

Decried by some, cheered by others, New Orleans's unusually liberal and relatively recent public drinking customs, for better or worse, keep alive this city's centuries-old reputation for indulgence—the likes of which were excoriated in one 1850 exposé, which denounced

grog shops . . . on three of every four corners . . . from street to street, every door leading into a drinking house. . . . Three-fourths of the men . . . are confirmed drunkards, [taking] up to twenty-five to thirty [drinks] a day, and yet these are all high-minded, *sober,* and respectable *gentlemen,* full of *Southern chivalry*[!]

GENTRIFICATION AND ITS DISCONTENTS
Notes from New Orleans

AUTHOR'S NOTE: *This essay was written in early 2013, at a time when post-Katrina population changes were beginning to manifest themselves in the cityscape and culture of New Orleans. Published online in the California-based* New Geography, *the essay "went viral" and precipitated widespread discussion and debate, much of it fervent. To my chagrin, I became the go-to person on the topic of gentrification, even more so when the* New York Review of Books *quoted extensively from the essay in July 2014. It is presented here in its original form.*

Readers of this forum have probably heard rumors of gentrification in post-Katrina New Orleans. Residential shifts playing out in the Crescent City share many commonalities with those elsewhere, but also bear some distinctions and paradoxes. I offer these observations from the so-called Williamsburg of the South, a neighborhood called Bywater.

Gentrification arrived rather early in New Orleans, a generation before the term was coined. Writers and artists settled in the French Quarter in the 1920s and 1930s, drawn by the appeal of its expatriated Mediterranean atmosphere, not to mention its cheap rent, good food, and abundant alcohol despite Prohibition. Initial restorations of historic structures ensued, although it was not until after World War II that wealthier educated newcomers began steadily supplanting working-class Sicilian and black Creole natives.

By the 1970s, the French Quarter was largely gentrified, and the process continued downriver into the adjacent Faubourg Marigny (a historical moniker revived by francophile preservationists and savvy real estate agents) and upriver into the Lower Garden District (also a new toponym: gentrification has a vocabulary as well as a geography). It progressed through the 1980s into the 2000s, but only modestly, slowed by the city's myriad social problems and limited economic opportunity. New Orleans in this era ranked as the Sun Belt's premier shrinking city, losing 143,000 residents between 1960 and 2000. The relatively few newcomers tended to be gentrifiers, and gentrifiers today are overwhelmingly transplants. I, for example, am both, and I use the terms interchangeably in this piece.

Everything changed after August–September 2005, when the Hurricane Katrina deluge, amid all the tragedy, unexpectedly positioned New Orleans as a cause célèbre for a generation of idealistic millennials. A few thousand urbanists, environmentalists, and social workers—we called them "the brain gain"; they called themselves YURPS, or Young Urban Rebuilding Professionals—took leave from their graduate studies and nascent careers and headed south to be a part of something important. Many landed positions in planning and recovery efforts, or in an alphabet soup of new nonprofits; some parlayed their experiences into PhD dissertations, many of which are coming out now in book form. This cohort, whose size I estimate to be in the low- to mid-four digits, largely moved on around 2008–9, as recovery moneys petered out. Then a second wave began arriving, enticed by the relatively robust regional economy compared to the rest of the nation. These newcomers were greater in number (I estimate fifteen thousand to twenty thousand and continuing), more specially skilled, and serious about planting domestic and economic roots here. Some today are new-media entrepreneurs; others work with Teach for America or within the highly charter-ized public school system (infused recently with a billion federal dollars), or in the booming tax-incentivized Louisiana film industry and other cultural-economy niches.

Brushing shoulders with them are a fair number of newly arrived artists, musicians, and creative types who turned their backs on Great Recession woes and resettled in what they perceived to be an undiscovered bohemia in the lower faubourgs of New Orleans—just as their predecessors did in the French Quarter eighty years prior. It is primarily these second-wave transplants who have accelerated gentrification patterns.

Gentrification in New Orleans is spatially regularized and predictable. Two underlying geographies must be in place before better-educated, more-moneyed transplants start to move into neighborhoods of working-class natives. First, the area must be historic. Most people who opt to move to New Orleans envision living in Creole quaintness or Classical splendor amidst nineteen-century cityscapes; they are not seeking mundane ranch houses or split-levels in subdivisions. That distinctive housing stock exists only in about half of New Orleans proper and one-quarter of the conurbation, mostly upon the higher terrain closer to the Mississippi River. The second factor is physical proximity to a neighborhood that has already gentrified, or that never economically declined in the first place, like the Garden District.

Gentrification hot spots today may be found along the fringes of what I have (somewhat jokingly) dubbed the "white teapot," a relatively wealthy and well-educated majority-white area shaped like a kettle in uptown New Orleans, around Audubon Park and Tulane and Loyola universities, with a curving spout along the St. Charles Avenue/Magazine Street corridor through the French Quarter and into the Faubourg Marigny and Bywater. Comparing 2000 to 2010 census data, the teapot has broadened and internally whitened, and the changes mostly involve gentrification. The process has also progressed into the Faubourg Tremé (not coincidentally the subject of the HBO drama *Treme*) and up Esplanade Avenue into Mid-City, which ranks just behind Bywater as a favored spot for post-Katrina transplants. All these areas were originally urbanized on higher terrain before 1900, all have historic housing stock, and all are coterminous to some degree.

The frontiers of gentrification are "pioneered" by certain social cohorts who settle sequentially, usually over a period of five to twenty years. The four-phase cycle often begins with—forgive my tongue-in-cheek use of vernacular stereotypes—(1) "gutter punks" (their term), young transients with troubled backgrounds who sneer at societal norms and settle, squatter-like, in the roughest neighborhoods bordering bohemian or tourist districts, where they busk or beg

67

in tattered attire. On their unshod heels come (2) hipsters, who, also fixated upon dissing the mainstream but better educated and obsessively self-aware, see these punk-infused neighborhoods as bastions of coolness. Their presence generates a certain funky vibe that appeals to the third phase of the gentrification sequence: (3) "bourgeois bohemians," to use David Brooks's term. Free-spirited but well-educated and willing to strike a bargain with middle-class normalcy, this group is skillfully employed, buys old houses and lovingly restores them, engages tirelessly in civic affairs, and can reliably be found at the Saturday morning farmers' market. Usually childless, they often convert doubles to singles, which removes rentable housing stock from the neighborhood even as property values rise and lower-class renters find themselves priced out their own neighborhoods. (Gentrification in New Orleans tends to be more house-based than in northeastern cities, where renovated industrial or commercial buildings dominate the transformation.) After the area attains full-blown "revived" status, the final cohort arrives: (4) bona fide gentry, including lawyers, doctors, moneyed retirees, and alpha-professionals from places like Manhattan or San Francisco. Real estate agents and developers are involved at every phase of transition, sometimes leading, sometimes following, always profiting.

Native tenants fare the worst in the process, often finding themselves unable to afford the rising rent and facing eviction. Those who own, however, might experience a windfall, their abodes now worth ten to fifty times more than their grandparents paid. Of the four-phase process, a neighborhood like St. Roch is currently between phases 1 and 2; the Irish Channel is 3-to-4 in the blocks closer to Magazine and 2-to-3 closer to Tchoupitoulas; Bywater is swiftly moving from 2 to 3 to 4; Marigny is nearing 4; and the French Quarter is post-4.

Tensions abound among the four cohorts. The phase-1 and -2 folks openly regret their role in paving the way for phases 3 and 4, and see themselves as sharing the victimhood of their mostly black working-class renter neighbors. Skeptical of proposed amenities such as riverfront parks or the removal of an elevated expressway, they fear such "improvements" may foretell further rent hikes and threaten their claim to edgy urban authenticity—the very ambience that attracted them here. They decry phase-3 and -4 folks through "Die Yuppie Scum" graffiti, or via pasted denunciations of Pres Kabacoff, a local developer specializing in historic restoration and mixed-income public housing. Phase-3 and -4 folks, meanwhile, look askance at the hipsters and the gutter punks, but otherwise wax ambivalent about gentrification and its effect on deep-rooted mostly African American natives. They lament their role in ousting the very vessels of localism they came to savor, but also take pride in their spirited civic engagement and rescue of architectural treasures.

Gentrifiers seem to stew in irreconcilable philosophical dissonance. Fortunately, they've created plenty of nice spaces to stew in. Bywater in the past few years has seen the opening of nearly ten retro-chic foodie/locavore-type restaurants, two new art-loft colonies, guerrilla galleries and performance spaces on grungy St. Claude Avenue, a "healing center" affiliated with Kabacoff and his Maine-born voodoo-priestess partner, yoga studios, a vinyl-record store, and a smattering of coffee shops where one can overhear conversations about bioswales, tactical urbanism, the klezmer music scene, and every conceivable permutation of "sustainability" and "resilience."

It's increasingly like living in a city of graduate students. Nothing wrong with that—except, what happens when they, well, graduate? Will a subsequent wave take their place? Or will the neighborhood be too pricey by then?

Bywater's elders, families, and intergenerational households, meanwhile, have gone from the norm to the exception. Racially, the black population, which tended to be highly family-based, declined by 64 percent between 2000 and 2010, while

Menu board on Dauphine Street in Bywater in 2013, at a time when post-Katrina gentrification became the single most radioactive issue in the city's civic discourse. *Photograph by Richard Campanella.*

the white population increased by 22 percent, regaining the majority status it had prior to the white flight of the 1960s–70s. It was the Katrina disruption and the accompanying closure of schools that initially drove out the mostly black households with children, more so than gentrification per se. Bywater ever since has become a kiddie wilderness; the 968 youngsters who lived here in 2000 numbered only 285 in 2010. When our son was born in 2012, he was the very first post-Katrina birth on our street, the sole child on a block that had 11 when we first arrived (as category-3 types, I suppose, sans the "bohemian") from Mississippi in 2000.

Many predicted the 2005 deluge would wash away New Orleans's sui generis character. Paradoxically, post-Katrina gentrifiers are simultaneously distinguishing *and* homogenizing local culture vis-à-vis American norms, depending on how one defines culture. By the humanist's notion, the newcomers are actually breathing new life into local customs and traditions. Transplants arrive endeavoring to be a part of the epic adventure of living here; thus, through the process of self-selection, they tend to be Orleaneophilic "super-natives," more local than the locals. They embrace Mardi Gras enthusiastically, going so far as to form their own krewes and walking clubs (though always with irony, winking in gentle mockery at the old-line uptown krewes). They celebrate the city's culinary legacy, though their tastes generally run away from fried okra and toward "house-made beet ravioli w/ goat cheese ricotta mint stuffing" (I'm citing a chalkboard menu at a new Bywater restaurant, revealingly named Suis Generis, "Fine Dining for the People"). And they are universally enamored with local music and public festivity, to the point of enrolling in second-line dancing classes and taking it upon themselves to organize jazz funerals whenever a local icon dies.

By the anthropologist's notion, however, transplants are definitely changing New Orleans culture. They are much more secular, less fertile, more liberal, and less parochial than native-born New Orleanians. They see local conservatism as a problem calling for enlightenment rather than an opinion to be respected, and view the importation of national and global values as imperative to a sustainable and equitable recovery. Indeed, the entire scene in the new Bywater eateries—from the artisanal food on the menus to the statement art on the walls to the progressive worldview of the patrons—can be picked up and dropped seamlessly into Austin, Burlington, Portland, or Brooklyn.

How will this all play out? History offers a precedent. After the Louisiana Purchase in 1803, better-educated English-speaking Anglos moved in large numbers into the parochial, mostly Catholic and francophone Creole society of New Orleans. "The Americans [are] swarming in from the northern states," lamented one departing French official, "invading Louisiana as the holy tribes invaded the land of Canaan, [each turning] over in his mind a little plan of speculation"—sentiments that might echo those of displaced natives today. What resulted from the Creole/Anglo intermingling was not gentrification—the two groups lived separately—but rather a complex, gradual cultural hybridization. Native Creoles and Anglo transplants intermarried, blended their legal systems, their architectural tastes and surveying methods, their civic traditions and foodways, and to some degree their languages. What resulted was the fascinating mélange that is modern-day Louisiana.

Gentrifier culture is already hybridizing with native ways; post-Katrina transplants are opening restaurants, writing books, starting businesses and hiring natives, organizing festivals, and even running for public office, all the while introducing external ideas into the local canon. What differs in the analogy is that the nineteenth-century newcomers planted familial roots here and spawned multiple subsequent generations, each bringing new vitality to the city. Gentrifiers, on the other hand, usually have very low birth rates, and those few that do become parents oftentimes find themselves reluctantly departing the very inner-city neighborhoods they helped revive, for want of playmates and decent schools. By that time, exorbitant real estate precludes the next wave of dynamic twenty-somethings from moving in, and the same neighborhood that once flourished gradually grows gray, empty, and frozen in historically renovated time. Unless gentrified neighborhoods make themselves into affordable and agreeable places to raise and educate the next generation, they will morph into dour historical theme parks with price tags only aging one-percenters can afford.

Lack of age diversity and a paucity of "kiddie capital"—good local schools, playmates next door, child-friendly services—are the hobgoblins of gentrification in a historically familial city like New Orleans. Yet their impacts seem to be lost on many gentrifiers. Some earthy contingents even express mock disgust at the sight of baby carriages—the height of uncool—not realizing that the infant inside might represent the neighborhood's best hope of remaining down-to-earth.

Need evidence of those impacts? Take a walk on a sunny Saturday through the lower French Quarter, the residential section of New Orleans's original gentrified neighborhood. You will see spectacular architecture, dazzling cast-iron filigree, flowering gardens—and hardly a resident in sight, much less the next generation playing in the streets. Many of the antebellum townhouses have been subdivided into pied-à-terre condominiums vacant most of the year; others are home to peripatetic professionals or aging couples living in guarded privacy behind bolted-shut

French doors. The historic streetscapes bear a museum-like stillness that would be eerie if they weren't so beautiful.

MAPPING THE GEOGRAPHY OF COOL

"Location, location, location," the real estate adage goes. In fact, a number of complex variables drive the value of land, particularly for residential areas. They range from schools and quality of life, to amenities and safety, to prejudices, perceptions, and social status.

In recent decades, a new variant of social status has entered the real estate equation, and it has since transfigured downtown New Orleans and other American cities. It's the curious cultural phenomenon known as "cool."

Neighborhoods that a decade or two ago were viewed as dirty, dangerous, and disregarded now rank among the region's hottest real estate markets, turned around courtesy of an emerging social charisma that may be described as "hip" or "cool." Among them are Bywater and adjacent areas down St. Claude Avenue; Faubourg Tremé and St. Roch; the Irish Channel; and Mid-City. A generation earlier, places like Faubourg Marigny and the Lower Garden District underwent the transformation.

True, these neighborhoods boast other advantages. They have history, architecture, walkability, high topographic elevation, and favorable flood zones, not to mention proximity to resources and employment. But they had these advantages years ago, yet few came a-bidding. What changed is that they became cool on the social scene, and that made them hot—on the real estate scene.

Coolness is elusive, and some might be inclined to scoff at the notion, as it smacks of affectation and brings to mind poseurs and "farceurs." To be sure, coolness is purely perceptual; it is constructed and superimposed, not innate. But any illusion that can so thoroughly change the character, composition, and property value of a neighborhood cannot be dismissed. Coolness is real in its effects if not in its posturing, and as such, it's a fairly recent phenomenon, though not entirely unprecedented.

New Orleanians in times past perceived certain spaces within their city to bear a particular dash, and it was based largely on class. The word "fashionable" appears in real estate ads in the nineteenth century, usually with respect to St. Charles Avenue or the Garden District. Other code words included "genteel" and "stylish." *Vanity Fair* explained in 1869 how "the Americans adopt the term of 'down-town' for the [Creole quarter], and dignify their own residential quarter as 'up-town.'"

But fashion, style, and dignity are not the same as cool; if anything, coolness sneers at such bourgeois aspirations. Coolness exudes an aloof poise and a confident sense of self-possession; it is never boastful or chatty, but rather vaguely mysterious, unknowable, and, above all, separate and apart from the masses. It explains why celebrities wear sunglasses, and why the smarter ones know to act taciturn and keep themselves scarce.

Coolness bears a certain set of attitudes, aesthetics, tastes, and politics which are framed not in absolute terms, but relative to the masses. That is, coolness constantly needs to be ahead of the mainstream, and if the mainstream catches up, coolness goes elsewhere. "The act of discovering what's cool," observed Malcolm Gladwell in an influential 1997 article titled *The Coolhunt*, "is what causes cool to move on." As it does, coolness often produces new cultural innovations and explores increasingly edgy terrain. Coolness thus becomes geographical: it occupies certain spaces, disdains others, and seeks new ones when uncoolness approaches.

And that's when, and where, it affects real estate.

Decades ago, for example, Bourbon Street was considered cool. But when corporate hotels and mass tourism made the strip all too plebian and crass in the 1960s, coolness moved on to new spaces such as lower Decatur Street in the 1970s, and extended in the 1980s–90s across Esplanade onto Frenchmen Street. By that time, the surrounding area, along with the blocks around Coliseum Square, became the city's coolest "new" neighborhoods. Both were rechristened, one with the revived historical moniker "Faubourg Marigny" and the other with a circa-1960s coinage, "Lower Garden District." Property values rose, renovation broke out all over, the areas gentrified, and coolness spread adjacently.

After Katrina, when a wave of cool youth from places like New York arrived in New Orleans in search of undiscovered bohemian coolness, they found places like Frenchmen (not to mention Bourbon) all too similar to what they had left behind. So they proceeded to push coolness into new spaces, down St. Claude Avenue, across Rampart, and beyond. Those areas are now changing as Marigny and the Lower Garden District did previously.

Lovers of Frenchmen Street now openly worry that their street is "becoming like Bourbon Street," an explicit fear that uncoolness may be knocking on their door. That's happened before too. When Bourbon Street became uncool and the white middle class moved en masse to Jefferson Parish, a new cool space popped up rather spontaneously (coolness is hard to choreograph) in the heart of Metairie. It was dubbed Fat City, and it peaked in the late 1970s with over seventy nighttime drinking, eating, music, and entertainment venues.

But in the 1990s, downtown New Orleans had regained the cool advantage, and Fat City soon found itself in a wilderness of uncool, catering to an aging demographic with musical tastes ranging from hair bands to the Yat Pack. Jefferson Parish authorities recently hired a consultant from Manhattan to advise them on how to revive the district. His advice: "create a 'cluster of cool'" in the heart of Fat City, "where you can really make it look and feel different." Managers are trying a similar strategy for the cool-challenged French Market. They've been running "Hip Scene, Historic Setting," ads in cool magazines like *Offbeat*, recruiting earthy craft vendors to counter the beads-and-T-shirts stigma, and piping in the very cool sounds of WWOZ into the flea market, like intravenous nourishment for the ailing.

Here and elsewhere, coolness has become an urban planning strategy, and planners today wield its trappings the way their predecessors once plied golf courses and gated subdivisions. "Real" cool, meanwhile, has a mind of its own.

The ever-changing geography of cool has brought with it a cycle of neighborhood change, introducing newcomers and new wealth, sometimes displacing nativity and poverty, and making the topic of gentrification one of the most acrid in local public discourse.

Some would argue that developers and a complicit local government instigate the cool-neighborhood-*cum*-hot-real-estate cycle, and that may well be true in some cases (such as the Warehouse District and newly christened "South Market District") and in other cities (such as New York). But I contend these forces, in most cases in New Orleans, are eagerly responding to the geography of cool, not initiating it.

Much has been written about gentrification, including by yours truly, and debates about its costs and benefits can be found elsewhere. My interest here is to contend that, while coolness is illusory, its effects upon the cityscape are quite real, and thus can be mapped.

Where is the geography of cool? To address this question, I devised a technique entailing the distribution of hundreds of points digitally throughout a Geographic Information Systems (GIS) map of downtown. Each point was then ranked 0 (uncool) through 10 (very cool), reflecting how that neighborhood, bar, restaurant, or venue is generally perceived, based on a wide range of observations,

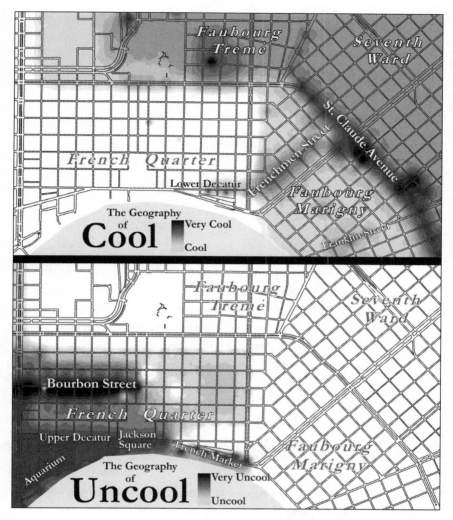

"Cool" may be an illusion, but its effects on real estate and neighborhood change are not. *Analysis and map by Richard Campanella.*

readings, conversations, and vibes from the zeitgeist. I then processed the ranked points into a "heat map" shaded by intensity of coolness or uncoolness. Yes, it's subjective; of course it's imprecise; but after bouncing the estimates off a number of other people, I found that a general consensus prevailed.

The resulting map does not represent my personal opinions of what's cool or uncool. Rather, it represents my attempt to estimate everyone else's opinions, as best as I can discern them. By no means should readers take offense at areas mapped in red which they think ought to be blue, or vice versa.

Where would you map coolness? Where do you seeing it going next? What impact will it have? For better or worse, the geography of cool may influence the future cityscapes of New Orleans.

MONKEY HILL AND THE GEOGRAPHY OF CHILDHOOD

Perhaps the highest return on investment ever earned on a few thousand federal dollars came in the form of a pile of dirt in a rather forlorn park at the depth of the Depression. The agency behind it was the Civil Works Administration, the park was Audubon, and the dirt is now known as Monkey Hill.

Contrary to popular belief, the Works Progress Administration did not build Monkey Hill; the mound was nearly complete before the WPA came into existence with the 1935 Emergency Relief Appropriation Act. Nor was the hill a goal of the project, much less a designed landscape feature with a name and purpose.

Rather, the CWA aimed to drain a wet thicket on the batture by digging a 1,200-foot-long lagoon and expanding the parkland around it, forming what are now the water bodies of the Audubon Zoo's Louisiana Swamp, Jaguar Jungle, and South American Pampas exhibits. Workers then used the spoil from the excavations to form a hill a few hundred feet inland. There appears to have been no plan to create a permanent landscaped hill: according to a biography written by Katherine Burt Jackson of her father, Henry F. Burt, regional head of the Federal Emergency Relief Administration in New Orleans at the time, "workers drained a brushy swamp to add usable dry land, and the mud formed a mound of dirt 35 or 40 feet high. People came to look at it—the first hill they had ever seen. Children began to play on it. Dad [Burt] suggested that it be left in place so the children of New Orleans could see what a hill looked like." Because parts of the batture had previously been used as a city dump, it may well be that, as one 1933 report anticipated, "broken bedsprings, cast-off tires, old shoes and other refuse" ended up in the mound, as they did in shored-up neutral grounds.

The project was one of many metro-area undertakings of the CWA, which used state-administered federal dollars to put people to work on civic improvements. Laborers earned at least thirty cents an hour for up to twenty-four hours per week improving the Lakefront, destumping City Park, beautifying Bayou St. John, planting trees along Chef Menteur Highway, restoring Jackson Barracks, and landscaping Audubon Park. Out of this last project came the moving of dirt that would fortuitously create one of the most beloved spots in the city. Like Henry Burt, locals at the time also suspected "Audubon Park Hill" would become a place where, according to a November 1933 *Times-Picayune* article, "native-born youngsters of New Orleans could run and boast that they had been on a real mountain."

By late March 1934, the lagoon and hill were nearly complete, having cost $59,000 in labor and $3,800 materials. At the time, Monkey Hill's summit lay higher than some riverfront levees, although it is difficult to ascertain the exact historical elevations of either.

That summer, children took to the unnamed mound like kittens to catnip. They scampered up and around it and rode bikes and go-carts down its steep slopes with reckless abandon. Adults called it "the Indian mound," for its resemblance to prehistoric middens. But kids called it "Monkey Hill," perhaps on account of how the tots frolicked upon it, or as a counterpart to Monkey Island, which was formally designed and named (and is now part of the Jaguar Jungle exhibit).

Whatever the reason, the name stuck. Planners took note of the hill's popularity, among them a 1929 Tulane University architecture graduate named Newtown Reeve Howard. When the WPA took over from the CWA, Howard oversaw $400,000 worth of construction projects throughout the park and zoo (which were both free and not separated as they are today), creating stately brick buildings and landscaping the hill and its surroundings. This probably explains why the WPA, which would soon supersede the CWA in size, impact, and in the public imagination, is almost universally credited for Monkey Hill today.

For decades to come, Monkey Hill would become an integral memory to generations of local children, as well as a rendezvous for uptown citizens—sort of an Audubon Park equivalent to "meeting under the clock at D. H. Holmes." But the renown was by no means universal. Monkey Hill was all but unknown to roughly one-third of the city's population, as segregation kept African Americans out of Audubon Park, not to mention many other spaces and opportunities.

In the 1960s, Monkey Hill became a spot for statements, politics, and protests. In 1965, for example, a Loyola ROTC battalion hoisted a flag atop Monkey Hill to publicize the university's pressing need to expand its cramped campus. Gubernatorial candidate Cy Courtney held a "Think In" at the spot in 1967 to encourage political engagement, and in 1969 people opposed to the hippie movement held a series of what they called "Square In's" at Monkey Hill.

Locals incorporated the mound into their vernacular as well. They'd use Monkey Hill as a metaphor for something comically puny, such as an undersized city budget, or for any manmade landscaping mound, such as the ones later built nearby on The Fly and in Brechtel Park on the West Bank. In a tradition that thrives to this day, New Orleanians would also use Monkey Hill as a term of endearment to poke fun at their city's cockamamy geography. Behold, a place so ridiculously flat that a manmade mound with so amusing a name would rank as its highest point! By this time, however, certain sections of riverfront levees had been built higher, and it's unlikely Monkey Hill ever truly formed the city's topographical zenith.

But Monkey Hill fell on rough times by the 1960s and 1970s. The zoo, hardly changed since the Depression, had become a local embarrassment, and Monkey Hill had become loved to death—trod bare of grass, furrowed with a deep gully, and, like coastal Louisiana, eroding, to its current height of 27.5 feet.

To add insult to injury, a new hill had been built in City Park's Couturie Forest from spoil excavated for Interstate 610, and it measured not only higher above sea level but much higher above grade. Now known as Laborde Mountain, the City Park peak rose 46 feet above its 3-feet-below-sea-level base, enough to peer above the tree line, whereas Monkey Hill measured only 16.5 feet above its 11-foot-above-sea-level base.

Planners devising a $5 million renovation of Audubon Zoo thought visitors were ready for something new. In 1974 they proposed fencing off Monkey Hill and letting goats graze on it, while building a new mound on the batture park (today's The Fly).

What they had not gauged was just how cherished Monkey Hill had become. Schoolchildren wrote letters of protest, and parents rebuked officials in indignant letters. "How can adults consider goats more important than children?" demanded one mother. "Haven't city officials taken away enough natural ground and woods from our children because of progress?" Another declared "every citizen would be happy to contribute a bucket of mud" to shore up the hill and give it back to children, and recommended the goats instead be "turned loose on Bourbon Street," where adults played.

The outcry helped raise funds and convinced planners to stabilize the original Monkey Hill and incorporate it into the zoo's Grasslands of the World (now Af-

Author's son climbing Monkey Hill in Audubon Zoo, for over eighty years a special experience in a New Orleans childhood. *Photograph by Richard Campanella.*

rican Savanna) exhibit. Unveiled in 1980, the renovation was a hit, and Monkey Hill became as popular as ever, so much so that zoo officials in the 1980s held an annual Ski Monkey Hill festival, in which ten tons of ice were trucked to the top—in September!—for a mini slalom, to promote Eastern Airlines flights to Canadian ski resorts. The gimmick became particularly popular when "a Cajun band and free beer" were added. Ever the entrepreneurs, some New Orleanians sold "Ski Monkey Hill" T-shirts, testament to the mound's role as an amusing prop highlighting the ironies of local geography and the eccentricities of local culture.

In 1999, Monkey Hill underwent another transformation, and adults again fretted whether its *je ne sais quoi* might get lost amid the progress. But the improvements only enhanced its appeal to children, who in addition to the climbable Pride of Lions sculptures on top and a rope bridge down its side, now found another feature of the natural world previously unavailable on their silty delta: a babbling mountain brook.

It is interesting to watch how children tackle Monkey Hill, especially tots just mastering the art of perambulation. To a tiny body experiencing it for the first time, uphill topography exerts an inexplicable but exultant resistance, one that fuels the spirit more than it taxes the body. To young eyes grappling with optical illusions for the first time, the view from the top amusingly turns Brobdingnagians into Lilliputians, and enables little ones to fit grown-ups between thumb and forefinger. To fledgling legs flexing for the first time, heading downhill unleashes the magical power of gravity, letting you go faster than you ever thought you could. You could also roll down like a log or somersault like a ball, and for once parents would not fuss about your gettin' all messy and dusty.

In essence, Monkey Hill is a place where all the staid restraints of the flat plane—and the deltaic plain—are tossed out, and the empowering forces of Make Believe become real.

The mound was originally built merely as lagniappe to a federal works project, but, through sheer youthful exuberance, it became a beloved part of local culture. Children discovered it, claimed it, named it, gave it character, and made it their own.

Monkey Hill may be an amusing quirk in the geography of New Orleans, but it is a veritable Everest in the geography of a New Orleans childhood.

ARCHITECTURAL GEOGRAPHIES
AND THE BUILT ENVIRONMENT

ON IMPORTATION AND ADAPTATION
Creole Architecture in New Orleans

"Creole" is a famously complex facet of Louisiana culture, whether as a noun implying an ethnic identity or an adjective describing anything from tomatoes to cooking. Ask ten New Orleanians to define "Creole" and you'll likely get thirty different answers.

So too Creole architecture: explaining what makes a house Creole defies one unequivocal answer. As an emergent tradition rendered by experimentation and adaptation rather than an inscribed order, Creole architecture is better understood through its evolution and transformation.

One thing is certain: most buildings in colonial New Orleans, at least until the 1790s, epitomized Creole architecture, and they exhibited an inventory of signature traits and construction methods. These included walls made of brick or mud mixed with moss (*bousillage*), set within a load-bearing timber frame covered with clapboards; an oversized "Norman" roof, usually hipped and double-pitched; and spacious wooden galleries supported with delicate colonnades and balustrades, which served as intermediary space between indoors and outdoors. Staircases were located outside on the gallery, chimneys were centralized, apertures had French doors or shutters, hallways and closets were all but unknown, and the entire edifice was raised on piers above soggy soils.

Such buildings were distributed across today's French Quarter by the hundreds in the mid-1700s and over a thousand later in the century. Roughly half were set back from the street, and nearly all had open space around them, used for vegetable gardens, chicken coops, and rabbit hutches and surrounded by picket fences. It was a rather bucolic environment, with the appearance of a French West Indian village. Wrote English captain Philip Pittman during his 1765 visit, "most of the houses are . . . timber frames filled up with brick" and "one floor, raised about eight feet from the ground, with large galleries round them. . . . It is impossible to have any subterraneous buildings, as they would be constantly full of water."

The best surviving examples of this early phase of Creole architecture in the French Quarter are Madame John's Legacy at 632 Dumaine Street and the Ossorno House at 913 Governor Nicholls, both of which date to the 1780s, and Lafitte's Blacksmith Shop on Bourbon Street at St. Philip, whose construction is undocumented but perhaps dates to the 1770s. A dozen or so similar buildings survive elsewhere in the city, including the Old Spanish Customs House (1784) and

Lafitte's Blacksmith Shop on Bourbon Street at St. Philip, probably built in the 1770s and one of the few surviving specimens of West Indian–influenced "first generation" Creole architecture. *Photograph by Richard Koch, 1934, Historic American Buildings Survey, Library of Congress.*

Pitot House (1805) on Bayou St. John and the Lombard House (1826) in Bywater. (The Old Ursuline Convent at 1111 Chartres, completed in 1753 and now the city's oldest structure, represents a French Colonial institutional style typical of France during the reign of Louis XV, and embodies many Creole traits, including the steep double-pitched hipped roof.)

Where did Creole architecture come from? Researchers generally agree this tradition was not "invented" locally in response to environmental conditions (hot weather, heavy rain, wet soils), as is often supposed. Rather, it arrived courtesy of newcomers who brought with them all their other cultural customs, including building know-how, and modified them to local conditions through incremental experimentation. But by what routes and from which source regions?

One theory views Louisiana Creole architecture as a derivative of French Canadian houses originating from the Normandy region of France (hence the term "Norman roof") and later modified to local conditions and needs. This proposition suggests Creole architecture diffused down the Mississippi Valley. Another theory emphasizes influences directly from France to Louisiana. A third and favored explanation sees Creole architecture as an extraction from a West Indian

Madame John's Legacy at 632 Dumaine Street, built in 1788 in the early Creole style and now one of the last best examples of eighteen-century New Orleans residential architecture. *Photograph 1930s, courtesy Library of Congress.*

cultural milieu, itself a product of European, indigenous, and African influences, such as the Arawak Indian *Bohio* hut and possibly West Africa's Yoruba hut. This hypothesis suggests that Creole architecture diffused primarily *up* the Mississippi Valley from the Caribbean and beyond, rather than down from Canada or directly from France. It thus situates New Orleans at the nexus of the "Creole Atlantic" and the North American interior. Louisiana State University anthropologist Jay D. Edwards viewed West Indian influence consequential enough to warrant recognition of the Caribbean region as "another major cultural hearth for the domestic architecture of eastern North America," along with England, France, Spain, Germany, West Africa, Holland, Scandinavia, and other places.

Circumstances changed in the late 1700s, and so would Creole architecture. A massive fire in 1788 destroyed 856 of New Orleans's Creole housing stock, and a second blaze in 1794 destroyed another 212. Spanish administrators responded with new building codes designed to prevent fires, mandating, according to Cabildo records, new houses to be "built of bricks and a flat roof or tile roof," and extant houses to be strengthened "to stand a roof of fire-proof materials," their

The Old Absinthe House (1806, seen here around 1900), corner of Bourbon and Bienville, representative of a second generation of Creole architecture, more urban and with greater Spanish influence. *Photograph courtesy Library of Congress.*

beams covered with stucco. "[All] citizens must comply with these rules," the dons decreed.

The fires and codes largely ended that first phase of rustic, wooden Creole houses in New Orleans proper, though they would persist in rural areas. They would become even more unsuitable in the years following the Louisiana Purchase and American dominion, during which the city's population quintupled by the 1820s. Land values rose, housing density increased, and picket fences and rabbit hutches disappeared from the inner city.

But Creoles—that is, locally born people, mostly francophones—still predominated, and Creole builders continued to erect "creolized" structures now exhibiting Spanish and Anglo-American influences, programmed to the needs of a budding metropolis.

Thus, in the early 1800s, a second phase of Creole architecture emerged, and it constituted the Creole cottages we know today (which are really an adaptation of first-generation Creole houses to more urbanized settings) as well as large brick

Typical courtyard of a "second generation" Creole townhouse on Royal Street, built in the early 1800s and seen here circa 1900. *Photograph courtesy Library of Congress.*

common-wall townhouses and storehouses featuring arched openings, wrought-iron balconies, an elegantly Spartan stucco facade, and a *porte cochère* carriageway leading to a rear courtyard. What once felt like a Caribbean village was now starting to look like a Mediterranean city. Wrote Scottish visitor Basil Hall in 1828, "[w]hat struck us most [about New Orleans] were the old and narrow streets, the high houses, ornamented with tasteful cornices, iron balconies, and many other circumstances peculiar to towns in France and Spain."

Contrast Hall's quote to that of Philip Pittman in 1765, above, and that's the difference between first-generation "country Creole" and second-generation "city Creole" architecture. There are, by my count, 740 examples of this latter phase still standing in the French Quarter, mostly dating to the 1810s–30s. We call them "Creole" today for two reasons: because they were creolized—that is, adapted to local conditions—and because folks regularly called them Creole back then. Among the most splendid specimens of these second-phase or second-generation Creole townhouses may be seen along 612–624 Royal Street.

But Creole people in this era increasingly found themselves competing with ever-growing populations of Anglo-Americans and immigrants, who imported their own cultural preferences. Architecturally, this meant the rise of Neoclassicism, particularly Greek Revival.

This was also the era when architecture developed into a specialized profession with standardized techniques, replacing the lay tradesmen and "housewrights" of old. Card-carrying architects such as James Gallier Sr. and Henry Howard, both from Ireland by way of New York, and the New York–born brothers James and Charles Dakin all set up shop in New Orleans in the 1830s, and they weren't designing Creole buildings.

To some researchers, the Neoclassical trend set the old Creole customs on a trajectory of decline. "The truly significant period of New Orleans architecture was brought into jeopardy by the [Louisiana] Purchase and brought to an end by the Civil War," wrote the late architect and preservationist James Marston Fitch. "The Americanization of the Crescent City has long been completed, at least architecturally; and the whole nation is the poorer for it."

An alternative interpretation holds that, rather than wiping them out, the city's mid-nineteenth-century Americanization drove Creole designs into yet another evolutionary phase. That phase entailed the dovetailing of one local innovation—the rotation of the traditional Creole cottage such that its roofline, typically parallel to the street, became perpendicular to it—with a related idea for elongated houses imported from Haiti starting in 1809, when over nine thousand Haitian refugees arrived at New Orleans. What resulted were long narrow houses, the type that would later be nicknamed "shotguns."

After the Civil War, as population density increased and demand for rental stock rose, builders erected shotgun houses by the thousands—singles, doubles, camelbacks, whatever the market demanded and space allowed. Those built in the late 1800s continued two key interior traits shared by that first generation of circa-1700s Creole architecture: center chimneys and no hallways. Our shotgun houses today retain a striking resemblance to the *Ti-kay* ("little houses") dwellings seen throughout modern Haiti, and the relationship is probably not coincidental.

Traditional shotguns went out of style in the early twentieth century, by which time we can fairly say that Creole architecture had faded away. Yet certain traits endure today in the form of pastiche, such as the Norman roofs popular in many modern Louisiana subdivisions, and the ample porches and galleries seen in New Urbanist communities.

More so, Creole architecture survives in modern New Orleans through the efforts of the preservationist movement, which recognized its value long before most residents and leaders did. New Orleanians are deeply indebted to preservationists for keeping within our stewardship the nation's largest concentration of this beautiful tradition.

SHOTGUN GEOGRAPHY
Theories on a Distinctive Domicile

Few elements of the New Orleans cityscape speak to the intersection of architecture, sociology, and geography so well as the shotgun house. Once scorned, now cherished, shotguns shed light on patterns of cultural diffusion, construction methods, class and residential settlement patterns, and social preferences for living space.

The shotgun house is not an architectural style; rather, it is a structural typology—what folklorist John Michael Vlach described as "a philosophy of space, a culturally determined sense of dimension." A typology, or type, may be draped in any style. Thus we have shotgun houses adorned in Italianate, Eastlake, and other styles, just as there are Creole and Federalist-style townhouses, and Spanish colonial and Greek Revival cottages.

Tradition holds that the name "shotgun" derives from the notion of firing birdshot through the front door and out the rear without touching a wall, a rustic allusion to its linearity and room-to-room connectivity. The term itself postdates the shotgun's late-nineteenth-century heyday, not appearing in print until the early twentieth century.

Vlach defined the prototypical shotgun as "a one-room wide, one-story high building with two or more rooms, oriented perpendicularly to the road with its front door in the gable end, [although] aspects such as size, proportion, roofing, porches, appendages, foundations, trim and decoration" vary widely. Its most striking exterior trait is its elongated shape, usually three to six times longer than wide. Inside, what is salient is the lack of hallways: occupants need to walk through private rooms to access other rooms.

Theory contends that cultures that produced shotgun houses (and other residences without hallways, such as Creole cottages) tended to be more gregarious, or at least unwilling to sacrifice valuable living space for the purpose of occasional passage. Cultures that valued privacy, on the other hand, were willing to make this trade-off. Note, for example, how privacy-conscious peoples of Anglo-Saxon descent who arrived at New Orleans in the early nineteenth century brought with them the American center-hall cottage and side-hall townhouse, in preference over local Creole designs.

Academic interest in the shotgun house dates from Louisiana State University geographer Fred B. Kniffen's field research in the 1930s on Louisiana folk housing. He and other researchers have proposed a number of hypotheses explaining the origin and distribution of this distinctive house type. One theory, popular with tour guides and amateur house-watchers, holds that shotgun houses were designed in New Orleans in response to a real estate tax based on frontage rather than square footage, motivating narrow structures. There's one major problem with this theory: no one can seem to find that tax code.

Could the shotgun be an architectural response to narrow urban lots? Indeed, you can squeeze in more structures with a slender design. But why then do we see shotguns in rural fields with no such limits?

Could it have evolved from indigenous palmetto houses or Choctaw huts? Unlikely, given their appearance in the Caribbean and beyond.

Could it have been independently invented? Roberts & Company, a New Orleans sash and door fabricator formed in 1856, developed blueprints for prefabricated shotgun-like houses in the 1860s to 1870s and even won awards for them at international expositions. But then why do we see "longhouses" in the rear of the French Quarter and in Faubourg Tremé as early as the 1810s?

Or, alternately, did the shotgun diffuse from the Old World as peoples moved across the Atlantic and brought with them their building culture, just as they brought their language, religion, and foodways? Vlach noted the abundance of shotgun-like longhouses in the West Indies, and traced their essential form to the enslaved populations of Saint-Domingue (now Haiti) who had been removed from the western and central African regions of Guinea and Angola. His research identified a gable-roofed housing stock indigenous to the Yoruba peoples, which he linked to similar *Ti-kay* structures in modern Haiti with comparable rectangular shapes, room juxtapositions, and ceiling heights.

Vlach hypothesizes that the 1809 exodus of Haitians to New Orleans after the Saint-Domingue slave insurrection of 1791–1803 brought this vernacular house

Late-nineteenth-century shotgun houses in the Fifth Ward, seen here in the 1930s. *Photograph by Walker Evans, courtesy Library of Congress.*

type to the banks of the Mississippi. "Haitian émigrés had only to continue in Louisiana the same life they had known in St. Domingue," he wrote. "The shotgun house of Port-au-Prince became, quite directly, the shotgun house of New Orleans."

The distribution of shotgun houses throughout Louisiana gives indirect support to the diffusion argument. Kniffen showed in the 1930s that shotguns generally occurred along waterways in areas that tended to be more francophone in their culture, higher in their proportions of people of African and Creole ancestry, and older in their historical development.

Beyond state boundaries, shotguns occur throughout the lower Mississippi Valley, correlated with antebellum plantation regions and with areas that host large black populations. They also appear in interior southern cities, most notably Louisville, Kentucky, which comes a distant second to New Orleans in terms of numbers and stylistic variety. If in fact the shotgun diffused from Africa to Haiti through New Orleans and up the Mississippi and Ohio valleys, this is the distribution we would expect to see.

Clearly, poverty abets cultural factors in explaining this pattern. Simplicity of construction and conservation of resources (building materials, space) probably

Shotgun houses in Donaldsonville, Louisiana. *Photograph by Richard Campanella.*

made the shotgun house type equally attractive to poorer classes in many areas. Indeed, it is possible that we may be artificially yoking together a wide variety of house types, unrelated in their provenance but similar in their appearance, by means of a catchy moniker coined after their historical moment.

Whatever their origins, shotgun singles and doubles came to dominate the turn-of-the-century housing stock of New Orleans's working-class neighborhoods. Yet they were also erected as owner-occupied homes in wealthier areas, including the Garden District. The case of the Garden District lends credence to the hypothesis that shotgun houses were designed to conform to narrow lots: properties in this affluent neighborhood were originally laid out in large sizes, with some blocks having only six or eight lots, leaving lots of space for gardens and outbuildings. Later in the 1800s, many owners decided to section off unneeded lawns into separate developable lots—which of course tended to be narrow, which in turn drove the architect to design a narrow house, which eventually we would call a shotgun house. But were these elegant Garden District shotgun-shaped minimansions really members of the same architectural family tree as the Caribbean and African longhouses? It's a tough question.

New Orleans shotguns exhibit myriad variations: as singles or doubles; with one or two stories; with hip, gable, or apron roofs; with grand Classical facades or simple ones; with or without elaborate Victorian gingerbread; and sometimes with "camelbacks" to increase living space. The Louisiana State University anthropologist Jay Edwards contends that camelback shotguns were formed after the Civil War, when, in an effort to make better use of courtyard space and to accommodate new kitchen technologies, builders fused previously separate two-story dependencies with the one-story main house, yielding a single elongated building that was one story in the front and two in the rear. New Orleans's wide range of shotgun houses can be explained as a strategy to address market demand with a multitude of options in terms of space needs, fiscal constraints, and stylistic preferences.

New Orleanians by the twentieth century, as part of their gradual Americanization, desired more privacy than their ancestors, and increasing affluence and new technologies, such as mechanized kitchens, indoor plumbing, air conditioning, automobiles, and municipal drainage, helped form new philosophies about residential space. Professional home builders responded accordingly, some adding hallways or ells or side entrances to the shotgun, others morphing it into the "bungalow" form. House buyers came to disdain the original shotgun, and it faded from new construction during the 1910s and 1920s. A *Times-Picayune* writer captured the prevailing sentiment in a 1926 column: "Long, slender, shotgun houses," he sighed, "row upon row[,] street upon street . . . all alike . . . unpainted, slick-stooped, steep-roofed, jammed up together, like lumber in a pile." Architectural historians also rolled their eyes at prosaic shotguns, and did not protest their demolition, even in the French Quarter, as late as the 1960s.

In recent decades, however, New Orleanians have come to appreciate the sturdy construction and exuberant embellishment of their shotgun housing stock, and now value them as a key element of the cityscape. Thousands have since been renovated, and the once-extinct typology has experienced a recent rebirth. Some homes in the Make It Right project in the Lower Ninth Ward, for example, were inspired by the shotgun (although rendered in contemporary styles), and some prefabricated "Katrina Cottages" and New Urbanist homes in recently rebuilt public housing complexes are made to look like the shotguns of old.

It's revealing to note, however, that among the renovations New Orleanians now make to their shotguns is something completely alien to their original form.

They add a hallway.

NEOCLASSICISM COMES TO THE CREOLE CITY
Greek Revival Architecture in New Orleans

Two hundred years ago, northerners started arriving by the thousands in New Orleans. Over the next century, these predominantly Anglo-Irish Americans would transform a mostly francophone city, whose cultural compass pointed toward the Creole Atlantic, into a mostly English-speaking metropolis firmly positioned within the American South. They would affect the cityscape in many ways, starting in the early to mid-1850s with the appearance of American building fashions along the streets of the Creole city. They reflected an architectural statement informed by the Enlightenment and traceable to Classical antiquity two millennia earlier, one that came to be known broadly as Neoclassicism.

Neoclassicism had a number of branches. One took form in the Georgian aesthetic popular in England and Ireland in the early 1700s. Another, called Empire and influenced by ancient Rome, became popular in France. Still another branch, called Hellenism, venerated Greek ideas and forms. Championing a new age of rationalism, liberty, tolerance, and democracy, Hellenism would affect everything from poetry and literature to art and architecture.

Not coincidentally, this was also a time when new archaeological discoveries in Athens came to light, intriguing populations in western Europe. Greek architectural ornaments—in porticos, pediments, columns, dentils, doorways, and lintels—subsequently began to appear in buildings throughout England and greater Germany.

The term "Greek Revival" would later be coined to describe this fashion, and the intellectual rationale behind it soon crossed the Atlantic (as did Georgian, which Americans modified into the Federal style). Public buildings, commercial houses, churches, and mansions resembling ancient Greek and Roman temples began to appear in places like New York and Virginia. As Americans from other areas began to trickle into New Orleans after the Louisiana Purchase, they at first had little choice but to conform to Creole architecture and hire local builders. But when the trickle grew to a torrent, Americans increasingly brushed aside localism in favor of their own ideas—and their own architects.

The earliest known surviving structure in New Orleans with prominent Greek traits is the Thierry House (1814) at 721 Gov. Nicholls Street, whose Doric columns and Classical proportions were designed by Henry Latrobe (son of Benjamin Latrobe, designer of the U.S. Capitol and an emissary of Neoclassicism) and

Arsène Lacarrière Latour. More followed, and by the 1820s, local draftsmen were producing Greek patterns for Louisiana townhouses, storehouses, institutions, country villas, and plantation houses. Edmund Hogan, for example, advertised in the *Courrier de la Louisiane* in 1822 his "architectural sketches . . . in the Grecian, Gothic and fancy styles . . . arranged on the most approved principles, with plans of public buildings of every description."

Greek Revival spread across the formerly Creole cityscape: Ionic porticos appeared on Canal Street; gable roofs came to outnumber hipped roofs; squared doorways replaced arched openings; heavy granite lintels were installed above apertures; delicate colonnades disappeared for Classical columns of the Doric, Ionic, or Corinthian order; and dentils appeared along entablatures. Interiors were affected too: staircases previously set outside on the gallery now came indoors; and hallways—a rarity in the Creole city—were designed into floor plans, indicating the Anglo value placed on privacy.

This was also the era when architecture developed into a specialized profession, and trained architects from out of state, nearly all Classicists of one vein or another, began to win contracts previously held by Creole builders. Among the newcomers were Irish-born James Gallier and Henry Howard, both by way of Manhattan, and New York–born brothers James and Charles Dakin, all of whom arrived at New Orleans in the mid-1830s and promptly set to work.

Two of Gallier's most important works were the original St. Charles Hotel (co-designed with Charles Dakin and built 1834–37, where the Place St. Charles skyscraper now stands) and Municipality Hall (1845–53, now Gallier Hall), fronting Lafayette Square. In his autobiography, Gallier describes each project in terms that betray just how exogenous these buildings were to New Orleans. His clients for the hotel, for example, were "Irish merchants" to whom he proposed a payment structure "as was usual . . . in England." He had "the stone work . . . joiners' work and iron work . . . prepared (up) north," and he struggled with New Orleans's "wholly alluvial" soil, into which his massive edifice would eventually sink by two and a half feet. A substantial number of his workforce, meanwhile, perished due to "sun stroke or yellow fever," the latter of which nearly killed Gallier himself.

But the result was stupendous: an immense Neoclassical dead ringer for Latrobe's U.S. Capitol, complete with a 185-foot-high dome and a "Corinthian portico," pointedly positioned on the American side of town.

For Municipality Hall, Gallier had his "portico and ashlar" (fine masonry) made of "white marble procured from quarries near New York," and the steps

The Dabney House at 2265 St. Charles Avenue, designed by James Gallier Jr. in the Greek Revival style and built in 1857. *Photograph from Historic American Buildings Survey, Library of Congress.*

made of granite from Massachusetts. "The style of the architecture is Grecian Ionic," he wrote, "and the portico is considered as a very chaste and highly-finished example of that style." Even the programming of the building bespoke the cultural changes afoot: it was slated to serve the Council of Aldermen for the Second Municipality, an area dominated by Americans. After 1853, it would become City Hall, today's Gallier Hall, a paragon of the Greek idiom.

Why did Greek Revival capture the American imagination? One reason is that its dignified majesty seemed to affirm the ideals of rationalism, order, and democracy stewarded by what the founding fathers presumed to be an enlightened aristocracy. Urban historian Lewis Mumford saw its appeal as indicative of "a desire for collective dignity and order, combined with the utmost decorum." Architectural historian James Marston Fitch viewed Neoclassicism's southern popularity in a darker light, seeing the reverence of "Imperial Rome [and] Periclean Greece [as a] reactionary use of the Classic idiom [which] regarded human slavery as the basis of Classic culture instead of . . . its blemish."

Practical reasons also explain Greek Revival's spread. Architects such as Minard Lafever sketched widely distributed pattern books of standard Greek motifs, which made their replication faster and cheaper. Ordinary folks came to expect that important buildings look this way, regardless of the theoretical rationale. Clients asked for the Greek look, and architects delivered it.

In Creole New Orleans, Greek Revival formed the first major American architectural contribution to the city's built environment, and specimens may be found citywide today. By my count, Greek Revival as well as Federal ornamentation may be seen in the facades of at least 614 structures in the Vieux Carré, more than one in every four street-fronting buildings—and this in the "French" Quarter! Most were erected between the 1820s and 1850s.

Greek Revival began to fall out of fashion as the agrarian America envisioned by Thomas Jefferson gave way to Alexander Hamilton's vision of commerce and industry, followed by the subsequent rise of Jacksonian democracy which championed the common man and spurned the notion of aristocracy. Mumford tied its decline to "the decay of public life, [which] became so painfully evident after 1840." Classicism would give way to Romanticism and its fêting of individualism and emotionalism, and by the 1850s, the solemn Greek temples dotting the landscape started to look passé. Clients instead began requesting a new and more effusive look, and it would be called Italianate. Greek Revival held on for a bit longer in the South, particularly in the plantation regions, but the demise of the slaveholding regime sealed its fate after the Civil War.

Years later, Greek Revival began to "re-revive" in a pastiche form sometimes described as Southern Colonial; specimens may be seen throughout uptown today, in buildings erected in the 1890s and early 1900s. Storybooks and cinema also helped resuscitate the association of Greek Revival with the Old South, and the style's motifs are commonly found in modern building pattern books.

So too survives the psychological link between Neoclassicism and gravitas: to this day, designers of institutional buildings whose clients want to communicate stability and order regularly invoke Grecian and other Classical forms. Evidence of Greek Revival's enduring credibility may be found all around Washington, D.C., in courthouses and government offices nationwide, and as close as your neighborhood's banks and churches.

BETWEEN BEAUTIFUL AND SUBLIME
Italianate Architecture in New Orleans

A stroll through New Orleans in the 1850s would have revealed a subtle but significant change in architecture. The austere Greek Revival style, which started to replace Creole aesthetics in the 1820s and flourished during the 1830s and 1840s, began to give way to a more ornate and luxurious look. Known as Italianate and later Victorian Italianate, this fashion would predominate in New Orleans for most of the latter half of the nineteenth century.

A number of factors brought forth the appeal of Italianate. One overarching driver was the rise of the Romantic movement, itself a reaction to the lofty ideals of the Enlightenment and the expanding domains of science and industry. Romanticism responded by celebrating emotionality, passion, the specialness of the individual, and the beauty of nature. Unlike Enlightenment thinkers, who found inspiration in Classical antiquity and thus took to Greek and Roman architecture, Romanticists fancied the glory of the Renaissance and the poignancy of medieval ruins, and embraced the panache of Italian buildings and gardens.

A second factor was an offshoot of Romanticism known as "Picturesque." This movement developed as budding scholars from England and elsewhere, taking advantage of improved roads and passenger ship service, increasingly spent time in the Tuscany and Romagna regions of Italy as part of their academic grand tour. They returned with paintings of lovely Italian landscapes. People found these pastoral scenes to be enchanting, and their properties came to be known as *pittoresco* in Italian ("like a painting")—hence, "picturesque" in English.

In her 1975 dissertation, architectural historian Joan G. Caldwell described the Picturesque aesthetic as bearing a certain "roughness, asymmetry, and irregularity" falling somewhere between the beautiful and the sublime. To English eyes, Picturesque exuded Italy's glorious past, and gardeners started incorporating the look into parks, installing scenic stone bridges, lagoons, and shrubbery to make them look like paintings.

Artists did the same with their art, and architects with their designs. In 1802 architect John Nash, according to Caldwell, "produced the first true villa in the Italian style" in England, at an estate named Cronkhill near Shrewsbury. Nash's design featured an asymmetrical rounded tower with an octagonal room and a loggia (arcade gallery) topped with a balustrade, all finished in white stucco, as if lifted from the outskirts of Rome. Nash would later design the hamlet of

The Luling Mansion (1865, seen here early 1900s), a grand example of the Italianate style, located near the New Orleans Fairgrounds and once owned by the Louisiana Jockey Club. *Photograph courtesy Library of Congress.*

Blaise, near Bristol, based on Picturesque philosophies. To this day it looks like a painting.

The Napoleonic Wars slowed new construction. But afterwards, with pent-up demand and an English upper class ready to embrace what Caldwell described as "sheer aesthetic enjoyment," Italianate gained popularity as the "aesthetic of luxury." Campaniles, loggia, bowed bays, arcades, bracketed eaves, decorative moldings, and segmented arches appeared throughout England. Pattern books made their reproduction efficient and inexpensive, and the style spread.

(It was during this era, incidentally, that Highclere Castle of *Downton Abby* fame was radically renovated from its original Classical form into the Renaissance Revival behemoth it is today. Its architect, Charles Barry, specialized in Italianate and incorporated its motifs into the redesign, which he described as Anglo-Italian.)

American architects, ever aware of their European peers, made their own pilgrimages to both England and Italy and returned doubly inspired. Caldwell credits Philadelphia architect John Notman with introducing Italianate to the United States with his 1839 design for a villa named Riverside in Burlington, New Jersey. Two years later, the landscape designer Andrew Jackson Downing published his

"Treatise on the Theory and Practice of Landscape Gardening," which conflated house and garden designs and edified Americans on both Italianate and Picturesque philosophies.

Italianate arrived in America at the right time. This was the Age of Jackson, and the nation was changing. Americans were moving west; individualism became a creed; and the genteel aristocracy of the founding fathers increasingly ceded power to the so-called "Jacksonian Man," that "hardworking ambitious person," according to historian Richard Hofstadter, "for whom enterprise was a kind of religion." Whereas the old-guard aristocracy, seeing themselves as the inheritors of Classical enlightenment, favored the majestic Grecian order, the rising Jacksonian Man scoffed at such haughty allusions and embraced instead a sumptuous look for his hard-won, self-made wealth.

Everywhere he went, wrote Hofstadter, the Jacksonian Man "found conditions that encouraged him to extend himself." Chief among such places was New Orleans, premier mercantilist emporium of western commerce and largest city in the South. Here, opportunity abounded—for empowered white males, that is. Vast sums of money changed hands, and fortunes were won and lost regularly. A new American upper class formed, and its members initially put their ample wealth into, among other things, capacious townhouses and mansions, usually of the Greek or Neoclassical style.

But by the booming 1850s, Greek Revival came to feel a bit stodgy and dated. The nouveau riche wanted that trendy new Italian look, like their peers elsewhere, and designers were eager to deliver. Among the style's local champions were architects William and James Freret, James Gallier Jr., Albert Diettel, and most of all, Henry Howard.

An early local example of a "magnificent Italian villa," as the *Daily Picayune* put it, was built on Prytania Street near Jackson in 1850 for local esquire Duncan Hennen. Costing twenty-two thousand dollars, the mansion featured a gallery and veranda amid an abundance of marble. Two years later and a few blocks away, the eccentric globe-trotting millionaire James Robb had erected an Italian palazzo on Washington Avenue between Camp and Chestnut. Surrounded by lavish landscaping suggesting Picturesque influences, the mansion sat "two stories high, eighty feet square, [on a] gently elevated terrace," wrote the *Daily Picayune*, and "had about it an air of quiet beauty, refined taste and substantial comfort. . . . No expense was spared[;] its fresco painting was particularly superb, [as are the] marble steps with massive railings [and] spacious hall." Inside were Robb's "large and choice collection of oil paintings, water colors, engravings, bronzes, marble statuary, vases, and other articles of *vertu*." Robb's gardened palazzo helped give the Garden District its name, and it's no coincidence that Italianate came to be a dominant style in this and other affluent neighborhoods.

We have since lost both the Hennen and Robb houses, but a comparable specimen survives in the form of the Luling Mansion near the Fairgrounds. Built for Florence Luling in 1865 and sold to the Louisiana Jockey Club in 1871, the house was originally surrounded by expansive manicured gardens and embodied Italianate and Picturesque aesthetics throughout. To this day it stuns the eye.

These and a few other grand Italianate villas, however, were the exception. Because local architects were mostly designing city houses on standard urban lots, they saw little reason to abide by the asymmetry and irregularity typical of the Italian order, much less the gardens and statuary. Instead, they designed standard house types already familiar to New Orleanians, including townhouses, center-hall cottages, and shotgun houses, and applied Italianate detailing upon them. This included segmented-arch doorways and windows, heavy molding, and an abundance of paired volute-shaped brackets lining roof eaves and galleries. Italianate was thus mostly manifested in New Orleans as an ornamental overlay to standard structural types, rather than a change in their essential configurations.

By the end of the century, industrialization, mass production, and a growing middle class had helped standardize what had previously been considered luxurious. New late-Victorian architectural styles such as Eastlake and Queen Anne absorbed Italianate's penchant for elaborate detailing, and builders of "catalog houses" milled brackets and quoins *ad nauseam* to spruce up the thousands of prosaic shotgun houses being erected for working-class families. Italianate by this time became Victorian Italianate, and along with parallel styles such as Renaissance Revival, it remained popular into the early 1900s.

Then came the Great War in Europe, and suddenly all of the above came to seem gaudy and decadent. Modernism would increasingly challenge the rationale behind Victorian and Italianate, not to mention the Picturesque movement, Romanticism, and Neoclassicism. After the Second World War, they were openly disdained in some circles.

Yet the architectural vessels of these aesthetic philosophies remain in the modern New Orleans cityscape, by the thousands, and they continue to inspire us in ways that were likely unforeseen by their philosophers.

THE REIMPORTATION
OF RICHARDSON ROMANESQUE

Much of New Orleans culture derives from outside influences imported by newcomers, whose traditions and tastes gradually syncretized locally into something distinct. The city has returned the favor, exporting its own indigenous innovations, such as Creole cooking, jazz, and bounce music.

Then there are cases of New Orleanians who went off to create great things elsewhere, and whose works subsequently found their way back home as part of a broader national diffusion. One such example of that cultural "reimportation" is the Romanesque architecture of Henry Hobson Richardson, a man so associated with this distinctive style that colleagues started naming it in his honor within a few years of his death, a rarity in architecture.

H. H. Richardson was born in 1838 on Priestly Plantation in St. James Parish, now the St. Joseph Plantation House in Vacherie. He grew up in a Julia Row townhouse in New Orleans and briefly attended the University of Louisiana, a predecessor of Tulane. He then set off for Harvard University and spent the Civil War years studying at the École des Beaux-Arts in Paris before returning to the United States to establish an architectural practice in New York City.

Over the next twenty years, Richardson would develop and refine a style he initially gleaned from the medieval churches and castles seen on his European sojourns. Stout and venerable, the ancient Roman-influenced edifices exuded strength and permanence, with their massive stone walls, broad semicircular arches and vaults, short columns, and fortress-like turrets and towers. Yet the stoic structures also retained a romantic quality, appearing graceful and picture-perfect in the landscape.

That sense of romance appealed to nineteenth-century eyes. As the Enlightenment gave way to modernization and industrialization, Western artists and philosophers shifted away from their fascination with classical antiquity, which helped inspire the revival of Greek architecture (Neoclassicism), and found a new muse in the aesthetics of the Middle Ages and Renaissance. The shift reflected a new spirit called Romanticism, which embraced beauty and emotionality and appreciated the picture-like qualities of the old ruins in the landscape—so much so that a "Picturesque movement" began to affect the design of English parks and villages.

Romanticist and Picturesque tastes steered architects toward a revival of the building styles of the Middle Ages, including Italian, Gothic, and Norman. These

Howard Memorial Library (1888, seen here around 1905) on Lee Circle, the city's only build-ing designed by Louisiana-born architect H. H. Richardson, creator of the "Richardson Ro-manesque" style. *Photograph courtesy Library of Congress.*

would become known respectively as Italianate, Gothic Revival, and Romanesque Revival architecture. (The term "Romanesque" here did not connote ancient Rome per se but rather the Norman buildings erected after the fall of the Roman Empire. Latter-day observers tended to "roman-ticize" these Roman-influenced edifices—thus the term.)

Richardson studied in Paris at a time when Romanticism and its architectural manifestations were peaking in Europe but still fairly new in the United States. He returned to a nation transformed by the Civil War, and the victorious North was ready for new ideas. Architecturally, English Gothic and French Second Empire styles were all the rage, and Richardson, in partnership with his business man-ager, Charles D. Gambrill, initially followed suit in his early work in New York.

But Richardson increasingly found himself experimenting with the Norman features he saw in Europe, adapting them to his own tastes and the ever-widening array of industrial materials now available. His efforts culminated with a break-through design for a church in Boston. Completed in 1874 to great acclaim, Trin-ity Episcopal Church made Richardson something of a "starchitect," and he moved to Boston, where commissions awaited him.

Universities in particular were in need of architects at this time: college cam-puses were being designed across the nation, and administrators sought a distinguished look to match the scholarship they cultivated. Richardson's brand of Romanesque seemed to nod to higher education in England, which American universities tended to emulate. Harvard University commissioned Richardson to design a number of campus buildings, and because other institutions of higher learning often followed Harvard's lead, "Richardson Romanesque" came into demand on campuses elsewhere. Other architects started replicating the look, and it spread.

Richardson also designed scores of train stations, government and commercial buildings, courthouses, residences, lodges, monuments and, most of all, libraries. According to biographer Jeffrey Karl Ochsner, Richardson and his firm designed at least 150 projects across the country, of which 85 were built.

In person, Richardson was the sort of man who left everyone dazzled. His portrait artist Hubert von Herkomer described the nation's most famous architect "as solid in his friendship as in his figure. Big-bodied, big-hearted, large-minded, full-brained, loving as he is pugnacious." Some might say he was pure Louisiana. But with so much success in the North, Richardson could hardly find time to return home to New Orleans or St. James Parish. It did not help that the region's tenuous postwar economy promised few opportunities for architects of his stature. Recalled writer Mariana Griswold Van Rensselaer, who knew Richardson personally, "he never even visited his native town again" after returning from France in 1865, "although I have heard him speak of a constant wish to do so."

Richardson did not realize that desire, as he succumbed to kidney failure at age forty-seven. Yet his work would nonetheless find a way home.

His most direct contribution came posthumously—and accidentally. While ailing, he submitted designs for a library competition in East Saginaw, Michigan. But because of a difference of design philosophy with the client, the job went to another firm. Shortly thereafter, Richardson died, and the partnership of Shepley, Rutan and Coolidge gained control of his commissions. The partners promptly reprised their mentor's East Saginaw plans for a new project: a building to house a private book collection slated for a site near Lee Circle in New Orleans. Howard Memorial Library, built in 1888 and now the Taylor Library of the Ogden Museum of Southern Art, is the only Richardson design erected in his home region.

But Richardson's main contributions to New Orleans came vicariously, as his nationwide popularity was reimported locally. Architects influenced by his work began designing similar structures for local clients. For one, a Romanesque annex was built adjacent to Howard Memorial Library in 1891; this would become Confederate Memorial Hall, Louisiana's first museum. Mansions with the same

Gibson Hall, designed by Harrod and Andry and built in 1894 as the first and principal structure on Tulane University's new uptown campus. Gibson Hall embodies the Richardson Romanesque style made nationally popular by New Orleans–raised architect H. H. Richardson.
Photograph courtesy Library of Congress.

colossal look later arose along St. Charles Avenue for clients such as businessman
and philanthropist Isidore Newman (completed in 1892 at 3607 St. Charles Ave.;
now gone) and cotton merchant and banker W. P. Brown (completed in 1904 and
now the largest house on the avenue, 4717 St. Charles). Some of the best local examples of Romanesque commercial, religious, and institutional structures include
present-day 201 Camp, designed by Thomas Sully and completed in 1888; St.
Paul's Episcopal Church, designed by McDonald Berthas farther up Camp Street,
completed in 1893 and demolished in 1958 for the Pontchartrain Expressway; and
the Jewish Orphans and Widows Home (1887), now site of the Jewish Community
Center on St. Charles and Jefferson. The city itself in 1892 selected Dallas architect Max A. Orlopp Jr., who specialized in Richardson Romanesque courthouses,
to unite judicial, constabulary, and punitive functions. Completed in 1893, the
Criminal Courts Building and Parish Prison, according to one *Picayune* journalist,
"reminds one of an old-time chateau or Norman country house, [with] circular
towers rising in the center . . . castellated, with turrets, battlements and slits for
the archers." "A closer view," he added, "shows . . . a mixing of the Romanesque
[and] the Gothic." Demolished in 1949, the courthouse occupied the site of today's
main location of the New Orleans Public Library.

Perhaps Richardson's premier indirect local contribution was to the university
he once attended, by this time renamed Tulane. Its administrators, including
President William Preston Johnston, toured peer institutions and had initially

considered an Italian Renaissance design for the new uptown campus. Instead, Johnston held a competition in which he requested "plain brick, pressed brick and stone" construction and a "unity of design" for the campus. Local architects dominated the submissions, and the winner was Harrod and Andry, whose emphatically Romanesque design for the Main Building (now the iconic Gibson Hall) and the Physics and Chemistry buildings (now Hebert Hall and the Richardson Building) went under construction in January 1894.

My office is in the Richardson Building, and as I look out my window, I see a veritable campus-scape of Richardson Romanesque amid live oak trees and a grassy quad: seven monumental buildings dating from 1894 to 1942, all of gray rusticated stone or pressed brown brick, with broad arches and a heavy horizontality to them.

Among the loveliest is Tilton Hall (1902), whose intricately carved facade features gargoyles and reptilian grotesques reminiscent of medieval buildings. Tilton Hall, originally the library, brings to mind Richardson's particular penchant for library projects. Tilton Library later merged its book collection with that of its Romanesque counterpart on Lee Circle, Howard Memorial Library, and today they form the core collection of Tulane's Howard-Tilton Memorial Library on Freret Street.

And whatever became of that project in East Saginaw to which a dying Richardson submitted one of his last designs, only to be rejected? That building, Hoyt Library, opened in 1887, remains in operation today.

Its style: Richardson Romanesque.

TOURO'S WILL
The Unexpected Life and Fiery Death of a Gothic Landmark

Sometimes we have to remind ourselves that for every historical landmark standing in New Orleans—and we are fortunate to retain so many—another building has disappeared, including some very grand ones. It is an exercise in speculative urbanism to ponder how these lost landmarks might have functioned in our cityscape today. Imagine, for example, heading down Chartres Street in Bywater and, between Piety and Desire, coming upon a colossal Gothic complex seemingly part cathedral, part fortress, and part castle.

In fact, the project began with more altruistic intentions: as an almshouse, or what today might be called an elder home or homeless shelter for what at the time were called the "honest poor." It was the brainchild of Judah Touro (1775–1854), the Rhode Island–born merchant of Sephardic Jewish origins who amassed a fortune in New Orleans through shipping and real estate.

Touro, who despite his wealth lived humbly, would endear himself to citizens through his generous donations for education, social aid, orphanages, health care, and houses of worship. His philanthropy continued after his death in 1854, as he bequeathed his $1 million estate ($27 million today) to sixty different social and religious causes.

Bequest number twenty on his long enumerated will allocated $80,000 "for the purpose of establishing an 'Alms House' in the City of New Orleans [for] the prevention of mendicity." Touro, who would die at age seventy-eight only twelve days after writing his will, further stipulated that control of the institution would eventually pass to "the Mayor of the City of New Orleans." In effect, Touro had, through his private gift, planted the seeds for public-sector social welfare, which hardly existed in this era. This was a time when most benevolence programs were funded not by the government but by civil society and religious institutions.

The "Touro Alms House" was incorporated by the state in March 1855, after which the executors devised an operational plan based on the best practices in northeastern cities and Europe. Prime real estate in the Third District was then acquired courtesy of an equally munificent donation by Touro's old friend Rezin Davis Shepherd, who forty years earlier had helped Touro recover from a grievous injury suffered in the Battle of New Orleans. The parcel spanned 318 feet from Piety to Desire streets and 556 feet from Levee Street (now Crescent Park) back to halfway between 3300 Chartres and Royal streets, the former not yet having been cleared through.

The executors then held an architectural competition, offering a $500 prize to the best design accommodating "400 to 450 pensioners" while costing no more than the bequeathed moneys, which by this time had swelled to $125,000. "When completed," predicted the *Picayune* upon perusing the thirteen submissions, "the Touro Almshouse will be one of the most noteworthy edifices of our city—a monument to the pure character, the genuine love of mankind and the true philanthropy of its immortal founder."

The winning architect, announced in January 1859, was a young local named William A. Freret Jr., son of a former mayor and recent graduate of engineering studies in England. Perhaps inspired by his travels, Freret sketched a rather

English-looking Gothic design for his proposed three-story masonry compound, featuring two crenellated four-story towers overlooking the river and stark walls with scores of tall narrow windows and parapets topped with ten-foot pinnacles. Freret left no explanation of his design rationale, but he likely aimed to bring dignity and pride to the indigent residents through a display of majesty and grandeur. A similar Gothic style, otherwise relatively rare in New Orleans, also adorned the U.S. Maritime Hospital (1848) across the river in Algiers, as well as a few other institutional buildings.

Construction by local builders Samuel Jamison and James McIntosh cost $206,000, the budgetary overrun having been paid by Shepherd, and took over three years to execute. What caused the delays and fiscal problems was an ongoing political crisis of unprecedented magnitude: the dissolution of the Union, formation of the Confederacy, and outbreak of the Civil War in April 1861. New Orleans was now the largest city in the Confederate States of America, and even as its port was blockaded, the city's largest private construction project persevered. By April 1862, the Touro Alms House was nearly complete but for some roofing and details.

Later that month, Captain David Farragut's Union fleet charged the Confederate bastions at the mouth of the Mississippi. After a great nocturnal naval battle, the warships broke through the gauntlet and sailed unmolested upriver to take the Queen City of the South. En route, sailors would have seen scores of plantation houses, warehouses, and sugar mills, but the first truly salient landmark within New Orleans proper would have been the Alms House.

Just beyond, sailors saw plumes of smoke and flame lofting skyward, the handiwork of rebels determined to deprive the enemy of spoils by igniting wharves and cargo. They landed shortly thereafter and entered the undefended city. A few days later, Union Maj. Gen. Benjamin Butler wrote to President Abraham Lincoln, "New Orleans . . . is at your command."

So too was the Touro Alms House, which made for a perfect federal base. Union troops occupied it almost immediately, completing the roofs and filling the interior with gun racks, bunks, and a kitchen. In August, Butler declared the Alms House to be an official "mustering headquarters for native guards," according to a later congressional investigation. This included the First Louisiana Native Guard, a federal fighting force comprising escaped slaves and free men of color. Within a few months, eighteen hundred African American men enlisted at the Alms House and mustered into twenty companies, whereupon some would see action at the Siege of Port Hudson in 1863 and elsewhere. Among them were Captain

Andre Cailloux, one of the first black Union officers killed in Civil War combat, and Captain P. B. S. Pinchback, future governor of Louisiana. In January 1864, the Alms House was used as a recruiting depot for the Corps d'Afrique.

By this time, Lincoln had issued the Emancipation Proclamation, changing the nature of the conflict from rebellion suppression to a war of liberation. Although Lincoln pointedly excluded federally controlled territories like New Orleans from emancipation, thousands of enslaved people nonetheless read the tea leaves of history and emancipated themselves as Union troops neared. Having nowhere else to go, they gravitated to federal encampments for food and shelter, including Camp Parapet in Jefferson Parish and probably the Touro Alms House as well. To wit, a December 1862 article in the *Daily Delta* mentioned African American women and children at the Alms House, suggesting that black civilians as well as soldiers experienced their first moments of freedom in the majestic Gothic edifice.

After the Confederate surrender in April 1865, New Orleans remained occupied even as many troops were sent home. Union officials no longer needed the Alms House, and aimed to vacate after the arbitrarily selected date of September 1, 1865.

It was an unlucky call by a matter of hours.

On the last afternoon of their occupancy, troops were baking beans in the oven they had installed three years earlier. Because Freret had not designed this particular room to be a kitchen, there was no chimney, so the troops connected their oven to a flue originally intended for ventilation. Unbeknownst to them, every time they cooked, sparks had been rising up an air duct replete with fissures and combustibles. They just didn't ignite.

At 10:40 p.m. on September 1, 1865, they ignited.

Flames burst from atop the Piety Street wall, straight above the oven. Alarms were sounded; the fifty-three remaining troops evacuated and formed a bucket brigade, while horse-drawn steam pumps were summoned. But coal sparks ignited tar on the roof, and the flames spread. To make matters worse, someone cried "Powder!"—erroneously, it turned out—but fear of a gunpowder explosion sent firefighters scrambling, which allowed the blaze to get out of control. "During the conflagration," stated writers of a later government investigation, "men . . . were heard to say that 'the baked beans had fired the building.'"

By dawn, Judah Touro's Gothic gift was a belated war casualty. The ruins stood until 1867, when the city cleared the bricks for the right-of-way of what is now 3300 Chartres Street.

Touro's "castle" was gone, but his gift endured. Remaining funds were supplemented by claims filed against the federal government, as well as by Mayor Joseph Shakspeare's "gamblers' fund" raised through steep licensing fees on betting houses. A new almshouse was built in 1895 on present-day Danneel Street between Joseph Street and Nashville Avenue, and like the original, it, too, was Gothic.

In 1901, control of the fund shifted to a city commission, and the almshouse was renamed Touro-Shakspeare. In 1927, the uptown site was sold and subdivided for residences, and a new home was established in 1933 at 2650 Gen. Meyer Avenue in Algiers. Though that building has been empty since 2005, the Touro-Shakspeare Home remains under city control today—just as Judah Touro stipulated.

As for the 1862 almshouse, its footprint has become obscured by bank erosion, levee realignment, and riverfront changes, all of which have subsumed old Levee (North Peters) Street. Had it survived, Touro's Alms House would be a major Bywater landmark today, looking something like the Old Louisiana State Capitol in Baton Rouge—another castle-like Gothic building of the 1850s involving architect William Freret.

Next time you climb Crescent Park's "rusty rainbow" pedestrian bridge, look toward the lake, the river, and Desire Street. These four acres were all within Touro's Alms House. Gothic arches would have surrounded you, and elegant pinnacles would have towered over your head.

"ORNAMENTS TO THE CITY"
Late-Victorian Architecture in New Orleans

"Victorian," in the strictest sense, refers to the years of Queen Victoria's lengthy reign over the United Kingdom, 1837 to 1901. By extension, it implies the society, mores, and tastes of that period.

In New Orleans and elsewhere, however, the adjective usually describes architecture, particularly the styles of the late 1800s. Their appearance, and eventual decline, may be understood in the context of the evolving philosophies and counterreactions regarding the relationship between people and buildings.

So let's back up a bit. Throughout the 1700s, structures in New Orleans were generally vernacular, created by local craftsmen who adapted traditions from

A typical late-Victorian frame house in uptown New Orleans. *Photograph courtesy Library of Congress.*

France, the Caribbean, West Africa, and Spain to the swampy conditions of subtropical Louisiana. The architecture was called Creole, and it was fundamentally functional.

During the early 1800s, New Orleans Americanized, its population diversified, and its building arts reflected the new order. Professional architects from out of town pushed aside old Creole customs in favor of new forms reflecting Enlightenment philosophies inspired by ancient Greece and Rome. The dignified architecture that resulted came to be known as Classical or Neoclassical, most prominently Greek Revival, and it heralded rationalism, order, and genteel aristocracy.

Too much aristocracy and order stirred a counterreaction, one that valued beauty, emotionality, and the spirit of the individual. That movement, called Romanticism, was paralleled in the United States by the budding frontier ethos of individualism and self-sufficiency, and the economic rise and political empowerment of the "common man." By the 1840s and 1850s, majestic Greek temples and townhouses started to look dour and passé. Architects rediscovered more recent medieval and Renaissance influences and breathed new Romanticist life into them—and found plenty of nouveau-riche clients eager to display their wealth through houses so designed.

What resulted in the early Victorian years were more luxurious aesthetics primarily of the Italianate order. The exuberance flourished later in the Victorian period, and it's probably the sundry panaches from those years, 1870s–1900s, that most New Orleanians picture when they think of Victorian architecture.

Among those styles were Stick, with its emphasis on wooden detailing ("stick work"), and its variants Queen Anne, distinctive for its towers and turrets, and Eastlake, with its brackets, quoins, railings, spindles, and skin-like shingling. There was also stony Romanesque with its stout rounded archways; francophile Second Empire and its mansard roofs; imposing Gothic, with its pointed arches; Tudor with its nostalgic rusticity; and a flamboyant expression of Classical and Renaissance motifs known as Beaux-Arts. Architecture blossomed in this era, almost literally, with florid embellishments and cornucopias of fruit bandied all over exteriors and interiors. It was not a time for understatement.

The trend did have some democratizing aspects. Mass production had made woodworking cheap, which enabled builders and owners of otherwise humble houses to spruce them up into charming mini-manses: thus our thousands of gingerbread-encrusted Victorian Italianate shotgun houses. Similarly, homes with modest adornment were featured in pattern books ("catalog houses") and mass-constructed for middle-class families, creating appealing neighborhoods such as today's Bayou St. John and Mid-City. Algiers Point particularly abounds in late-Victorian homes because a terrible fire laid waste to its ten core blocks at precisely the time—1895—when these styles peaked in popularity for new construction.

It was the housing stock built for the upper classes that would become the iconic specimens of late-Victorian residential architecture: huge, vertically massed frame houses with busy roofs, deep-set wraparound porches, and detailing galore. Architects peddling such blueprints found the right clientele in uptown neighborhoods, which boomed in the years following the 1885 World's Industrial and Cotton Centennial in present-day Audubon Park. "The present season in New Orleans has been one of exceeding activity in . . . building and improvements," reported the *Daily Picayune* in an 1888 real estate article subtitled "The Sound of the Saw and Hammer Is Heard in the Land." "The architecture," noted the journalist, "is much more elaborate and original than formerly, the prevailing style for cottages and residences being the Queen Anne, the Eastlake, old colonial, etc.[,] all of which will prove to be ornaments to the city."

Victorian ornamentation was also applied to new commercial and institutional buildings, causing parts of downtown to shed their antebellum scale and distinction for the latest look of other American cities. The Mercier Building on Canal at Dauphine (1887, home to the original Maison Blanche) and its rival Godchaux's (1899) on Canal at Chartres, visually splendid as they were, nevertheless could be picked up and dropped seamlessly into Cincinnati or Boston or Detroit. Most New Orleanians did not see this as a problem; they saw it as progress.

A number of factors drove late-Victorian exorbitance. Raw materials such as lumber, quarried stone, and coal for calefaction were inexpensive, given the largely unregulated extraction of natural resources at this time. Mechanized mills and expanded rail lines brought down production and transportation costs. Skilled labor and domestic help were cheap; federal income tax did not yet exist; and real estate taxes were minimal, all of which freed up household income to sink into the house. There were no zoning regulations limiting size or style, and because municipal water, gas, and electrical services were either nonexistent or nascent, utility bills were hardly an issue.

Furthermore, this was the Gilded Age, when industry and economic expansion swelled the ranks of the upper classes and yielded a new American elite. Unlike its counterparts from earlier times, this generation proudly displayed its wealth, and there was no better way to do so than through one's residence. For a wealthy family in the late 1800s, there was no reason not to build big and grand. Motifs got mixed and matched ad nauseam, and home sizes grew ever larger, as if to say more is always better, and too much is never enough.

And that's what drove the counterreaction.

It began in England in the 1880s, and took root in the United States by the early 1900s. Its philosophy was, by its very nature, low-key and understated, eschewing machine production and frivolous detailing in favor of handcrafted natural simplicity. The movement came to be known as Arts and Crafts, and at its core, it held that less was more, and too much was not only more than enough; it was vulgar.

To be sure, the extravagance continued even after Queen Victoria died in 1901 and Prince Edward ascended to the throne. The Modernist movement, emerging since the 1870s and intensifying after World War I, probably played a greater role in killing Victorian and Edwardian architecture, as did the rising costs of owning a big drafty wooden house. The shift in taste got underway locally around 1910, when more and more architects and home buyers found refreshing charm in simpler, earthier designs. The styles arrived not from the Northeast or England, nor from medieval or ancient precedents, but rather from twentieth-century California.

Yet late-Victorian architecture has left a lasting impression throughout the nation, becoming almost the archetype, in many Americans' minds, of what beautiful houses and idealized domesticity are "supposed" to look like. Christmas cards, children's books, and toys such as dollhouses and model-train layouts feature Victorian houses with striking regularity, and cinema has used them as props to evoke everything from hope (*It's a Wonderful Life*) to horror (*Psycho*).

The Victorian period left a considerable structural mark on the New Orleans cityscape. Despite the fame of the city's Creole legacy, far more extant buildings date to the late 1800s than the 1700s and early 1800s combined, and late-Victorian stylistic specimens substantially outnumber those of Creole or Greek. The aesthetics of that era also live on in the facades of new construction. A study I conducted of hundreds of residences built after the 2005 Katrina flood revealed that nearly three out of every four facades had a historical pastiche—and of those, most paid homage, either partly or largely, to late-Victorian tastes.

CALIFORNIA, HERE IT CAME
Golden State Architecture in the Crescent City

In the early 1800s, the United States gained a new coast, along the Gulf of Mexico, and it beckoned to thousands of migrants. By the early 1900s, it was the Pacific Coast that beckoned, and to California's golden shore arrived migrants by the millions, their dreams in tow. What followed was a westward shift in the engine rooms of American cultural innovation, away from the older eastern cities and into places like Los Angeles and San Francisco. These metropolises would become disproportionately influential worldwide; think how much Hollywood and Silicon Valley affect our daily lives today.

One of the most significant early cultural exports of California was not entertainment or technology, but architecture. Two forms would predominate: one was the California Bungalow, which was both an architectural "style" (fashion) and a residential building "type" (spatial design). The second was more purely stylistic, applicable to residential, commercial, or institutional uses, and its variations would become known as Mission, Spanish, Moorish, Churrigueresque, and Mediterranean.

The primary originators of the California Bungalow were the brothers Charles S. and Henry M. Greene. Born in Ohio and educated at MIT, the twosome launched their careers in Boston but sensed their destiny was in California, where in Pasadena they established Greene and Greene Architects in 1894. Dazzled by the region's sunny, mild climate and intrigued by Japanese and Indian building customs, Greene and Greene created distinctive residences with a horizontal, low-slung massing, somewhat like a ranch house. Interiors featured sedate wooden finishing, sparse but tasteful detailing, mantels and chimneys made of uncut stone, and an abundance of doorways, windows, and porches with overhanging eaves. They called these sprawling yet cozy houses "bungalows" (from "Bengali," meaning the region in India), and they embodied the ideals of the American Arts and Crafts movement, which favored handcrafted simplicity over machine production and gaudy extravagance.

Booming southern California formed perfect *terroir* for these appealing homes, which could be prepared as kits, sold through catalogs, and scaled up or down and adapted to any environment, including neighborhoods designed for automobiles. The American bungalow came to be associated with halcyon California, and the California Bungalow would soon diffuse across America.

Around the same time, California began to discover its own past, and found inspiration in its crumbling Franciscan missions from Spanish colonial and Mexican times. Their native materials and august aura befit California's environment and history, and the state made them its own in 1893 when it designed its pavilion at Chicago's World Columbian Exposition to look like a giant Spanish mission. A revival of "Mission" architecture ensued, and it soon expanded into a Spanish revival, which in turn broadened into a Mediterranean revival, drawing inspiration from Spain and its Baroque (Churrigueresque) and Moorish elements, as well as from southern France, Italy, Greece, Persia, and beyond.

In 1901, architect Bertram Goodhue, known in New York City for his Gothic Revival work, toured these regions with a California client in what proved to be a transformative journey. In the words of urbanist Wade Graham, the two men "drank in the architecture and gardens of this prelapsarian Oriental dream world" and brought home what they saw. Goodhue later completed for that client a villa outside Santa Barbara called El Fureidis, "arguably the first 'Mediterranean' house in California."

The style caught on, largely for the region's Spanish heritage but also for its

A typical California bungalow, the likes of which were often sold as kits through catalogs and built throughout early-twentieth-century neighborhoods such as Gentilly Terrace and Broadmoor. This example is on Maple Street near Carrollton. *Photograph by Richard Campanella.*

geography. The Golden State's dry, sunny landscape of woodlands, scrub, orchids, and vineyards resembles those of the Mediterranean Basin, and buildings of that region look at home in California.

Goodhue would become the supervisory architect of the 1915 Panama-California Exposition in San Diego, which showcased California's emerging architectural idiom to the nation. Soon, Americans everywhere were falling in love with terra-cotta, ironwork, tiles, heavy stucco walls with rough-hewn wooden doors and windows, loggia with Solomonic (spiral) columns and rounded arches, and courtyards with fountains. The Spanish aesthetic spread into the same milieus as the California Bungalow. Both forms celebrated clean, simple lines and natural materials, eschewed frilly ostentation, and made good use of light and ventilation. Importantly, they exuded California—where America was moving, and where the future lay.

That's where New Orleans comes in. The Crescent City had just drained its vast backswamp, allowing for new development all the way to Lake Pontchartrain. Middle-class New Orleanians were eager to move out of the cramped old river-

Palm Terrace (1926), a block of Spanish-Moorish Revival cottages seemingly lifted out of Los Angeles and dropped just off St. Charles Avenue in uptown New Orleans. *Photograph by Richard Campanella.*

front neighborhoods and into modern subdivisions. Developers, home builders, mortgage lenders, public utilities, and city officials all had vested interests in making it happen.

Folks wanted "the latest" in these spaces, and California Bungalows fit the bill. They had curb appeal, scalability, ample porches for hot summer nights, and lots of windows to make up for the low ceilings (something new for locals). They could be built with "New Orleans basements" or on piers, fitted with modern appliances and set among auto-friendly streets and driveways. This was the era when the shotgun house, long the vernacular residence of the working class, was becoming passé on account of its lack of privacy and its awkward linearity. Bungalows offered a familiar yet superior alternative—and with the cachet of California instead of the stigma of southern poverty.

Starting around 1909, California Bungalows would be built citywide by the thousands, in places such as Broadmoor, Lakeview, and Gentilly Terrace, which was billed as "Little California" when it launched in 1909. "THIS IS A REAL CALIFORNIA BUNGALOW IN ALL ITS BEAUTY—Make It Yours," proclaimed a 1912 *Times-Picayune* ad for a Music Street house built by the Gentilly Terrace Company. Its copy bespoke the style's attributes: "The interiors are finished in natural woods, polished wood floors . . . white enameled woodwork . . . all such refinements are handsome. City water and electricity are in. . . . Pay $250 and move in!"

Broadmoor developers erected so many California Bungalows on either side of Napoleon Avenue, from South Claiborne to Broad, that the area gained the same nickname, "Little California," used earlier for Gentilly Terrace. "Justification for the name," explained the *Times-Picayune* in 1920, "was the fact that most of the new homes . . . were bungalows . . . built close to the ground, after the California practice. The Louisiana modification adds a basement, which yields all the advantages of the two-story model."

At the same time, Mission, Spanish, Moorish, Churrigueresque, and Mediterranean Revival facades started to appear on everything from auto dealerships to theaters, funeral homes, schools, churches, municipal markets, and pumping stations. The styles also lent themselves to opulent new homes along uptown boulevards, particularly in Fontainebleau and lakefront neighborhoods.

Perhaps the most charming local example is an unusual one: Palm Terrace, a specially cut block between St. Charles and Carondelet near Marengo. Designed by California architect William E. Spink and landscaped by Swiss designer Sigmund Tarnok, Palm Terrace comprised twelve "architectural gems [in the] beautiful Spanish and Moorish" style, nestled together amid tiny sloped lawns and driveways—"a slice of paradise [be]neath the shade of the palms," according to ads. Opened in 1926, Palm Terrace is arguably the only place in New Orleans with an integral Mediterranean streetscape. A stroll down its narrow confines is a trip to Los Angeles in 1926. It also feels a bit like a Hollywood movie set, as do many of southern California's Spanish villas and estates.

Spanish Revival and its affiliated idioms waned after World War II, though they remain fairly popular for new residences today, especially in the Southwest. California Bungalows, on the other hand, took the brunt of the Depression-era decline in new construction, and found themselves superseded by the slab-at-grade ranch house in the decades after World War II.

Recent decades have seen renewed appreciation for this sturdy and staid style, here and nationwide. When you see bungalows in our cityscape today, anywhere from Old Arabi to Old Metairie, Marrero to Mandeville, they testify to local aspirations of a century ago, to the philosophies of architecture and urbanism in that era, and to California's nearly mythic allure in the early 1900s, as a new American promised land.

WHEN NEW ORLEANS EMBRACED MODERNISM— AND WHY IT STOPPED

"How many New Orleanians does it take to change a light bulb?" goes a local joke. Answer: three. One to change the light bulb, the other two to discuss how much better the old light bulb was.

The insinuation that local society tends to glance backward for its inspiration is often invoked to explain, among other things, the apparent distaste many New Orleanians feel for Modernist architecture. Evidence suggests, however, that Modernism was not originally spurned here. Quite the opposite: throughout the middle of the twentieth century, local society embraced new thinking in architecture, as it had with earlier trends dating back to colonial times. That acceptance would completely redraw the New Orleans skyline, all within thirty or so years.

Modernism's origins may be traced to the late 1800s, when intellectuals began to challenge Western assumptions in science, religion, art, literature, and beyond. They spurned Romanticism, with its glorification of the past and maudlin notions of beauty, and were ready to move on from the stalled progress of the Enlightenment. Rejecting the old and craving the new, the adherents became known as Modernists. In subsequent decades, radical new ideas emerged, ranging from Darwinian evolution to Freudian psychology, from Pablo Picasso's Cubist paintings to James Joyce's stream-of-consciousness writing. The Modernist zeitgeist also helps explain why a New Orleans export known as jazz, which challenged Western musicality with its improvisation, syncopation, and sheer style, would find receptive audiences in places like Paris and Berlin.

Architects, for their part, jettisoned Victorian gaudiness and opted for simplicity over detail, openness over clutter, function over form, and new materials like steel frames and sheet glass. The most prominent American architect advancing this new design thinking, Frank Lloyd Wright, did some of his most influential work in this turn-of-the-century era.

Initially optimistic, the tone of Modernism intensified after World War I, which seemed to affirm every suspicion Modernists had of the Western establishment. Surrealism and absurdism began to appear in the arts and philosophy; theater experimented with the avant-garde; and architects infused their profession with ever-bolder aesthetics. Chief among them was Le Corbusier of France, who spearheaded the horizontal massing of buildings and the use of flat roofs and nonloadbearing walls, which gave greater flexibility to layouts and facades and allowed for open floor plans and wide windows.

Such cutting-edge designs were a bit too much for most Americans in the 1920s, who were hardly Modernists but nonetheless open to modern thinking. For homeowners, this meant the clean, simple Arts-and-Crafts feel of a California bungalow or an American "foursquare," which was sold through catalogs and erected nationwide. For commercial and government builders, it meant a fusion of Modernist traits with traditional architecture. Local examples include the modernized Gothic of the Pere Marquette Building on Common and Baronne (1925, now the Renaissance Hotel), the former Masonic Temple on St. Charles and Perdido (1926, now the Hilton Hotel), and the modernized Neoclassicism of the Orleans Parish Criminal Courthouse (1929) at Tulane and Broad. Similarly amalgamated styles would become known as Moderne, Streamline Moderne, and most famously, Art Deco, of which New Orleans boasts splendid examples, among them Lakefront Airport Terminal (1934), the F. Edward Hebert Federal Building on Lafayette Square (1939), and the now-empty Charity Hospital (also completed in 1939).

The catastrophe of World War II further pushed Modernist thinking. Art Deco and any hint of Neoclassicism came to look ominous for their association with fascism, whereas their antitheses—taut surfaces of aluminum and glass, crisp edges and smooth curves, capacious sun-lit interiors—looked refreshing, even liberating. The International Style of buildings, though it originated before the Second World War, became the primary Modernist aesthetic, and it found good *terroir* in postwar New Orleans.

The city at the time strove to modernize and expand. Projects included new bridges and highways, a new railroad station and a proposed monorail, the replacement of streetcars with buses, and an ambitious Civic Center featuring a new City Hall, courthouses, and library, all built in International Modernist style. Commercial interests were also gearing up for the future—this was the beginning of the oil boom—and they too wanted the latest. The Modernist idiom reflected the optimistic mid-century spirit, and architects responded in kind. Over the next two decades, writes Tulane architecture professor John Klingman in his 2012 book *New in New Orleans Architecture,* "New Orleans was receiving national and even international attention for its then contemporary Modernist design"—quite contrary to the stereotype of backward-looking New Orleanians resisting new ideas.

Modernism in New Orleans had a variety of geographies. Its skyline signature was the array of Central Business District skyscrapers erected starting in 1965, when a new technique of coupling concrete pilings allowed engineers to build higher by driving supports deeper into the hard-clay suballuvial surface. Three prominent examples were the Plaza Tower (1965), designed by Leonard Spangenberg; the International Trade Mart (1965, now the World Trade Center), designed by Edward Durell Stone; and One Shell Square (1972), by Skidmore, Owings and Merrill, the city's tallest building at 697 feet. All were International in style, as were most other new office buildings erected in the 1950s through 1970s, and together they gave the city a new Modernist skyline, particularly after the visually astounding Curtis and Davis–designed Louisiana Superdome opened in 1975.

The French Quarter, by contrast, was a Modernist lacuna, because its legal preservation in 1937 had officially prohibited contemporary exteriors. But even here, Modernism made inroads, in its Art Deco and Commercial Style forms, in interiors not covered by Vieux Carré Commission regulations, and in certain North Rampart blocks removed from commission jurisdiction from 1946 to 1964. One striking Modernist example built here in 1955 is the WWL-TV Studio at 1024 North Rampart.

Modernism and the International style also appeared in public housing, such as the Guste apartments, as well as religious, educational, and civic structures. The Catholic Church was a particularly amenable client, as the ecclesiastic changes set forth by the Second Vatican Council (1962) seemed to call for a new parochial look. Perhaps the best example was St. Frances Cabrini Church (1963, demolished amid controversy in 2007) on Paris Avenue in Gentilly, whose worship space was designed by Curtis and Davis to accommodate greater liturgical participation.

If there is one neighborhood where Midcentury Modern came the closest to forming an integral cityscape, it's Lake Vista. Designed by the Orleans Levee District in 1936 upon artificial land pumped in from Lake Pontchartrain a decade earlier, Lake Vista reflected "Garden City" concepts in its layout—long, curving superblocks in a radial pattern, with centralized greenspace and community amenities, plus varied lot shapes designed to diversify the housing stock. After World War II, Lake Vista became an ideal place for new residential architecture, and dozens of Modernist homes were built here in the 1950s and 1960s. Some have since been demolished, but the streetscapes still exude the aesthetic spirit of Modernism's midcentury zenith.

If there was one building that symbolized that spirit—as well as its subsequent souring—it was the Rivergate Exhibition Hall. Designed by Curtis and Davis in the Expressionist brand of Modernism and sited dramatically where Canal and Poydras met the Mississippi, the great pavilion opened in 1968 in time for the city's 250th anniversary.

The dazzling Rivergate Exhibition Hall (1968), designed by Curtis and Davis Architects and built at the foot of Canal and Poydras streets, came to a contentious demise in 1995. *Photograph from author's NOPSI/Entergy collection.*

At first, the Rivergate was a success. Architects here and elsewhere admired its stunning freeform arches and vaulted ceilings, and the business community saw both the exhibition hall and the adjacent International Trade Mart as a sign of New Orleans reasserting itself on the world stage. By one estimate, a steady stream of bookings for floor shows, special events, and Carnival balls at the Rivergate generated $170 million during the first five years.

Yet only twenty-seven years after its celebrated opening, the Rivergate Exhibition Hall met the wrecking ball, to be replaced by a building whose design was the utter antithesis of Modernism: Harrah's Casino. While architectural aficionados were outraged by the loss of the Rivergate, many New Orleanians, including some historical preservationists, were indifferent if not glad to see it go.

What changed was the arc of the city's destiny. After well over a century as the largest city in the South, New Orleans saw its population begin to decline in the 1960s, as school integration triggered white flight to suburban parishes. The exodus intensified in the 1970s and 1980s as the loss of the tax base and subsequent divestment exacerbated structural and social woes. Containerization, meanwhile, sapped most port jobs, and the oil bust thinned the ranks of petroleum employment. Crime soared, blight mounted, and civic spirit sank.

With a mediocre present and a bleak future, New Orleanians sensed their best days were behind them. So they turned their heads in that direction, and found what they were looking for: a source of civic pride in the past, even if it needed some burnishing and selective amnesia. And what most convincingly evidenced that the past was something to be proud of was the city's vast inventory of splendid old buildings, in elaborate styles and integral distributions unlike any other American city. Houses formerly spurned as archaic now had admirers and defenders across a remarkably wide span of society, such that nearly everyone spoke lovingly of how neighborhoods "used to be" and wistfully shook their heads at "progress." Historical buildings, with their fanciful ornamentation, seemed to emote warmly of the familiar and the known; Modernism, in its eschewing of detail, seemed to do the exact opposite. In the minds of many folks, New Orleans architecture *was* historical architecture, and if a historical building was razed for a cutting-edge Modernist replacement, the loss was not mitigated; it was doubled.

Into this extraordinary turnaround arrived Postmodernism, which showcased historical motifs in otherwise contemporary structures and appealed to those who found Modernism to be icy and supercilious. Likewise, for residential construction, home buyers increasingly opted for neotraditionalism and retro-revival designs. Architects created pastiche designs for developers and builders, who featured them in pattern books. The trend only intensified after Hurricane Katrina: a study I conducted of hundreds of new homes erected after the 2005 deluge revealed that historical styles prevailed overwhelmingly, by a fourteen-to-one ratio, over contemporary designs.

For better or worse, a populist consensus seems to have emerged that the new New Orleans ought to look like Olde New Orleans, even though the city during its zenith had itself exhibited a completely different sensibility, importing new ideas, experimenting with the bold, craving the latest thinking.

THE URSULINE NUNS' LOST LANDMARK ON THE MISSISSIPPI, 1824–1912

On the morning of September 7, 1912, fifty-two veiled women in black habits boarded a streetcar on Dauphine Street in New Orleans's Ninth Ward. For some it was their first venture into the city since before the Civil War; for others, it was their first ride on an electric streetcar. They were cloistered Ursuline nuns, and they were heading uptown because their downtown home since 1824 was about to be demolished.

The Sisters of the Order of Saint Ursula came to New Orleans from Rouen,

France, in 1727, a few years after the arrival of the Capuchins and Jesuits. They were part of an attempt to "civilize" the roguish colony with the Catholic faith, education, health care, and the presence of women. After living for six years in provisional quarters, including Governor Bienville's house at present-day 301 Chartres Street, the nuns in 1734 moved into their own building eight blocks downriver on the same street (called Condé at the time). Designed by Ignace Broutin and Andre de Batz and built by Michael Zeringue, the original three-story Ursuline Convent had cross-timbered walls, a steep hipped roof with a double pitch, and a towering cupola. But its lack of protective stucco led to the rapid deterioration of its *colombage*. Broutin redesigned the convent in 1745, and Claude Joseph Villars Dubreuil rebuilt it, sans the cupola, by 1753. The new building exhibited a majestic French Colonial institutional style typical of the reign of Louis XV. Inside, the nuns would operate their school and control the four surrounding blocks as well as rural parcels throughout the French and Spanish colonial eras.

By the early American years, population growth had put urbanization pressure on these and other city lots. It also made the nuns' life, dedicated to prayer and education, increasingly untenable in these inner-city environs, especially with the City Market and lively riverfront being but two blocks away. So in 1821, the Ursulines acquired a rural parcel in the lower banlieue—that is, the downriver outskirts—and had erected, according to the designs of architects Gurlie and Guillot, a graceful convent dramatically fronting the Mississippi River roughly two miles from their old locale. They took occupancy of the new building in 1824, making it New Orleans's third Ursuline Convent.

Over the years, ancillary buildings and landscaping would make the site into a campus-like compound, comprising the distinctive St. Ursula Chapel (1829, later renovated), the boarding academy for girls, a cloister, a chaplain's residence (likely a preexisting plantation house), space for an orphanage and other evolving social and religious needs, and dependencies for everything from cooking and dining to steam laundering, storage, and even a dairy. When streets of neighboring faubourgs were extended through the area in the 1840s, the convent found itself set back from North Peters Street (formerly the River Road) by about one hundred feet, with Dauphine Street three blocks to its rear and the spaces for Royal and Chartres subsumed by the compound. The convent itself was renovated in the 1850s with a mansard roof and a baroque clock, which would become a riverfront landmark for generations.

From the 1820s to the 1910s, the Ursuline nuns lived, prayed, worshiped, taught girls, welcomed visitors, aged, and died among the oaks and gardens of

Main building of the third Ursuline Convent, built in 1824 at what is now the mouth of the Industrial Canal and seen here a few years before its 1912 demolition. Its baroque clock was a landmark for travelers on the Mississippi River, to the right. *Photograph courtesy Library of Congress.*

their Old World–style nunnery. Once she took her vows, a sister would circulate for the rest of her years in and among fifteen buildings distributed between the levee and Dauphine Street, and from Manual to Sister streets. Life inside was structured, simple, and pious: "Rising early for their matins [morning liturgies]," described K. K. Blackmar in 1912, "attending early mass in the convent chapel, long hours in the classrooms or the sewing-rooms, with brief recreation in the handsome parks or in the well-stocked libraries, with vesper office and long night prayers: these things represent the sum total of the day of the cloistered Ursuline nun." Students came from the elite families of the city and region, but despite their privilege, the girls dressed in simple blue uniforms, lived Spartan lives alongside their mentors, and emerged with the best education attainable for girls in this time and place.

Like other plantations in the lower banlieue, the Ursuline parcel extended all the way back to the Forty Arpent Line, now Florida Avenue. An *arpent* measuring 192 feet, forty arpents usually marked the full 1.5-mile-wide span of the higher, more fertile natural levee in this region, behind which lay cypress swamp. Over the decades, those forty arpents transformed from sugarcane and rice fields, or multi-use French working farms and pasturelands, to street grids with low-density housing, and finally, in the closing years of the 1800s, to fully urbanized neighborhoods. The Ursulines likely would have eventually sold off their unneeded rear arpentage and retained their riverfront compound, from North Peters to Dauphine, where they lived and worked.

But the Mississippi River, and the New Orleans Levee Board, had other designs. River currents had long scoured these particular banks, and the Levee Board had decided that the levee had to be realigned, heightened, and strengthened. Authorities expropriated the nuns' main convent and annexes for demolition—a fate shared by a number of other historic riverfront structures, including the two front turrets of Jackson Barracks—but left the chapel and buildings in the rear of the complex. This undertaking also explains why North Peters Street, which fronts the French Quarter as well as the Lower Ninth Ward and Arabi, does not exist between Press Street and Andry Street: the artery and its edifices got wiped out by the levee realignment.

Resigned to the project and aware that most of their students lived uptown, the order decided to donate part of their land to the city and, selling the rest to raise funds, erected a new institution on State Street and South Claiborne Avenue. On that September morning in 1912, the nuns took a special streetcar directly to their new uptown campus, New Orleans's fourth Ursuline Convent, carrying with them sacramental records and religious treasures dating to the early 1700s.

Demolitions ensued along the Ninth Ward riverfront, but they would be the least of the changes to come. City leaders and the maritime industry, inspired by the recent opening of the Panama Canal and an envisioned canal connecting Chicago with the Mississippi system, had long been clamoring for the construction of a new "inner harbor" with a fixed water level for industry and shipbuilding. In July 1914, the city received authorization from the state to build a deep-draft canal linking the Mississippi River and Lake Pontchartrain. Where exactly? Sufficiently wide and perfectly positioned, the Ursuline parcel provided the answer, and because it was largely undeveloped, its acquisition precluded costly expropriations and house relocations. All remaining buildings formerly owned by the order were acquired and razed, and with the Dock Board in charge and the renowned George W. Goethals Company as consulting engineers, ground was broken on June 6, 1918. Over the next year and a half, the Ursuline land and other properties along the right-of-way were literally wiped off the face of the earth. On May 5, 1923, the Inner Harbor Navigation Canal, which would come to be known colloquially as the Industrial Canal, was formally inaugurated.

The Ursulines thrive today on their State Street campus, with the oldest continually operating girls' school in the nation. As for the circa-1753 Chartres Street convent, it became the residence of the bishop of the archdiocese of New Orleans and would later serve as a school, rectory, office, archive, and today a Catholic center and museum. Inside, visitors can see the circa-1727 cypress staircase from the original convent, arguably the oldest structural artifact in the city. Now known as the Old Ursuline Convent (1112 Chartres Street), the edifice is the oldest documented complete building still standing in the lower Mississippi Valley and deltaic plain, and the most aged in New Orleans by a margin of about thirty years.

Of the circa-1824 third Ursuline Convent, however, only the adjacent five-block-long Sister Street recalls its century-long presence. So eradicated is the old estate that it's hard to say whether it would be in today's Bywater/Upper Ninth Ward or in Holy Cross in the Lower Ninth Ward, because the waterway that obliterated the land also gave rise to the very division between the Upper and Lower Ninth.

Next time you head down St. Claude Avenue and cross the canal, look two thousand feet to your right. While much of the nuns' six-block compound is now mostly water, the site of the main building sits partially on that spit of land jutting into the mouth of the canal. Locals call the spot "World's End," and for good reason.

LESSONS LEARNED FROM THE DELORD-SARPY HOUSE, 1814–1957

Two centuries ago, one of New Orleans's most imposing residences arose on a recently subdivided upriver plantation. Known as the Delord-Sarpy House, the graceful manse would witness vast transformations of its environs and survive as probably the oldest house above Canal Street—only to meet its fate over a matter of feet.

The Delord-Sarpy House was a product of eighteenth-century Creole society at a time of accelerated change. The recently Americanized city was growing rapidly: over nine thousand Haitian refugees had arrived via Cuba in 1809, and they would be followed by thousands of foreign and domestic migrants starting in the 1810s. With New Orleans's urbanized footprint—limited since 1788 to today's French Quarter and Central Business District (Faubourg Ste. Marie)—increasing in population density, owners of adjacent plantations began to subdivide their parcels to cash in on the real estate boom. First came the Faubourg Marigny in 1805, followed over the next few years by parts of present-day Bywater and Bayou St. John, Faubourg Tremé, and five upriver plantations comprising today's Lee Circle and Lower Garden District area.

The parcel closest to Faubourg Ste. Marie belonged to the Delord family, who in 1806 had it surveyed by Barthélémy Lafon and sold in part to Armand Duplantier. The area became known as Faubourg Delord and Faubourg Duplantier, and its lowermost street was named Delord, today's Howard Avenue and Andrew Higgins Place.

Still bucolic in its setting yet proximate to the expanding urban core, Delord Street formed the perfect spot for a spacious and comfortable country home—a villa of sorts. According to the researchers of the *New Orleans Architecture* series, a surgeon named Joseph Montegut acquired a lot on what would later be 534 Howard and erected what was described at the time as "a beautiful new master house . . . brick and terrace roofed, [with] a flanking gallery on pillars and in the rear a small gallery."

True to the West Indian–influenced design instincts of local French Creole builders, Montegut's house had no hallways, an exterior staircase, airy verandas, stucco walls with no frills, and a flat-tiled hipped roof with a slight double pitch punctuated by center chimneys and commanding dormers. It looked like something plucked from Port-au-Prince or Havana, with elements reminiscent of the French countryside or a Mediterranean port. Circumstances suggest the architect may have been Jean Hyacinthe Laclotte, who is thought to have also designed the famous Girod (Napoleon) House at 500 Chartres Street. Indeed, the two buildings bear an uncanny resemblance but for the gallery, and both were started in 1814.

Dr. Montegut's financial troubles delayed completion until 1818, by which time the house came into the possession of Madame Delord-Sarpy. It would remain in the hands of her descendants, namely the Burthe family, for the next forty years, even as the once-pastoral upper banlieue (outskirts) became enveloped by downtown urbanization.

Over the next century, residential land use would shift upriver, the port would modernize, and the Delord-Sarpy (or Sarpy-Burthe) House, having changed hands four times, would find itself hemmed in by storage and industry. Photographs from the 1920s show a poignantly weathered edifice, still resplendent despite peeling paint and cinema posters, with an incongruous repair garage squeezed inches from its majestic pillars. The house struck an odd pose in that its left flank now fronted Howard Street, while its magnificent facade and main gallery, having been originally oriented to view the distant Mississippi, now overlooked the garage. Conditions deteriorated by the Depression: "Pitifully out of place," wrote the authors of the WPA *New Orleans City Guide* (1938), "with one gallery gone and its wide entrance ways boarded up, the plantation home, at present a boardinghouse, stands surrounded by warehouses." (Delord-Sarpy was not technically a plantation home, in that it was never affiliated with an agricultural operation. It was erected

The Delord-Sarpy House, built 1814–1818 on what was then the genteel outskirts of New Orleans, seen here in 1928 hemmed in by light industry. *Photograph by Arnold Genthe, courtesy Library of Congress.*

on an urban street grid, though as a villa once on the edge of town, it certainly looked like a plantation home.)

The Delord-Sarpy House, a product of the Napoleonic Age, had become by the Atomic Age an artifact of a different time and place, appreciated only by preservationists and architectural historians, faded and ragged but sturdy and enduring nonetheless.

Then came the bridge.

In 1952, the state legislature created the Mississippi River Bridge Authority, and with civic advocate Neville Levy as its chair and modernization-minded

Mayor deLesseps "Chep" Morrison in City Hall, planners got to work selecting a route.

They decided to utilize the recently filled New Basin Canal right-of-way, already state-owned and devoid of structures, to bring traffic from points west into downtown. That trajectory dictated that a swath would have to be cleared through the Calliope and Gaienne corridors, from Simon Bolivar Boulevard to Camp Street. What followed were two years of land acquisitions under eminent domain, $3.5 million in compensatory payments, and, starting in 1956, demolitions of fifty-two historical buildings. Construction of the bridge, meanwhile, was well underway.

What threatened the Delord-Sarpy House was not the main Pontchartrain Expressway to the bridge but a forked off-ramp that brought West Bank traffic curving onto Howard Street (right lane) or heading down Camp Street (left lane). The old house sat within the interstice of the two lanes—but, alas, too close to the left lane by a matter of feet.

Could the ramp be relocated? Could the Camp lane be redesigned? Could the house be moved? In May 1955, alarmed members of the Louisiana Landmarks Society met with bridge officials and made their case. But for reasons of funding, engineering, viability, and perhaps just plain intransigence, authorities would not budge. Bridge construction was proceeding at a rapid clip, and with little public support for preservation beyond the French Quarter and a postwar prioritization for modernization, the 140-year-old monarch didn't stand a chance.

In early 1957, the Delord-Sarpy House was dismantled to salvage some components and then cleared away. Ramps were built, and on April 15, 1958, what was described as the world's largest cantilevered highway bridge opened for traffic. Ever since, every motorist exiting onto Camp Street from the West Bank has passed within feet of Delord-Sarpy's space.

In 2012, in preparation for its latest expansion, the National World War II Museum commissioned a local archaeological firm to excavate the corner at Higgins and Camp. Researchers found an abundance of artifacts, from newspapers and shoes to patios with herringbone bricks, plus the house's foundation, cistern, kitchen, privy, and outbuildings. Today they lie beneath another piece of history: the museum's Road to Berlin and Road to Tokyo Campaigns Pavilion.

As for the Delord-Sarpy House, two of its mantels were rescued and donated to the Louisiana Landmarks Society's Pitot House, where they remain today. But perhaps its lasting legacy was the experience of its defenders. The loss helped galvanize and embolden preservationists: no longer would advocates for historic buildings only play defense and negotiate without leverage with unyielding officials. The city's preservation movement was not born in the ruins of the Delord-Sarpy House, but it in part came of age there, and the experience helped steel the movement for the larger battles of the 1960s and 1970s.

IF THE SAINTS LOSE, DON'T BLAME THE GIROD STREET CEMETERY

Every whodat has heard the folklore, and it is usually told in tones ranging from jest to rue: that the travails of the New Orleans Saints can be traced to their home having been built over a cemetery.

In fact, the story of that not-so-final resting place, the Girod Street Cemetery, suggests that street improvements pose more risks to cemeteries than cemeteries do to football teams. Origins of that now-gone graveyard date to two hundred years ago, when Anglo-Americans began to migrate into what had previously been an overwhelmingly Catholic city with a francophone Creole population. The newcomers brought with them all their cultural traits, chief among them religion. Within two years of the Louisiana Purchase, transplanted Episcopalians founded Christ Church.

Congregants of New Orleans's first Protestant church had to make space for themselves in the Catholic city. For the living, this meant a series of temporary houses of worship. For the dead, it meant being relegated to the unkempt rear of St. Louis #1 Cemetery. Vestrymen gained permission to oversee that marginalized space, and over the next fifteen years they brought a little more dignity to the city's first Protestant burial ground.

But then came the first street improvement. In 1820, the city reclaimed most of the Protestant section of St. Louis #1 to lay out what would become Tremé Street plus adjacent blocks. (Many years later, this area would become the heart of Storyville, and afterwards, the Iberville Housing Project.)

So the vestrymen of Christ Church looked elsewhere for a new burial space. They cast their eyes uptown, to Faubourg St. Mary where most Protestants were settling, specifically to an undeveloped 256-by-594-foot parcel at the terminus of Girod Street. On August 10, 1822, the City Council authorized Mayor Joseph

Roffignac to sell to Christ Church, for $3,140.67, that grassy lot situated between two dirt roads named Perrilliat and Cypress. The latter was aptly named, because from it one could see the soggy cypress swamps in various stages of deforestation.

There was a twist. Recalling its need two years earlier to cut Tremé Street through the downtown cemetery, the city stipulated that the congregation could use the new uptown tract "until the Council of the City of New Orleans sees fit to change the location of this Cemetery by virtue of its proximity to the City." Even though the deed allowed Catholics to be entombed there, most people called the new resting place "the Protestant Cemetery." Others called it "the American burying ground," and Creoles called it "Cimetière des Hérétiques." The city named it the Girod Street Cemetery, and for the next 135 years, it would become the final resting place for twenty-two thousand New Orleanians.

Tombs were erected among three main walkways intersected by twenty-two cross aisles. Wall vaults with over 2,300 "ovens" were built along the perimeter, while over a thousand family crypts, more than 500 smaller vaults, and around 100 society tombs formed the interior. Families paid Christ Church fifty dollars for a vault, substantially more for a family tomb, and next to nothing for the mass burials made during times of epidemic. One particular 400-square-foot area came to be known as the "yellow fever mound," although historians Leonard V. Huber and Guy F. Bernard, who authored a monograph on the cemetery in 1961, found evidence that the bodies buried here were actually victims of the calamitous 1832–33 cholera outbreaks.

That Anglo newcomers as well as German and Irish immigrants adopted the Spanish-influenced local custom of above-ground entombment—a rarity in the societies from whence they came—speaks to the cultural syncretism transpiring in New Orleans in the early nineteenth century. According to Huber and Bernard, however, the crypts at Girod fell short of the imposing mausoleums found in the older Catholic grounds, while the space itself always seemed to want for maintenance. In part this was due to the area's soggy soils, which frequently flooded; one illustration likely depicting the 1849 Sauvé Crevasse flood shows a man paddling a pirogue among the tombs.

More so, maintenance problems derived from the lack of a perpetual care policy, in which families would pay a lump sum to fund future upkeep. Instead, sextons rested on the faulty assumption that descendants would care for their ancestors' final resting places. Despite a city ordinance penalizing those who did not, all too many families either moved away or lost interest. Because Christ

Church only owned the land and the walls, it had no legal right to touch the tombs, and more and more fell into disrepair.

It did not help that this section of town had always been rather seedy. The infamous flatboatmen's lair known as "the Swamp" lay only a stone's throw away, as did the malodorous New Basin Canal. Girod itself ranked among the toughest streets in the city, and nearby Phillippa (now O'Keefe) was home to many saloons and brothels. By the end of the nineteenth century, gas works, industry, railroad tracks, and garbage dumps formed a backdrop to the Girod Street Cemetery. Once along the backswamp, its location was now decidedly the "back-of-town."

As a result of these changing physical circumstances, a social transformation began to affect those entombed. White families started taking their recently deceased loved ones to the bigger and more fashionable new cemeteries along the Metairie Ridge. Black entombments increased markedly, especially in the wall vaults and society mausoleums. "Latterly," commented an 1899 *Picayune* article, "the [Girod Street] cemetery has been relegated almost entirely to the colored people, except such white families as have tombs therein." In a peculiar predecessor to the white flight that would occur among the living later in the twentieth century, the Girod Street Cemetery in the early 1900s became less known for its religious affiliation and more for its racial disassociation, with white remains moving out and black bodies coming in.

Attempts by Christ Church to improve maintenance policies failed, and the cemetery grew increasingly derelict. The city's Health Department condemned it as unsanitary in 1945, though illegal burials continued. Hoping to relocate the remains of its deceased congregants elsewhere, Christ Church engaged in a protracted legal battle to clear its title to the cemetery so that it could control the tombs as well as the land.

After workers removed a wall and carted off five truckloads of bricks in 1948, vagrants and looters entered and left in their wake open tombs, stolen ironwork and statuary, and human bones scattered amid jungle-like vegetation. "A perfect setting for a horror movie," wrote the *Times-Picayune* in 1954, "the old graveyard hides bums, vandals [and] ghouls in its overgrown expanse." The eerie eyesore worked against the modernization agenda of Mayor deLesseps "Chep" Morrison. Prioritizing for downtown urban renewal and street improvements, Morrison welcomed plans for a new federal building and post office near South Liberty and Cypress streets, both of which would be widened.

Those projects intersected with the ruinous Girod Street Cemetery.

An aerial view of the Girod Street Cemetery (*upper center*), a few years before its 1958 deconsecration and removal. The area (Lasalle Street at Girod/David Dixon Drive) is now occupied by ancillary features of the Superdome. *Photograph from author's NOPSI/Entergy collection.*

With title to the entire cemetery now legally in the hands of Christ Church, the city in late 1954 filed expropriation proceedings in the Civil District Court. What cinched its legal case was that prescient line written back in 1822—that the Episcopalians could use this land "until the Council . . . sees fit to change the location of this Cemetery," a clause itself motivated by the city's 1820 seizure of the original Protestant tract within St. Louis #1. Cleared title paved the way for Christ Church to relocate the bodies, and the expropriation greenlighted the city's takeover of the land.

On a dreary morning in early January 1957, a small group of religious leaders gathered inside the Girod Street Cemetery to witness Rt. Rev. Girault M. Jones, bishop of the Archdiocese of Louisiana, revoke and annul the Sentence of Consecration that, according to Episcopalian canon, had made this ground sacred. Workers then began extracting thousands of cast-iron and cypress caskets and readied them for their final journey. Racial segregation persisted even in death: black corpses went to Providence Memorial Park on Airline Drive, and the white dead, including the skeletons unearthed in the so-called yellow fever mound, went to Hope Mausoleum on Canal Street. For some of the bodies, this was their second crosstown move, the first having occurred between St. Louis #1 and Girod 135 years earlier.

By the early 1960s, the cemetery's footprint had been obliterated and the surrounding cityscape had been thoroughly redesigned. By the early 1970s, work commenced on the Louisiana Superdome. Gleaming skyscrapers arose on Poydras Street, crowds packed the stadium, a new hotel and shopping mall opened across Lasalle Street, and the oil boom pumped millions into the Central Business District.

What revived fading memories of the Girod Street Cemetery was the discovery, in the late 1980s, of twenty skeletons on a worksite between the Hyatt Regency Hotel complex and the Superdome. News coverage brought the obliterated cemetery to the attention of a new generation. Given the Saints' dismal performance in this era, many sports fans, with their penchant for jocular superstition, spoke woefully of their team's home being haunted by the spirits of the graveyard it displaced.

Alas, it did not. Today, the Girod Street Cemetery's unmarked footprint straddles Lasalle Street immediately upriver from Champions Square, half lying under the Superdome's garages 2 and 2A, and the other half beneath the structure housing the Club XLIV and Encore event spaces.

A two-time victim of city street improvements, New Orleans's first Protestant cemetery lives on today in the form of local folklore, resurrecting in local conversations whenever the Saints' performance declines.

THE ST. LOUIS AND THE ST. CHARLES
New Orleans's Legacy of Showcase Exchange Hotels

No account of nineteenth-century New Orleans's Creole-Anglo ethnic rivalry is complete without reference to each group's showcase hotel. For the Creoles, it was the St. Louis, in the heart of the French Quarter; for the Anglos, it was the St. Charles, in the epicenter of the Faubourg St. Mary, or American sector, today's Central Business District. Plenty other places to board could be found, and they served visitors of all classes; many functioned additionally as "exchanges," which in addition to lodging provided guests with financial services and meeting spaces for everything from auctions to business transactions to dining, drinking, and entertaining. But the St. Louis and the St. Charles topped them all, in grandeur and amenities, and either or both of their respective sites have hosted iconic lodges nonstop from 1837 to today.

Architect J. N. B. de Pouilly, commissioned by the Improvement Bank in 1835, designed the St. Louis Hotel and Exchange to occupy an entire block in the heart of the original city. The Panic of 1837 forced a reduction to slightly more than half that size, with the frontage along the lower side of St. Louis Street between Chartres and Royal. But grand it was nonetheless, especially with Exchange Alley leading from Canal Street all the way to its doorway.

For its first two years, the St. Louis (1838) would form, according to the *Daily Picayune*, "the pride of New Orleans and of Louisiana, the wonder and admiration of strangers, the most gorgeous edifice in the Union," featuring a "magnificent hall where merchants congregated, the saloon where beauty gathered for the dance, the elegantly furnished hotel, the bar room, the billiard room [and] numerous offices and stores." The journalist wrote in the past tense because a terrible conflagration the previous morning, February 11, 1840, had completely destroyed the building, its timber-supported rotunda collapsing spectacularly.

So brisk had been the hotel's business that the owners speedily rebuilt, this time funded by the adjacent Citizens Bank at a cost of $600,000 and executed with fire-resistant components such as a lightweight dome made of a honeycomb of hollow clay pots. "We rejoice in seeing its lofty dome soaring again to the sky," beamed the *Picayune* in May 1841, "and we hope to hail it . . . once more a proud architectural boast of New Orleans."

For the next twenty years, the St. Louis would form the nucleus of Creole business and society. Auctions of every conceivable form of property, including enslaved human beings, were conducted within the 88-foot-high rotunda surrounded by towering Tuscan columns, like a scene out of ancient times.

The Civil War altered the St. Louis's destiny. The hotel had closed, its rooms having been used by troops, and in 1874 the building came into the hands of the New Orleans National Building Association, which promptly sold it to the State of Louisiana to serve as the de facto state capitol. It returned to its original use in the 1890s, when, as the Hotel Royal, it featured a ladies' entrance on Royal, a restaurant under the rotunda, a kitchen behind it, and a steam laundry in the adjoining Greek Revival edifice (facing Toulouse Street) of the now-defunct Citizens Bank, funder of the earlier hotel.

But hardly was the Hotel Royal regal, and with gradual divestment in the French Quarter, its patronage declined until the business shuttered. The building soon found itself, according to a 1906 retrospective penned by Charles Patton Dimitry, in a state of "silence, neglect, emptiness and gloom." Tourists would explore its labyrinthine interior and, amid the ruins, come across vagrants and,

The former St. Louis Exchange Hotel, rebuilt in 1841 after a fire and seen here as the Hotel Royal around 1906, ten years before its destruction. *Photograph (detail) courtesy Library of Congress.*

on one occasion, a horse. After the Great Storm of 1915 further disheveled the landmark, the building was sold to the lowest bidder, the Samuel House Wrecking Company, which proceeded to dismantle it between October 1915 and early 1916. But for a few storefronts left standing along Chartres Street, the prime real estate would serve as nothing more than a salvage yard for decades to come.

After World War II, with tourism on the rise, the Vieux Carré Commission— which, despite its preservationist mission, worked closely with commercial interests in this era—floated the idea of a major new French Quarter hotel. According to a 1946 article in the *Old French Quarter News,* the commission deemed there were "numerous potential sites and places were buildings could be torn down without any great loss to historic character of the quarter." One site was the salvage yard on St. Louis Street. The idea lay dormant until 1957, when the owner of the parcel, Edgar B. Stern, envisioned a major hotel for his property. With assistance from Lester B. Kabacoff and the collaboration of Roger Sonnabend, chairman of the Hotel Corporation of America, a massive modern hotel was erected in a style highly reminiscent of the circa-1840 St. Louis. The city's premier architectural historian and historical architect at the time, Samuel Wilson Jr., designed the exterior, while the comparably talented Arthur Davis planned the interior.

The Royal Orleans Hotel opened in 1960, and, according to pioneer preservationist Mary Morrison, "exceeded everyone's expectations, [becoming] overnight practically, a very, very popular hotel." Demand was so high that architects three years later added a mansard roof with additional rooms and a penthouse, which the Vieux Carré Commission permitted on account of the antebellum predecessor's lofty dome. Wilson had also embedded into the hotel's flank a fragment of the old arcade left standing on Chartres Street, including a palimpsest of the word "Exchange," the only remnant of the 1841 St. Louis Exchange Hotel. The Royal Orleans does brisk business to this day.

Six blocks upriver, on the second block of St. Charles Avenue, architects James Gallier Sr. and (probably) Charles Dakin sketched plans for what would become one of the most splendid structures in the nation. The St. Charles Exchange Hotel, opened in 1837, bore a resemblance to the later-completed U.S. Capitol. Under its 185-foot dome and cupola, by far the highest point in town, were elegant accommodations and services catering to a mostly American clientele. Like the St. Louis, guests at the St. Charles could congregate, negotiate, dine, recreate, socialize, and board in luxury, all under one roof.

Hundreds of guests and workers, day and night, meant a constant presence of candles, oil lamps, calefaction, and cooking pits. Hotels were therefore infamously prone to fire, as the owners of the original St. Louis could testify. Just before noon on January 18, 1851, a blaze broke out in the north wing just beneath the eaves and spread faster than firemen could contain it, their hoses incapable of reaching so high. In a report written in real time, a *Picayune* journalist described "a scene of confusion that baffles description . . . with boarders . . . busy packing up . . . husbands looking for their wives, and wives wringing their hands in agony." Winds shifted the flames southward, and upwardly they swept. "At 1 o'clock the dome fell in with a tremendous crash[;] the pride of our city gradually [became] a mass of ruins."

Attesting to its commercial success, the hotel was promptly rebuilt and reopened in January 1853 under the same name, and according to the *Picayune,* in "the same imposing architectural display that delighted every beholder of the old one"—only this time without the front steps and the costly dome. Like its predecessor, the new St. Charles served as a focal point for anglophones in St. Mary throughout the so-called "Golden Age" of the 1850s, and it bore silent witness to the subsequent Civil War, occupation, Reconstruction, and modernization.

But fire remained a risk. At 11 p.m. on April 28, 1894, a kitchen fire ignited wooden beams, spread laterally, and sent deadly smoke upward toward slumber-

The second of the three St. Charles Hotels (opened 1853 and seen here a few years before its 1894 destruction by fire), each standing at present-day 200 St. Charles Avenue. The hotel occupied that spot from 1837 to 1974. *Photograph by George François Mugnier, courtesy Library of Congress.*

ing guests. Shortly after midnight, sections of the building began caving in, and by dawn only the massive columns and pediment remained. It was a harrowing sight, and the toll of four lives could have been much higher.

Once again, investors endeavored to rebuild, but only with new safety technologies as well as modern luxuries. They sent architect Thomas Sully on a nationwide tour of comparable hotels, and, finding particular inspiration in the Planters' Hotel in St. Louis (1894), Sully designed what the *Picayune* described as "a hotel containing all [the] latest modern conveniences, built especially for light, comfort and ventilation." The third St. Charles, bearing an Italian Renaissance aesthetic, opened just in time for Carnival on February 1, 1896, and for the next eight decades, its reddish brick color, rooftop garden, 500 guest rooms, and arcade of street-level shops formed the veritable heart of the Central Business District. It was sold in 1959 to Sheraton for $5 million and continued in service as the Sheraton–St. Charles.

By the 1970s, two factors put the third St. Charles in a defensive position. One was the rise of skyscraper hotels with all the latest amenities; the other was the petroleum industry, which exerted pressure for office and parking space in the CBD. In 1973, a local businessman partnered with an Italian financier to replace the aging lodge with what would have been a fourth hotel, fifty-two stories high, containing 1,080 guest rooms as well as office space. With the land title in their hands and zero preservation rules holding them back, they razed the 1896 building in 1974. (Two years later, the Planters' Hotel met the same fate in St. Louis.)

The lot remained empty until the Place St. Charles skyscraper, designed by Moriyama and Teshima Architects with The Mathes Group, was completed in 1984. Postmodern in style, Place St. Charles has a spacious triple-level veranda overlooking the avenue, ideal for viewing Mardi Gras parades, and boasts more stories (fifty-three) than any other building in the city (although One Shell Square's fifty-one stories rise higher—697 feet to Place St. Charles' 645 feet). But initial plans for lodging fell by the wayside, and today Place St. Charles is home to finance, banking, legal, and energy offices.

Thus ended the long history of hotels on the St. Charles site, even as it continues at the Royal Orleans on St. Louis Street—a dual lodging legacy traceable to 1837.

THE POYDRAS AND PILIÉ MARKETS, 1838–1932

New Orleans during the 1830s saw its population more than double, to over 100,000, as migrants predominantly from Ireland, Germany, and the northeastern United States made their way to the banks of the lower Mississippi. Increasingly, the human geography of the city shifted away from the largely francophone lower city and toward the predominantly anglophone upriver precincts of the Faubourg St. Mary (now the Central Business District and "South Market District") as well as the neighborhoods we now call the Warehouse District, Lower Garden District, Central City, and Irish Channel.

As the population shifted, so did food retail. The buying and selling of food-stuffs took a number of forms in this era, both lawful and illicit. Peddlers were ubiquitous: Benjamin Latrobe reported in 1819 that "in every street during the whole day black women are met, carrying baskets upon their heads calling at the doors of houses." Hunters and fishermen, meanwhile, would sell their catch on the canal docks and by the riverfront. Along the uptown wharf, flatboatmen would earn the wrath of licensed merchants by turning their rafts into illegal pop-ups, selling wholesale to retail consumers. "The owners of the flat-boats no sooner arrive," growled one businessman in 1847, "than they open their floating shops for the sale of their respective cargoes; and as their prices average little more than one-half of those [in] stores[,] there are always numbers of customers thronging the levee." Corn, wheat, smoked hams, barrel pork, and other up-country exports typically sold along the flatboat wharf.

For most New Orleanians most of the time, "making groceries" meant a trip to the neighborhood market. These open-stall bazaars were owned and operated by the city so that inspectors could enforce sanitary regulations and collect fees from a centralized space. The French (Creole) Market was the first and largest unit, dating originally to 1780–91 and expanded to four blocks by the early 1800s.

To outside eyes, the market was among the most interesting spectacles of the city, and travelers regularly commented on the scenes they saw. Basil Hall, who came from Edinburgh in 1828, noted that "the fishermen were talking Spanish," likely Isleños from St. Bernard Parish, "while amongst the rest . . . was a pretty equal distribution of French and English." His inventory imparts an idea of the city's foodways at the time: "cabbages, peas, beet-roots, artichokes, French beans, radishes . . . potatoes both of the sweet and Irish kind;—tomatoes, rice, Indian corn, ginger, blackberries, roses and violets, oranges, bananas, apples;—fowls tied in threes by the leg, quails, gingerbread, beer in bottles, and salt fish." He noticed at "every second or third pillar sat one or more black women, chattering in French, selling coffee and chocolate [and] smoking dishes of rice. . . . I found it was called gumbo, a sort of gelatinous vegetable soup, of which . . . I learnt afterwards to understand the value."

The urban expansion of the 1830s forced authorities to create new food retail spaces in new areas, particularly uptown. What resulted was a municipal market system which, over the next eighty years, would form one of the largest in the nation.

The first to serve the upper faubourgs was the St. Mary's Market (1836), lo-cated off Tchoupitoulas Street in what is now the Warehouse District. "For quite a number of years after its erection," noted J. Curtis Waldo in his 1879 *Illustrated Vis-*

itors' Guide to New Orleans, St. Mary's Market "was considered very far up town." Because of the ethnic predomination of this area, some people jokingly called the emporium "the Irish French Market."

Two years later, the city acquired space from the Carrollton Railroad Company on Poydras Street for a market to serve what at the time would have been the rear of the Second Municipality. Known as the Poydras Market (1838), the two-block-long building ran in the middle of an extra-wide section of Poydras Street from Penn to South Rampart. It offered every conceivable foodstuff and household goods via hundreds of open stalls, all under a pavilion-like roof with a picturesque wooden cupola. The gables of the structure were finished in ornate detailing, and a passageway beneath the cupola allowed mule-drawn drayage and (later) streetcars to move beneath the structure.

Markets in the antebellum era were owned by the city, sold by stall (rather than leased) to vendors, controlled by ordinances, and managed by a market commissary, who oversaw regulations regarding sanitation, suppliers, stall keepers, deliveries, and the building itself. Records indicate the Poydras Market kept its commissary busy: according to an 1858 *Daily Picayune* report, the emporium was "intolerably filthy, from the want of facilities for obtaining water," which left the public "often disgusted at the uncleanliness," not to mention "so crowded as to be almost impassable" in the section "devoted to the sale of vegetables, coffee and refreshments."

The area around the Poydras Market made matters worse. Markets in general tended to attract loiterers and vagrants, and nearby Dryades Street, which was called Phillippa at the time, bore witness to a remarkable concentration of saloons and brothels—and along with them all the affiliated scams and crimes. Worse yet, a few blocks upriver was a sketchy purlieus known as "the Swamp," a notorious lair where flatboatmen debauched. The delinquency sometimes found its way into the market proper: in 1860, for example, an unemployed woman lingering around the bazaar, likely a prostitute, exchanged words with what she described to the *Daily Delta* as "a beautiful looking man with a gold watch around his neck." She ended up getting shot in the abdomen by him.

Mostly, however, ordinary law-abiding people patronized the marketplaces for their everyday sustenance, and found an abundance of fresh victuals amid well-arranged stalls. Despite its problems, the Poydras Market prospered to the point that in May 1866, the city purchased the adjacent neutral ground from South Rampart to Basin (now Loyola) to create the Pilié Market, to relieve overcrowding in the original pavilion. A reorganization of the market system in 1868

A view under the cupola of the Poydras Market, looking up present-day O'Keefe Street, captured by famed photographer of the West William Henry Jackson in the 1890s. *Courtesy Library of Congress.*

occasioned the selling of stands and stalls to a new set of owners—although many proprietors both before and after the change subleased their spaces, a source of constant dispute at the time. Renovations in 1898 included more permanent walls between outdoor and indoor space, and the installation of a long rooftop monitor for ventilation.

By the late 1800s, source regions of immigration to New Orleans had shifted to southern and eastern Europe. Among them were Orthodox Jewish families from Russia and Poland, some of whom would find work at the Poydras Market. Because Dryades Street ran through the market and accessed the 325-stall Dryades Market (1849) a mile uptown, both emporia would become central to the residential settlement and economic ascendency of this population. Into the 1960s, Dryades Street would be known as New Orleans's "Jewish neighborhood," and while this ethnic enclave is mostly traceable to commercial opportunities on Dryades Street (now Oretha Castle Haley Boulevard), the connection originated with the Poydras Market.

In 1911, New Orleans's municipal market system added its thirty-fourth unit, double the number from 1880 and over tenfold since the establishment of the

Poydras Market. The city at the time boasted the highest per-capita number of public markets in the nation, and possibly the largest absolute number as well.

It was an apex that would not last. Municipal markets grew increasingly ill-suited for twentieth-century city life, as corner grocery stores offered convenient alternatives and as populations moved into new automobile-based subdivisions. The rise of supermarkets after World War II sealed the fate of the system, and by the 1960s it was reduced to its original member: the French Market.

Vendors did not go down without a fight. They formed merchants' associations, developed competitive strategies, and lobbied authorities for facility improvements. But the city had other designs: in 1927, the St. Louis–based firm Bartholomew and Associates, consulting for the recently formed City Planning Commission, identified Poydras Street's "present width of 74' [as] hardly sufficient to meet the demands of trucking" and recommended broadening it to 100 feet along its downtown flank. The extra-wide section occupied by the Poydras Market, which the planners scorned as an obstructing relic, provided an idea of how a widened corridor might improve traffic flow and help modernize downtown. Bartholomew's emphasis on trucking pointed to the fact that Poydras Street, first laid out in 1788, had long been something of a blue-collar cousin to Canal Street, attracting wholesalers, shippers, warehousing, and light industry. It was the sort of environment that planners ached to "improve," and Step One was the removal of the Poydras Market.

In January 1930, the Dryades-to-Penn section of the ninety-two-year-old pavilion was torn down explicitly to make more street space for vehicular traffic. Two years later, the city officially abandoned the market because it "was no longer needed and it constitutes a serious traffic hazard." The remaining structure was unceremoniously cleared away in June 1932; Dryades was later renamed O'Keefe, and both it and Poydras were widened in the 1950s and 1960s for precisely the reasons identified in 1927 by Bartholomew: traffic efficiency.

No trace of the Poydras Market survives today, but there are some clues. For one, the former home of famed Maylie's Restaurant, founded in 1876 by two market workers and in business for 110 years, remains standing and now hosts an Irish pub. Across the street at 900 Poydras are three surviving antebellum storehouses, the likes of which once surrounded the Poydras Market. And a few blocks upriver is a booming new mixed-use neighborhood centered on the Rouse's Market, which opened in 2011. Developers christened this area with the neologism "South Market District," meaning south of the old Poydras Market.

No one called it that during 1838–1932, but if the name catches on, so too will endure the memory of the Poydras Market.

A STORIED GEM LOST TO PYROMANIA
Gallier and Dakin's Merchants' Exchange

At their most basic level, "exchanges" were places where people met to conduct business. But because the assembled parties usually had other needs and desires— for financial and legal services, reading rooms, lodging, recreation, entertainment, victuals, and libations—entrepreneurs created ornate multi-use, multi-service complexes catering to itinerant businessmen. As such, exchanges became key nodes in the social and economic geography of antebellum cities. Most of the larger hotels in antebellum New Orleans billed themselves as exchanges—roughly the equivalent of modern conference hotels—as did many "coffee houses" (saloons). Some catered to Creoles on the lower side of town, others to Anglos on the upper side.

It was in this milieu that an Anglo-American banker and merchant named Samuel Jarvis Peters recognized an opportunity. Peters realized the city's commercial core was spreading upriver from the old Creole-dominant Chartres-Royal corridor and into the American sector on the other side of Canal Street. An exchange built in the heart of this expanding but bifurcated commercial district, he reasoned, might prosper for its convenience to both Creole and American populations and their visiting colleagues.

So motivated, Peters amassed $100,000 through a joint stock company and acquired a parcel at 18 (now 124–132) Royal Street, steps off Canal and with key rear frontage along the recently created Exchange Place (later Alley). In 1835, the company commissioned the architectural partnership of James Gallier Sr. and Charles Dakin to design an exchange for merchants. This was the Irish-born Gallier's first summer in New Orleans, and the former New Yorker was already busy designing what would become two of the city's foremost landmarks, the St. Charles Exchange Hotel in the American sector, and now the Merchants' Exchange.

The St. Charles had an entire block at its disposal, with arteries and open air all around. Not so the site for the Merchants' Exchange: extant buildings hemmed in the parcel, blocking natural light, and the narrow confines of Royal Street and Exchange Place could hardly showcase a prominent structure. But because the site was large, 80 feet long by 120 feet deep, Gallier and Dakin made up for the limited frontage by shifting the design emphasis away from the horizontal dimension and exterior, in favor of the vertical dimension and interior.

What the duo devised were two separate three-story wings united by a capacious rotunda topped with a splendid dome and florid skylight. While the fenestration on the Royal and Exchange facades exhibited what one observer described as a rather "plain and bold" Greek Classicism—four sets of deeply inset and squared-off apertures on either side of a centralized main entrance—what awaited inside would stun the visitor. Architectural historian Samuel Wilson Jr. described it as "one of the first great monumental interior spaces ever seen in New Orleans," a soaring atrium bathed in natural light surrounded by walls with towering pilasters and Corinthian capitals.

The plans initially drew skepticism. "The design for the dome and roof over the large room was somewhat peculiar and caused a good deal of criticism among the builders," recalled Gallier in his 1864 autobiography. William Nichols, an architectural emissary of Neoclassicism in the South and lately Louisiana's state engineer, "pronounced that the building . . . would be insecure and the dome could not stand." But Gallier, who had followed the guidelines of noted English structural engineer Thomas Tredgold, stood his ground and convinced his clients and builder Daniel H. Twogood his plans were sound. "Everything was finished in due time," Gallier reported, "and has remained firm and secure to the present day. My reputation having gained some advantage by this discussion, I soon had . . . as many . . . contracts as I could possibly attend to."

Opened in 1836, the Merchants' Exchange would host a head-spinning array of programs and occupants. In today's parlance, it was "shared space": flexible multi-use public space held in the private domain for varied patrons day and night. In addition to auction rooms, meeting areas, and trading floors, the ground floor of the Merchants' Exchange became the U.S. Post Office, a key tenant that made the building relevant to residents citywide. (According to the *Daily Picayune*, letters in English were delivered in the Exchange Place entrance, "while letters in foreign languages, and those addressed to ladies, were delivered in Royal Street.") There was also a barroom right next to the post office, which surely benefited from the foot traffic, and offices throughout the two wings were leased to various agencies

Difficult to fully appreciate from narrow Royal Street or Exchange Alley, the Merchants' Exchange (1836; dome at center right, seen here around 1900) was most prominent when viewed from afar. *Photograph (detail) courtesy Library of Congress.*

and enterprises. The second floor hosted a popular reading room, stocked with the latest tomes and newspapers and frequented by a loyal patronage paying ten dollars annually. "There are two bulletin boards in the room," reported the *Daily Picayune* in 1840, "one for ship . . . arrivals and clearances; the other . . . containing the latest and most important news." For years the second floor also housed a city court and the Federal District Court, and it was here in 1857 that filibuster William Walker was tried but acquitted for violation of neutrality laws in his notorious adventurism in Nicaragua. On the third floor was a billiard club and parlors for chess games, smoking, and general socializing, all with the business of business at hand. (As for Gallier and Dakin's original skylight, it had been destroyed by a lightning bolt in 1841 and replaced with tin.)

147

The Merchants' Exchange had a particularly sumptuous atmosphere at night. Observed Abraham Oakey Hall after perambulating inside the gaslit chambers one evening in 1850, "yonder is the cotton broker, with the fluctuations of the market . . . penciled on his face[;] near him is a sugar broker, fat with perpetual tasting of the sweets of his life. . . . In one corner the banking agent [chats] familiarly with the jolly planter who has just doffed his hat [to] a passing factor[;] in another corner [sits] a sallow-faced man versed in the tobacco mysteries [of] the London market. . . . Of all the crowd, perhaps not one calls the city his home, from birth or choice. . . . All [are gathered here] intent on speculation and accumulation, working for them all the day, dreaming of them by night."

As for slave auctions, a bookseller who worked in the exchange in the 1850s told the *Daily Picayune* many years later that after the U.S. Post Office moved to the Customs House in 1861, the rotunda "was rented to the Associated Auctioneers of the city, who used it as a place for the sale of real estate and slaves at auction." Incredibly, even after federal troops seized Confederate New Orleans in May 1862, "the sale of slaves went on briskly for several weeks. There seemed to be no restriction put on these sales." An 1864 article in the *Daily True Delta* referred to the building as "the Merchants' and Auctioneers' Exchange."

All that, of course, would change. The fall of the planter regime and the disruption of trade during and after the Civil War upheaved the commercial community and its spaces. Chief among the victims was the Merchants' Exchange, which had already lost its main postal and judicial tenants and, unlike its competition, had no hotel income to fall back on. By the time commerce began to revive, the city's industrial sectors each wanted their own exchange rather than a shared space. Cotton firms formed the Cotton Exchange in 1871; food merchants created their Produce Exchange (now Board of Trade Plaza) in 1880; sugar merchants formed the Louisiana Sugar Exchange in 1883 and included rice in 1889; and a Stock Exchange formed among the brokers of Gravier Street in 1906. There was also a Mechanics, Dealers and Lumbermen's Exchange; a Mexican and South American Exchange; and a Fruit Exchange. The antebellum model of the all-purpose exchange had become a victim of its own success, and the former Merchants' Exchange became just another downtown commercial building.

Rent went downward, and so did the quality of the renters. Some rooms became an illegal gambling hall (probably keno or faro, which were popular on Royal Street), while a restaurant and cheap boardinghouse filled other rooms. Known by the shady euphemism "No. 18 Royal Street" (news flashes from an 1892 *Daily Picayune* crime report: "*row in a Gambling House [at] No. 18 Royal Street . . .*

crowded with people . . . attacked . . . with a knife . . . previous trouble in the place . . . second disturbance within a week"), the aging gem found itself sandwiched between a dicey gaming house and the ribald New Tivoli Varieties Concert Saloon. Other incongruous tenants in the 1890s–1900s included the Fourth Battalion of the Louisiana State National Guard, a Chinese laundry, and the Audubon Athletic Club (1890), which put on boxing matches in the rotunda. A fire in 1903 damaged the graceful dome and led to its remodeling into a standard rooftop monitor.

What breathed new life into the old building was the enterprise of a man named Henry Gluck, who opened an eatery downstairs around 1903. Gluck's Restaurant would become a favorite epicurean rendezvous, known for its German, French, Italian, and Louisiana cuisine, and it brought a moneyed clientele into the building. The Gallery Circle Theater would later open on the second and third floors, and by the 1940s–50s, shops filled the Royal Street storefronts, among them a Mexican curio vendor, a shoeshine, and Aunt Sally's Original Creole Pralines. The old Merchants' Exchange had once again become multi-use, and patrons would often frequent both the restaurant and theater during a night out on the town.

Such was the case on December 2, 1960, when the recently renovated Gluck's did a brisk Friday night business and 225 people enjoyed a comedy called *The Front Page* in the playhouse upstairs. Shortly after the curtains fell, at 11:40 p.m., employees smelled smoke and spotted flames in the theater. Over the next four hours, according to a front-page *Times-Picayune* report, 140 firemen used thirty-three pieces of equipment to douse the inferno, as sparks erupted into the sky and black smoke enveloped Royal Street. The roof caved in and the floors below pancaked, injuring four firemen. By dawn, Gallier and Dakin's gorgeous interior was open to the street and strewn with charred debris among tenuous exterior walls. Enough remained to give cause to the Louisiana Landmarks Society to advocate for its stabilization and reconstruction, but because the 100 block of Royal lay outside the Vieux Carré Commission's jurisdiction, no legal means could prevent its demolition. The site was cleared in April 1961, sold that December for $300,000, and redeveloped in 1969 with a Holiday Inn, now the Wyndham Hotel.

Investigators determined that a transient pyromaniac had ignited the blaze in the restroom of Gluck's after ordering a hamburger—a pointless and banal end to a storied gem.

KING COTTON'S CRESCENT CITY THRONE
The New Orleans Cotton Exchange, 1871–1964

Though it dates to 1921, the building known as the New Orleans Cotton Exchange on Carondelet and Gravier streets speaks to antebellum history on many levels. It evokes the city's historical role as a transshipment port, and recalls the South's plantation economy and the enslaved labor on which it depended. Financially speaking, the Cotton Exchange marks what had been one of the most powerful spaces in the South, an area locals dubbed "the Cotton District" and "the Wall Street of New Orleans." It also represents the gradual decline of southern cotton and its lucrative futures market.

The southern cotton industry emerged in the late eighteenth century from a series of technical breakthroughs. On the demand side, the invention of the steam engine, mechanical spinners, and the power loom drastically reduced the production costs of cotton fabric, thus lowering its price and raising demand. On the supply side, the introduction of Sea Island cotton and upland varieties expanded the plant's growing range, while Eli Whitney's "cotton engine" (1793) enabled workers to separate lint from seed and trash ten times faster than by hand. With plans to grow cotton, settlers from the Atlantic Seaboard migrated to the fertile lower Mississippi Valley, which, along with the strategic transshipment port of New Orleans, were now under American dominion thanks to the Louisiana Purchase.

Cotton plantations were established throughout the fertile bottomlands and loess bluffs between Baton Rouge and Natchez and would expand throughout the lower valley and its tributaries. By the 1810s, yet another technological advancement abetted the blossoming cotton industry: steamboats. Within a few years, cotton rose from a minor regional crop to a major Mississippi Valley export. The 2 million pounds of cotton raised in Louisiana in 1811 quintupled in ten years, which in turn nearly quadrupled to 38 million pounds in 1826. By 1834 the harvest was over 62 million pounds. New Orleans would serve as a key node in the Cotton Triangle, in which northern-owned ships would ferry cotton to ports like Liverpool, continue to New York with cargos of fabric or immigrants, and return to New Orleans with northern manufactured goods or ballast.

The cotton boom in what was then called the Southwest also breathed new life into the institution of slavery. Over the next half-century, well over 750,000 African Americans were sold out of the upper South, where tobacco had depleted soils and manufacturing had expanded, and sent to the wharves of New Orleans, where the nation's largest slave market would route the captives to the cotton or sugarcane fields.

Depending on the season, those same wharves would have been crowded with cotton bales in transit. Here toiled the working-class end of the New Orleans cotton industry: first were the roustabouts, who handled the bales on the steamships until the vessel docked, at which point cotton screwmen took over, unloading the bales on the wharf for the longshoremen to organize them into shipments and pass them on to draymen, who hauled them to the cotton presses. There, cotton rollers moved the bales to the scalemen, who loaded them onto scales for the cotton weighers and pulled samples for the cotton classers, who in turn graded the lint by color, cleanliness, and fiber length, and gave it a rating that would influence its price and sellability.

That was the key piece of information needed by the professional cotton men. At the top were cotton brokers, merchants, and agents, who kept records, tracked bales, and decided whether a client's cotton should be sold locally, warehoused in anticipation of better prices, or shipped overseas to a buyer client. Cotton factors, a particularly powerful profession, accepted cotton on consignment from planters and sold it at the highest prices obtainable, supplied planters with agricultural equipment, provided financial services, and generally represented planters' interests in the marketplace. Anglo-Americans predominated among cotton men, and many were either born or based out of state.

Each tier of players on the New Orleans cotton scene had its support echelons. The professionals dealt with insurers, bankers, and lawyers; the presses needed machinists and engineers; the dock workers needed tools and equipment. Ancillary parties such as cottonseed oil manufacturers; ginneries; pickeries (which salvaged scrap lint); makers of screws, ties, and presses; and myriad others serviced the industry, creating thousands of jobs throughout New Orleans.

The nature of trading a commodity like cotton entailed personal interaction and information sharing, which tended to drive firms to cluster spatially to form industry districts. As the districts grew, so too did their clout—which thus attracted ever more firms. Entries from *Cohen's City Directory* for 1854 indicate that cotton professionals had by this time aggregated around the intersection of Carondelet and Gravier in what was then called the Faubourg St. Mary or the American sector, today's Central Business District. Of the 147 cotton firms listed that year, 46 had addresses on Carondelet, and another 24 operated on Gravier Street, far more than any other street. Nearby Common, Camp, St. Charles, and

The original New Orleans Cotton Exchange, built in 1881 and replaced in 1921, marked the financial epicenter of the southern cotton industry, at Carondelet and Gravier streets in downtown New Orleans. *Photograph courtesy Library of Congress.*

Union streets accounted for another 42. In all, about 90 percent of the city's professional cotton concerns were situated within a four-by-four block area centered on Carondelet and Gravier. By 1861, fully 174 of the city's 465 commission merchants and cotton factors had addresses on Carondelet or Gravier. The draw of the district was so strong that even dealers in cotton gins and in slaves set up shop nearby. Gravier Street had seven slave dealers operating pens or compounds, where recently arrived slaves were prepared for auction. Nearby Baronne Street was home to another seven.

What was lacking in the cotton district was one centralized place for professionals to gather and transact. "Most of the cotton business was conducted in the open air, up and down Carondelet Street," recalled one veteran merchant, or "in saloons, which called themselves 'exchanges,'" such as the Merchants' Exchange

on Royal Street. The need for central exchange only grew after the Civil War, when cotton men had to rebuild both an industry and its labor force.

Toward this end, in February 1871, a group of a hundred cotton men and a few bankers organized the New Orleans Cotton Exchange. They chartered the organization with the objectives of providing meeting space, arbitrating disputes, establishing regulations and standards, serving as an information clearinghouse, and promoting and marketing the industry while reducing risks wherever possible.

After operating out of rented rooms for a while, the Cotton Exchange contracted for a three-story building on the corner of Gravier and Theater Alley (Varieties Alley, or Varieties Place) about one hundred feet off Carondelet. A decade later, the growing organization decided to erect a larger and more ornate building squarely on the corner of Carondelet and Gravier.

Costing $380,000 and opened in 1883, the New Orleans Cotton Exchange was strikingly florid, with elements of Second Empire, Renaissance, and Italianate styles. Inside was a large Exchange Room with Corinthian columns, gold ceiling medallions, fresco murals, sculptures, and a fountain around which cotton futures were sold. Numerous well-appointed offices and meeting rooms were on the four upper floors, serviced by an elevator. For almost four decades, this building functioned as the "capitol" of New Orleans's cotton district, just as New Orleans served as the "capital" of Mississippi Valley cotton production. "Carondelet and Gravier streets are considered the centre of the cotton business, and in this neighborhood are clustered all the large houses dealing in cotton," declared one writer in 1893. Of the 283 Cotton Exchange members listed in the organization's 1894 charter, fully 94 percent worked within two streets of the Cotton Exchange.

Edward King captured the ambience of a typical day in the cotton district in his 1875 book, *The Great South*. "In the American quarter, during certain hours of the day, cotton is the only subject spoken of; the pavements [by] the Exchange are crowded with smartly-dressed gentlemen, who eagerly discuss crops and values, and who have a perfect mania for [cotton]; with young Englishmen . . . with (their) slang of the Liverpool market; and the skippers of steamers from all parts of the West and South-west, each worshipping at the shrine of the same god. From high noon until dark the planter, the factor, the speculator, flit feverishly to and from the portals of the Exchange, and nothing can be heard above the excited hum [but] the sharp voice of the clerk reading the latest telegrams."

While the number of cotton businesses in New Orleans gradually declined by about three or four per year from the 1880s to the 1920s, gross receipts continued to rank the crop near the top of the city's moneymakers, and the city at or near the top of the nation's cotton markets. The Cotton Exchange remained the most important financial spot in the city.

The Great War in Europe brought with it rocky times for American cotton, as overseas markets closed and market quotations ceased. But demand for lint increased (for uniforms), and the movement of matériel to the front rejuvenated Mississippi River shipping. The South produced its first billion-dollar crop during these years, and doubled it in 1919. Counting on a rosy future, the New Orleans Cotton Exchange in 1920 had its aging building demolished, for its general inadequacy and for structural problems traceable to its lack of foundational pilings. The laying of the cornerstone for the new eight-story steel-frame corner building, designed with a Renaissance flair by Favrot and Livaudais and costing $1,222,520, occurred on the organization's fiftieth anniversary in 1921. Festivities marked the occasion, and the future looked bright.

But the optimism proved to be ill founded. Government regulations, foreign competition, a shift in domestic production to drier western environs, plus the rise of railroads and trucking and the emergence of Dallas as a business hub, all conspired to topple New Orleans's domination. Of the ninety-three cotton factors listed in the *New Orleans City Directory* in 1880, fifteen operated in 1921, and only one remained by 1949. "We went from trading thousands of contracts in the early '50s to maybe five contracts in all of 1962," recalled Eli Tullis, a retired cotton broker from one of New Orleans's last active cotton families.

In the cotton fields, floods and boll weevils took their toll, and planted acreage in Louisiana declined from almost two million acres in 1930 to a few hundred thousand in later decades. (In 2013, only 130,000 acres of cotton were planted in the state.) As cotton planting moved westward, so too did the movement of bales, leaving riverfront wharves and sheds to switch to bananas, coffee, lumber, rubber, and metals. Today, only Staplcotn and Kearney Companies keep cotton moving through New Orleans, the latter leasing federally licensed cotton warehouses at the Napoleon Avenue Container Terminal for shipments destined for Pakistan, Turkey, Latin America, and elsewhere. The bales are packaged and hidden from view, and most New Orleanians have probably never seen one.

As for the New Orleans Cotton Exchange, in 1962 the organization sold its landmark building on Carondelet and Gravier to the Universal Drilling Company, as if to signal the upcoming oil boom, and became a renter in its own home. What finally killed the Cotton Exchange was the Agricultural Act of 1964, which subsidized domestically consumed cotton and controlled once-volatile prices, thus eradicating the futures market. When the exchange finally closed on July 9, 1964, its last president, C. Layton Merritt, wistfully told the *Dallas Morning News,* "We cede our role in the market place to the Secretary of Agriculture, the cooperatives, and history."

IF WALLS COULD TALK, THIS STARBUCKS WOULD SPEAK OF LINCOLN

In 2014, a new Starbucks coffee shop opened in the Pickwick Club on the corner of Canal Street at St. Charles Avenue. Though it's hard to tell from the interior, this prominent landmark retains structural elements dating as early as 1826, the year of its original construction. It was remodeled into a hotel in 1858 and a billiard hall in 1865, and all but reconstructed in 1875 as the Crescent City Billiard Hall according to grand designs by architect Henry Howard. Thomas Sully finished off the interior in 1886, and since then, it's become known to generations of New Orleanians for its Carnival viewing stands and for the varied retailers renting its street-grade spaces.

When I bike past the Pickwick Club each morning en route to my office at Tulane, I think not so much of the coffeehouse or of architectural history, but of a little-known incident involving Abraham Lincoln on the eve of this nation's greatest drama.

Lincoln never set foot in the building, although he may have strolled past its earlier incarnation during his 1828 and 1831 forays to New Orleans as a flatboat-man. Rather, the incident occurred in the 1850s, when Lincoln was a country lawyer working the "mud circuit" around Springfield, Illinois, and when New Orleans, at the peak of its mercantilist power, roiled over the mounting sectional tensions regarding slavery.

Springfield at that time was home to twenty-seven free African American families. Among them was a woman named Polly Mack, who had arrived years earlier after her Kentucky master freed her upon moving north. Polly raised her son John Shelby in Springfield, and as the lad reached manhood, he yearned to stretch his legs, make some money, and see the world. In this time and place, that usually meant working the rivers, the arteries of western commerce.

In late 1856, Shelby ventured to St. Louis and took a deckhand job aboard a southbound steamboat. Upon arriving at the Crescent City, Shelby, like any country chap, eagerly stepped ashore to explore the enticing metropolis. What Shelby did not realize was that New Orleans, finding itself increasingly on the defensive regarding slavery, had become ever more resistant to the rights of free blacks. To be sure, the city since colonial times had been known as something of a haven for native-born free people of color, who enjoyed certain legal rights, attained skills and education, and prospered to degrees unimaginable in the interior South. But times were changing, and the white establishment by the 1850s endeavored to curtail their rights, proscribe their influx into the city, and expel those recently arrived. A contemporaneous *Picayune* editorial angrily described "free negroes" as an "evil," a "plague and a pest" responsible for "mischief to the slave population," and recommended deporting them to Liberia and cracking down on further emancipations. Authorities viewed out-of-state free black males in particular as potential subversives whose very existence threatened the institution of slavery. Those in the city unsupervised and undocumented were routinely arrested and jailed.

Shelby set out into the streets of New Orleans blissfully ignorant of all this, not even having procured a pass from his captain. In short time he found himself detained by police, tossed in jail, tried, and fined. Because his steamboat by then had departed, he had no way to pay his penalty. Shelby was "thrown [back] into prison," according to an 1866 letter between involved parties, and "as no one was especially interested in him, he was forgotten. After a certain length of time, established by law," the writer explained, Shelby "would inevitably have been sold into slavery to defray prison expenses." Months passed, and he languished in prison.

Somehow, in early 1857, Shelby managed to establish contact with a sympathetic young New Orleans attorney named Benjamin F. Jonas, who, like Shelby, had been raised in Springfield. Jonas visited his childhood neighbor in jail, and the two conferred as to whether a particularly capable lawyer back home, a man by the name of Abe Lincoln, might adopt his case.

Shelby may have known Lincoln through William Florville, a Haitian of mixed Franco-African ancestry who himself had escaped possible enslavement in New Orleans decades earlier before settling in Springfield. Florville became Lincoln's barber, as well as a pillar of the local black community, and thus likely knew both Shelby and his mother. Jonas knew Lincoln well: Abe was a close friend of his father, Abraham Jonas, a leading citizen of Springfield and one of the first Jewish settlers in the region. Everyone thought highly of Lincoln, and the two agreed to involve him.

Jonas sent word of John Shelby's desperate situation upriver. An 1866 historical narrative by Josiah Gilbert Holland described Lincoln's response:

Mr. Lincoln was very much moved, and requested [his law partner] Mr. Herndon to . . . inquire of Governor Bissell if there was not something that he could do to obtain possession of the negro. [T]he Governor regretted to say that he had no legal or constitutional right to [act]. Mr. Lincoln rose to his feet in great excitement, and exclaimed, "By the Almighty, I'll have that negro back soon, or I'll have a twenty years' agitation in Illinois, until the Governor *does* have a legal and constitutional right."

Lacking further recourse and all too aware that New Orleans had the law on its side, Lincoln and William Herndon drafted $69.30 out of the Metropolitan Bank of New York and, on May 27, sent the funds from their law office at South Sixth Street and East Adams in Springfield to Benjamin Jonas at his law office in New Orleans. According to city directories of this era, that office was located at 3 St. Charles Street, or 103 St. Charles Avenue on the modern address system— precisely the space of today's Starbucks. There, Jonas would have received Lincoln's paperwork and arranged to pay the fine.

The plan worked. Within days, Shelby won his release and returned as swiftly as possible to Springfield. "[S]hould he come south again," Jonas warned Lincoln in a letter dated June 4, 1857, and probably written in the same office, "be sure [he has] his papers with him—and he must also be careful not to be away from the boat at night—without a pass [from] the captain."

What makes the incident more intriguing is the situation in which the Jonases would find themselves when war broke out four years later, by which time Lincoln was president of the United States. The Illinois-based Jonas family had many relatives in New Orleans, some of whom served as Union spies who secretly informed patriarch Abraham Jonas of Confederate activities, who in turn passed the intelligence directly to President Lincoln. Others, however, sided with the Confederacy—including, paradoxically, the same Benjamin Jonas who helped liberate John Shelby in 1857.

Despite the divided loyalties, President Lincoln maintained his affection for the Jonas family, unionists and rebels alike, demonstrating the better angels of his own nature. Benjamin once recalled that "Mr. Lincoln always asked after us when he saw any one from New Orleans during the war." The president even granted a three-week parole to Benjamin's imprisoned Confederate brother Charles so he could visit his dying father. Benjamin Jonas himself would later serve as a Louisiana senator.

As for John Shelby, we may justly view him as among the first African Americans, if not *the* first, ever freed by Abraham Lincoln—from a New Orleans incarceration that may well have led to his enslavement.

I think about this every time I pass that Starbucks.

THE RISE AND FALL OF THE OLD SHOT TOWER, 1883–1905

For twenty years, an eerie medieval-looking obelisk known as the Old Shot Tower loomed over the gritty late-Victorian cityscape of downtown New Orleans. Despite its salience, the edifice floundered structurally and economically, went curiously unrecorded by photographers, and rates today, over a century after its demise, among the least-remembered, most-prominent elements of New Orleans's historical cityscape.

An ingenious invention of the late 1700s, shot towers used physics to manufacture ammunition without specialized machinery. At the top of a high hollow pillar, molten lead would be poured through a sieve and dropped over a hundred feet. The plummet exerted surface tension upon the globules, which cooled into spheres and plunged into a tank of water. Smaller pellets would be sorted for birdshot or buckshot, while larger ones—which needed a coarser sieve and more drop time, thus a higher tower—might end up as grapeshot for artillery. Irregular pellets would be remelted and dropped again.

Philadelphia erected the first major American urban shot tower in 1808, and by 1813, three big operations served the lead mines near St. Louis. In subsequent years, shot towers advanced technologically and spread across the nation. Steam elevators would replace staircases; cast-iron frames would buttress brick walls; and rail lines would supplant mule-drawn carts.

A shot tower of unknown dimensions once operated in New Orleans in the 1830s–40s on the Carondelet Walk along the Old Basin Canal (now the Lafitte Greenway). Little is known of this and other local towers, probably because of their small sizes and improvised construction.

Fifty years later, investors from New York and New Orleans detected an opportunity. While ten shot towers processed lead mined from Colorado, Missouri, and Arizona, none were located in the lower South, even though most of the final product made its way down the Mississippi. Hoping to boost profits by saving on freight, the investors bought two lots at St. Joseph and Foucher (now Constance) and made designs for a massive enterprise.

We call it the Warehouse District today, but in the late 1800s, this neighborhood was dedicated more to making things than warehousing them. Here toiled skilled workers in foundries, machine shops, engine and boiler yards, chain and rope walks, even an electric-light factory. Industry was drawn here for its spur connections to the Illinois Central Railroad and extensive wharf-side shipping access, as well as for its steam-powered generators and water service. A shot manufacturer fit in perfectly.

Completed in 1883, the St. Joseph Street Shot Tower, run by the Union Company and later the Gulf Company, was impressive. A stout 900 square feet at its base, the 214-foot-high octagonal obelisk resembled a hollow, eight-sided, brown-brick Washington Monument, 40 percent as high and perforated with small windows. Its massive load rested upon cast iron and wooden beams as well as citadel-like brick walls, which rested upon a cypress mat topped with an iron plate for stability. Cauldrons and water pools filled the ground floor, next to the polishing casks and sacking rooms. The tower's interior had two chambers, one for the steam elevator to lift the molten lead, and the other for the dropping stations. A new rail spur coming up St. Joseph Street connected the operation to the shipping wharves.

Its prominence and novelty of purpose made the Shot Tower locally renowned. Citizens used it as a spatial reference (for example, "near the Shot Tower," "between the Shot Tower and Lee Circle"), as we use landmarks like the Superdome or bridge to orient ourselves today. Sometimes it served as neighborhood nickname or adjective. Few things struck more fear in New Orleanians than the Shot Tower Gang, notorious hoodlums who terrorized this area from the 1880s to the 1900s.

The tower's unique form also inspired innovations. When the Muller Company started manufacturing high-powered electric light bulbs on the same block, its owner in 1884 arranged to illuminate the Shot Tower's window-filled interior with 132 bulbs and its summit with a 36,000-candle-power arc lamp. The first-of-its-kind light show dazzled residents far and wide. Not just a marketing stunt, Muller's experiment tested the best way to illuminate a city, whether by a

The Shot Tower (1883, at center, to the right of the obelisk at Lee Circle) appears prominently in this 1885 Currier & Ives bird's eye illustration of New Orleans. *Lithograph (detail)
courtesy Library of Congress.*

few gigantic spotlights mounted aloft or by hundreds of smaller lampposts lining
every street. The Shot Tower spotlight fared well enough, because in subsequent
years enormous steel light towers were erected to illuminate arteries throughout
downtown, making for an amazing nighttime spectacle. The strategy, however,
eventually proved impractical.

As the only shot tower in the lower South, the St. Joseph Street venture
seemed poised to control regional demand. But because its proprietors also
owned towers elsewhere and worried about cannibalizing their own market
share, they ran their New Orleans asset sporadically. So idled, operators in 1885
switched to the tourism industry: for twenty cents, pleasure-seekers could ride
the elevator daily from 9 a.m. to 5 p.m., much like any modern tourist attraction,
and enjoy the scenery. An 1885 tour guide described the summit as "decidedly the
best view obtainable of the city, [where] old canals known from childhood, when
looked down upon from above, insist upon running in tangents to their supposed
course[,] streets curl up and decline in almost semicircles, [and the Mississippi]
staggers about in loops and curves."

The Shot Tower ranked as the highest building ever erected in New Orleans
until the completion of the Hibernia Bank Building in 1923. One enthusiastic
writer in 1897 called it "one of the twelve or fifteen highest structures in the
world" and among the loftiest "ever erected by man in ancient or modern times."
(It should be noted that he also called Avery Island "quite mountainous.")

When the Shot Tower did perform its eponymous function, it was no leisurely sight. Roaring fires, steam-spewing boilers, rickety elevators, and molten lead flying through the air made for myriad occupational hazards. In the tower's first year, for example, a worker had his heel badly mangled by the steam elevator and later died of lockjaw. In 1887, an electrical fire spread beyond the reach of fire hoses, creating a terrifying spectacle. The blaze destroyed interior timbers, knocked iron columns out of plumb, and threatened neighbors with falling debris.

The tower was eventually repaired, but its reputation was not. Dangers, coupled with a national outcry against tower companies and other industries for forming trusts and colluding, made New Orleans's shot tower something of a neighborhood nuisance. One *Daily Picayune* editorialist hoped to kill two birds with one stone by wishing "the shot tower should fall on the gang of hoodlums that infest its base." It almost did fall in 1895, when a freight train on St. Joseph Street "acting as a battering ram, pushed [a] derailed car through the [Shot Tower] and sent the bricks [upon] a dozen men." People started to call the landmark, despite being barely a dozen years old, the "Old" Shot Tower.

By the new century, the property had come into the hands of the American Shot and Lead Company, a trust that had, once again, idled the plant for the benefit of its other holdings. In 1904 the firm sold the asset—or rather, liability—to the United Lead Company for $10,000, which in turn sold it to a New York–based meat-packing company in need of a cold-storage facility. Having no need whatsoever for what a *Picayune* journalist called a "grim old tower . . . most familiar of all of the old city's landmarks," the company had the curious pillar dismantled in 1905.

Construction materials were reused elsewhere. The cypress timbers, for example, were unearthed and used in 1913 as a platform to construct the Queen and Crescent Building on Camp Street, now a hotel. Bricks from the tower's walls likely remain in Warehouse District buildings today, perhaps even in the former cold-storage facility currently under renovation as apartments on St. Joseph and Constance today.

Shot towers would soon fade from the American landscape as modern manufacturing techniques were developed. But the concept of pelletizing by gravity persisted: an ammonium nitrate pelletizing plant, complete with a shot tower, was built in Luling in 1954.

One would think such a salient landmark would attract legions of photographers. At least one man did lug a camera up the Old Shot Tower to capture a bird's eye vista published in an 1892 sketchbook, and some street photographers unintentionally captured it from a distance. Perhaps its most prominent treatment appears in a well-known Currier & Ives lithograph of the city, released in time for the 1885 World's Cotton and Industrial Centennial, at which time the tower was open for sightseers. But close-range or interior photos are exceedingly rare, if they exist at all. Perhaps this oversight can be explained by its industrial use and isolation from the more famous and romanticized precincts of the city. Whatever the reason, the Old Shot Tower stands alone among the city's many famous historic structures in its fall from renown, having been universally known in the late 1800s and all but forgotten by the early 1900s.

Too bad, because had it survived, the strange pillar would have become a nationally recognized element of the New Orleans cityscape.

"OMINOUS"
The Old Criminal Courts Building and a Brief History of Penal Architecture

The adjective "ominous" often accompanies descriptions of the prisons of New Orleans's past. Though the word does not necessarily express the architectural intentions of the city's five major penal facilities, it does fairly well characterize the reputations they would earn. Chief among these storied institutions was the Old Criminal Courts Building and Parish Prison, which brooded over the "back-of-town" from 1893 to 1949. But first, a brief history of prior penitentiaries.

A series of *calabooses,* under various jurisdictions and incarcerating everyone from escaped slaves and prisoners of war to petty thieves and murderers, operated directly behind the present-day Cabildo (1799) for the city's first hundred years. By the 1820s, population density and economic prosperity made an inner-city prison impractical, and a new facility was erected seven blocks toward the swamp, on Orleans Street in the Faubourg Tremé. Consequently, the Cabildo's calaboose was demolished and replaced by the Arsenal, although a police station and small jail remained on-site into the early 1900s.

The geography of the new prison reflected a tendency in historic New Orleans to shunt stigmatized or otherwise unwanted features (prisons, hospitals, cemeteries, dumps) out of the more empowered riverfront neighborhoods and backward toward the swamp. The architecture of the new prison was nonetheless a bit more progressively informed. Designed by prominent local architects Joseph Pilié and A. Voilquin and built during 1831–36, the compound occupied an entire block and had a majestically austere Franco-Spanish aesthetic, featuring long arcades with arched openings, stuccoed walls, interior courtyards with galleries, and separate sections for different offenders and offenses. The design communicated strength and stern discipline to the streetscape, but not without touches of beauty, perhaps intended to signal mercy and rehabilitation: two graceful cupolas were set atop the hipped roofs, and sycamore trees were planted in front to soften the austerity.

Prison operations and conditions were hardly fiscal priorities for the city, and the Orleans Parish Prison in Tremé soon took on an aura that was perfectly ominous. That reputation was further sullied when, in 1891, its walls and wardens failed to prevent an angry mob from lynching eleven suspected Sicilian mobsters recently acquitted of the murder of Police Chief David C. Hennessy. The incident provoked an international crisis between the United States and Italy and hastened efforts to replace the sixty-year-old prison.

The city used the need for a new prison as an opportunity to centralize judicial, constabulary, and punitive functions, and in February 1892 issued a call for a challenging architectural proposal. On the square bounded by Gravier, Common (now Tulane Avenue), Basin (South Saratoga, now Loyola Avenue), and Franklin (now gone), authorities envisioned a complex with five interrelated programs: a parish prison with cells for three hundred men and fifty women, plus "condemned cells," a chapel, and a mortuary; a criminal courthouse with courtrooms and dozens of ancillary chambers for judges, attorneys, clerks, and juries; a citywide headquarters for the Police Department; a First Precinct Police Station for the local neighborhood; and a Recorder's Office to handle the bureaucracy generated by the agencies. "Particular attention," read the request for proposals, "must be given to the ventilation and lighting of the entire premises, as well as full provision for water closet and sewerage and drainage with distinction for both sexes." Indoor plumbing was new at the time, and the city wanted the latest amenities. Total expenditures would be $350,000 for design, supervision, and construction. As before, the complex would be located in what locally born Louis Armstrong described as the "back-a-town" and what other folks called "the Battleground," for its rampant vice.

The winner of the competition was Max A. Orlopp Jr., a Brooklyn-born German American architect/builder based in Dallas who specialized in Romanesque-style brick and stone courthouses. Orlopp devised for New Orleans something that would stun the eye and cower any criminal. Wrote a *Times-Picayune* colum-

The imposing yet structurally unsound Criminal Courts Building and Orleans Parish Prison (left), built 1893, seen here in 1906, and completely eradicated in 1949. *Photograph courtesy Library of Congress.*

nist, the design "reminds one of an old-time chateau or Norman country house, [with] circular towers rising in the center . . . castellated, with turrets, battlements and slits for the archers." "A closer view," he added, "shows a sort of hybrid architecture, with a mixing of the Romanesque, the Gothic and the nondescript of hurried get-through-quick style of the later day." High above was a reconnoitering clock tower visible for miles.

The design and siting of the complex, completed in 1893, were clearly intended to send a message of judicial power and social order to the tough neighborhoods of the Second, Third, and Fourth wards. Chinatown, known for its opium dens, sat directly across the street, and the vice zone that would become Storyville in 1898 lay only two blocks downriver, within the sightlines of the imposing—and ominous—tower.

Inside could be found all the proscribed programming except the Orleans Parish Prison, which was in an adjoining set of buildings on Gravier at Basin (now Loyola). To its rear was a fenced yard where, until a change in law moved executions to the state penitentiary, convicts were hanged—the last such spectacles in New Orleans history. Stylistically, the courthouse, prison, and dependencies were all unified by Orlopp's "Romanesque . . . Gothic" design and salmon-red brickwork, such that the entire massing when viewed from a distance looked like one colossal citadel-city. It was quite a sight.

Then came to light a litany of problems which literally undermined Orlopp's architectural display of power. Just as officials were settling into the new building, nearly half of City Council members, according to a *Times-Picayune* report, "were indicted for bribery and graft . . . in connection with the construction of the building." News of the financial shenanigans was followed by reports of cracks developing in the walls and foundations of both the courthouse and prison. Floors tilted, doors stuck, and windows jammed. Something was wrong.

One wonders if Orlopp, who did most of his work in the interior South, did not understand the specialized requirements of New Orleans's soft deltaic soils (he served as both designer and builder on this contract). But according to an 1892 report in the *American Architect and Building News,* the problem was not Orlopp but his client, and the fact that "the competition was held under one administration and the execution of the work left to its successors." Confusion and incompetence, the reporters surmised, paved the way for a sloppy competition, hasty approval, design changes, budgetary shortfalls, misunderstandings galore, opportunities for corruption, and animus all around. "We can hardly understand how Mr. Orlopp deserves all that has been said against him," the journal lamented, "except perhaps that he should be on his guard next time, and look before he leaps into such enticing opportunities." Fiscal, political, and architectural troubles became indistinguishable, and the project became a fiasco.

Making matters worse, the facilities swiftly became obsolete. As the city expanded and new technologies such as radio communications and automobiles came to the task of policing, the headquarters found itself increasingly inadequate, not to mention leaky and listing. The new City Planning Commission in the 1920s, like its counterparts in the 1820s, came to feel this downtown location was inappropriate for incarceration, and employees inside wanted out. In 1931, prison and court functions were relocated to new facilities at Tulane and Broad, leaving only the precinct station in the 1893 building. Folks began calling it the "Old" Criminal Courts Building.

To add injury to insult, further deterioration necessitated the humiliating removal of the landmark tower in 1940, leaving a rambling hulk used for ministerial banalities like permitting and driver's licenses. The building became something of a city joke when, in 1948, "hoboes" were discovered living—rather sumptuously, and for six years—in "the ancient catacombs under the old criminal courts building at Tulane and S. Saratoga," which a *Times-Picayune* journalist dubbed "Hotel de Bastille."

Unloved by citizens and a liability to the city, the complex was unceremoniously dismantled during Christmas and New Year's 1949–50. As a measure of the building's unpopularity, Mayor deLesseps "Chep" Morrison cited its demolition as evidence that his administration truly cared about the adjoining neighborhoods. Later in his term, the entire "back-a-town" of Louis Armstrong's childhood, including his birthplace on Jane Alley and the footprint of the penal complex, would be declared a slum and targeted for a massive urban renewal project. Out of this came today's Civic Center, including City Hall, Duncan Plaza, and the Public Library.

The 1931 Orleans Parish Prison on 531 South Broad would, like its predecessors, also earn an ominous mystique, and by the 1960s, the City Planning Commission called for a modern replacement at Gravier at South White. That prison, opened in the late 1970s, gained a reputation as among the worst in the nation, and was itself replaced recently amid a growing nationwide debate on incarceration—in a place regularly described as the most incarcerated city, state, and nation on earth.

As for the circa-1893 courthouse and prison, their footprints today lie beneath the Main Branch of the New Orleans Public Library and the adjacent green space, plus half of widened Loyola Avenue. To get a sense of the lost citadel, New Orleanians now have to travel to Max Orlopp's home base of Dallas, where the architect designed another turreted Romanesque courthouse. Affectionately known as Old Red, it is now a city museum—and anything but ominous.

COURT DECISIONS
The Neighborhood Rivalry behind Two Massive Government Buildings

Spring 2015 marked the hundredth anniversary of the John Minor Wisdom U.S. Court of Appeals Building. Home to the Fifth Circuit, the resplendent landmark at 600 Camp Street was initially conceived for a different purpose and nearly ended up at an alternative location. Its origins and destiny were intertwined with those of another massive government building, and our cityscape would look quite different today had decisions played out otherwise.

It was the 1890s, and New Orleans was in the throes of modernization. Engineers had drained the backswamp and installed new water and sewerage systems; the recently reorganized Port of New Orleans renovated wharves and streamlined shipping facilities; and more and more households had running water, electricity, and telephones. Population neared the 300,000 mark, and New Orleans held its rank as the largest city in the South.

But there was one thing it didn't have: a real post office.

Certainly, postal services were available, in the U.S. Customhouse at the foot of Canal Street. But that building, commenced in 1847, had been designed for other purposes, and the postmaster himself called its mail facility "a damp semi-cellar which often smells like a tomb [where] yellow fever can, perhaps, never find better encouragement."

In 1899, the New Orleans Board of Trade and the Cotton Exchange took up the cause for a new federal post office. That same year, state officials called for a new state courthouse to replace the small and crumbling circa-1799 Cabildo on Jackson Square.

Siting these two big government buildings, one federal and one state, would form a topic of constant controversy between the historically rival neighborhoods on either side of Canal Street. On the upper side was the present-day Central Business District, which had in earlier times been called Faubourg Ste. Marie, St. Mary, or the American sector, but in this era was usually referred to as the First District. On the lower side of Canal Street was the old neighborhood broadly referred to as "downtown" or the Second District, else the French or Creole quarters. (Unlike today, New Orleanians in those days did not use "downtown" to include what we now call the CBD.)

In 1901, the New Orleans Progressive Union, a predecessor of the Chamber of Commerce, lobbied to add $1,250,000 to a congressional bill "for a site and Federal building worthy of the first city of the South," according to the *Daily Item*. A year later, Congress enacted legislation to acquire the land, pending local identification of a parcel matching certain criteria. The city thus organized a "Postoffice Commission" and tasked it to find a convenient space of at least 62,500 square feet, surrounded by streets on all sides, for no more than $200,000.

Councilman James Zacharie reminded the commissioners that the city had also recently created a Courthouse Commission to site the state supreme court.

Perhaps the two committees might, as a *Picayune* article reported, "confer [so that] valuable data and information could be obtained."

Everybody seemed to have an opinion. Some commissioners felt it might be better "to have the two buildings standing near by." Another suggested "that the post office should be closest to the newspaper offices" around 300 Camp—an area nicknamed Newspaper Row—for they had "to fetch and carry . . . to the post office, instead of having mail delivered." That helpful suggestion would fuel later suspicions that the press had vested interests in this story, and as it became clear that both projects would raise property values and generate economic activity, neighborhood advocates would also march to the beat of self-interest. Rival factions vied to land either asset—or both—on their side of Canal Street.

Those advocating for the First District argued, according to *Picayune* reports, that "the growth of the city is upstream, and not towards the cemeteries [or downstream]. The Camp Street site is suited to the business interests of the city." Concurred another, "all the big public buildings [should be] grouped around a park," namely "Lafayette Square, having the City Hall there already."

Citizens weighed in. One "old retired merchant" with "an ax to grind" proclaimed "the wholesale-trade . . . is altogether *above* Canal Street" and that the optimal site was clearly "Baronne, Union, Perdido and Dryades. . . . I would like to see things done right for New Orleans." Another declared, "we do not want a Post-Office in the *rear* of the city, surrounded by houses of prostitution. . . . There will be no Mardi-Gras business with Uncle Sam's money[!]"

Uptown-minded commissioners thought investing federal money in downtown was preposterous. "I have the highest . . . admiration for the residents below Canal Street," said one. "But," he added aloofly, "the great majority of the letter-writing residents live above Canal Street." Downtown had a glorious past, he allowed, but the future was uptown: "If we were selecting a site sixty years ago it might have been well to locate the Postoffice down there, but now things are different."

Not so fast, responded downtowners. French Quarter merchants reasoned their lower land values would ease budgetary constraints, and new investment would buoy neighborhood competitiveness. Besides, both the post office and state courthouse had always been downtown. Why not site the two buildings adjacently, perhaps on 800–900 Customhouse (now Iberville), or 200–300 Bourbon?

Those suggestions emanated from the prominent clothier John Anselmo Mercier, whose elegant emporium at Dauphine and Canal (predecessor of Maison Blanche) would profit handsomely from the foot traffic. So motivated, Mercier took out a front-page ad in the *Picayune* preemptively declaring, "Hurrah for

Downtown. Downtown is Taking the Lead. Downtown Will Have the New Post-office. Downtown Will Have the New Court House."

Then there were those everyday folks who just wanted service, never mind the spoils. "I write on behalf of the working women of the city," wrote one weary citizen, "who do not have the time to go six and eight blocks to the post office, and trust you will be our friend and locate the post office on Canal St."

By the time federal authorities visited in November 1902, the Postoffice Commission had narrowed down the list to 600 Camp, 1100 Canal (today's Loew's Theater), and 900 Iberville. While it mulled, the Courthouse Commission in February 1903 finally decided on 400 Royal for the state supreme court. Demolitions of a full block of century-old Creole townhouses began on June 1, 1903, and, seven years later, the Louisiana State Supreme Court would move into its gigantic new home.

As for siting the post office, commission members were, as the *Picayune* put it, "quite at sea." To the list of potential locales were added two Canal Street sites around the Basin intersection, Union at Dryades, the north or south side of Lafayette Square, and a number of other parcels proffered by eager real estate agents. As for 600 Camp, the commission had actually recommended that space, but the City Council rejected it because it contained two key city properties, a firehouse and a library, for which the feds would be paying outrageously low prices.

People protested. Only a few years earlier, an ordinance had merged two donated book collections to create the New Orleans Public "Fisk Free" Library (1896)—and now citizens would lose their only public reading room, as well as a firehouse, for so little in return? The undervalued land prices incurred additional objections from the New Orleans Taxpayers' Protective Association, a fiscal watchdog group.

The breakthrough came in the form of Leslie M. Shaw, President Theodore Roosevelt's secretary of the treasury. Shaw, who visited in 1903 and took a carriage tour of all sites, found Camp Street to his liking, as it fulfilled the government's criteria and benefited uniquely from its dignified position across from City Hall, today's Gallier Hall. The commission and the council acquiesced, and in 1904, the federal government purchased the site for $199,808.12, just under the $200,000 cap.

The president of the Library Commission, Frank Howard, hardly enthused over the impending doom of the Fisk Library, used the opportunity to advocate for a bigger, better library. In 1908, an imposing Roman Revival library opened at Lee Circle and would serve readers until the late 1950s, when the modern branch opened on Loyola.

The John Minor Wisdom Fifth Circuit Court of Appeals Building (1915) on Camp Street fronting Lafayette Square, originally designed for the U.S. Post Office as its main tenant. *Photograph courtesy U.S. Fifth Circuit Court of Appeals.*

In 1907, the 600 Camp site was cleared and Capdeville Street was created, to
fulfill the requirement that the building be completely surrounded by arteries. At
the same time, a competition led to the selection of the New York architectural
firm Hale and Rogers to design the structure. After Hebert D. Hale died unexpectedly in 1908, partner James Gamble Rogers secured the contract.

Rogers set forth to design the First District's newest landmark, with programming to include not only a post office on the ground floor, but also the Federal
Court of Appeals, circuit and district courts, the U.S. Marshal Office, and the
Weather Bureau. Excavation of the basement, for wagons depositing and delivering
mail, began in 1910, after which wooden pilings were hammered into the soil by
steam-operated pile drivers and a load-bearing frame of steel beams was erected.

On January 28, 1911, a ceremony marked the laying of the cornerstone. Most
of the edifice arose over the next two years, although budgetary and material
needs delayed completion until spring 1915. Everyone seemed to agree the splendid three-story Italian Renaissance Revival behemoth, measuring 198 by 323 feet
and replete with the latest technologies, was worth the wait.

The Louisiana Supreme Court Building (1910), sited on 400 Royal Street in an attempt, along with the new Post Office, to inject new investment into two rivalrous downtown neighborhoods. *Photograph courtesy Library of Congress.*

Rogers's edifice would evolve in its roles and position in the cityscape. Federal tenants came and went; the U.S. Post Office moved out in 1961, as did government offices and courts in 1963. It served as a high school for youths displaced by Hurricane Betsy in 1965, and after an early-1970s renovation, the U.S. Fifth Circuit Court of Appeals became the edifice's sole occupant.

While Rogers's taste was impeccable, his timing was not. His majestic brand of Neoclassical exuberance fell out of favor among architects after World War I, and his work, as well as that of his counterpart who designed the Beaux Arts–style Supreme Court on 400 Royal, came to be seen by some as dated. That view has since matured to one of admiration and preservation, as well as historical appreciation of the roles that both buildings have played in the city's legal heritage.

Consider how different things might be today had either edifice ended up on Bourbon Street, or Iberville Street, or if the federal building were placed on Canal Street—or if the state building were squeezed onto the narrow Elk Place neutral ground, as was seriously proposed.

Instead, the John Minor Wisdom U.S. Court of Appeals Building and the Louisiana Supreme Court each landed in the heart of the two historically rival neighborhoods that today, together, comprise downtown New Orleans.

A LEGACY OF LUXURY LODGING
The Original Cosmopolitan Hotel

For the third time in a decade, a developer has floated outsized plans for 121 Royal Street, this time for a high-rise hotel and condominium complex to be called the Royal Cosmopolitan. Although technically outside the jurisdiction of the Vieux Carré Commission, the proposed building's height—two towers measuring 164 and 190 feet, well above the 70-foot height limit for this zone—and adjacency to the French Quarter have raised the ire of preservationists and neighborhood advocates. A coalition of organizations has filed suit to stop the City Council from considering the proposal on the grounds that it violates the city's recently approved master plan.

I will leave it to my preservationist colleagues to critique the proposal. This article instead recounts the legacy of lodging at this site, which, I contend, helped usher in a new age of luxury hotels in the late 1800s and laid the groundwork for the modern tourism economy.

That story begins in the years after the Civil War, when residential wealth in the urban core began shifting uptown, leaving downtown more commercial in its land use and grittier in its social environs. A rambunctious nocturnal entertainment scene had developed, where a man on the town could find concert saloons, keno halls, bars, restaurants, clubs, and theaters catering to every taste, particularly on upper Bourbon and Royal streets. Elegant retail emporia operated on the main arteries, principally Canal Street, even as the ubiquitous sex trade carried on its business but steps away. Streets teemed with pedestrians, and ships and trains arrived at all hours of the day and night, depositing travelers with pent-up desires into a city more than willing to accommodate them.

Part of the action could be explained by emerging trends nationwide in the *fin de siècle*. Postbellum industrial growth in the Northeast had expanded the ranks of the middle class and its disposable income and time, and higher levels of education made many Americans increasingly curious about their rapidly developing country. Folks ventured farther from home, enabled by an ever-growing network of railroads with increasingly fast and comfortable trains. Gone were the frontier days of old, when travel was treacherous and destinations were dicey; these new leisure tourists were now sportingly exploring new national parks and playing cowboy at dude ranches. Readers of nostalgic local-color literature, meanwhile,

The original Cosmopolitan Hotel (1891, upper right) on Royal Street, and its Bourbon Street annex at left (seven-story building with white façade and smoking chimney) viewed around 1900. *Photograph (detail) courtesy Library of Congress.*

grew intrigued about seemingly exotic places like Louisiana and New Orleans, and many bought train tickets to see for themselves.

As demand for travelers' services mounted, supply rose to meet it—and encourage it. The 1885 World's Industrial and Cotton Centennial Exhibition at present-day Audubon Park had particularly abetted New Orleans's nascent tourism industry, and entrepreneurs took note that profits could be made from "hospitality," namely luxury lodging. In 1891, investors made plans for a fancy hotel at the heart of the action, what is now 121 Royal, and hired noted architect William Fitzner for the designs. It would be called the Cosmopolitan.

The selected parcel happened to occupy the footprint of the old colonial fort line, which like all French defenses had slightly angled ramparts to maximize firing lines. The makeshift fortification had been obliterated by the early 1800s, after which its right-of-way found a new use as a *corderie*—a ropewalk, for the laying and twisting of twine. The swath was finally subdivided in 1810, creating Canal Street and adjacent parcels, but remarkably, the crooked interstice persisted, yielding odd-shaped lots with oblique rears. Over the years, owners of most such parcels had them rectified to more manageable rectangles. But not the Cosmopolitan's, with its 150-foot-long flank awkwardly tilted 20 degrees off plumb. Undaunted, the architect Fitzner skillfully fitted into that idiosyncratic space a handsome five-story structure with a cast-iron facade of twelve bay windows, a design reminiscent of Manhattan but strikingly modern for Royal Street. With the Café Restaurant on the ground floor and 125 well-appointed rooms upstairs, the Cosmopolitan Hotel aimed to live up to its name as it prepared to open in early 1892.

Then disaster struck. On the night of February 16, 1892, amid what the *Daily Picayune* described as "a ceaseless procession [of] merry, happy" people patronizing "saloons [and] restaurants," a fire started one block from the Cosmopolitan, "crossed [Bourbon] street in a bound," and enveloped half the block. Crowds fled; steam pumps arrived, and plumes of water arched into the sky. By morning, both sides of 100 Bourbon were reduced to smoldering embers. Damages exceeded $2 million, and thirteen major enterprises were out of commission. Not among them was the Cosmopolitan on Royal Street, which had only its rear wall seared.

One person's disaster, the adage goes, is another person's opportunity. Owners of burned lots found they had an eager buyer in the form of famed Canal Street department store D. H. Holmes, which purchased the parcels at the corner of Customhouse (now Iberville) and expanded its enterprise onto Bourbon Street. Owners of the river side of the Bourbon ruins, meanwhile, had an equally eager neighbor: the Cosmopolitan on Royal, whose owners envisioned a valuable second entrance on Bourbon. They purchased the parcel of an old piano store, cleared the wreckage, and commissioned architect Thomas Sully to design an annex.

Sully's Bourbon annex would rise seven stories high and boast an imposing granite facade with a grand entrance for long-term-residency guests, while the main entrance on Royal would continue to welcome short-term guests. Sully also added a third wing opening onto Customhouse Street for service workers. Now the tallest structure in the vicinity, the enlarged Cosmopolitan Hotel would attract a steady flow of moneyed visitors who in turn would accelerate the formation of a nocturnal entertainment district in the upper French Quarter. The complex's Royal-to-Bourbon lobby, not unlike the Roosevelt Hotel's lobby connecting Baronne and Roosevelt Way today, became a famed rendezvous of local and state politicians. The hotel's cadres of patrons, overnight guests, and long-term residents created demand for dining, entertainment, potations, games of chance, and "Turkish bathes" (saunas, a new fad in this era), and to accommodate them, enterprises specializing in food and drink opened nearby, among them what is now Galatoire's (1905).

The mounting bustle inevitably attracted sex workers. Prostitutes in this era tended to live in group quarters up Customhouse Street toward Franklin (which would become Storyville after 1898), and found johns aplenty in the various venues of the upper French Quarter. Women "notoriously abandoned to lewdness" would visit the Cosmopolitan Hotel so regularly that the Customhouse doorway became a segregated women's entrance. One evening in 1914, a curious fifteen-year-old girl ventured through that doorway. "I could see all these girls decked out in diamonds and beautiful clothes," she recalled later in life, "eating sumptuous meals in the dining room, having drinks, having a ball." Intrigued, she sought entrée into their demimonde, only to be dissuaded—on account of her young age, they said, but more likely because "they weren't about to let me hustle on their territory." Instead the women directed her to a "landlady" on Dauphine Street. "Why don't you go [there], learn how to do it?" She did, and later became the French Quarter's last and longest-working madam, subject of Christine Wiltz's book *The Last Madam: A Life in the New Orleans Underworld*. Norma Badon Wallace's career in the downtown sex industry lasted over half a century, and it began at the ladies' entrance to the Cosmopolitan Hotel.

The Cosmopolitan's success ushered in a new era of handsome high-rise hotels appealing to affluent leisure travelers. Among them were the Grunewald (1893) on Baronne (now the Roosevelt), the Denechaud on Perdido in 1907 (now Le Pavillon), and, five years later, the Monteleone, towering twelve stories above 200 Royal and family-owned to this day. On a smaller scale were the Country, the Commerce, the Henrietta, and the Planters hotels, all within two blocks of the Cosmopolitan. At least sixteen additional luxury hotels were operating downtown by 1920, among them the venerable St. Charles, which adapted to the new leisure market.

All the competition cost the Cosmopolitan its marketplace advantages, as did the turmoil of the Great War in Europe, which sapped the high-end leisure travel trade. In 1919, the owners sold part of the Bourbon annex for $215,000 to the Chess, Checkers, and Whist Club. One year later, the Eighteenth Amendment passed, forcing a popular drinking hole named the Gem to close its doors on the ground floor of the Cosmopolitan. In an attempt to reposition itself in the new marketplace, the Cosmopolitan in 1920 underwent a complete interior renovation, including an elevator, telephone exchange, steam heat, and new decor. It reopened as the Hotel Astor.

While the Royal side of the Astor survived structurally, the Bourbon annex met a different fate. Older members of Chess, Checkers, and Whist had died off, and new members failed to fill their shoes. In 1935, the club closed its books and auctioned off its property. The now-vacant Bourbon annex came to be viewed as valuable real estate, especially after the 1937 legislative preservation of the French Quarter. That constitutional amendment designated Iberville Street as the district's boundary, which ergo made parcels on the unprotected side prized for new construction. Developers amassed adjacent parcels on 100 Bourbon throughout the 1940s, and in 1953, Sully's 1892 annex finally met the wrecking ball for the expansion of Woolworth's, formerly Kirby's. The Royal Street end of the old Cosmopolitan/Astor, however, managed to survive.

Economic pressure to accommodate modern New Orleans's ever-growing tourism sector in the more recent *fin de siècle* attracted the attention of a new generation of corporate hoteliers to 100 Bourbon. In 2000, work began on a massive new Astor Crowne Plaza Hotel, which not only revived the Astor name and used portions of its space, but also replicated the profile of the old Bourbon annex. Skyscraper hotels had previously opened on adjacent blocks fronting Canal as far back as 1973, to the dismay of preservationists and the delight of promoters of tourism—an economy traceable, in part, to the original Cosmopolitan.

ON THE CULTURAL POWER OF PRESERVATION
The Old French Opera House

Preservationists need not be reminded of the power of old buildings. They recognize them as testaments of social memory, artifacts of architecture, and vessels of culture, and know all too well how their razing leads to historical amnesia. In some cases, their destruction can also accelerate cultural decline, or at least reify it. A case in point comes from one of the most important buildings in historic New Orleans, the Old French Opera House in the French Quarter. Its magnificent rise, colorful career, and fiery demise testify to the relationships among people, place, culture, and structure.

In the late 1850s, in this town smitten with performance and sprinkled with rival venues, Bourbon Street—an otherwise rather middling artery with a mixed population and motley commercial scene—scored a cultural coup. A new owner from Paris had taken possession of the Théâtre d'Orléans, a venue renowned for featuring touring European companies under the management of New Orleanian Charles Boudousquié. The Parisian planned to keep that success going, but because he failed to negotiate a lease acceptable to the local impresario, Boudousquié decided to open a superior venue himself. In early March 1859, he formed the New Orleans Opera House Association, quickly raised well over $100,000 from affluent aficionados, purchased a 193.5-by-191.5-foot lot, and contracted to build a splendid edifice, according to the original building contract, "at the corner of Bourbon and Toulouse Streets, in accordance with the plans and elevations made by [architectural firm] Gallier and Esterbrook." Work commenced in May and, striving to open in time for the late-autumn social season, proceeded round the clock, with nighttime lighting coming from bonfires. It must have been a magnificent sight, as yellow-orange illumination danced off the rising walls of what the *New Orleans Delta* predicted would be "a handsome structure of the Italian order [that will] rise like a Colossus over everything in that vicinity."

The grand opening occurred on the evening of December 1, 1859, with a performance of Rossini's *Guillaume Tell*. It was a triumph that would be remembered for years. "Superb . . . magnificent . . . spacious and commodious . . . a spectacle . . . richly worth viewing [at] a scale of great elegance," raved the *Picayune* of the gleaming white New French Opera House.

Theaters were a big deal in this era. Featuring opera and plays as well as reenacted historical and current events, magicians, "natural philosophers," orchestras, balls, and dances, these venues were a premier locus of social activity in a time when all performance entertainment was live. The French Opera House, and nearby competing venues such as the St. Peter Street and Orleans theaters, stoked the twilight bustle of downtown and gave entrepreneurs an opportunity to serve that gathered pool of potential clients with food, drink, lodging, and other forms of diversion. Antoine's Restaurant, for example, noted on its calling card how it catered to patrons of nearby theaters, and other places benefited from the foot traffic. In this manner, a nocturnal entertainment district began to form in the central French Quarter, and because the grandest of all venues was the French Opera House, Bourbon Street found itself as the axis. Thus was planted one of the seeds from which, decades later, the modern-day Bourbon Street night scene would germinate.

For the next sixty years, despite Civil War, occupation, declining fortunes, managerial turnover, and a few missed seasons, what became beloved as the "Old" French Opera House played host to a litany of famous names and performances, not to mention countless Carnival balls and society events. It served as a home away from home for a steady stream of French and other European performers at a time when New Orleans's connection to the Old World was growing increasingly tenuous, and when Gallic syllables became less frequently heard in local streets. And magnificent it remained, particularly at night: wrote one observer in the postbellum years, "the building, with its fresh coat of whitewash, glimmers like a monster ghost in the moonlight." Its prominence persisted despite the economic woes of the late-nineteenth-century French Quarter. Wealth had moved uptown in the aftermath of the Civil War, and advocates envisioned ways to revive the old neighborhood. One proposal floated in the *New Orleans Tägliche Deutsche Zeitung* suggested widening Bourbon Street into a boulevard from Canal Street to the French Opera House at Toulouse, to showcase the venue and "raise hope in the French Quarter of new vital business life." The newspaper correctly predicted that the widening project "will probably not get enough support to be realized [because] such a project needs [finances], public spirit, community initiative, and energy, and these are exactly [what is lacking] in the French Quarter."

Perhaps the greatest significance of the Old French Opera House came not from its architecture or performances but from its enthusiastic patronage by local French Creoles, who simply adored the place. While many members of this deep-rooted local ethnicity had departed the French Quarter after the Civil War, enough remained to maintain a francophone society in this and adjacent neighborhoods at least two decades into the twentieth century. Critical to the precarious cohesiveness of this culture were cherished local structural landmarks, which gave French Creoles space and a sense of place against the forces of assimilation. St. Louis Cathedral and other downtown Catholic churches, for example, bonded them religiously, and about twenty tiny private institutes, so-called "French schools" taught by aging Creole society gentlemen like Alcée Fortier, kept alive their language and heritage. The French Opera House, meanwhile, unified them in the arena of civic rituals and French-language entertainment. Quarter children would routinely attend Sunday matinees for 25 cents, and were seated in a special section downstairs. "I was brought up in that way[,] to enjoy music," recalled Madeline Archinard, born in 1900; "even as young children[,] we learned to love music in that way." Interviewed by the Friends of the Cabildo in a 1982 taped session archived in the New Orleans Public Library's Louisiana Division, Mrs. Archinard recalled how she spent Carnival around 1910:

There was a Mrs. Parmaris who lived on Bourbon Street who had a home on the parade routes, and while all of our parents used to go there before the balls [at the Old French Opera House], the children were taken [by] our nurse to see the parades. . . . We always knew on what floats our relatives were and they would always throw us a lot of beads. . . . It's a little shop now, but it reminds me of the past every time I go there.

The Old French Opera House on Bourbon Street (left) at Toulouse, built in 1859 and destroyed in a structurally and culturally calamitous blaze in 1919. *Photograph courtesy Library of Congress.*

Mildred Masson Costa, born in 1903 into a strictly French-speaking household in the Quarter, described the Old French Opera House as "my second home. . . . I practically lived there[,] three nights a week, and then we had the matinee on Sunday." Because she arrived early with her grandfather, little Mildred would run around in the dressing rooms and get free ballet lessons from the dancers. Then came the performance. Recalled Mrs. Costa with a laugh, "The very first thing I saw was *Faust*, and when the devil came out, with the smoke and the drumbeat, yours truly got panicky and I *flew* backstage to my grandfather! . . . I was two years old; it was more than I expected. I met the devil afterwards, and he was very charming."

Even better was what came *after* the performance. "The foyer was right in the front, upstairs, on the second floor," she recalled three-quarters of a century later; "and there they used to always serve punch for the ladies[;] there was never a man in the place." The men went "down in the bar in the basement" on Bourbon Street—and that's where Mildred wanted to be. She "used to slip underneath . . . the double swinging doors" of the saloon to visit her granddaddy in the bar, where they would "sit me on the bar, and I was given a glass of Maraschino cherries . . . in a Sazerac glass . . . at nine or ten o'clock at night!" By the time the performance ended, it was nearly midnight, but perish the thought that this meant bedtime. Rather, Mildred would accompany her granddad to Johnny's, a little eating place across Bourbon Street: "All my grandfather's cronies would gather at Johnny's . . . and at one o'clock in the morning, I was eating fried oysters and . . . rum omelets. I *loved* rum omelets! I loved to see these little purple flames go up and down and I can still see it there. Then we walked home."

Everyone in the Quarter went to the Old French Opera House on Bourbon; patronage transcended the lines of class and race, although black patrons were relegated to inferior seating. There was another reason, however, for Mildred's regular attendance: her grandfather belonged to a volunteer organization, les Pompiers de L'Opéra (Opera Firemen), whose members pledged to attend operas nightly and, in exchange for enjoying the production gratis, would check for fire hazards before, during, and after the performance. The Opera Firemen took their jobs very seriously. "When there was a fire to be built upon the stage," explained Mrs. Costa in 1985, "they were the ones who built it, and they were the ones who put it out. . . . Before they went home—well, me too because I was there—they used to go over *every single seat* to see that not a cigarette was left under those seats." Because fire hazards came when there was an audience, the Pompiers worked only during performances, not rehearsals. That policy, which seemed rational, would prove to be fatal.

Just before midnight on December 3, 1919, the concert master of the Old French Opera House and his colleague from the New Orleans Grand Opera Company went out for drinks following a rehearsal of *Carmen*. As the two men returned home down Bourbon Street at 2:30 a.m., they noticed a plume of smoke wafting from the theater's second-story window. To a nearby saloon they darted to alert the central fire station. Flames of unknown origin had proceeded to ignite highly combustible props, costumes, and scenery, and soon engulfed the upper floors. Neighbors awoke to witness the terrible sight, and fire crews struggled to prevent the blaze from spreading. By dawn, "[t]he high-piled debris, the shattered remnants of the wall still standing, the wreathing smoke" reminded an *Item* journalist of "a bombarded cathedral town."

The allusion to the recent fighting in Europe was apropos. The Great War weakened the already-fragile exchange that French cultural institutions struggled to maintain with the former colonies of their fading empire. New Orleanians at the receiving end of that exchange took special pride in their French Opera

House on Bourbon Street—"the one institution of the city above all which gave to New Orleans a note of distinction and lifted it out of the ranks of merely provincial cities," wrote a *Times-Picayune* editorialist. It represented an "anchor of the old-world character of our municipality . . . without [which] will be the gravest danger of our drifting into Middle-Western commonplacity."

Mildred Masson, by this time a teenager, was among those devastated by the loss, particularly since her own grandfather toiled *pro bono* as a Pompier to ensure this would never happen. "You see, the fire burned the night after a rehearsal, not after a performance." Her voice betraying agitation and indignation even sixty-six years later, she iterated that the Pompiers "were *not* responsible for being there during rehearsals because you weren't supposed to use the rest of the theater, you were supposed to be on the stage, and they thought the actors or the singers would have the sense enough not to smoke. You can't very well smoke and sing anyway."

Now, with the destruction of the city's last best French cultural toehold, even the Grand Opera Company admitted in a special notice posted in the *Item* that it had suffered "a severe blow to the artistic and social life of New Orleans." The aforementioned editorialist fretted whether the fire would "sound the death knell of that entire quarter of the city, with its odd customs that charm the stranger." Recent evidence suggested he might be right. Just three years earlier, another major Creole landmark, the former St. Louis Exchange Hotel on St. Louis Street, was razed for damage inflicted by the Great Storm of 1915. A few years before that, officials leveled an entire block of Creole townhouses across from the hotel and replaced it with a gigantic Beaux-Arts courthouse. Newspaper editors received hundreds of letters pleading the Grand Opera Company to rebuild at the same site, but all too aware of its decaying vicinage, the owners demurred. When officials finally erected a comparable multi-use venue ten years later—today's Municipal Auditorium—they located it *outside* the French Quarter. Many New Orleanians by that time viewed the neighborhood as a dangerous, dirty slum—"Little Palermo," they called it, and not flatteringly—and some called for its wholesale demolition. Two Creole girls born in the Quarter around 1900, Madeline Archinard Babin and Marie Pilkington Campbell, testified emphatically in their elder years that it was after World War I, which coincided with these losses, that the last wave of old French Creole families finally departed the French Quarter.

Would francophone Creole society have persevered had the Old French Opera House not burned? No. But the building's destruction eliminated a major cultural bastion and incubator, and the vacuum it left behind was never refilled. The loss punctuated and hastened the decline of French Creole culture in the French

Quarter, and enabled its subsequent assimilation, or hybridization, with larger national culture.

Charred ruins stood throughout the 1920s in the hope of a restoration, but they were eventually cleared away. The lot, owned by Tulane University on account of an earlier donation, would become a storage yard for the Samuel House Wrecking Company. Ironically, this and other Quarter wrecking yards became meccas for first-generation historical renovators, who, according to pioneer preservationist Mary Morrison, would go "nosing around the sidewalks[,] beachcombing[,] swapping hardware. . . . You'd buy some beautiful particular fine wood or something, and you'd just drag it home!" The anecdote serves as a reminder that, while the loss of major landmarks came at great cultural cost, they also catalyzed preservationist intervention and helped inspire the legal protection of the French Quarter in 1937.

As Bourbon Street grew more popular and valuable in the midcentury decades, entrepreneurial eyes envisioned better uses for the weedy lot where sopranos and ballerinas once performed. In 1964, investor Winthrop Rockefeller of Arkansas teamed with corporations in Memphis and Houston and received permission from the Vieux Carré Commission to erect a $3 million five-story hotel with 186 rooms on the site of the Old French Opera House. The Downtowner Motor Inn opened on December 4, 1965, forty-six years to the day since the fire.

Today, only a handful of clues of the grand old venue remain. A nightspot across Toulouse Street calls itself the Old Opera House Bar, and the circa-1964 hotel, now the Four Points by Sheraton, heralds the site's heritage and occasionally features opera singers at its club. Perhaps the most salient relic is the widened span of Bourbon Street, reflecting a building setback Gallier and Esterbrook had designed in 1859 to allow horse-drawn carriages to deposit patrons en route to an evening at the opera.

150 YEARS AFTER A GREAT MILITARY VICTORY, TWO CULTURAL DEFEATS

While much deserved attention has gone to the two-hundredth anniversary of the January 8, 1815, American victory at the Battle of New Orleans, the year 2015 also marks the fiftieth anniversary of two less-remembered losses near the Chalmette Battlefield. They were elements of opposite ends of antebellum Creole society, one a tiny hamlet of poor black families, the other a magnificent plantation mansion. Both survived a century after the Civil War, and both were obliterated in 1965.

The hamlet developed on a rice field owned by Pierre Fazende, a free man of color who appears to have inherited a portion of the Chalmette plantation on which the Battle of New Orleans was fought against the invading British. In 1856, his son subdivided the elongated parcel, positioned roughly parallel to the American firing line, and sold the thirty-three lots of "Fazendeville" to other free people of color and (later) emancipated slaves. By the turn of the twentieth century, three to four dozen black families called Fazendeville home. According to local historian Roy Chapman, the linear village featured a one-room school, two barrooms, a grocery, church, dance hall, ball field, and a single straight access road paralleling an old millrace used to drain runoff. All houses were positioned on the downriver "British side" of the road, and one practically overlaid the spot where British Maj. Gen. Sir Edward Packenham is thought to have fallen wounded in 1815.

In form, Fazendeville resembled dozens of other one-street African American communities perpendicular to the banks of the lower Mississippi River. But this was the only one in predominantly white St. Bernard Parish, and it was uniquely positioned between two historic sites that would come under the jurisdiction of the National Park Service: the 1815 battle's American rampart eight hundred feet upriver, and, equidistant downriver, the circa-1864 Chalmette National Cemetery.

Fazendeville residents were proud of the history in their backyard; they named their house of worship the Battleground Baptist Church and saw themselves as part of the area's legacy. Others, however, saw them as, quite literally, an intrusion on history and, in the early 1960s, sought to oust them.

The move to eliminate Fazendeville is viewed through two interpretative lenses today. One holds that well-intentioned but thoughtless history buffs, with the battle's sesquicentennial on the horizon, aimed to unify the American firing line and the national cemetery into one military historical park. Local and federal governments supported the concept, and after persuading local industries to donate their parcels in the sliver of land in between, attempted next to buy out the two hundred or so denizens of Fazendeville. When those offers were declined, expropriations ensued, and what began as historical memorialization turned into ham-fisted forced displacement. Most Fazendevillians ended up settling in New Orleans's Lower Ninth Ward or the community of Violet farther downriver in St. Bernard Parish, and few if any received fair market value for their homes.

Aerial photograph (1940) of Chalmette Battlefield in St. Bernard Parish, with the linear village of Fazendeville appearing at center, perpendicular to the Mississippi River. Note also jagged Confederate-era ramparts at center right, immediately adjacent to Chalmette National Cemetery. *Aerial photograph from author's personal collection.*

The other interpretation holds that local officials, in this era of civil rights protests and resistance to integration, covertly sought to dislodge a poor rural black outpost from a potential tourist attraction in the heart of their rapidly suburbanizing parish, and carried out this hidden agenda under the subterfuge of historical remembrance. Wrote LSU anthropologist Joyce Marie Jackson in her study of the community, "It could be coincidental that [the civil rights tensions] and loss of their land to the government happened around the same time. [But] the confluence of events was close enough that it was certainly logical for villagers to see them as connected." That they hired famed civil rights attorney A. P. Tureaud to make their case attests to this viewpoint.

But precedence and power were on the side of the government. The National Park Service, after all, had a long record of displacing locals—usually the rural poor—in the name of protecting and preserving the nation's heritage; prior examples included the removal of Native Americans from Yellowstone and Glacier national parks, and rural whites from the Shenandoah and Great Smoky mountains. Millions nationwide may have benefited from these decisions, but they came at a dear cost for those removed, and among them were the folks of Fazendeville.

Three Oaks Plantation House at right, photographed a few years after the American Sugar Refining Company opened its Chalmette Refinery (left) in 1912. *Photograph (detail) courtesy Library of Congress.*

The Park Service closed the village's road in 1963; the last residents moved out in 1964; and by March 1965, the last remaining structures were relocated or bulldozed. Fazendeville, in more ways than one, was history.

At the same time, a half-mile upriver, a very different situation was playing out toward a similar end. It involved the resplendent Three Oaks mansion, built around 1831 for Sylvain Peyroux, a Creole sugarcane planter and French wine importer. As one of the largest homes below New Orleans, Three Oaks would become a local landmark, distinguished by its towering pearl-white Doric columns and prominent hipped roof. Legend has it that, after Admiral Farragut's Union fleet dodged forts St. Philip and Jackson in April 1862 and sailed up the Mississippi River to New Orleans, a Confederate battery fired on the warships at Chalmette, and a return volley knocked down one of Three Oaks's columns. The brief action represented the last and only exchange of fire just prior to the Union's capture of Confederate New Orleans.

Three Oaks's destiny shifted from the raising of cane to the refining of cane juice when the American Sugar Refining Company bought the manse and surrounding land in 1905. In 1909, the company opened its towering Chalmette Refinery (where Domino Sugar is made today), and proceeded to draw to these rural precincts the industrial refining which previously occurred on the upper French Quarter riverfront. By this time, the adjacent community of Arabi (Friscoville) had been laid out with streets (1906) and houses, and Three Oaks found itself on the industrializing fringes of a growing metropolis.

Because Three Oaks was secured on the refinery property, it managed to stave off the capricious speculators, absentee ownership, vagrants, and vandals who precipitated the demise of so many other aging plantation houses in this era. But the mansion also languished in isolation, inaccessible to the tourism circuit and largely unknown outside the historical architecture community. Company officials would occasionally open the house to admirers, but they had other priorities, and they would later point out that only seven visitors came to see the century-old building over ten years.

On February 15, 1965, an explosion ripped through the Chalmette Refinery, killing one worker, injuring dozens, and causing over $1 million in damage. Shaken company officials devised a recovery strategy that prioritized for modernization. Among the obsolete assets targeted for demolition were three old barrel-making buildings, a molasses factory, a lime-storage shed, old oil tanks, a former clock-in office—and Three Oaks, which company officials said suffered from a bad case of dry rot.

Not unlike what had transpired in Fazendeville, the situation pitted ostensibly good intentions against the wrong problem and led to a regrettable decision. One day in late June 1965, company officials had the 134-year-old landmark hurriedly bulldozed. Stunned preservationists, who were given no notice, reported a few days later that the mansion had been so rigorously eradicated that its footprint was all but indiscernible. The sudden razing led to calls for public notice laws requiring owners to post plans for demolitions of historic buildings before they were executed. These rules have led to the last-minute rescue of numerous historic buildings slated for the wrecking ball.

Three Oaks's destruction left only a handful of intact antebellum plantation houses in upper St. Bernard Parish. In 2013, one of them, the LeBeau House, burned to the ground in an act of drug-induced arson. The remaining two are, ironically, in the hands of the two entities responsible for the demise of Fazendeville and Three Oaks. They are the circa-1830 Rene Beauregard House at the Chalmette Battlefield unit of Jean Lafitte National Historical Park and Preserve, and the circa-1844 Cavaroc House, owned by Domino Sugar.

Today, the only vestiges of Three Oaks are its eponymous trees, and until recently, the only evidence of Fazendeville was its faint footprint in the now-unified battlefield. This changed a few years ago when the National Park Service, in an institutional mea culpa of sorts, erected a sign commemorating the lost hamlet. The twin losses provide cause for reflection among preservationists today, whose predecessors were outraged by the destruction of one local historical legacy—even as they were complicit in the other.

THREE EXHIBITION HALLS, THREE FATES

Business travel in New Orleans predates leisure travel. Businessmen flocked by the thousands to the city during its autumn-through-spring "commercial season," and exchange hotels such as the St. Charles and the St. Louis, which were specially designed for extended-stay guests, may be considered the forerunners of modern convention hotels. For industries holding annual conferences and trade shows, need also arose for exhibition space, and investors and architects rose to the challenge of creating them. Three particular New Orleans exhibition halls, spanning from the 1870s to the 1990s, illustrate the differing purposes and designs of such structures, and the difficulties of adaptively reusing them when circumstances changed.

In an effort to revive industry after the Civil War, business leaders in the late 1860s aimed to attract commerce by creating a space to convene and display wares. They conceived a vast hall where meetings could be held and, as a *Picayune* reporter explained, "objects of interest to the planter, the mechanic, the merchant, or the mere amateur of inventions" might be showcased "all the year round . . . under one roof." It would be called Exposition Hall, and it would be unlike anything New Orleanians had seen.

Designed by Albert Diettel and built by William Ames in 1870–71, Exposition Hall measured 80 feet wide and spanned the entire 340 feet from St. Charles to Carondelet Street between Girod and Julia. While its exterior was "a simple but elegant adaptation of *renaissance* style of architecture," inside it was perfectly spectacular. A visitor entering from St. Charles would encounter two grand staircases leading up to a foyer separated by a glass partition. On the other side was the main Concert Hall, which at 160 feet deep and 35 feet high ranked as "the largest hall in the city." On the Carondelet side was the Fine Arts Hall, 170 feet by 20 feet, and to the sides were four "refreshment rooms" (restrooms), four cloakrooms, a dining hall, and a library. Actual exhibitions, which usually in-

Washington Artillery Hall (1871), an early multi-use exhibition space. The building spanned an entire block from St. Charles to Carondelet, between Girod and Julia. *Photograph courtesy Library of Congress.*

volved heavy objects, took place on the ground floor with the aid of a railway system. Huge windows allowed air and light to circulate throughout the cavernous interior.

Part conference center, part concert venue, and part ballroom, Exposition Hall was a success, having landed the 1872 Grand Industrial Exposition and many other major clients. Its size and location also attracted the interest of the Washington Artillery, the famed local battalion which found itself in need of a headquarters and arsenal. Exposition Hall had all the right attributes, and in 1878 the organization purchased the building and renamed it Washington Artillery Hall (upstairs) and Washington Artillery Armory (downstairs). Locals also called the whole outfit the St. Charles Armory.

Under the management of the Washington Artillery, the building had two distinct programs. Upstairs continued to be used for elegant society balls, including for Rex and other Carnival organizations, as well as for reunions, expositions, political conventions, conferences, fraternal get-togethers, and any other clubby merriment able to pay the rent. Downstairs, however, was reserved for the business of war. There the battalion stocked rifles, cannon, uniforms, ammunition,

Horticultural Hall, the only edifice of the World's Industrial and Cotton Centennial Exposition designed to be permanent. It measured 600 feet long and had a 105-foot tower. A storm in 1906, a tornado in 1909, and the Great Storm of 1915 led to its demise, but not before it planted the seeds for today's Audubon Zoological Gardens. *Photograph courtesy Library of Congress.*

and matériel of all sorts; it even had a live shooting range—in the heart of downtown New Orleans, in this era of rudimentary safety codes and no zoning.

What pushed the arsenal out of downtown was the congestion of a modern Central Business District. In 1922, the Washington Artillery moved its equipment to Jackson Barracks at the lower city limits, and retained the St. Charles hall for social uses. After World War II, it moved all of its functions to Jackson Barracks and sold the landmark. Drafty, costly to maintain, difficult to adapt, and without the advocacy of the nascent preservationist community, the eighty-year-old hall entered that tenuous phase when a building is worth less than the land it occupies. A Buick dealership was its last tenant, and in 1952 the former Exposition Hall was demolished. Today a stout Modernist office building occupies the site.

Five miles upriver, a comparable hall built in a very different design arose in what is now Audubon Zoo. It was called Horticultural Hall, and it was one of the most distinctive buildings in the region.

Much like Exposition Hall, Horticultural Hall came about as an attempt by commerce interests—in this case the National Cotton Planters' Association—to put to rest rumors of lingering postbellum turmoil by shining light on the city's incipient modernization. The idea, approved by Congress in 1883, was to stage a World's Industrial and Cotton Centennial Exposition at Upper City Park, today's Audubon Park. Construction delays, sparse funding, erratic participation, and a "sadly unfinished" opening day got the event off to a rocky start in 1884, and matters hardly improved during the main run in 1885. But the fair had its share of wonders, and Horticultural Hall topped the list.

Described by one visitor's guide as "the crowning glory of the Exposition," Horticultural Hall was neither the largest nor the most elaborate structure at the fair; the Main Building measured ten times its size. Nor did it hold the most extravagant attractions. But it was likely the most beautiful, a gigantic glass conservatory bringing to mind the famed Crystal Palace at London's Great Exhibition of 1851. Over 600 feet long, 120 feet wide, and 46 feet high with a 105-foot tower, the wood-timbered greenhouse displayed plants from throughout the Western Hemisphere, and with newfangled electrical lights above, live oaks all around, and a grand illuminated fountain at its center, it cut a splendid sight both night and day. Inside, everything from tropical ferns to Sonoran cacti to "bananas, cocoanuts, palms, coffee trees, pineapple and cotton plants, ginger plants, cinnamon and clove trees, vanilla plants [as well as] apples, oranges and other fruits" were displayed. Horticulturalists from all over the world met in the hall and inspected each other's handiwork for awards for "best variety," "handsomest plate," and "best collection," a sort of scientific conference and national competition amid the festivities.

Because of its beautiful design and price tag of $100,000, Horticultural Hall, unlike the other fair buildings, was designed for long-term use. Organizers struck a deal with the City Council to donate the conservatory to the newly renamed Audubon Park (1886) after the exposition closed. For the next two decades, Horticultural Hall would continue to serve as an indoor botanical garden around which many of the park's new recreational features would be clustered.

What doomed Horticultural Hall were three episodes of fierce wind: a storm in 1906, a tornado in 1909, and the Great Storm of 1915, which utterly destroyed the greenhouse and buried its collections. Some members of the public advocated for its reconstruction, but the $10,000 insurance claim was used instead to build a dedicated flight cage for birds. To that initial aviary would be added larger displays for birds and other animals, and from them would grow today's lovely Audubon Zoological Gardens. The footprint of Horticultural Hall today lies between the Audubon Tea Room and the Sea Lion Exhibit. Nothing remains except for some underground foundations.

Fifty years after Horticultural Hall's demise, New Orleans once again found itself in need of display space. What resulted, the Rivergate Exhibition Hall, tells a story of midcentury optimism, progressive planning, and architectural daring. That it is now disappeared tells a very different story.

In the years after World War II, New Orleans ambitiously modernized its infrastructure, building bridges, unifying rail lines, widening arteries, separating grade crossings, and creating a bold Civic Center. By the 1960s, in the midst of a petroleum boom, leaders sought to lure industry by putting New Orleans on the map as a "World Trade Center." That imprimatur, among other things, entailed the building of a complex dedicated to international visitation, exhibition, and commerce.

In siting the skyscraper and exhibition hall, the City of New Orleans and the state-run Port of New Orleans eyed the most valuable land in town, six parallelogram-shaped blocks between lower Canal and Poydras. Convoluted land titles led to an arrangement in which the port would own the lion's share of the facility, and the city the remainder—but the port alone would bear the cost of operation. Starting in 1964, the area was cleared, pilings were driven, and workers erected the International Trade Mart, designed by Edward Durell Stone, which became one of New Orleans's first two truly modern skyscrapers. What arose subsequently across the street would stun the collective eye of the city: an enormous pavilion of sweeping freeform arches and vaulted ceilings, designed by the stellar local architectural firm of Nathaniel Curtis and Arthur Q. Davis and representing a rebirth of Expressionism within the context of Modernist architecture. Officially known as the Port of New Orleans Rivergate Exhibition Hall, the space was designed for floor shows as well as Carnival parades and balls, such that trucks and floats could drive directly into the hall. Because of its affiliation with the International Trade Mart overlooking the Mississippi, the hall faced not the city, but the mart and the river. Built over a period of three years, the Rivergate and Trade Mart were known together as the International Center, and both got an elaborate dedication ceremony on April 30, 1968, themed to the city's 250th anniversary.

A steady stream of bookings got the Rivergate off to a good start. By one estimate reported by Wilbur Meneray, the hall generated $170 million during its first five years. The next decade, however, would see the opening of the Louisiana Superdome (1975) and the Louisiana World Exposition (the 1984 World's Fair), whose Great Hall would afterwards become a full-service conference center with exhibition floors, food facilities, and even a theater. Business tourism did well as a result, but the new venues outcompeted the Rivergate, whose bookings dropped.

These aerial views of the foot of Canal and Poydras streets at the Mississippi River show the area's change in land use from port industry (left, 1952) to the Rivergate Exhibition Hall (built in 1968 and visible in the center image, 1989) and Harrah's Casino (opened in 1999 and seen at right in 2006). *Aerial photographs from author's personal collection.*

The hall had other problems. From the perspective of pedestrians downtown, the Rivergate's towering block-long flanks and river-facing orientation made it seem inaccessible and overwhelming, as if reminding locals they had no business there. At the same time, many architects in this era were casting their eyes away from Modernism and toward Postmodernism, while preservationists never warmed to Modernism in the first place and remained enamored with historicity. As the Rivergate lost fans, it also lost clients: revenues declined, and, stuck as it was with cost of operations, the Port of New Orleans looked to get out of the exhibition business. Economically, the city in the 1980s suffered the worst oil bust in memory, costing the state vital revenue and wiping out petroleum jobs on Poydras Street. Leaders looked to new ways to fill the gap, and legalized gambling rose to the top of the list. Promoters sought not the tacky barges moored along the riverfronts of second-tier cities, but rather a big Vegas-style land-based casino in the heart of downtown.

What ensued in the early 1990s was a complex caper involving chicanery on the part of promoters and politicians, and a gross overestimate of just how successful a downtown casino might be. What got sacrificed was the Rivergate Exhibition Hall, whose prime location and ample footprint had the casino people salivating. The architectural community spoke passionately of the building's remarkable design and urged its adaptive reuse, but they failed to inspire many rank-and-file preservationists, not to mention government or business interests.

Sadly, the battle to save the Rivergate marked the last chapter in the six-decade career of the father of architectural history and preservation in New Orleans, Samuel Wilson Jr., who died shortly before testifying to the City Council to save the Rivergate.

In January 1995, demolition began on the barely twenty-seven-year-old building, and by April, the Rivergate joined Exposition and Horticultural in the halls of architectural memory. Today it is the site of Harrah's Casino.

ARNAUD CAZENAVE AND THE REINVENTION OF BOURBON STREET

Ninety years ago, a new type of business opened on Bourbon Street. It was called a nightclub, and it both reflected and affected the changing social mores of the 1920s. It would also permanently transform Bourbon Street.

Nightclubs represented a variation of the concert saloon of the late nineteenth century. First appearing on Bourbon Street in 1868, concert saloons typically featured cancan dancers or other ribald entertainment for male audiences, who were served a steady stream of alcohol by comely waitresses. Associated with gambling and prostitution, concert saloons were not the sort of places where respectable women or couples would want to be seen.

Nightclubs, on the other hand, catered to respectability. Featuring fancy dinners and classy entertainment, they cultivated an air of swanky exclusivity through the use of thematic decor, memberships or cover charges, a velvet-curtain barrier, and a doorman, all of which made patrons feel special just to be there. Both owners and patrons wanted prices to be high—that made it all the more exclusive—and everyone dressed to the nines.

The most significant social aspect of nightclubs involved gender. Whereas women were usually servants, performers, or prostitutes in concert saloons, in nightclubs they were pampered patrons as well. Many were participants in the emerging social trend of "dating," in which young men courted flappers with bobbed hair and cloche hats with a night on the town. Nightclubs created spaces in which these newly permitted social interactions could take place, while their private ambience enabled them to evade Prohibition agents.

Nightclubs emerged during the Belle Époque in Paris, in venues such as the famous Maxim's on Rue Royale (1893), and diffused to other European and American cities. While the Grunewald Hotel's "Cave" (1908, now the Roosevelt Hotel) was probably the first modern nightclub in New Orleans, Bourbon Street—already home to theaters, bistros, and saloons—offered the perfect environment for the concept to take root.

In Louisiana, nightclubs got an unintended boost from a 1908 state law known as the Gay-Shattuck Act, which, in addition to racially segregating bars, prohibited female patronage and musical performances wherever alcohol was served. But the law did not prohibit women, alcohol, and live music in establishments that also served meals, thus creating a legal loophole—and an economic opportunity. Cuisine, couples, libations, and entertainment were the key ingredients to a "club," and because few people drank and danced during the day, the enterprise became a "night" club. The terms "supper club" and "dinner club" also were used.

What first brought nightclubs to Bourbon Street was the creative mind of Arnaud Cazenave, a flamboyant French-born wine merchant who, finding New Orleans to his fancy in 1902, decided to make it home. Cazenave established a French café in the Old Absinthe House and in 1918 expanded into a larger space diagonally across Bourbon on Bienville Street. This is today's Arnaud's Restaurant.

Ever the entrepreneur, "Count" Arnaud (as he liked to be called) sought to enlarge his empire. Ever the Parisian, and contemptuously dismissive of the American legal nuisance of Prohibition, he looked to the City of Lights to inspire the City That Care Forgot. He came up with an idea and shared it with singer Babe Carroll, who recounted the conversation in a 1949 *New Orleans Item* interview with Thomas Sancton. "One night he called me over to his restaurant," recalled Carroll, "and told me of his plans to open a club on Bourbon and Bienville and call it 'Maxime's,' after the famous spot in Paris. He wanted me to sing."

Situated at 300 Bourbon Street in a rather functional one-story building rented from the American Brewing Company, the Maxime Supper Club opened its doors in late 1925 but saved its formal inauguration for the new year. In retrospect, 300 Bourbon Street on the evening of January 13, 1926, may be considered the birth of Bourbon Street's "golden age" of swanky clubs and elaborate floor shows. According to the advertisement in the *Times-Picayune*, it was quite a night, with the Princeton Revelers' Orchestra providing "that dancy music" and featuring Joe Manne's Chicago blues, "Golden Voiced Tenor" Anthony Beleci, and Babe Carroll as "Cheer-up-odist."

Cheerful perhaps, but Carroll initially had her doubts. "Rampart was the street in those days," she said in reference to the "Tango Belt" in the upper-lakeside corner of the French Quarter. "I wondered for a while if a night-club could really go on Bourbon." But the sheer force of Cazenave's "personality"—and his sixth sense as an entrepreneur—"could make a club go anywhere. And he did. Maxime's became a great success," she added. "He was the real Columbus of Bourbon St."

Maxime's was, in Carroll's interpretation and in Sancton's paraphrasing, "the first full-fledged Bourbon St. night club in the style that eventually made it one of the most famous streets in the country." To be sure, there were similar venues nearby, such as Peter Casabonne's club in the Old Absinthe House. But "in those days," countered Carroll, "the entrance was on Bienville." How about Turci's? And Toro's? "[T]hose were restaurants," she said. "I'm talking about night clubs." Keyword searches on digitized newspaper archives corroborate Carroll's argument: Maxime's was the first of its type on Bourbon Street.

Carroll's description of Maxime's serves as a checklist for what made a nightclub special. Opening night was by invitation only, and a hatcheck took patrons' garments. Alcohol was served in demitasses, grudgingly acknowledging Prohibition but otherwise defying it. The floor show included a master of ceremonies, and from behind a black velvet curtain emerged blues singers, triple pianos, comedians, jazz orchestras featuring names such as Max Fink, and dancers with "brief costumes" and "sex appeal" but absolutely no "sporting house" behavior. Patronage was "traveling men, salesmen, businessmen [as well as] wives and daughters [and] good decent kids" on dates.

Carroll herself came to be viewed as "the first singing star of Bourbon Street" when she "walked out in the spotlight one night in 1925 and put it on the maps." It helped that the Tango Belt on North Rampart had been raided incessantly by police, and, losing ground to expanding Canal Street department stores, saw its night scene lose steam. A critical mass, meanwhile, had formed a few blocks toward the river, and that momentum would soon make Bourbon Street the city's premier space for hedonism and indulgence.

Cazenave's impact on Bourbon Street would last a long time, but Maxime's would not. It got padlocked for Prohibition violations later in 1926, and Cazenave himself got arrested for two carloads of booze in 1927. By 1928, his club was known as Frolics, and it would clash with the law repeatedly despite its classy aspirations. A few years later, its biggest problem was not the law but the marketplace: new nightclubs had opened throughout the first three blocks of Bourbon, employing well over a hundred musicians. Carroll would herself open a nightclub—but in St. Bernard Parish, away from all the competition on Bourbon. Cazenave remained an entrepreneur and Bourbon advocate until his death in 1948, having lived long enough to see the street become nationally famous during and after World War II.

The curtain would eventually fall on Bourbon Street's "golden age" in the 1960s, when police cracked down on illicit activity and many old-line clubs closed. Corporate hotels opened; tourists began to outnumber locals by wide margins; and the club action shifted to drink-toting pedestrians in the street.

Maxine's original building was demolished in 1966 to make room for the Royal Sonesta Hotel, and no evidence of the club remains today. But Count Arnaud's flagship restaurant on Bienville is still going strong, as is the momentum he helped impart to Bourbon Street's nocturnal entertainment scene—starting on that winter night, ninety years ago.

MOTOR CITY IN THE CRESCENT CITY
Arabi's Ford Assembly Plant

The New Orleans metropolis we recognize today largely took shape during the 1890s through 1920s, when most modern urban infrastructure was installed and drained swamps gave way to spacious car-friendly neighborhoods. Comparable transformations were going on nationwide, and as both their cause and effect, the American automobile industry grew commensurately.

Contemplating how to satisfy this mounting demand, Ford Motor Company founder Henry Ford realized that, if all parts were manufactured identically, there was no need to assemble and test automobiles in Detroit and ship the unwieldy cargo to dealers nationwide, as was done previously. Better to ship parts to plants across the country, which would then assemble, test, and deliver the autos to regional dealers. So after World War I, Ford built or expanded fifteen auto plants across the nation, and by 1925, new Model Ts were rolling off assembly lines from Cambridge to Los Angeles, from Louisville to Salt Lake City, and from the uppermost city on the Mississippi River, Minneapolis–St. Paul, to the lowermost—not New Orleans proper, but Arabi in St. Bernard Parish.

Ford's selection of Arabi made sense. New railroads, superb river access, abundant fresh water, open land, and proximity to the urban core had attracted investors here since the late 1800s. Thereafter, upper St. Bernard Parish steadily transformed from a mostly agrarian landscape of plantations and pastures to a mixed-use cityscape of industry, shipping, warehousing, railroads, truck farms, and low-density housing. Chief among the employers was the vast slaughterhouse complex where citywide *abattoirs* had been concentrated since the 1870s. The Chalmette Slip, opened in 1907, gave St. Bernard a deep-draft harbor, and after petroleum was discovered onshore and offshore, oil and gas facilities followed. In 1912, the American Sugar Refining Company completed its Chalmette Refinery, which quickly supplanted the upper French Quarter riverfront as the fulcrum for regional sugar processing.

All the new jobs occasioned, starting in 1906, the subdivision of today's Old Arabi (also called Friscoville at the time) where, in this era before zoning, traditional cottages and shotgun houses were erected practically within the shadows of both antebellum plantation houses and modern factories.

There was another reason Ford invested here: New Orleans at the time formed the nation's premier commercial entrepôt with Latin America, a market Ford previously served through New York City. Arabi would make for a superior perch to access the Caribbean Basin and South America, not to mention the Gulf Coast.

The corporation purchased ten acres at 7200 North Peters Street along the Arabi riverfront and in 1922 erected a 225,000-square-foot plant "built to the standard Ford specifications for branch buildings," as the *Times-Picayune* reported, "of brick and white stone, with special provisions for lighting and ventilation." Two stories in the front, one in the rear, raised above the grade, and replete with all the latest technologies, including a freight elevator, Ford's Arabi plant looked like a bit of the Motor City in the Crescent City. The designer was Albert Kahn, the famed industrial architect whose technique of steel-reinforced concrete allowed for the creation of vast floor space obstructed minimally by pillars. Kahn became the favored designer of the automotive industry, and his distinctive buildings earned him the sobriquet "architect of Detroit." Kahn also designed the Packard Motor Company Building on 1820 St. Charles Avenue.

Not precisely a factory because parts would still be manufactured in Detroit, the Arabi facility, which opened in 1923, operated as an assembly, testing, and distribution plant. Auto components arrived by barge and were unloaded at Charbonnet Street Wharf in the Lower Ninth Ward, where they were moved onto the Public Belt Railroad and brought down to the plant.

The old Ford Motor Assembly Plant (1922, left) and Domino's Sugar Refinery (1912, right), in Arabi and Chalmette, St. Bernard Parish. *Photograph by Richard Campanella.*

Within two years, four hundred skilled workers were outputting 150 autos per day, and demand only increased. Getting the inventory to dealerships meant Ford had to invest also in railroads and ships; Ford's freighter SS *Oneida*, for example, would run back and forth to Tampa, Florida, with loads of 300 completed automobiles, each "Made in Arabi." All those men working all those hours needed facilities, and one of the distinguishing aspects of Kahn's design, still in place today, was industrial-scale bathrooms with circular trough urinals—and raised above the assembly floor, so as not to waste production space.

The nationwide Ford plants were not without their problems. For one, machinery in each one had to be revamped every time a new model rolled out, a time-consuming process which forced the Arabi operation to go offline for a year. But the plant reopened in May 1928, and with pent-up energy, hundreds of men working three shifts cranked out Model A Fords round-the-clock. The Arabi operation broke company-wide records when it averaged 300 autos per day throughout the month of October 1929.

That was the month the U.S. stock market crashed, and the Roaring Twenties slipped into the Great Depression. The plant shuttered in 1930, then reopened and expanded in 1931–32 on account of sound demand in Central America and Cuba, only to convert in 1933 to a sales branch and in 1934 to a parts-and-distribution branch for cars assembled elsewhere. That was another problem of the national plants: they tended to cannibalize each other's workload during times of belt-tightening. Ford kept the Arabi facility viable by using it as a training school and meeting space for regional car dealers.

World War II ended the Depression, but the economic revival went mostly to military production. In 1942, the U.S. Army port quartermaster seized the Arabi plant and put it to work as a warehouse, even as Ford sued the Army for the $70,000 annual "fair rent" it paid the auto giant, seeking $30,000 more. The plant resumed its function as a sales-and-distribution node in the late 1940s and 1950s, by which time ownership had transferred to Capital City Ford of Baton Rouge.

In December 1960, one of the property's sheds took on an incongruous new use: as temporary space for the segregated Arabi Elementary School Annex, used by those white children whose parents had withdrawn them from the nineteen recently integrated William Frantz and John McDonogh public schools in New Orleans's Ninth Ward. The incident was a harbinger of a major demographic shift about to hit the parish: in ensuing years, white families from New Orleans relocated in large numbers to new suburban subdivisions in Arabi, Chalmette, and Meraux, where decent blue-collar employment could be found at enterprises like Kaiser Aluminum, Murphy Oil, Amstar's sugar refinery, and the Tenneco gas plant. Interstate 510 (Paris Road), which connected to the national interstate system, further improved the area's fine port and railroad transportation access.

The boom gave new life to the old Ford plant, which was purchased in 1971 by the auto distributor Southern Service Company. Four years later, Southern Service's parent company, Amco, was taken over by Toyota. With the New Orleans area enriched by an oil boom and the rest of the nation buying smaller imports to save gas, Toyota saw its sales accelerate, and Amco brought the Arabi plant back online to receive, clean, repair, accessorize, and test newly arrived Toyotas from Japan. Throughout the mid-1970s, thousands of Celicas and Corollas rolled through Arabi, like the Model T's and Model A's fifty years earlier.

What killed the business, according to former building co-owner Jack Bertel, was the advent of screen-covered freight cars designed to protect new autos during rail delivery. The innovation reduced handling damages and led to a shift in distribution points of Japanese cars to more convenient West Coast locations, costing the Arabi plant its business. In 1977 Southern Service sold the Arabi building to Hayes Dockside, a public warehouse owned by Bertel and his business partner Cliff Miller. So quickly did the operation lose its value, Bertel told me in an interview, the prior managers "handed us the keys and walked away, leaving behind papers on the desk, machinery, and even some Toyota cars and trucks."

From 1977 until 2005, Hayes Dockside stored freight in transit such as coffee, twine, rubber, hardwood, burlap, and cotton. When Hurricane Katrina's surge inundated St. Bernard Parish in 2005, around two feet of saltwater swamped the building, despite its high riverfront elevation, and ruined the boric acid and wax stored inside. Today, the property is leased out to trucks for parking, and owner Cliff Miller has put the building up for sale.

As for Arabi, the century-old Domino Sugar Refinery continues to be a major employer, and the charming century-old cottages and shotguns of the Old Arabi and Friscoville historic districts are starting to see the first hints of gentrification diffusing from downtown: architectural restoration, newcomers, artist studios, "discovered" dives, and so forth. The old Ford plant, now over ninety years old, today lies dormant, much like its sibling buildings all over Detroit. But with its solid construction, unusual history, and great location amid the budding interest in Old Arabi, it may not remain that way for long.

IN THE ASHES OF THE LEBEAU PLANTATION HOUSE, A LESSON IN *CARPE DIEM*

In the wee hours of November 22, 2013, one of the lesser-known grand historical treasures of greater New Orleans disappeared from the cityscape. The LeBeau House, the last large unrestored antebellum plantation mansion within metropolitan limits, ignited in a fire set by inebriated arsonists and was reduced to ashes before sunrise.

Earlier that year, I took my Tulane architecture students inside this impressive Arabi landmark. We were joined by Chris Haines of the Arlene and Joseph Meraux Charitable Foundation (which owned the building), pioneer preservation architect Gene Cizek, and St. Bernard historian Bill Hyland, whose resounding baritone and imposing presence—he's a direct descendant of the famed Bernard Xavier Philippe de Marigny de Mandeville—seem to summon the past.

Our hosts guided us through the darkened interior of the 10,000-square-foot circa-1854 manse. We gingerly ascended the precarious staircases into the attic and onto the roof, even into its prominent cupola. We saw the house's Creole-style brick-between-post interior walls and America-style center hall, a rare fusion for so late in the antebellum era. We viewed a room full of cast-iron railings from when the house was a country residence in the late 1800s, and armored peepholes from when it was a not-so-secret gambling club in the early 1900s. We saw the damage of a 1980s fire, and inspected the stabilization work done in 2004, which

The author's Tulane students visiting the LeBeau Plantation House (1854) in Arabi, St. Bernard Parish. A few months later, in November 2013, arsonists burned the weathered mansion to the ground. *Photograph by Richard Campanella.*

fortified the building against a half-dozen subsequent hurricanes. From the rooftop, we enjoyed rarely seen vistas of historic Arabi abutting the Mississippi River, with the downtown skyline to our right, the sprawling Domino Sugar Refinery to our left, and behind it, the little-known Ford Assembly Plant. Swirling midwinter clouds and a setting sun made for an unforgettable experience, one now denied future generations.

The students wrote reflective essays on their visit. Some proposed restoring the house as a living-history museum, with exhibits on slavery and sugarcane cultivation. Others saw it as an opportunity to showcase St. Bernard Parish history and tell stories too often left out of the New Orleans–centric narrative. Still others viewed LeBeau as a marquee stop on a cultural heritage trail linking downtown with Hopedale and Delacroix in the eastern marshes, along with the Lower Ninth Ward, Bayou Bienvenue, Jackson Barracks, Chalmette Battlefield, St. Bernard State Park, and the Isleños Museum.

Imagine a historic mansion, nearly as large as Oak Alley in Vacherie or Houmas House in Burnside, only ten times closer to the city and surrounded by an abundance of diverse attractions: the students marveled that this opportunity had not been seized upon long ago, and at least one, a native daughter of St. Bernard Parish, contemplated making it her mission.

No more.

If a lesson may be rescued from LeBeau's ruins, perhaps it should be *carpe diem*. Nearly every historically aware person who knew of this building had a sense of its exceptional nature, as well as its gross underappreciation. We also recognized its vulnerability to any number of threats. Yet we did not seize the moment and save it.

We knew that it would be a costly undertaking to restore—at least $5 million for the basic renovation, much more for the envisioned complex—and that it was not our call to make. The foundation that owned LeBeau, we were told, had other priorities for the social needs of the parish, and had at least stabilized the structure to the tune of $1 million. It too failed to seize the moment.

As for leaders and authorities, they could well point to the ongoing effort of St. Bernard to recover from having been the single most devastated parish or county in the nation (99.9 percent flooded in 2005), even as its BP-oil-stained coastline continues to fray into the sea. Thus, they too did not seize the moment.

None of us did, myself included. And we all seemed to have "good" reasons.

Missed opportunities come with costs. To a remarkable degree, the identity and economy of our region rest on the aged timbers and piers of our historical structures. If you don't believe this, try and imagine what metro New Orleans would be like today had the French Quarter been razed a century ago, as was routinely suggested, and had not the success of its preservation inspired the restoration of thousands of other old buildings citywide.

Without large-scale historic preservation, our main source of employment—tourism—never would have germinated. The sense of exoticism instilled by legions of local-color writers would have dissipated. Culinary and musical traditions would have been deprived a space for paying customers. Lacking a structural basis, our social memory would have faded, and New Orleans might have ended up with a civic character more like that of Mobile or Houston. Instead, key actors seized the moment before it became too late, starting in the 1920s and continuing in the present. As stewards of this historical legacy, we all stand as beneficiaries today.

If you go out to 7200 Bienvenue Street in Arabi, you'll see what happens when that moment is missed. What could have become a cornerstone of St. Bernard Parish's collective memory is instead a smoldering pile of cinders.

URBAN GEOGRAPHIES

BENEATH NEW ORLEANS,
A COASTAL BARRIER ISLAND

Ever been to Ship Island off the coast of Mississippi, or nearby Cat, Deer, and Horn islands? Dauphin Island near Mobile, Alabama, or our own Grand Isle in Jefferson Parish?

Unbeknownst to most of the 165,000 people who live above it, a similar sandy atoll exists beneath greater New Orleans. Were it not for this feature, southeastern Louisiana would look very different today, and its largest city likely would have been established elsewhere. The subterranean peculiarity came to the attention of scientists as the result of a 1937 soil study conducted by a team of engineers and architects working with the Works Progress Administration. "It is a fine white sand," wrote the researchers in an excerpt appearing in the *Item-Tribune*, "mixed with sea shells of various kinds and sizes, at varying depths of one to fifteen feet below the surface." Coastal geographer Roger T. Saucier called it the Pine Island Beach Trend, and it originally looked much like our present-day barrier islands except that its easternmost tip probably joined the mainland south of Slidell, making it more like a peninsula, thirty to forty miles long and one to two miles wide.

Pine Island formed around forty-five hundred years ago as the Pearl River, which separates southern Louisiana and Mississippi, deposited quartz sand into the Gulf of Mexico in an era of slowed sea-level rise. Longshore currents subsequently swept the shoal westward, sculpting it into an island—until a few centuries later, when a much larger river, the Mississippi, began depositing far greater quantities of sand, silt, and clay particles from the opposite direction.

The Mississippi, for the prior three thousand years, had been lunging about in what is now southcentral Louisiana, spreading alluvium over hundreds of square miles—"like a pianist playing with one hand," as geographer John McPhee put it, "frequently and radically changing course, surging over the left or the right bank to go off in utterly new directions." When that "hand" leapt eastward, however, it found itself blocked on the north by Pine Island, whose bulk effectively routed the river's meandering channel on a continued eastward path. Wherever the river went, it deposited sediment and raised the delta's elevation. For this reason, Metairie Road, City Park Avenue, Gentilly Boulevard, and Old Gentilly Road/Chef Menteur Highway all follow a topographic ridge, even though the river has long since abandoned this channel for the present one. (The lagoons in lower

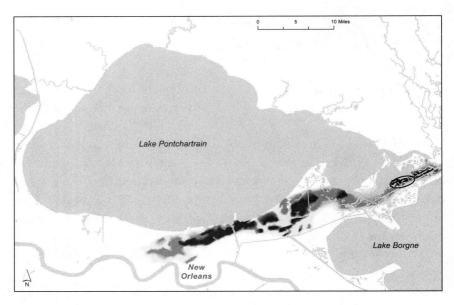

The darkly shaded area is the subterranean Pine Island Trend, 0 to 30 feet below the land surface. Circle at right shows location of the relic barrier island's only sizable surface expression. *Map by Richard Campanella based on geological data by Roger Saucier.*

City Park and Bayou Sauvage in eastern New Orleans are the last relics of this earlier course.)

The blockage created by Pine Island also had the effect of hemming in a bay and separating it from the rest of the Gulf of Mexico. Today we call this brackish tidal lagoon Lake Pontchartrain, and were it not for Pine Island, river-borne sediments likely would have converted much of its water body into marsh and swamp, just as they were doing to the south and east.

Such depositions gradually landlocked Pine Island, and its sandy beaches began to consolidate under constant overlays of river alluvium. No longer an atoll in the Gulf of Mexico, the old shoal was now a relic "trend"—the geological term for an elongated feature—lying anywhere from one to thirty feet below present-day Metairie, Lakeview, City Park, and Gentilly, across New Orleans East and out the Rigolets land bridge. That the former island is situated between the Metairie-Gentilly Ridge and the Lake Pontchartrain shore speaks to its role in guiding the formation of both features.

Without Pine Island, southeastern Louisiana would have a radically different geography today, and we would have a very different history. Lacking the convenient backdoor access that Lake Pontchartrain and Bayou St. John afforded to the banks of the Mississippi River, French colonizers probably would have gone elsewhere in seeking an ideal site for New Orleans. Eastern Lake Pontchartrain would look more like the Maurepas Basin; Slidell would have swamp rather than open water to its south and west; and the Mississippi may never have jumped into its current channel.

Humans have utilized Pine Island for centuries. From roughly 500 BC to AD 200, members of the Tchefuncte tribe built mounds of shells and bones atop the sandy atoll, either as ceremonial sites, encampments, hunting and fishing perches, or as middens (debris heaps). Now known as Little Oak and Big Oak islands, these mounds rise up to fifteen feet above the marshes of eastern New Orleans, and were used by natives, hunters, trappers, and possibly maroons (escaped slaves) well into the 1800s.

The Pine Island Trend also figured in recent history. Residents of Gentilly got a rude awakening to its presence after Hurricane Katrina, when floodwaters gushing from the London Avenue Outfall Canal floodwall breach at Mirabeau Avenue excavated the ancient sands and piled them up like dunes among destroyed houses and cars, nearly covering some. Mollusk and clam shells, some as large as four inches across, lay strewn about, mystifying residents as they inspected their wrecked homes. Some speculated that the sand came in from the lake or Gulf, but in fact it came from below. Tulane geologists Stephen Nelson and Suzanne Leclair characterized the resulting fluvial formations, which were cleared away in spring 2006, as "a rare but spectacular example of crevasse splay deposits in an urban environment."

In subsequent discussions of post-Katrina rebuilding, planners cited the Pine Island Trend as an opportunity for a compacted, sturdy geological foundation upon which major infrastructure could be footed. It also figured into arguments to save New Orleans East from "green spacing."

In the ongoing planning for improved urban water management, the architectural firm Waggonner and Ball envisioned a Gentilly Resilience District with a Mirabeau Water Garden where "wetland terraces, rain gardens, bioswales, and a woodland wash [would] divert runoff[,] infiltrating it into the sandy substrate of the Pine Island Trend and filtering it for use in recreational and ecological features."

Want to see the Pine Island Trend? There is only one major spot where the feature emerges from its depths and breaks the surface, like the back of a swimming alligator. Next time you drive Highway 90 eastward toward Mississippi, look to the south into Lake Catherine as you climb over the Rigolets Channel Bridge by Fort Pike. You will see on the horizon the smattering of mature pine trees for which the feature was named. Pines are extremely unusual in a saline marsh of mucky organic matter and thin clay, and the only reason they grow here is because of another rarity in this area: sand. I visited this area by boat a few years ago and found artifacts all around—what appeared to be pottery shards, pipe stems, and a human skull fragment—suggesting itinerant human occupancy much like Big Oak and Little Oak islands, only without the shell mounds.

This remote spot is the only part of New Orleans's natural land surface not created by the Mississippi River; it was created by the Pearl River. And when it first formed, it looked much as Dauphin Island, Ship Island, and Grand Isle do today: white sandy beaches nudged ever westward by the longshore currents of the Gulf of Mexico, strewn with tall grass and scrub trees, windswept beneath a subtropical sun.

PAUGER'S SAVVY MOVE
How an Assistant Engineer Repositioned New Orleans on Higher Ground

Students of New Orleans know how engineer Louis-Pierre Le Blond de la Tour and his able assistant Adrien de Pauger designed and laid out the street grid for the original city of New Orleans. What many may not realize is that their work did not represent the city's first surveyed line, nor was their plat, today's French Quarter, originally supposed to front the river. It took some field reconnoitering and on-the-fly reconsidering before the envisioned grid got shifted into the position it holds today.

Bienville's men started clearing vegetation for New Orleans in late March and early April 1718. That effort had been preceded by over half a dozen prior projects, dating back to 1699 and scattered across hundreds of miles, to establish toeholds in France's vast Louisiana claim. Among them was an attempt by Bienville and his older brother Iberville to establish Fort Louis de la Louisiane on the Mobile River in 1702. Flooding, however, forced its relocation to a point downriver in 1711. There, officer Jacques Barbizon de Pailloux designed a bastion according to the principles of French military engineer Sébastien Vauban, and laid out a rectilinear urban grid, traces of which remain today in downtown Mobile, Alabama.

Unlike in Mobile, urbanization in New Orleans began without the initial surveying of a street grid. But nor was it completely indiscriminate. Aiming to bring some initial order to the cleared forest, Bienville, probably with the collaboration of Mobile planner Pailloux, laid out a perfectly straight baseline running behind the crest of the natural levee about seven hundred feet from the river. Today this invisible trajectory would run between and parallel to Chartres and Royal streets, tracing through the rear wall of present-day St. Louis Cathedral. Bienville and his surveyor angled their baseline by 37 degrees, roughly southwest to northeast, so that it fronted the sharp meander of the river like a board balanced atop a bent knee. The angled baseline thus faced approaching river traffic, as if Bienville expected a fully articulated urban grid and defensive fortification to be forthcoming. That rotation angle would later drive the orientation of the entire city and set it famously awry of the cardinal directions. Bienville correctly foresaw the curvaceous river as being far more pertinent to the geography of his city than the distant stars and poles behind the points of the compass.

This rudimentary urban planning, however, did not prevent early development from occurring rather haphazardly. A number of factors explain why. For one, skepticism prevailed as to whether Bienville's flood-prone site would ever survive. Worse, John Law's land-development company—the financial impetus behind the New Orleans project—imploded in 1720, instigating riots in Europe and wreaking havoc on Louisiana's already shaky reputation. Further affronting New Orleanians was the company's recent decision to designate New Biloxi as headquarters and colony capital rather than their outpost. Chief Engineer La Tour proceeded to design the new coastal capital, sketching a star-shaped fortification system surrounding a symmetrical grid with a *place d'armes* and a church.

La Tour soon fell ill and, with orders from Paris, dispatched his assistant Pauger to plan New Orleans. Described by anthropologist Shannon Lee Dawdy as "proud [and] proper . . . one part idealist engineer and one part hot-tempered rogue," Pauger did not see eye-to-eye with his boss, to which La Tour responded with feelings of envy and competition. According to historian Lawrence Powell, Pauger seems to have gotten along better with Bienville, who also locked horns with La Tour. Sharing a common adversary and collaborating on a common problem (Pauger, like Bienville, granted himself nearby land concessions and thus stood to benefit personally if the project succeeded), the two men would play key roles in creating New Orleans.

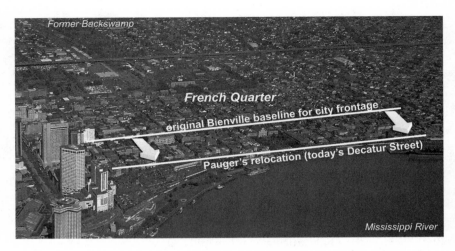

Assistant Engineer Adrien de Pauger's decision to shift the city's street grid toward the river by 700 feet had the advantageous effect of moving it to higher ground, thus reducing the risk of backswamp flooding. *Graphic by Richard Campanella.*

Pauger arrived at New Orleans on March 21, 1721, carrying La Tour's Biloxi plans in his baggage. He proceeded to explore the terrain and observe its relationship to the Mississippi. The front of the new plat, it was presumed, would be aligned with the preexisting Bienville-Pailloux baseline. But over the next few weeks, as Pauger adapted La Tour's plan for New Biloxi to the New Orleans site, Pauger sensed such an alignment would be ill advised. He decided to move his street plan seven hundred feet closer to the river, to today's Decatur Street. Pauger explained "the changes I have been obliged to make because of the situation of the terrain, which being higher on the river bank, I have brought the town site . . . closer to it, so as to profit from the proximity of the landing place as well as to have more air from the breezes that come from it."

In doing so, Pauger had apparently prevailed upon two superiors, his boss and rival La Tour, and La Tour's boss and rival, Bienville. Perhaps the alliance between Pauger and Bienville paved the way for the underling's professional judgment to win the day. Or perhaps all three recognized that it would be in everyone's best interests to shift the plat riverward.

Indeed it was: it gave the city two extra feet of topographic elevation, enough to largely evade floodwater rising from the lowlands in the rear—the type that inundated the city in 1816, 1849, 1871, and 2005. As for riverfront space, there was still plenty for shipping activity even after the move, and even more would be created decades later, when the river fortuitously deposited alluvium along the levee to create a valuable batture. Today, these are the lands riverside of North Peters and Tchoupitoulas, roughly from Conti to Felicity streets.

But Pauger had a problem on his hands before he could execute his prudent plan. Since 1718, residents had erected houses and planted gardens hither and yon, and many of them obstructed his envisioned streets. "Pauger . . . has just shown me a plan of his own invention," wrote Father Pierre Charlevoix at the time, "but it will not be so easy to put into execution, as it has been to draw [on] paper." Indeed, Pauger nearly got into fisticuffs with neighbors who resisted his call to clear the way, and went so far as to produce a map illustrating the conflicts. (It is this map that shows the Bienville-Pailloux baseline, labeled *Alignement Suiuant le projet de Mr. de Bienville des premieres maisons*: "alignment following Mr. Bienville's plan for the first houses.")

Nature resolved the conflict. According to documents found by famed architectural historian and preservationist Sam Wilson, Pauger wrote that, at 9 a.m. on September 11, 1722, "a great wind" swept the settlement, "followed an hour later by the most terrible tempest and hurricane that could ever be seen." "With this impetuous wind came such torrents of rain," wrote another eyewitness, "that you could not step out a moment without risk of being drowned[;] it rooted up the largest trees, and the birds, unable to keep up, fell in the streets."

New Orleans's first hurricane destroyed or damaged thirty-four houses, the entire flotilla of five ships, flatboats, and pirogues, plus cargo and cannons. Yet, in accordance with the axiom that one man's disaster is another's opportunity, the tempest cleared the way for new urban order. Wrote La Tour, "all these buildings were temporary and old, not a single one was in the alignment of the new town, and they were to have been pulled down. Little harm would have been done."

The final map that was actually surveyed into the landscape, titled *Plan de la Ville de la Nouvelle Orléans*, beautifully depicted a nine-by-six grid of perfectly square blocks immediately recognizable as today's French Quarter. Angled to match the Bienville-Pailloux baseline and brought forward as Pauger had decided, the orthogonal grid neatly exploited the higher, better-drained natural levee while positioning corner bastions to confront approaching enemy vessels. In the principal cell, Pauger created a *place d'armes*, to be fronted by edifices of church and state in perfect symmetry. Pauger also split the blocks evenly behind the church with an additional street (Orleans)—a feature that, taken together with the positioning of the church and *place*, resembled La Tour's plan for Biloxi and suggests a mentor-protégé influence despite whatever animus existed. Surrounding the grid was the *de rigueur* Vauban-style fortification, its bastions (never quite fully built) commanding clear firing lines in all directions.

The naming of the streets possibly alludes to the relationships among Pauger, La Tour, and Bienville. Note, for example, the self-flattering *Rue de Bienville*, and the likelihood that *Rue St. Pierre* and *Rue St. Anne* discreetly inscribed La Tour (whose first name was Pierre) and his wife Marie-Anne Le Sueur into the map. These are today's Bienville, St. Peter, and St. Ann streets. Adrien de Pauger attempted to do the same with *Rue St. Adrien*, but he seems to have been trumped— perhaps by an indignant La Tour—because that name was soon changed to *Rue de l'Arsenal*, now Ursulines. Other names (*Dauphine* and *Burgundy*) were added shortly thereafter, and a few have since been relocated or coined anew. With the exception of *Rue Quay* (today's Decatur), all original street names paid homage to the monarchy in general or to key Crown figures or their relatives, lineages, titles, or patron saints. Most remain in place today, changed only by orthography and an anglicized pronunciation.

And thanks to Pauger's savvy move, they all sit two feet higher in elevation than originally planned.

WHY PRYTANIA JOGS AT JOSEPH
The Colonial Surveying System Undergirding Local Streets

If you glance at a map of New Orleans, streets seem to emerge from a nebulous mid-crescent origin and radiate outwardly toward the arching Mississippi, like blades in a handheld fan. Viewed from the river, the pattern resembles the skeleton of a sinuous snake. The striking morphology happened neither by chance nor by plan, but rather by the inadvertent momentum that occurs when human beings survey lines upon the landscape and organize lucrative activities therein.

Undergirding the pattern, which appears on the older, riverside half of the city everywhere except the French Quarter, is the "long lot" or *arpent* surveying method introduced by the French in the early 1700s. The system, possibly first used in Babylonian times, appeared in the lowlands and mountain valleys of north-central Europe around the end of the first millennium. It spread to present-day Belgium and northern France in later centuries, where, according to historian Carl J. Ekberg, it formed agrarian landscapes known variously as *en arête de poisson* (herringbone), *village-route* (street-village), or *hameau-allongé* (string town). Whether this cadastral system—that is, a procedure of land subdivision and documentation of tenure—derived from tillage practices or from an organized effort of settlement and ownership, the resulting cadasters (land parcels) were usually shaped as elongated lots with depth-to-width ratios anywhere from 3:1 to 10:1 or more.

It was primarily the French who transferred this spatial concept to the New World, establishing their long lots in the St. Lawrence Valley, the Detroit region, the Illinois Country around present-day St. Louis, and throughout the alluvial and deltaic regions of lower Louisiana. The rationale behind the method is compelling: given (1) a valued linear resource at one end (a waterway in our case, else a road), (2) unproductive land at the other end (backswamp here, mountains elsewhere), and (3) an expanse of arable terrain in between (natural levees here, valley bottoms elsewhere), then the optimal way to create a maximum number of parcels accessing both resources is to delineate narrow strips *off* the linear resource and *across* the arable terrain. If the lots are too wide, only a few farms would be created. If the lots are demarcated as a grid rather than strips, then numerous lots may be created, but many would lack access to the linear resource, for transportation or irrigation. Long lots represent an optimal allocation of two scarce resources.

The unit used to measure long lots throughout French America was the arpent. This measurement emerged as an estimate of the amount of land one farmer can till in one day. Many cultures have equivalent units; in the Spanish-speaking world it's called a *manzana*; in the English-speaking world, an *acre*. Unlike the manzana or acre, however the arpent can be used as a linear measurement (approximately 192 U.S. feet) or an area (192 by 192 feet), depending on context.

The initial years of French imperialism in Louisiana were characterized by a weak and distant authority amid an abundance of land; hence a stable cadastral system did not immediately take form. Instead, vast concessions were made rather liberally by company officials to wealthy and important colonialists, and most were inconsistently sized and shaped, rarely surveyed, and often used more for timber extraction than for their desired intention, which was the development of an agricultural economy. But concessions did have some key features that connected them with their ancient antecedents: they were oriented perpendicularly to the river, they extended backward toward the *ciprière* (cypress swamp), and they were generally deeper than they were wide.

When the Crown learned of the excessive concessions in Louisiana and wor-

New Orleans's cityscape abounds in quirky intersections and offset streets, such as Prytania at Joseph; more often than not, they mark centuries-old plantation lines. *Photograph by Richard Campanella.*

ried about their impact on agricultural production, it intervened with a new law. The Edict of October 12, 1716, provided for the return of certain lands to the public domain for distribution to inhabitants "in the proportion of two to four arpents front by forty to sixty in depth." The edict ended the era of vast concessions and formally established the long-lot system in lower Louisiana. As local authority increased, as populations grew, and as the plantation system created new wealth, that system became increasingly codified and documented, with professional surveyors and bureaucrats turning it into a bona fide cadastral system. A typical Louisiana long-lot cadaster measured two to eight *arpents de face* (frontage arpents) along the river or its distributaries, and extended forty or eighty arpents (roughly one-and-a-half or three miles) to the backswamp—that is, across the varying width of natural levees in southern Louisiana. To this day, features such as canals, roads, and levees are sometimes named for the Forty Arpent Line or Eighty Arpent Line.

By the 1720s, most riverine land near New Orleans had been delineated into arpent-based long lots. Straight portions of the river yielded neat rectangular long lots, while curving stretches rendered lots that, like isosceles triangles with their tips cut off, converged on the concave side of the river and diverged on the convex side. Indigo, rice, tobacco, and food crops were raised on these early plantations, but following the 1788 Good Friday fire, which charred four-fifths of New Orleans, a new land use seemed viable: urban expansion. Starting with the Gravier family, which subdivided its plantation into Faubourg Ste. Marie (present-day Central Business District) shortly after the conflagration, planters throughout the upper and lower banlieue (outskirts) independently contemplated whether they could make more money by continuing in agriculture or by developing their plantations for urban expansion.

One by one, over half a century, planters eventually made the decision to develop, and hired engineers and surveyors to design and lay out street grids. Those professionals, of course, had to confine their plats to fit within the limits of their client's property; the upper and lower limits of the long lot thus became the edge streets of the new subdivision, the middle was usually reserved for a grand avenue, and all other spaces became interior blocks.

Where the river ran straight and the abutting plantations formed elongated rectangles (such as below Elysian Fields Avenue, in present-day Bywater and the Lower Ninth Ward), surveyors had no problems fitting orthogonal street networks snugly into the cadaster.

But uptown, where the river meandered broadly, surveyors were forced to squeeze rectilinear grids into cadasters that were shaped like wedges. Slivers and ever-narrowing blocks resulted, and street jars and jogs occurred whenever one surveyor attempted (or resisted) to align his plat to that which a colleague had designed adjacently at an earlier time. This explains why Prytania Street jogs at the Joseph Street intersection, why St. Charles angles at Felicity Street, why Maple Street doesn't quite align with itself on either side of Lowerline—and why Lowerline and Upperline are so named, as they were "lower" and "upper" plantation lines. And why is Lowerline *above* Upperline? Because the former was the downriver property line of a plantation (Macarty) that happened to be upriver from the Bouligny plantation, whose upriver line lent its name to the latter.

The only exceptions to the rule actually validate the rule: when adjacent plantations were purchased and subdivided together, surveyors were free to ignore the now-erased lines that once separated them—and ignore them they did. Case in point: the plantations of Delord-Sarpy and Duplantier, Solet, Robin, and Livaudais were all purchased, conflated, and subdivided in one fell swoop (1806–10), obsolescing the lines that once separated them and giving us today's Lower Garden District.

Because of this piecemeal development and the lack of a central planning authority—the city had a chief engineer but no city planning commission until the 1920s—the geometry of the colonial-era arpent system got inadvertently burned into the expanding street network of the growing city. Although full housing density would not occur until the late 1800s, most long lots within the uptown New Orleans crescent had transitioned from plantation to faubourg between 1788 and the Civil War.

It may seem paradoxical that arbitrary and cryptic cadastral patterns often have a greater and longer-lasting impact on cityscapes than massive buildings of brick and mortar. But buildings are subject to the elements and the whims of their owners, whereas cadastral systems are inscribed in legal and political realms and root deeply into fundamental national philosophies. Excepting revolutionary changes of government, cadastral patterns usually endure under new administrations and continue their imprint upon the landscape. The French arpent system persisted even when Spanish dominion replaced French, and when American replaced the Spanish. Its geometry survived after plantation agriculture gave way to faubourgs and eventually became urban neighborhoods.

The term *arpent* appears frequently in French colonial documents of North America, and despite being largely unknown in modern France, still appears in real estate signs and transactions in rural Louisiana. Long-lot fields and farms, meanwhile, persist in eastern Canada, the Great Lakes region, the central Mississippi Valley, and most conspicuously throughout the francophone region of Louisiana, where the American cadastral system of township-and-range respectfully left them in place. Urbanization has since subsumed those agrarian parcels from New Orleans proper, but their ancient geometrical rationale continues to affect the daily life of citizens today—as they negotiate quirky intersections like that of Prytania and Joseph.

THINGS AT ODD ANGLES TELL INTERESTING TALES
Explaining a Seventh Ward Urban Artifact

Things at odd angles, I teach my geography students, tell interesting tales. The New Orleans cityscape abounds in such eccentricities—misaligned streets, odd-shaped blocks, off-axis houses—and like archaeological artifacts, they shed light on conditions and decisions from centuries ago.

Such is the case for one of the most peculiar quirks of our map, a dizzying labyrinth of streets in the heart of the historic Seventh Ward. On the outside, it's bounded by St. Bernard Avenue, North Galvez, Allen, and North Roman streets, all of which extend into adjacent neighborhoods like any rational urban grid. But on the inside one finds disconnected street fragments with curious names, such as Old Roman, Old Prieur, New Prieur, and a short narrow public alley named Old St. Bernard. Strewn about are irregular blocks and neutral-ground shards that, in maps, look like the floor of a mismanaged tailor shop.

New Prieur is especially elusive. It's one of the few places on earth that has managed to evade Google Maps, nor does it appear in the city's official street gazetteer. But assessor records and street signs indicate New Prieur is no apparition. As for Old St. Bernard, well, that artery got superseded in the mid-1800s by a nearby New St. Bernard Street. But don't presume New St. Bernard is today's St. Bernard Avenue; in fact, it's now Allen Street.

So, in other words, old New St. Bernard Street, which no longer exists, supplanted Old St. Bernard Street, which still exists, and neither of them is today's St. Bernard Avenue (formerly White Street), which once hosted the New St. Bernard Canal—the successor to the Old St. Bernard Canal.

How and why this vortex fell into place has long perplexed me. But some historical-geographical sleuthing, aided by rare surveys at Tulane's Southeastern Architectural Archive, has shed new light on the mystery.

First, it's important to understand how French colonials surveyed land here. They did so by delineating elongated lots perpendicularly from waterways and ridges, such that each landholder attained valuable frontage as well as a slice of the arable land behind it. The resulting long lots were measured by the French unit *arpent*, equaling 192 English feet. A typical French long lot measured six to ten arpents wide by forty arpents deep, roughly a mile and a half, the typical span of the higher terrain before it petered out into backswamp.

Most modern riverside neighborhoods can trace their street patterns to their prior long-lot plantations, whose elongated shapes lent themselves to urban grids fairly effectively. But things got a bit messy when long lots converged in the uptown crescent. If you've ever gotten lost in Gerttown, for example, join the club.

Things got messier still in the area that is today's Seventh and Eighth wards. They were bounded by the Mississippi River to their south, Bayou Road and Bayou St. John to the west, and Gentilly Road to the north. All were key transpor-

This twisted checkerboard of blocks (center), circumscribed within the broader street network of the Seventh Ward, can be traced backed to a 1721 property line. *Satellite image courtesy Digital Globe/author's collection.*

tation arteries in colonial times, all had fertile land along their flanks, and all had been surveyed into long lots. And they would all converge around our Seventh Ward labyrinth.

As early as 1720–21, a few years after the founding of New Orleans, a land concession was made to Stephen Langlois and Daniel Provanchez fronting a bend of Bayou St. John and extending forty arpents eastward into the backswamp. The rear lines of other colonial-era plantations emanating off curvaceous Bayou St. John and Gentilly Road reflected these features' bending frontages. Together with the Langlois-Provanchez rear edge, the property lines formed a zigzagged sequence of boundaries across otherwise undeveloped swampland in today's Seventh Ward between Interstate 610 and Interstate 10.

On the opposite side of that zigzag line lay the rear holdings of the famous Creole aristocrat Bernard Marigny, whose plantation fronted the Mississippi River just below the city proper. In 1805, Marigny had the front of his property subdivided, becoming today's Faubourg Marigny. A few years later, he contracted Joseph Pilié to do the same for his back lands, creating the Faubourg Nouvelle Marigny, or New Marigny. Pilié ran his street system all the way up to the zigzag line, which by this time hosted a drainage ditch, called the St. Bernard Canal.

New Orleans subsequently spread primarily upriver and downriver from the original city. But it also expanded lakeward, up the Bayou Road, in the form of

A closer look at the Seventh Ward "labyrinth." *Satellite image courtesy Digital Globe/author's collection.*

the Faubourg Tremé, which had been surveyed by Jacques Tanesse in 1810. It additionally spread into the Faubourg New Marigny, whose street grid, because of the bend of the river, met the Tremé grid at a 40-degree angle.

All this encroaching development left open a space in between—that is, between Bayou Road and that old zigzag property line and canal. It pertained to Pierre Gueno, who ran a brickyard on it. After Gueno died, his heirs in 1832 had it subdivided by surveyor Louis Bringier as the Faubourg Gueno.

Bringier, quite rationally, took Tanesse's Tremé streets from the other side of Bayou Road and extended them straight to the St. Bernard Canal along the zigzag line. But when the city aimed to expand drainage capacity, it dug a new canal through the middle of Bringier's street plan. The centrally positioned ditch, named the New St. Bernard Canal (today's St. Bernard Avenue) would supersede the zigzag canal, which became known as the Old St. Bernard Canal.

It would also form a clear and obvious new neighborhood axis, to which Bringier probably should have responded by abandoning his use of the Tremé grid. For the between-the-canals area, he should have extended the New Marigny grid up to the New St. Bernard Canal. Had he done so, all of Faubourg Gueno's streets would then meet neatly at 40-degree angles, as most do today.

Enter at this point an Irish-born Kentucky polymath named Maunsel White. A veteran of the Battle of New Orleans who married into a wealthy French Creole

219

family, White became an influential planter, politician, businessman, civic leader, and, in typical New Orleans style, a connoisseur of pepper sauces. He was also an original board member of the University of Louisiana, the precursor to Tulane University. In the 1840s, White purchased fifty-six lots within the between-the-canals section of Faubourg Gueno, and in 1848 donated them to the university with instructions to sell them in thirty years for "the establishment of a chair of Commerce and Statistics."

White's actions appear to have locked in place Bringier's Tremé-influenced plan and made it difficult to "correct" to the New Marigny system. Reworking all those separate land titles would have been bureaucratically complex, and the thirty-year no-sell stipulation put the area in a holding pattern.

The result: one twisted checkerboard circumscribed within another, with the rogue streets prefixed "Old" to distinguish them from their compliant counterparts preceded with "North." Things got even messier when London Avenue, today's A. P. Tureaud Avenue, was cut through, leaving behind erratic blocks and helter-skelter neutral grounds. Perhaps for this reason, residents call this area "The Cut."

In time, White's donation would form what may be the first professorship of business in an American university; and White's heirs, a year after his death in 1863, would capitalize on their patriarch's penchant for pepper by launching Maunsel White's Concentrated Essence of Tobasco [sic] Pepper, derivatives of which are still available today. (Food historians debate whether White ought to be credited for the Tabasco sauce recipe and trademark, a notion tersely rebuked by the McIlhenny Company—in no less a place than the "Myths" section of its Web page, first item listed.)

As for the tangled enclave White inadvertently created, both canals have long since been filled, houses have been erected, and the area now comprises the heart of the Seventh Ward. A visit there today is a trip into the fascinating idiosyncrasies of our urban geography. Inspecting it from above, through aerial photographs and property maps, brings the cryptic past to life even more vividly.

Remember Old St. Bernard? That little back alley, still an official city street today, falls precisely on the Forty Arpent Line of the circa-1720 Langlois-Provanchez concession. Part of the old zigzag line, Old St. Bernard also once hosted the channel of the eponymous canal that precipitated much of the confusion. The rest of that archaic zigzag persists today not as streets, but in tellingly angled fence lines and driveways of dozens of Seventh Ward residents, having been unknowingly passed down—from colonial surveyor, to planter, to subdivider, to real estate agent, to homeowner—across nearly three hundred years. It is a true urban artifact, an undiscovered relic from early colonial times, and incredibly, you can even see it in satellite images.

These are some of the tales told by things at odd angles.

"FORT-PRINTS" OF THE FRENCH QUARTER

The past leaves behind clues in present-day cityscapes. Sometimes they are plain and clear, as our vast inventory of historical buildings attests. In other cases the clues are subtle and seemingly mundane: an inexplicably crooked street; an incongruously curving road within standard suburban subdivisions; an apparently random cluster of businesses. Only upon understanding their backstory do these relics become rational and elucidating.

That crooked street, for example, came from a misalignment of two different faubourgs laid out in separate plantations platted by two surveyors at different times. That curving road followed an ancient river channel which left behind a topographic ridge—and a convenient footpath through the swamps. That business cluster formed around a public market to take advantage of the foot traffic it generated, and while the cause has long since disappeared, the effects remain.

So too a handful of slightly angled property lines at the edges of the French Quarter. I call them "fort-prints," and their story goes back three centuries.

When assistant engineer Adrien de Pauger and his boss Le Blond de la Tour created the French Quarter in the early 1720s, they had two urban-design principles in mind. One was for an orderly grid of blocks and streets, a city-planning idea traceable to ancient Greece which later became a template for colonial settlements. The second principle recognized that these outposts were vulnerable to attack and had to be walled and armed.

French engineers fortified their cities in accordance with the guidelines of Sébastien Vauban, the Crown's chief military engineer. Vauban's *New Method of Fortification* (1693) instructed "How to make the Draught of a Square" and "the Streets in a Fortress," and told "of the principal Angles of a Fortress." Vauban also

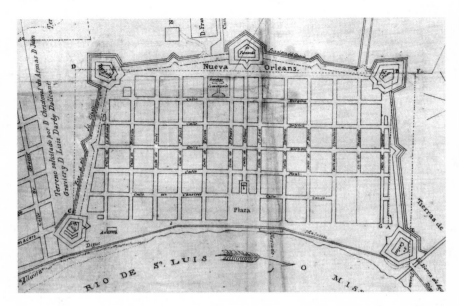

This 1804 map shows the fortifications and bastions surrounding New Orleans. Though meager in actual construction and completely eradicated by 1821, the defense system nevertheless left imprints on the modern-day French Quarter. *Map (detail) by Vicente Sebastián Pintado and Carlos Trudeau, courtesy Library of Congress.*

advised on "the Advantages and Disadvantages of a Place situated on the side of great River." Suffice it to say the early engineers of New Orleans had much to learn from Sébastien Vauban.

When Pauger adapted de la Tour's earlier plan (for Biloxi) to the environs of New Orleans, he sketched a grid of six by eleven squares and surrounded it with angled fortifications (walls, or ramparts) connecting five forts (bastions). The straight streets gave authorities visual control over the city and allowed troops to be summoned and dispatched efficiently. The angled fortifications increased the length of the weaponized perimeter, and thus exposed attackers to maximal firepower.

Those angled ramparts sliced diagonally across what are now the 100 blocks and 1300 blocks of the French Quarter, between Canal and Iberville and between Barracks and aptly named Esplanade. In the rear of the city, along eponymous Rampart Street, the wall had the shape of an inverted delta wing.

Maps from the French colonial era make the walls look intimidatingly impenetrable. But this was cartographic deception, aimed to scare off scheming enemies or, more likely, impress distant bosses who had been sending funds for defenses.

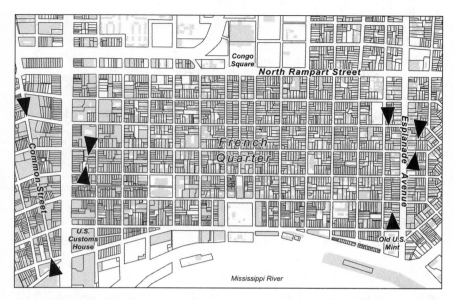

Present-day vestiges of the old fort system take the form of street names (Rampart, Esplanade, and Common, which marked the edge of the open commons fronting the fortification) and land uses (the spaces of three of the five old bastions remain government-owned: the federally owned U.S. Customs House, city-owned Congo Square, and state-owned Old U.S. Mint). The arrows mark slightly angled property lines and buildings which align with the old fortifications or their affiliated commons. *Map by Richard Campanella; imagery courtesy DigitalGlobe.*

In fact, hardly anything was built until the 1729 Natchez Indian uprising, after which authorities erected a palisade and dug a shallow moat. When emplacements were finally erected thirty years later, for fear of a British attack during the French and Indian War, the Crown came to realize their earlier funding had been misspent, and a Louisiana corruption crackdown ensued.

Spanish authorities later erected the five bastions, named San Louis, Borgoña, San Fernando, San Juan, and San Carlos. Only the last of these, facing approaching river traffic, could be called formidable. As it turned out, New Orleans did find itself under relentless attack in the Spanish colonial era—but from floods, hurricanes, and fire. So thoroughly did the Good Friday Fire of 1788 char the city, the Spanish decided to start afresh by laying out a new subdivision upriver, called the Suburbio Santa Maria (Faubourg Ste. Marie, today's Central Business District).

In doing so, they duly left open a commons for artillery fire between the upper fortification and present-day Common Street (thus the name), even though the new subdivision sat on the wrong end of the defensive fire. The same situation happened downriver in 1805, when the Faubourg Marigny was surveyed outside the lower fortification between present-day Barracks and Esplanade. It was becoming clear that nineteenth-century New Orleans was outgrowing its eighteenth-century defenses.

Louisiana had by this time transferred to American dominion, and the commons became federal property. New Orleans needed that land more than the feds, so in 1807 Congress passed an act transferring the commons to the city. The Americans retained Fort San Carlos, now called St. Charles, but cleared all other ramparts and commons and subdivided them to become the Canal Street and Esplanade Avenue corridors. But because the fortifications had been angled and their adjacent parcels inside the city were already developed with structures, surveyors had no choice but to retain the angled lines into dozens of new exterior parcels.

For a while, the interstitial space on the Canal Street side was used as a rope walk, an elongated area for twine-making. As they were built up in ensuing years, many of the odd-shaped parcels were fused or subsumed with adjacent parcels, and the old angled fortification line disappeared. In other cases, the angle became a straight alley so that the rest of the parcel would then have structure-friendly 90-degree angles. Over time, these too were subsumed. In still other cases, architects simply conformed to the odd-shaped lots and built edifices or courtyard walls to fit them. In those cases, some fragments of the circa-1720s fortification right-of-way became frozen into the legally documented property lines of the 1800s, 1900s, and 2000s. Thus, "fort-prints."

The best-preserved fort-prints may be found in the rear lines of properties between Barracks and Esplanade, from the middle of the 500 block through to the 700 block (Bourbon Street). These lines, which today are marked with courtyard walls or fences and are generally not visible from the street, align perfectly with the right-of-way of the colonial defenses. A slightly tapered driveway on the 1300 block of Royal is probably the best place to see a fort-print from the street.

Additionally, there are some likely fort-prints in the 1300 block of Burgundy as well as in the 100 blocks between Chartres and Bourbon, including the rear of the Acme Oyster House on Iberville Street, although some of these angles lines are parallel to the old fortification rather than precisely upon it.

Because the fortifications required open space to fire their cannon, the commons also left behind fingerprints in our modern cityscape. Common Street marks the upper fortification's firing area, and a few property lines on the Fau-

The slightly angled wall on the right side of this driveway at 1300 Royal Street aligns with the old colonial fort line. *Photograph by Richard Campanella.*

bourg Marigny side of Esplanade reflect the edge of the lower firing line. Those along North Rampart Street left no imprints.

The old colonial fortification effort did manage to play an unintended role in military history. In late 1814, as Major General Andrew Jackson arrived to save New Orleans from the advancing British, he found Fort St. Charles (formerly San Carlos under the Spanish) in abysmal condition and the rest of the city all but unprotected. For this reason he shifted his emphases downriver, by building earthworks and stationing troops throughout today's Bywater, Lower Ninth Ward, St. Bernard Parish, and the West Bank. When the long-expected battle finally occurred, it did so on the plains of Chalmette, over four miles downriver from the city's never-quite-adequate original defenses.

Demolished in 1821, Fort St. Charles left no fort-print, nor did the other four Spanish bastions. However, it's worth noting that three of them sat on spaces which remain in the public domain to this day. Fort San Louis's site is now the U.S. Customs House; Fort St. Charles is now occupied by the Old U.S. Mint; and Fort San Fernando marks today's Congo Square.

THE ACCIDENTAL FOREST

Some of history's toughest questions are those that ask, "Why not?" Many features in our cityscape, for example, can only be explained by understanding why certain decisions were not made, and why things did not happen.

A case in point is a remarkable remnant of what was once our region's dominant ecology. Tucked along the western side of the London Avenue Canal, lakeside of Virgil Boulevard in the Fillmore-Dillard section of Gentilly, lies a last fragment of the storied New Orleans backswamp, that vast, damp, dense forest which has long since been felled by axes, drained by pumps, and populated by us.

To be sure, this twenty-seven-acre woodland is by no means virgin old-growth. Aerial photographs attest that it was a second-growth thicket in the 1940s, and its oldest oaks today appear to be at most a century of age. Nor is it still truly "swamp"—that is, forested wetland—although one section, at four feet below sea level, appears to impound rainwater during heavy downpours.

But this nameless city-owned forest is nonetheless dense and robust, with vines dangling from a full canopy and palmettos rising from a shady open floor. It exudes the same bewitching subtropical aura that fascinated and frightened our forebears. Exploring it today, one can easily be transported back in time, as there are no sounds or sights therein of the surrounding metropolis.

Why did it survive? It's probably easier to explain why it never urbanized— that is, why things did not happen there. The reasons are partly geographical, partly historical, and largely accidental, and they start with the curving shape of nearby Gentilly Boulevard, which, as a topographical ridge, constituted the main pathway through the backswamp.

As early as the 1720s, French surveyors delineated parcels perpendicularly to the narrow ridge, creating a snake-like array of lots which over the next century would host small farms, dairies, pastures, and orchards. Dense stands of cypress swamp, meanwhile, stood in the low country to the rear. By the 1830s, Creole families with names like Martin, Bermudez, Martel, Lebeau, and Darcantel owned these rural properties. But it was only the Darcantel clan who, by 1834, planned to subdivide their land into a faubourg. Reason: the new Pontchartrain Railroad (1831) gave it direct access to the city and thus increased its land values. This is today's busy intersection of Gentilly Boulevard at Elysian Fields Avenue.

What the Pontchartrain Railroad also did was establish a perfectly straight north-south axis across an otherwise wild region defined previously by Gentilly

The "Accidental Forest," a 27-acre remnant of full-canopy woodlands in Gentilly, where once stood a vast cypress swamp. *Photograph courtesy Jaap van der Salm, used with permission.*

Road. When engineers began developing this area, they positioned new infrastructure relative to the orderly rectitude of the railroad on Elysian Fields, rather than the wending ridgetop road. For this reason, the Darcantel street grid was laid out parallel with Elysian Fields. Likewise, when the London Avenue Outfall Canal was dug forty years later, engineers aligned it too with Elysian Fields, slicing the channel across a corner of the angled Bermudez parcel. So detached, this patch would, in time, become our "accidental forest."

By the early 1900s, as that outfall canal and the associated pumping station lowered the groundwater, Gentilly's backswamp became dry land—and prime res-

How the "Accidental Forest" got its shape—and evaded development for nearly three hundred years. *Graphic by Richard Campanella; photograph courtesy Jaap van der Salm, used with permission.*

idential real estate. Large expanses came under the ownership of the New Orleans Land Company, whose surveyors laid out an orderly street network within the preexisting framework of Elysian Fields and the London Avenue Canal. One by one, subdivisions filled the checkerboard, and former woodlands became modern neighborhoods.

For some reason, the old Bermudez property did not get subsumed into the company's holdings, and thus retained its original shape abutting Gentilly Boulevard. Instead it came into the hands of the real estate partnership of Bassich and DeMontluzin, which in 1917 began laying out the Rose Hill Cemetery upon it. It's likely that whatever ancient trees still stood in our present-day woods were felled for the cemetery—a bit ironic, because the city would purchase the next lot east on Gentilly Boulevard for its municipal tree nursery.

Progress on the burial ground moved slowly, possibly because the project, according to one allegation detailed in the *Times-Picayune*, "was not in reality a cemetery"; rather, "a body . . . had been obtained from Charity Hospital and buried there as a ruse to avoid paying taxes." Whatever the case, the increasingly valuable Rose Hill tract attracted other interests. One organization in 1923 proposed a tuberculosis hospital for the land. Four years later, trustees for Dillard University, the product of a recent merger of two predecessor institutions of higher education for African Americans, envisaged the site as their new campus.

In 1931, Dillard purchased seventy acres of Rose Hill for $339,750 and, after a few bodies and markers were removed from the cemetery (among them the Dreux Monument now on Jefferson Davis Parkway), workers proceeded to construct a campus east of the London Avenue Canal, fronting Gentilly Boulevard.

The western portion, however, remained undeveloped because it was too far from the boulevard and on the wrong side of the canal. Sections were sold off in the 1940s for small subdivisions, and by the 1950s, what remained was a trapezoidal patch of open land which Dillard might have eventually sold to a developer.

But circumstances changed in the 1960s. The population exodus shifted new development to the suburbs, and land values declined in the city proper. Dillard found itself stuck with a forest too inconvenient for campus use, too far from the boulevard, and too late to sell for a subdivision. In 1982, university officials made a deal with the city, swapping their isolated forest for the front of the old municipal nursery. Dillard subsequently expanded its campus eastward, to where the Cook and Nelson buildings are now located.

The city, meanwhile, had no particular plans for its new arboreal acquisition, except for a school that would be built on its northern tip. (This was F. W. Gregory Junior High, recently demolished.) The rest gradually returned to nature, slipping through the cracks of three hundred years of urbanization. Today it forms the last substantially sized remnant of wild forest in the heart of New Orleans's East Bank, outside of parkland or batture.

Urbanization evaded these twenty-seven acres because they constituted interstitial space—that is, small, undesignated, and highly idiosyncratic areas wedged amongst larger planned areas. Through serendipity and happenstance, this tract ended up getting left behind by human endeavors, like a sliver of king cake sliced at odd angles and left uneaten on the plate.

This is not to say that the forest has completely evaded attention. According to Dillard urban planning professor Robert Collins, the university in the early 2000s expressed interest in reacquiring it for campus use. But, largely for the cost of erecting an Army Corps–approved pedestrian bridge over the London Avenue Canal, Dillard abandoned the idea. The city, which labels the woodland as Parcel 41109359, has also eyed the area. When planners behind the recent City Zoning

Ordinance proposed changing its status from Single Family Residential to Educational Campus, one citizens' group expressed concerns about neighborhood impacts, and suggested either keeping the status quo or zoning it as Regional Open Space. Others have recognized the forest's ecological and hydrological value: the Greater New Orleans Urban Water Plan spearheaded by local architect David Waggonner envisioned a London Avenue Canal Wetland Park with siphons from the canal feeding "a circulating water system to nourish the wetland habitat" plus "boardwalks [to] allow visitors to engage the diverse flora and fauna." Professor John Klingman's studio at the Tulane School of Architecture saw similar potential, and students in the Dillard Department of Urban Studies, according to Collins, use the forest for field mapping projects.

Perhaps someday things will happen here. But after exploring in and around this fortuitous little Eden, and at one point following a rather contented turtle marching stridently toward the emerald refuge, I'd be satisfied if things continued not to happen in the Accidental Forest.

"SO UNSAVORY A SMELL"
Managing Streets and City Services in Historic New Orleans

On any given day in the French Quarter, workers at select locations cut into the asphalt to service underground utilities and expose to inquisitive eyes millennia of alluvial strata—and centuries of municipal artifacts. They evidence, among other things, the attempts of our forebears to harden these stubbornly soft deltaic soils, by draining, grading, planking, leveling, paving, repaving, and eternally repairing city streets. You'll see fragments of soft red river bricks and hard clay lake bricks, rangia and oyster shells, a layer of old paving stones, an occasional rough-hewn wooden board recycled from a barge or flatboat, and more recent strata of concrete and asphalt. What you're not seeing is an intricate network of electrical and gas lines, water and sewerage mains, and wires and optical fibers that are also buried. Our finely textured alluvium, abundant rainfall, and once-high, now-dried groundwater have made street management an additional challenge here ever since Adrien Pauger first laid out the French Quarter.

Like today, streets in colonial New Orleans required constant maintenance, and because of the small and largely improvisational nature of French colonial government, authorities often had to task residents to help do the maintaining. Officials in the 1730s, for example, mandated that proprietors dig drainage ditches five *pieds* from their lots, to dry out a corridor as a primitive sidewalk. Few complied and even fewer mastered local hydrology, and ended up creating backed-up and overflowing pools. Intersections were particularly problematic in this regard, as filthy water puddled deeply and backed up into gutters. Stagnant watery ditches were a source of great nuisance and inconvenience throughout colonial times, and necessitated the development of raised wooden walkways (*banquettes*) in lieu of earthen sidewalks. According to historian Marcel Giraud, the King of France himself, informed of conditions in New Orleans by *ordonnateur* Edme Gatien Salmon, sympathized with inhabitants of this *aquatique* environ who were obliged to "dig little ditches in front of their houses, one or two feet in width by a foot or a foot and a half in depth in order to drain off the water that seeps through the levee [or] from the rains which are frequent." Because elevations diminished away from the river, the ditches had to be excavated longitudinally to usher runoff toward the woods. Thus, "these ditches cross the streets" and force "inhabitants [to] build bad wooden bridges which must be repaired at least every year." As financial officer and paymaster, Salmon proposed constructing three varieties of brick bridges, together with brick-lined drainage ditches, but his plan might have proven unpopular once white residents realized it would be funded by, according to a letter written by the king to Salmon and city founder Bienville, a tax of "five livres per head of negroes."

Spanish administrators inherited New Orleans's street problems from the French, and drainage remained at the top of the list. Records of the Spanish Cabildo (City Hall) in the 1780s–90s are replete with discussions of *puentes* ("bridges"), wooden paving planks built across cross-street drainage ditches to give drayage and pedestrians dry passage, "thus avoiding the odor of corrupted and stagnant waters." Authorities mandated that property owners were responsible for constructing puentes in front of their properties, but widespread noncompliance forced the Cabildo to let the work to city contractors (publicans) funded by property owners, a tax levied on cart proprietors, or by the Cabildo itself. A typical New Orleans street in this era constituted packed earth paralleled by ditches and banquettes and lined with rustic cottages. On it were pedestrians, frolicking children, stray dogs, occasional livestock, the Cabildo-paid town crier, and peddlers offering, in sing-song French Creole, everything from "fresh beef, fresh pork, salted meat and sausages . . . mutton, venison . . . , rice, fresh and dry vegetables" to "wild fowl of all kinds and fresh fish." Foodstuffs that went bad en route were unceremoniously dumped in the gutters.

Hoofs, heels, wheels, weather, and water eroded streets unevenly. In response, the city tasked publicans to regrade the streets, using fill and a water-level device to ensure proper inclinations. Grading was also required to shore up the elevation of the blocks so that runoff flowed into the gutters. This placed a premium on sediment, a scarce and treasured resource (to this day) in this flat and silty land. Citizens preferred to excavate dirt as close as they could find it, robbing Peter to pay Paul. The problem, of course: "pools will be formed and the water will become stagnant which is detrimental to the public health." So the Cabildo required that residents "bring [earth] from the outskirts of the city, instead of . . . the central section . . . for the construction of houses or for repairing the sidewalks." The best source for sand was the batture along the banks of the Mississippi, where the river's flow ran slack and its coarsest suspended sediment got deposited onto a beach. Some citizens took it upon themselves to "[make] their own ditch and sidewalk, without paying attention to grading it to the proper level of the city," which, once again, compelled the city to hire engineers to intervene. Excavating, transporting, filling, shoring, paving, bridging, draining: the streets of modern-day New Orleans hide strata from sundry sources, stirred and relayered relentlessly during the course of its first century alone.

The Spaniards also created a street sanitation service by funding horse- or mule-drawn wagons, food for the animals, and wages for hired-out slaves to gather and haul refuse to the town dump. The beasts, of course, fertilized the streets with their droppings, as did those pulling carriages or bearing riders. Coupled with the mud and stagnant water, a stroll about New Orleans in the late 1700s could be a hazardous and disgusting adventure—worse so at night. When "loiterers or people of bad character" successfully evaded authorities one too many times, the Cabildo acted on the need for nighttime illumination by mandating owners of corner properties to erect "reflectors," gas lanterns with reflective tin backing. They cast about as much light as an alacritous firefly. Two years later, the Cabildo ordered eighty-six oil lamps from Philadelphia and hired Brion the blacksmith to determine their best placement at intersections citywide. They agreed to install wooden posts at each corner, with an iron arm extending the glass-encased lamp into the intersection and a counterweight at the opposite end. Costs for the "oil, cotton, sulphur, wicks, flints, and steel . . . to make sparks," plus nightly lighting and maintenance, was borne by property owners based on their frontage, although this was later changed to a chimney tax and a flour tax. Fuel for lamps included fish oil, bear oil, and pelican grease (costly whale oil, which burned clean and bright, was reserved only for indoor lighting). To minimize costs, street lamps were lit only twenty-two nights monthly pending "the light of the moon."

American dominion brought no sudden improvement to the streets of New Orleans. By some accounts they were rougher than ever, a failure that Anglo newcomers tended to blame on the Creole political establishment. One Anglo-American, pointedly signing his name AMERICANUS in an 1805 *Louisiana Gazette* letter to the editor, advised the mayor that "New Orleans . . . might be rendered as cleanly and healthy as most towns in the United States" if only it adopted his plan to excavate brick-covered canals down streets from the river to the backswamp so that fresh water could be flushed throughout. The anglophone newspaper that carried that letter animatedly reported another Anglo-American native of Kentucky who, "attempting to cross the street of the [Anglo-dominated] Fauxbourg St. Mary" after a heavy summer rain in 1806, "got out of his depth, and not being able to swim, was unfortunately drowned." The editors pondered "whether . . . the 'accidental death' . . . ought to be [held] against the corporation of the city." (One wonders if too much of another liquid may have played a role in the demise of the hapless Kaintuck.)

It took another eleven years before the city finally paved its first street—Gravier, between Tchoupitoulas and Magazine in the American sector—and an additional five years before it launched a citywide paving campaign starting with Royal Street. That 1822 effort, however, hardly spread citywide, and residents continued to hop among puddles, trenches, mud pits, and feces much like their ancestors did a century prior. Even worse were the sidewalks, which were called footpaths, footways, and causeways in English, and *trottoirs* and *banquettes* in French. Old wooden sidewalks were replaced with brick ones starting in 1820, but the project proceeded only when funds became available. An 1827 city ordinance taxed property owners whose parcels abutted already-improved streets to pay for new sidewalks, and, in keeping with the de facto prioritization of the front-of-town at the expense of the rear of the city, specified that work begin on Royal first, then Levee, then Bourbon, Dauphine, Burgundy, and finally Rampart.

Two years later, Bourbon's trottoirs continued to generate complaints. An item in the *New Orleans Argus* in 1829 noted, "the sidewalks on Bourbon st. from one extremity to the other are in the most wretched state. The bricks are torn up, the gutters sunk and the edgings of the walks rotten, and in many places the walking at night is dangerous." In the street proper, hackmen and their passengers had their teeth rattled as carriages bounced along washboarded surfaces. Wheels and hoof beats deepened the potholes, which collected water, which in turn stagnated and produced mosquitoes, algae, slime, and stench. "We were the whole of yesterday assailed by so unsavory a smell," bemoaned one informant in the *Louisiana Gazette* in 1826, "the whole street from Bourbon to Royal suffered alike. . . . Such nuisances . . . will give us yellow fever in abundance."

Bourbon Street, despite its center-of-town position, seemed to suffer back-of-town street conditions, and became something of a rallying cry for street improvements. An ordinance in 1835 resolved to contract Mr. Claudot-Dumont "to pave, according to his method, Bourbon street from Canal to Esplanade street," using granite curb and gutter stones (measuring four inches thick and at least thirty-six to forty-two inches long) for the street edges, and "hard square paving stones" (twelve by eight by eight inches) for the surface. Whether Claudot-Dumont did his job is unclear; what is clear is that Bourbon Street's rough condition continued to generate a disproportionate number of citizen complaints. The city in 1838 sent around men in carts loaded with sediment to smooth over perturbations, but this too proved problematic. "Bourbon street, between Canal and St. Louis . . . is in filthy condition," growled a local newspaper; "the dirt carts not having been along for several days. This is wrong, and the person to whose charge this business is entrusted, should attend to his duty."

To equalize improvements among the competing neighborhoods of the First Municipality, the City Council in the late 1830s used Bourbon Street as an experiment for a new type of paving. It involved brick and bitumen, a viscous tarlike petroleum that, when mixed with mineral aggregates, formed asphalt. "The paving of Bourbon street . . . from Canal to Toulouse . . . , so far, promises success," reported the *Picayune* in 1839; "we would not be surprised to see the plan adopted throughout the city."

The new technique worked well at first—to the point that, according to the *Picayune*, "many a drayman, hackman, or cabman [goes] squares out of his way" to glide across Bourbon's smooth surface. Problem was, the bitumen crumbled, in part because it attracted heavy traffic but mostly for reasons of application, material, and subsurface. It had to be done again. "They are *re-bitumenising* Bourbon street," huffed a reporter, as workers tried to fix the problem. In 1841 the municipality council abandoned the great Bourbon Street "asphaltum experiment," resolving instead to pave it with the simpler but bumpier round stones imported as ship ballast or on flatboats from "the upcountry." Other paving materials used on antebellum streets included cobblestones, square block and flat granite stones, rangia shells dredged from the bottom of adjacent lakes and bays, bricks, and wooden planks and gunwales stripped from flatboats.

Paved streets meant smoother and faster-flowing traffic, but that too engendered danger. Horses and mules, often driven by free people of color or hired-out slaves, pulled wagons, trucks, and drays at speeds fast enough to injure or kill unwary pedestrians. For "the Safety and Facility of traffic in the Streets," the city in 1827 prohibited anything faster than "a stepping pace." Speeding penalties, which were posted on walls and corners, ran five to fifty dollars for free people and ten lashes for slaves if the master failed to pay the fine. Another ordinance banned the hitching of horses and mules to posts along the banquette, because of the damage they could inflict. Nor could one wash horses on the street. Inner-city streets were generally spared the herds of cattle and hogs corralled through public arteries, but not so the suburbs: those of the upper banlieue, where the flatboats docked (today's Irish Channel), regularly suffered this stinky, noisy invasion.

Even more critical to folks' daily lives was domestic water. New Orleanians needed it to drink, cook, bathe, and clean both inside and outside; an 1817 public-health law mandated that residents water down dusty streets and banquettes fronting their houses daily. Denizens obtained water from a variety of sources; some would purchase it from street vendors—one *picayune* for four buckets—or task their domestics or children to scoop it directly from the Mississippi. Others would collect rain off their roofs or dig wells in courtyards and store the water in cisterns. For drinking water, residents would remove impurities with stone, alum, or charcoal filters in earthen jars stored in courtyards or kitchens. Each method required much labor and yielded little water, creating a niche for entrepreneurs: enter the private water system. One attempt worthy of biblical times came in 1810 on the levee at Ursulines Street. Slaves pumped river water into a raised tank, which thence flowed by gravity through hollow cypress logs to subscribers. Famed architect Benjamin H. B. Latrobe designed a better system a few years later, in which a steam engine mounted in a three-story pump house would draw water from the Mississippi, store it in raised cast-iron reservoirs, and distribute it to nearby basins and through a network of cypress pipes to subscribers or to cast-iron boxes at street corners. Latrobe's waterworks served the city from 1823 to 1836. Subsequently, the Water Works Company assumed responsibility for water distribution, and in spring 1853 installed "large new main pipes . . . in place of the old small ones" from Latrobe's system. "We have been struck," wrote a *Picayune* reporter, "with the depth to which the workmen dig without reaching water."

Garbage was collected in antebellum New Orleans six days a week by a city contractor in a horse- or mule-drawn cart, into which residents deposited "dirt, filth and kitchen offals" brought out in "tubs, hampers, [or] baskets." Citizens had to bring their household detritus outside just as the cart approached; the contractor did not pick it up from the curb, except for dead animals and street litter. The policy kept garbage off the street but forced residences to wait endlessly listening for the cart to approach. An 1819 ordinance corrected this flaw by allowing the storage of garbage in containers "placed near the gutter of the foot way, opposite to their respective building." Strictly forbidden by city ordinance were "dung, chips, shavings and feculent matter," which individuals had to remove themselves. Human feces could only be moved through the streets at night and "emptied into the current of the river"—the same river that served as water source for folks downstream.

No wonder, then, that New Orleans recorded some of the highest death rates in the nation throughout most of the nineteenth century—making it all the more remarkable that most of these municipal hardships were significantly improved over the course of a single generation. During the Progressive Era of the 1880s–1920s, a sophisticated drainage system and modern water-treatment plant were installed; streetcar lines were expanded and electrified; automobiles came onto the streets and necessitated their paving with smooth asphalt; steel frame and pilings allowed buildings to rise higher; and modern electrical, telephone, and gas utilities reached more and more houses. But with some of the roughest streets of any American city, modern New Orleanians are reminded all too often of their soft deltaic underlay, and a headlong ram into a foot-deep pothole can bring a resident of the twenty-first century to empathize with their counterparts of the colonial era.

"A FOREST OF MASTS"
The Port of New Orleans in Antebellum Times

Security regulations and a massive concrete floodwall now isolate the people of New Orleans from the Port of New Orleans, although some residents live as close as a thousand feet from global shipping activity. While that proximity is as old as the city, the current barricaded condition is relatively recent. Until containeriza-tion arrived in the 1960s and the floodwall went up in the 1970s–80s, the port was no mystery to locals; pedestrians could freely stroll the wharves—if, that is, they managed to get past the tangle of riverfront sheds and railroad tracks.

Prior, and since colonial times, "the levee"—or "the quay," "the wharf," or "the landing," as the downtown riverfront was called—seamlessly adjoined the front of town, and people would enjoy its breezes and bustle like a tourist attraction. Nearly every educated person in the Western world knew about the New Orleans levee; it ranked as famous, and as notorious, as the city itself. There a visitor would see "the most extraordinary medley" of vessels, as one spectator put it in 1832, docking at a port that "rated . . . as the fourth port in point of commerce in the world, exceeded only by London, Liverpool, and New York." By another account, New Orleans represented "the leading export city of the United States and one of the leading ports of the world."

How did it all work?

Maps of the era show scores of "docks" protruding into the river every hun-dred feet for three miles. The docks adjoined the "wharf," a plank-covered plat-form over 120 feet wide, thousands of feet long, and open to the sky. The wharf overlaid the artificial levee, which lay at the crest of the natural levee, upon which most of the city was built. On the city side of the wharf ran Levee and New Levee streets, now Decatur and North Peters, along which people, beasts, and cargo moved about with purpose and order.

Masts, spider-web-like rigging, and plumes of smoke and steam beclouded the downtown riverfront, where docked the larger vessels of sea and river, while smaller craft clustered along the upper and lower fringes. A specialized nauti-cal lexicon—part English or Old English, part French, part American—could be heard: there were *ships* (three masts, oceangoing), *barks, brigs* (two masts), something called *hermaphrodite brigs, schooners* (one mast), and *sloops*. Rafts could be *barges, flatboats,* or *keelboats,* the last of these designed to be rowed against the current. There were also *feluccas, galliots, ketchers, luggers, pettiaugers, brigantines,* and *batteaux.* Then there were steam-powered vessels: *steamboats* and *steamships, steam ferries, steam tugs,* and *steam schooners.*

Crews moored vessels to the docks and arranged "flying bridges" to discharge cargo, and to their sterns tied up additional ships in parallel "tiers," two, four, sometimes six deep. Waiting vessels anchored sixty fathoms (360 feet) away, fighting currents and evading traffic. The curving river dealt different hydrologi-cal challenges to sections of banks: those above the Place d'Armes (now Jackson

This 1851 bird's eye depiction of New Orleans captures the bustle of shipping activity during the city's late-antebellum economic boom. *Illustration (detail) by J. Bachman, courtesy Library of Congress.*

Square) grappled with sandbars; those below constantly battled bank erosion. The St. Mary batture, subject of a lingering legal dispute in the antebellum era, created so wide a beach along lower Tchoupitoulas Street that the city in 1819 had to invest in "flying-bridges [for] unloading of commodities aboard the flat-boats."

Port conflicts were a source of constant public griping. Why are some agents allowed to hog wharf space with sloppily arranged deposits? Why are certain captains permitted to impede others by mooring inconveniently? Why are some wharves rotting, unplanked, insufficiently extended, or not properly numbered? How can those flatboats get away with "remain[ing] permanently on the beach as fruit stores and haunts for villains of every cast and color[?]" "The committee of the city council on levees," growled one editorialist in 1835, "appear[s] to be very negligent."

Everyday grievances aside, port activity—a chief source of government revenue in this era before income taxes—was carefully regulated by federal and local officials. The collector of customs, a prestigious presidential appointment, represented the federal government. He collected duties owed by foreign importers, controlled outbound vessels, and policed against smugglers, pirates, filibusters, illegal slave traders, and rumrunners. Locally, the City Council enacted regulations while the governor appointed a harbor master to enforce those rules and oversee day-to-day operations. Among his charges were the skilled ship pilots who boarded incoming sea vessels at Pilot Town (Balize) and guided them up to the city, a practice that continues to this day. Also beneath the harbor master were the wharfinger, who collected duties from oceangoing sailing ships, and a wharfmaster, who did the same for interior vessels.

Abundant regulations, and a rotating horde of transient sailors willing to test them, kept the wardens busy. Every ship had to have at least one capable hand— by law, a white man—on board at all times. No ballast, wastewater, pitch, or tar could be discharged. On-board kitchen fires were closely regulated, as were cargoes of hay, gunpowder, and other combustibles. Discharging of cannon and firearms was forbidden. Excessively heavy cargo like granite pillars or lead bars could not be piled upon wooden planks. The master warden, keenly aware that time meant money, ensured that port calls were quick and efficient. *Moor, unload, load, and depart. No dillydallying. No vending. No upkeep, repairs, or tinkering. Dismantle and remove broken-down craft immediately. Unload merchandise swiftly, arrange it unobtrusively, and carry it off after no more than five days.* Penalties included steep fines or seizure.

Behind the wardens were teams of inspectors for flour, beef and pork, tobacco, and other perishables. Inspectors seized damaged goods, examined vessels, and verified weights and measures, as duties were based on tonnage. In 1830, a sea vessel would pay a twelve-dollar wharfage fee for a hundred tons of cargo, and up to sixty dollars for over 450 tons. Steamboats owed six to twelve dollars for 80 to 160 tons. A loaded flatboat, regardless of weight, paid six dollars.

Behind the chief officials toiled a much larger private-sector workforce of agents, factors, brokers, traders, merchants, lawyers, bankers, and others stewarding the transfer of wealth. When things went awry—when vessels sunk, crews were robbed, cargo went bad, or livestock died—shippers trekked over to the notary public to file a Ship Captain's Protest. This document evidenced the legitimacy of the loss to the captain's clients, insulating him from legal action and enabling them to file an insurance claim. Thousands of antebellum Ship Captain's Protests lie filed to this day in a Poydras Street skyscraper that houses the New Orleans Notarial Archives.

The port never closed. While activity waned in summer and early autumn—yellow fever season—and waxed in the business season of October through June, vessels nonetheless arrived year-round, seven days a week. Wharf action slowed down on Sundays to about one-third normal levels. Nightfall precluded much activity, but lanterns, torches, gaslights, and moonlight allowed shipmen to squeeze additional hours of work out of their port call. It must have been a dazzling sight.

Heavy traffic, limited space, and cargo of varying value meant officials had to regulate where certain vessels were allowed to dock, called "stations." Generally, oceangoing sailing ships arriving from the Gulf of Mexico were assigned to the downriver stations, while river vessels bearing bulk commodities from the "up-country" docked in upriver stations.

The advent of the steamboat in 1812 brought a major new player to the riverfront stage. By 1819 they totaled 287 per year, and by 1830, steamboats arrived at a pace of one per hour, with 50 docked at any one time. Where exactly they should dock was a matter of neighborhood rivalry. The City Council in 1824 adopted a sweeping new ordinance which divvied up stations with an eye toward ethnic settlement patterns and political tensions. On the American side of town, oceangoing vessels were stationed at and below Common Street, while steamboats controlled the docks from Common to Poydras Street, and barges, flatboats, and keelboats up to St. Joseph. On the Creole side of town, steamboats controlled from Elysian Fields Avenue down to Mandeville Street, but, with permission, could also dock along a 460-foot-wide flatboat landing at Conti Street. Another stretch by the French Market allowed for "smaller vessels doing the coasting trade" to deliver foodstuffs, while an 80-foot stretch at Conti was reserved for a ferry landing. Oceangoing sailing ships controlled most other sections of the Old City riverfront, creating a spectacle visitors described as a "forest of masts."

Flatboats, the notorious bearers of nuisance-emitting cargo, required special handling. Those carrying "horses, hogs, oxen, or other animals" or rotting cargo "emitting disagreeable odors" were exiled to the nuisance wharf. Citizens themselves regularly dumped "filth in the current" using ramps built of recycled flatboat timber. The city acknowledged that "the banks . . . are in a most unsanitary condition," replete with "dead animals and an accumulation of filth whose pestilential effluvia may be prejudicial to public health." Its solution: task "the negroes of the city work shop to empty and clean said river bank."

Daily dynamics played out along the riverfront among buyers and sellers, transients and locals, shipmen of various stripes, competing laborer castes and classes, and between all of the above and the dues-collecting, rules-enforcing officials. Inevitably, conflicts and tensions arose. One flashpoint involved "retailing flat-boats," in which boatmen vended cargo directly to residents, a practice that enraged local merchants who paid high rent and taxes only to lose business to the loathsome squatters. After flatboatmen sold their cargo, they proceeded to dismantle their vessels—another point of contention, as this noisy task cluttered valuable wharf space endlessly, at the expense of incoming vessels. The scrap flatboat wood went into everything from banquettes to barge-board cottages, and some of it survives today.

For all the discord, order prevailed at the Port of New Orleans; there was too much money at stake to allow chaos to reign, and captains exercised constant diligence to ensure it did not. Negotiating the Mississippi's tricky currents amid heavy traffic, shifting winds, sandy bottoms, and cantankerous steam engines tested the very best captains as they awaited their berth, tied up, paid dues, unloaded, conducted business, managed their ornery crews, serviced their vessels, loaded, and departed—all while avoiding danger, vice, and virus. For most shipping expeditions, benefits far outweighed costs, and more and more vessels called—making overcrowding yet another pressure point. An editorialist in 1831 called on authorities "to look to widening the . . . wharfage and the landing of articles [to handle] immense additional tonnage. . . . The evil, of want of room and convenience, is felt sufficiently at this moment."

However complex port activity was in the 1820s–30s, it would only heighten after 1836, as New Orleans separated into three semiautonomous municipalities and tripled nearly all its functions, including port management. After reunification in 1852 came even busier days, when port activity seemed destined to fulfill the circa-1820s predictions that New Orleans would "one day become the greatest [on the] continent, perhaps even in the world."

But northern canals and railroads by that time had been quietly diverting much traffic away from the lower Mississippi, and after war clouds gathered on the horizon in 1861, the flatboat trade disappeared, the forest of masts thinned, and the great New Orleans quay would never quite be the same.

ADDRESSING URBAN ORDER
A History of House Numbers

American cities transformed around the turn of the twentieth century. The agrarian days before the Civil War had become a distant memory, supplanted by rapid industrialization, railroad building, and dazzling technological breakthroughs. Income and education levels rose, expanding the size of the middle class. More Americans took time and money to explore their vast country, as well as engage its problems—and there were plenty: high rates of immigration and urbanization had brought to light the problems of the inner city, while wanton exploitation of natural resources did the same for wild areas. A spirit of citizen-led intervention arose, and politicians followed. What resulted was a remarkable set of reforms and infrastructure advancements from which emerged the modern nation. Historians call it the Progressive Era, and it helped launch the American century.

New Orleans was no exception. In terms of livability, the city ended its nineteenth century muddy, malodorous, and insalubrious and entered the twentieth century cleaner and healthier. Drainage systems, water and sewerage treatment plants, street paving and park landscaping, telephones, incandescent lighting and electrified streetcar networks, automobiles, steel-frame construction, urban planning and zoning—even playgrounds—all came to fruition from the 1890s to the 1920s. Yellow fever and cholera epidemics became bad memories, death rates dropped, and life expectancies rose.

One of the lesser-known but most emblematic Progressive Era improvements stares you in the face when you come home each evening. It's the number on your door. The seemingly trivial task of enumerating houses took nearly two centuries for New Orleans to perfect—and that's faster than many cities. Like zoning ordinances and preservation statutes, logical and consistent house-numbering systems come about only when a certain level of civic agency passes to the hands of authorized professionals charged with oversight of the entire city.

House addresses became problematic because New Orleans's colonial founders, having bigger problems on their hands, did not establish a logical framework for such a system when they first laid out the city plat. Thus, unlike places like Salt Lake City, they missed the opportunity to create a regularized method from the start. Not until the early American years did an organized enumeration attempt materialize. To design it, authorities tasked a man named Matthew Flannery, probably because he had also been contracted to conduct the 1805 door-to-door population census.

Unfortunately, Flannery, an American newcomer to the Creole city, brought some ill-fitting outsider's assumptions to the task. He imposed neat orderly cardinal directions upon the curvaceous city, which wore them like a cheap suit. He anointed Orleans Street as the principal axis, which made sense only on paper—and not even then, once Canal Street became the chief artery in the 1810s. He also decided to enumerate existing houses sequentially in disregard of vacant lots and future changes in density—then overcompensated by arbitrarily doubling all the numbers.

What resulted was a herky-jerky jumble that became even less popular when homeowners were mandated to pay Flannery two and a half bits for a tin house-number plaque. People rejected Flannery's over-engineered mess and replaced it with imprecise but reliable descriptions, such as "Dauphine corner Orleans," "St. Peter at the Square," or "at the Exchange on Chartres."

The city intervened in 1831, requiring every twenty feet of street space to be enumerated regardless of structural development, with odd and even numbers placed consistently on either side of the street. No other system-wide rule was stipulated, although the ordinance did specify how houses should post their signage. Finding an address in circa-1840s New Orleans would have entailed seeking an oval-shaped tin or iron plate above each door, on which the number was supposed to be painted at least three inches high in black oil and varnished to protect it from the elements. Street signs had black lettering on a yellow field if the street ran perpendicular to the river, and white lettering on a black field for parallel. The system was never fully adopted, nor documented, and it frustrates researchers to this day.

The year 1852 brought major changes to the administration of New Orleans, including the adoption of modern municipal districts and wards. The reshuffling also provided an opportunity to rework once again the problematic house-numbering system. Mostly this effort took the form of fixing quirks and smoothing over anomalies rather than a wholesale redesign. While the reworked system did maintain odd-and-even street siding and increased the numbers with distance from Canal Street or the river, it neglected to distribute the numbers consistently, and paid no heed to the significance of a block. Irregularities were small and tolerable on inner-city blocks, but they propagated as one went outwardly. Buildings on today's 3100 Magazine Street, for example, were labeled in the 800s, whereas a parallel block on Constance numbered in the 500s, and nearby Tchoupitoulas counted five solid blocks all in the 900s. Mailmen delivering letters to homes, which the U.S. Postal Service started during the Civil War in some northern cities, would have endured this erratic system when home delivery reached New Orleans in the late 1800s.

Mail delivery plus the emerging progressive spirit of the 1890s demanded that the house-numbering problem be fixed fundamentally. Following an 1893 ordinance, City Engineer L. W. Brown, the same man in charge of infrastructure improvements, took the lead. His staff kept what worked in the two prior systems—the Canal Street/Mississippi River axes and odd/even siding—and wiped away everything else.

The new design, developed in 1893 and deployed in 1894, utilized the Philadelphia-inspired "decimal system," in which numbers consistently incremented by 100 per block, such that location and distance could be pinpointed just by looking at an address. "One does not have to hunt for a number," beamed a supportive *Picayune* editorialist. The system also followed Philadelphia's protocols for parcels and blocks of varying sizes, multiple-unit buildings, and similar anomalies. Other American cities followed suit, driven by a spirit of municipal improvement as well as national standardization. It's no coincidence that the house-numbering reforms occurred at the same time the Mendenhall Order of 1893 formally converted the U.S. Coast and Geodetic Survey to the metric system. The decimal system of house numbering is essentially the metric system of measurements inscribed into the cityscape.

One of the biggest stakeholders in the conversion project was the publisher of the *New Orleans City Directory*, L. Soards, who strongly advocated for the reform. "In the past there [have] been many proposals . . . that came to naught," he wrote to readers of the *Picayune* in 1893. "I can truthfully say that the present proposed ordinance is the most sensible, practicable, the simplest and best of any yet framed." His business dependent on it, Soards nervously tracked the progress of the conversion in 1894, at one point admonishing readers of the *Daily Item*, "Caution[:] former or old numbers . . . should and must be retained till the New City Directory comes out, otherwise serious inconvenience would arise!" "Will you ask your readers not to remove the old numbers from their houses?" pleaded one letter writer to the *Picayune* during the transitional period. "Mail is still sent to them[!]"

Normally such civic change brings with it resistance—and there was some; citizens successfully fought the requirement to purchase official metal plates on concerns about monopoly, a sensitive issue in the Progressive Era (which, of course, partially coincided with the Gilded Age). But the system itself, which represented so vast an improvement, won swift and widespread acceptance from residents and particularly merchants.

While the decimal system succeeded in the streets of New Orleans, the Mendenhall Order fell flat in converting the nation to the metric system, an effort on which the U.S. government would eventually give up many years later. Other cities also fell short of New Orleans's success. Parts of lower Manhattan and Paris, for example, never adopted the decimal system, and seeking an address there today can entail canvassing numerous blocks, lest one invokes a smartphone. Some European cities got stuck between the two systems Soards worried about, and post both the old and new numbers on houses to this day. Cities in less-developed countries commonly endure the sort of ad-hoc systems New Orleans had in the early 1800s.

The 1894 decimal-based "Philadelphia system" remains the system we use today, having been successfully extended into twentieth-century subdivisions and serving as a model for the addressing of adjacent suburbs. It represented a rational solution to an old problem, and attests to the Crescent City's progressive spirit in matters of municipal improvement at the dawn of the American century.

A "WEIRD AND GHOSTLY APPEARANCE"
The Great Light Tower Experiment

A nighttime stroll through the streets of late-nineteenth-century New Orleans would have presented many memorable sights: retail emporia with lavish window displays; rambunctious concert saloons spilling music into the streets; sailing ships and steamboats preparing for next morning's journey. But perhaps the most striking spectacle would be overhead, where spindly steel towers loomed over key arteries, each topped with blinding electric suns casting an ethereal glow upon the cityscape below.

"Tower lamps" were a radically different approach to urban illumination than the strategies employed since colonial times, which, given the technology of the day, were highly localized and thus widely distributed. The Spanish Cabildo in the

1790s, for example, called for owners of every corner property to mount lanterns with tin reflectors against their walls. When these proved inadequate, the Cabildo purchased glass-encased oil lamps from Philadelphia and installed wooden posts with iron arms extending over key intersections. Expenses for fuel, flint, and wicks were borne by property owners in proportion to their frontage, and to minimize costs, administrators ordered lamps to be lit twenty-two nights monthly, the remaining being sufficiently illuminated gratis by "the light of the moon."

By the 1820s, lighting came from oil lamps suspended from chains or ropes crisscrossed over downtown intersections. The picturesque scene caught the attention of the visiting Englishman James S. Buckingham, who explored the Faubourg Marigny in 1839. "The lamps were hung from the centre of ropes passing across the streets, as in France," Buckingham wrote. "The shops, signs, gateways, pavements, and passengers moving in the streets, all seemed so perfectly Parisian." A team of city-employed lamplighters serviced the devices, doubling as security guards as they made their daily rounds.

In 1834, the New Orleans Gas Light and Banking Company opened a gas plant in the vicinity of today's Superdome and laid distribution lines to paying subscribers for domestic cooking and lighting—quite the status symbol at the time. By the 1850s, stately iron posts with glass-encased gas lamps were installed by the hundreds throughout the urban core, while old-fashioned suspended oil lamps remained throughout the faubourgs.

Electrification arrived at New Orleans around 1880 and was adopted enthusiastically by a remarkably wide range of private-sector entities. Canal Street department stores glowed yellow every night, and theaters and hotels electrified their chandeliers. "Even dingy back streets and narrow alleys are illuminated," reported *Harper's Weekly* in March 1883, "and it is not uncommon to find the brilliantly lit globe of glass swinging in front of some picturesque tumble-down shop."

Along the levee, the wharfmaster installed "high poles" keeping aloft rows of bulbs, each color-coded to mark certain docks and stations, while gigantic spotlights were mounted atop the cupola of the Canal Street Ferry House. On clear nights, the lighting enabled the loading and unloading of vessels, and when fog rolled in, "the effect is then wonderful," wrote *Harper's*, giving the scene "an uncertain, weird, and ghostly appearance."

Wonderful as it was, the city realized piecemeal lighting eventually had to be replaced with permanent electrical infrastructure for street illumination. Engineers debated a fundamental question: should the city install a distributed system of hundreds of lampposts citywide, illuminating streets at the pedestrian level using Thomas Edison's incandescent bulbs? Or would it be more effective to install a few dozen soaring towers and light entire neighborhoods with powerful arc lights favored by Edison's rival, Charles Brush?

The distributed strategy had been practiced for years with oil and gas lamps. But building a whole new network of high-voltage wires and specially designed lampposts would be slow and costly. Centralized towers, on the other hand, would get light on the streets quicker and cheaper, including the low-density fringes of the city, and make constituents happier sooner.

Other cities had been experimenting with electric tower lights, including Aurora, Cleveland, Detroit, and New York City, which in the early 1880s erected a 250-foot-tower over Madison Square and a similar structure to guide ships up the East River. Liverpool lit its port in this manner, as did France for parts of its coastline. New Orleans wanted to remain a leader in electrification, and towers seemed to be where the technology was going. Certainly the need and opportunity were here: stated a feature article in *Scientific American,* "It is doubtful whether there is in the whole of the country another space . . . so largely benefited by the new method of lighting as the busy crescent of the New Orleans levee."

That 1882 article introduced an ambitious proposal by local inventor William Golding for a pencil-like cast-iron cylinder rising 500 feet above the foot of Canal Street. It would be erected section by section, from the bottom up, its zenith tethered by guy wires to the four street corners. Inside the cylinder, Golding designed a rather claustrophobic elevator for a "light trimmer" to be lifted daily to the top, like a human bullet moving slowly up a vertical barrel. There, he would insert new carbon rods into the lamps—a wildly dangerous job called "trimming"—to cast the equivalent light of 40,000 candles over the course of the next evening.

Golding's needle was never built, but the idea of centralized towers moved forward. In 1884, the Committee on Fire Department and Lighting advised the City Council to allow the Brush Electric Light Company to erect a light tower uptown. It would save the city the expense of fifty existing gas lamps, the committee noted, and not cost a dime, because Brush offered to erect the first tower gratis—and then get paid to build many more.

At the same time, the owners of the Shot Tower, a 214-foot-high pillar on St. Joseph Street from which molten lead was dropped to form pellets, fitted their medieval-looking brick tower with 132 electric lights in the windows and a 36,000-candle-power arc lamp at the top, using bulbs manufactured on the same block by the Muller Company. The results dazzled residents, and the city was sold: it would build light towers all through the "suburbs," meaning just about every-

ELECTRIC LIGHT TOWER FOR CANAL STREET AND LEVEE NEW ORLEANS.—DESIGNED BY WM. GOLDING, M.E.

This 1882 proposal to illuminate lower Canal Street was never realized, but a comparable system of gigantic light towers was installed throughout downtown later in the decade. It eventually proved impractical, and all traces were removed by the 1910s. *Illustration courtesy* Scientific American *magazine.*

where outside the French Quarter. Because the committee approving the towers included the Fire Department, authorities, according to the national *Electrical Engineer* journal, "stipulated that an iron pipe should be run up each tower, to be used in extinguishing fires . . . which cannot be reached by the fire-engines."

The first tower was erected in 1884–85 across from the Dryades Market on present-day O. C. Haley Boulevard at Martin Luther King. The Detroit Iron Tower Company installed the triangular 175-foot-high structure, while Brush handled

This ungainly steel tower, seen here in 1892, was used to illuminate the busy intersection of Bourbon and Canal streets as well as uphold transmission wires serving adjacent neighborhoods. *Photograph from author's personal collection.*

the 12,000-candlelight-power lamps. That same year, the World's Industrial and Cotton Centennial Exhibition at present-day Audubon Park was lit by ten 25,000-candlepower towers, and its exhibits proudly showcased electricity in all its uses.

More towers followed: on Canal at Bourbon; along Poydras, Carondelet, Camp, Dryades, and Carrollton Avenue; on North Tonti and Lapeyrouse; on Galvez at Dumaine. The concurrent spread of telephone and telegraph wires as well as electrical cables meant that some of these towers were used for both lighting and utility wiring, whereas others transitioned over time from one to the other use, or were designed exclusively for either. Plans called for over 250 towers throughout town.

By the early 1890s, however, the novelty of the midnight suns had worn off and the public began to see the towers' drawbacks. For one, the arc lamps were absolutely blinding to a direct gaze, and the glow on the street faded to pale as one moved farther from the source. The lamps also created hard shadows and left areas not directly aligned with the towers in complete darkness. Maintenance was another problem: whereas a lamppost with an incandescent bulb could be tended by any worker on a ladder, tower-mounted arc lamps required a trimmer to climb to the top daily, or the lamps to be lowered to the ground, both of which entailed dangerous and specialized jobs. Safety questions arose regarding live wires falling to the streets, and city dwellers found the spindly apparatus to be "beauty spoilers . . . great, cumbersome, unsightly affairs," as the *Daily Item* stated in an 1894 editorial titled "Remove the Towers." This was an era when citizens increasingly called for municipal improvements and urban beatification, and these metal monstrosities were anything but.

The towers themselves became urban nuisances. Pedestrians and conveyances had to navigate around their bases; migrating birds crashed into them; kids scampered up them and drunks fell off them. One "foolhardy climber . . . under the influence of liquor," reported the *Daily Picayune* in 1890, scaled the 150-tower on Howard and Carondelet and ended up "tumbling down . . . dash[ing] out his brains [and landing] in an inert heap." Others raised concerns about monopoly, as the tower companies increased their leverage in the utility marketplace when more and more wires were strung upon them.

By the early 1900s, it became clear that the tower approach to both urban illumination and utility wiring was a mistake. Without much fanfare or coverage, the steel structures were dismantled one by one, and, along with suspended lamps, were gradually replaced by curbside electric lampposts, telephone poles and, in parts of downtown, underground wiring. By the 1910s nearly all towers were gone. Arc lamps, meanwhile, were gradually being replaced by incandescent lights, whose "effect," according to one 1919 source, "is much more beautiful, and the light more evenly distributed."

Whereas many street scenes photographed in the 1880s to 1900s capture towers in the distance, only a couple of artist sketches show the arc lamps in action at night. No traces of the towers remain today, but New Orleanians can get an idea of how they might have looked, at least during the daytime, from the giant transmission towers currently lining the riverfront, particularly the one at the foot of Oak Street.

As to how they appeared at night, one must travel to Austin, Texas, home to the world's last operating system of "moon towers," in service since 1895.

EARLY AERIAL PERSPECTIVES OF NEW ORLEANS

With a compelling built environment straddling the sinuous Mississippi and surrounded by complex marshes and bays, New Orleans begs to be viewed from above. For the first century of the city's existence, however, the human eye could rise no higher than the tallest structure to gain a remote perspective. Ballooning, which became a popular stunt in the early 1800s, afforded loftier perches, but only for the "aeronaut" aboard. One such adventurer, a "Mr. Robinson," thrilled New Orleanians in 1827 with a flight that started from the French Quarter levee, rose, according to local press coverage, "into the regions of the upper air," and crash-landed in waist-deep mud around Madame Coriocourt's Gentilly Road plantation eight miles away. A newspaper described the day's events as "wonderful, glorious and sublime beyond expression," as surely were the vistas enjoyed by Mr. Robinson.

By the 1830s–40s, structures such as the 185-foot-high St. Charles Hotel and 140-foot St. Patrick's Church afforded artists a perch from which they could observe and sketch accurate bird's eye views of the cityscape below. Early daguerreotypists and photographers, such as Jules Lion, Jay Dearborn Edwards, and Theodore Lilienthal, followed in their stead in the 1840s–60s, using rooftops and towers as platforms for their bulky equipment. This was also the era in which the first genuine aerial photographs were captured: downtown Boston was photographed from a balloon in 1860, as had been Paris a few years earlier, although no such image was ever made of New Orleans in this era. Additionally, kites, messenger pigeons, and tethered balloons were used as early remote-sensing platforms in the late 1800s and early 1900s. During the heyday of aviation experimentation in the 1910s, individuals lugged cameras aboard aircraft and snapped photographs of the cityscape on either side of the cockpit. Local archives retain a handful of these magnificent "oblique" views of New Orleans, including a unique view of

Storyville taken around 1914 and a collection of breathtaking downtown scenes captured by *Item* photographer Edward E. Agnelly eight years later.

While oblique aerials render spectacular vistas, they are not particularly useful for the purposes of mapping. If cartography is the goal, a specialized camera must be pointed straight down in a "nadir" (base) view and held as stable as possible. Military uses of nadir aerial photography during the Great War in Europe led to the refinement of wide-format lenses, shutter speeds, specialized film with fiducial marks, and custom-made mounts on the airborne platform. On the ground, photogrammetric engineers developed tools such as stereo plotters to view overlapping frames in three dimensions, remove distortion, and turn the photographs into geometrically accurate cartographic products called orthophotos.

After the war, the Fairchild Aerial Camera Corporation discovered there were lucrative civilian applications in photo mapping. These were the early days of city planning and zoning, and with new auto-friendly subdivisions expanding metropolitan footprints nationwide, planners and developers eagerly consumed this new and informative type of spatial data. In 1921, Fairchild successfully photographed all of Manhattan Island, producing a first-ever mosaic of the nation's largest city. The firm extended its business elsewhere.

A number of years ago, I acquired a copy of a rare aerial photo mosaic of New Orleans from an obscure 1920s Port of New Orleans report. It appears to date from around the time of the Fairchild project in Manhattan, and it's certainly the earliest comprehensive nadir-view photographic coverage of New Orleans I have ever seen. I've since scanned and geo-referenced it for use in my geographical research, and have published it in two of my books. But I have not been able to ascertain its provenance.

Conversations with my colleague Keli Rylance of Tulane University's Southeastern Architecture Archive have since shed more light on this unique city portrait. Keli discovered in the archive's vast collections a few individual frames from the same era, and found news articles from the early 1920s on early aerial missions.

The mosaic, it appears, was not a Fairchild project but rather an idea hatched in 1920 by the city planning committee of the Association of Commerce, which had learned of the power of civilian aerial photography from its counterparts in other cities and wanted a similar data set for New Orleans. The association found a willing partner in the U.S. Navy, which had developed a seaplane with a specialized mount and was eager to test its new equipment.

New Orleans's first full aerial portrait, 1922. Note as-yet-undeveloped land in present-day Broadmoor (upper center), the rural nature of pre-bridge West Bank (bottom), and the old French long-lot plantations still under sugarcane cultivation at left. *Photo mosaic from author's personal collection.*

Photographing New Orleans, however, proved frustrating, indeed nearly disastrous. The first attempt, in 1920, was thwarted by weather: the mission required that all skies over the city be clear below an 8,000-foot ceiling, literally a tall order for this region. A second mission in 1921 never quite photographed the city because it first flew down to map the mouth of the Mississippi River—only to run out of gas, forcing the pilot to land in the Gulf of Mexico. He and the photographer were finally found two days later, alive but suffering from exposure. The third mission completely failed to get off the ground, as a storm in Lake Pontchartrain, according to newspaper reports, tore the seaplane "from its moorings off the Southern Yacht Club [and] ground [it] to bits against the sea wall."

The fourth attempt proved the charm, and in 1922, under perfect weather conditions, one Ensign Keene piloted a plane which, with the help of chief photographer Daniel W. Culp and a flight crew, had been rigged with "an automatic camera operated by a wind motor from the streamline of the propeller, at the rate of one every thirty-five seconds, with a 50 percent overlap in each [frame]. These photographs measure 7 inches by 9." It appears that the film was developed at the Pensacola naval base and mosaicked—that is, strategically subsetted within the overlap regions and pasted together like a puzzle—to form a first-ever photographic map of the City of New Orleans. In all likelihood, this is the origin of the copy I found.

Later in the 1920s, commercial interests routinely sent up aircraft to photograph, either in oblique or nadir format, the subdivision development of present-day Gentilly and Lakeview. A circa-1920s nadir photograph of the area around the Fairgrounds and DeSaix Circle, which Keli Rylance found in her archive's Weiss, Dreyfous and Seiferth Office Records, probably derives from one of these real estate development efforts.

Nadir-view aerial photography effectively replaced field surveys for the making of maps within a decade of the New Orleans mosaic, and it would dominate cartography until the end of the century. Since then, digital sensors mounted on space-borne satellite platforms have largely replaced film-based airborne imagery. Today we have a wealth of spatial data about our region—you can view detailed satellite imagery of your house for free on the Internet—which adds all the more value to those first mapping-quality nadir-view photographs captured nearly a century ago.

POLYMNIA STREET GOES TO WAR

"New Orleans is not an industrial town," we are told. True enough: manufacturing here never attained the scale of northern and midwestern cities, and nowadays, aside from petroleum and chemical processing, making things falls well behind shipping things and serving things in the rankings of economic sectors.

Thus it comes as something of a surprise to consider, regardless of other cities, just how much industry *did* exist in New Orleans. From the late 1800s to the mid-1900s, factories dotted the skyline, and New Orleanians did everything from assemble automobiles and brew beer to produce aluminum, paint, furniture, ships, and assorted foodstuffs.

The greatest chapter in local manufacturing history came courtesy of Andrew Jackson Higgins's boat-building business, which employed tens of thousands of people and built as many vessels to, quite literally, help win World War II. If any one moment encapsulated that homegrown industrial miracle, it involved a little-known episode in June 1941 on, of all places, residential Polymnia Street just off St. Charles Avenue.

Higgins, a Nebraska-born builder who specialized in shallow-draft vessels capable of navigating Louisiana's waters, contemplated a pressing tactical problem facing the Allies. How do you land millions of troops on two overrun continents when all deep-draft harbors are in enemy hands? Higgins saw the answer in flat-bottomed landing craft dispersed along sparsely defended beachfronts, rather than traditional troop ships concentrated dangerously at a port which first had to be captured.

Reading the tea leaves of world events, Higgins massively scaled up his operation even before the war began. With a mix of brilliant vision, dazzling managerial skills, and lordly arrogance—"his presence is imperative, his gaze steady," reported *Fortune* in 1943; "he radiates belligerent authority . . . and swears beautifully and easily"—Higgins won over East Coast–inclined military bureaucrats ("s.o.b.'s," he called them) and landed lucrative contracts to build vessels in his adopted hometown of New Orleans.

Higgins's production line kicked into high gear with the fall of France in 1940 and Axis domination of Western Europe by 1941. President Roosevelt foresaw Hitler's next move as possibly aimed at the Portuguese Azores or, worse, French Martinique in the Caribbean, which would give the Germans stepping stones to the American mainland. With or without a declaration of war, the U.S. military was not about to let that happen and made plans to land heavy tanks on those atolls. An operation like that needed a specialized craft, called a tank lighter.

On May 27, 1941, military contractors challenged Higgins to design a tank lighter within the impossibly short span of three days. Higgins, who liked designing *by* building rather than *before* building, promised instead to construct a working model. "It can't be done," the Navy replied. "The hell it can't," Higgins growled; "you just be here in three days." According to historian Jerry E. Strahan, whose seminal biography of Higgins planted the seeds for our National World War II Museum, Higgins and his team got to work and "designed, built, and put in the water [a] 45-foot tank lighter [within] sixty-one hours." The craft passed all tests in Lake Pontchartrain, "climbing halfway up the concrete sea wall [and] riding over tree trunks," according to *Fortune*.

Marine Corps and Navy brass were thrilled. They had their prototype. Now, on June 7, they wanted the full order—fifty tank lighters, nine of which were to be delivered combat-ready to Norfolk, Virginia. And they wanted them by June 21.

Fifty new craft never before mass-produced, in two weeks? Plus delivery? A prudent man would have shaken his clients to their senses. But Higgins relished the challenge and jumped into action, resolving seemingly show-stopping obstacles with creative, bold, and at times barely legal solutions. Low on steel, he "chartered a fleet of trucks and armed plant guards," wrote Strahan, "to persuade [a Baton Rouge] consignee to release the metal to Higgins Industries." Requiring bronze shafting, he sent his men to raid a Texas depot, and arranged for complicit Louisiana police to placate livid Texas law enforcement as his trucks crossed the state line heading back to New Orleans. Needing more steel, Higgins begged and borrowed from a Birmingham plant, then sweet-talked Southern Railway officials into bending the rules to deliver the metal to New Orleans. "Never before or since," wrote Strahan, "has a Southern Railway passenger train pulled freight cars."

Higgins's chief problem was where to build the fifty tank lighters. His makeshift headquarters at 1755 St. Charles Avenue could only handle modest civilian projects, and his big City Park plant, still under construction, was already fully tasked with other war deliverables.

Higgins cast his eyes down the avenue and found the answer. It was called Polymnia Street.

Never mind that 1600 Polymnia was residential, or that it was neither equipped nor positioned for heavy manufacturing. In an extreme example of spot zoning, Higgins got Mayor Robert Maestri to permit the requisitioning of this public space for his private use, and blew past any dissent.

Higgins's workers next roped off the street, strung lights, and erected giant tarps to create an all-weather work yard and assembly line. Machinery, power supplies, and actual construction took place in an old stable which Higgins had acquired. Because the ceiling was too low for a crane, "bull gangs" of the strongest men (depicted in the accompanying graphic from a Shell Oil advertisement, the only known illustration of the project) were used to lift heavy sheets of metal into the stable.

For two weeks, a steady stream of trucks brought the Alabama steel, the Texas bronze, a forest's worth of plywood, and other raw materials into the Carondelet end of 1600 Polymnia, and with at least eight hundred employees (possibly many more) working three shifts nonstop twenty-four hours a day, battle-ready tank lighters came out the St. Charles Avenue end.

All the bustle did not go without complaint. The United States was not yet at war, and a patriotic sense of sacrifice had not fully developed; besides, it wasn't as if Higgins was going broke on all these government contracts. Neighbors protested about obstructed streets, blocked access to homes, interrupted garbage

This wartime Shell Oil advertisement featured the June 1941 Polymnia Street boat-building story and may represent the only illustration of the episode. *Courtesy National World War II Museum, 2002.067.001; special thanks to Lindsey Barnes, Senior Archivist.*

pickup, and loss of commerce. In one only-in-New-Orleans case, the irate madam of a Polymnia Street brothel "argued plausibly that the racket destroyed romance," and, according to the *Fortune* article, "threatened to take up the matter with the authorities."

The last of the vessels was completed right on time; now came rail delivery to Norfolk. According to historian Peter Neushul, "seven railroad bridge clearances had to be raised or strengthened in order to transport the craft." By June 21, all the Polymnia Street tank lighters—"ugly but fast," Higgins proudly described them—were done and delivered, right on schedule. Navy bureaucrats who were oftentimes at the receiving end of Higgins's temerity now praised the man for his "zeal, efficiency and splendid cooperation."

The very next day, Hitler's war machine did indeed open a new front in the war—but it aimed eastward to attack the Soviet Union, not westward onto the Atlantic atolls. Higgins's tank lighters proved unnecessary for their original purpose, but they would come in handy elsewhere. Within six months, the Japanese

Polymnia Street today, with St. Charles Avenue in foreground. Higgins's headquarters was located in the block to the left. *Photograph by Richard Campanella.*

would attack Pearl Harbor, prompting the United States to enter a two-front war. Higgins Industries would have lots more work to do.

The company ended up producing 20,094 boats—most of the Navy fleet—and employing as many as thirty thousand people, including African Americans and women, across seven gargantuan plants citywide. Its most famous vessels included the Patrol-Torpedo (PT) Boat and the Landing Craft Vehicle–Personnel, or LCVPs, which deposited troops at Normandy on D-Day and elsewhere in both theaters of combat.

That fortnight on Polymnia Street in June 1941 portended the critically important manufacturing that would come, and it demonstrates that even a nonindustrialized city like New Orleans can whip into action swiftly and efficiently if need be—oh, and perhaps bend a few rules in the process.

MONORAIL DERAILED

Imagine entering a spaceship-like terminal on Loyola and Poydras, boarding a futuristic bullet train suspended high above the street, and relaxing in sleek comfort as you speed to the airport in fourteen minutes. When might you foresee such a vision becoming a city project? The 2030s? 2050s? Never?

Try the 1950s.

New Orleans's monorail initiative, which garnered national attention in 1958, reflected a number of veins in midcentury municipal machinations, ranging from regional growth and modernization to old-fashioned rivalries and power politics.

New Orleans had since World War II embarked on strident transportation improvements, a priority for Mayor deLesseps "Chep" Morrison as well as City Council President Victor "Vic" Schiro. Both men of political ambition, Mayor Morrison cast his eyes toward the governor's mansion while Councilman Schiro eyed the office of mayor. Everyone's eyes, meanwhile, were fixated on booming Houston, which had recently surpassed New Orleans's long-held rank as the largest city in the region and billed itself as the metropolis of the future.

In response, Morrison spoke boldly of making New Orleans the "Gateway to the Americas." He also spearheaded a new Civic Center on Loyola Avenue, oversaw the construction of the city's first bridge and expressway, streamlined key arteries, and unified disparate train routes into the new Union Passenger Terminal. But regional traffic circulation remained problematic. The national interstate highway system was in its infancy, and enough suburbanization had occurred by the mid-1950s to clog traffic on Airline Highway, River Road, and Metairie Road.

One way to abet both downtown renewal and regional transit was to build a light-rail system connecting the city and airport—and why not make it dazzling? This was, after all, the Space Age, and what better way to beat Houston at its own game than to entertain the plan of a Houston-based firm to install a first-in-the-nation monorail right here in New Orleans. Named Monorail, Inc., the company requested a seventy-five-year franchise to build a raised track from New Orleans to Kenner, on which it would run high-speed trains funded by $16.5 million of entirely private capital. Revenue would be earned via the 75-cent fare to the airport, $1.00 round trip, and 50 cents for shorter legs.

To some, it sounded too good to be true.

To others, it sounded too good to pass up. Monorail, Inc., hired a local front man named Thomas J. Lupo to persuade city leaders of the latter.

259

Lupo, who had longtime connections in city government, found a champion in Council President Schiro. It's fair to say that Schiro genuinely thought the monorail was in the public's best interest, but that did not prevent some from suspecting that Schiro also viewed it as a political vehicle on which he could almost literally ride into the mayor's office. Schiro availed Lupo of the resources of his position, going so far as to give him keys to his council office.

Councilman James "Jimmy" Fitzmorris, who also had mayoral aspirations, viewed the monorail dubiously on practical grounds, all the more because his chief rival Schiro had endorsed it. When Mayor Morrison threw his support behind the monorail, and by extension Schiro, Fitzmorris hardened his opposition.

By early 1958, the word "monorail" was on everyone's lips. New Orleans would be first among cities again, the envy of the nation. Take that, Houston!

But the monorail also raised the eyebrows of professional planners. The Bureau of Government Research questioned the project's feasibility, and the City Planning Commission flat-out opposed it, citing its experimental nature and lack of preliminary research.

Yet the City Council voted unanimously in April 1958 to grant Monorail, Inc., its conditional franchise. In deference to their colleagues' concerns, however, the legislators attached a number of no-nonsense amendments to the motion, chief among them the need for a feasibility study done by an independent expert.

Up for the challenge, Monorail, Inc., hired rail-transit expert Colonel Sidney Bingham, a former New York City subway chief and the man who figured out how to get three thousand locomotives and fifty thousand loaded freight cars into Normandy in the wake of the D-Day invasions. Bingham proceeded to investigate technical issues, and in January 1959 submitted his "Report on the Feasibility of a Monorail System for the New Orleans Metropolitan Area."

Bingham's report detailed three proposed routes, all with termini in downtown and the airport but with spur lines as far out as River Ridge, Gentilly, and the Lower Ninth Ward. Routes included Veterans Boulevard and the lower Canal Street shopping district, Orleans Avenue through the Fifth Ward, even the French Quarter riverfront. Each would be lined with gigantic concrete pillars upholding a single track forty feet above grade, from which would hang an "asymmetrically suspended type monorail" rolling on rubber wheels and powered by diesel engines.

Over fifty thousand people per day would use four trains from predawn to midnight, Bingham estimated, bringing in more than $3.7 million annually. Numerous stops suggested the vision had grown beyond that of a mere airport connection to become a true metropolitan light-rail transit system.

Bingham declared the project feasible and finished off his report with futuristic graphics inspired by the heady days of the Space Race.

But to hear doubters tell it, the whole notion might well have been phoned in from outer space. Led by monorail skeptic and Schiro rival Jimmy Fitzmorris, council members questioned the routes and predicted vociferous public dissent. Engineers challenged the design, and planners recoiled at the interjurisdictional complexity. The whole concept seemed a bit too ahead of its time—to which supporters responded, well, that was the point.

The monorail's Achilles' heel was its business plan. "Simple arithmetic" exposed the flaw, explained one *Times-Picayune* editorialist. "If one million Moisant Airport passengers . . . take one express trip each [year], the gross revenue . . . will amount to only $750,000, which will be less than the interest on [the] $16.5 million." Local ridership would hardly make up the difference. "Clearly, the promoters of the venture propose to use New Orleans as a showcase," wrote the editorialist, "from which to display their product . . . to sell it to other communities." If Monorail, Inc., went bankrupt, what then?

Many saw an imbroglio in the making, and Morrison seemed to admit as much when he diffidently sought public financing for the project, ratcheting up the risk to be borne by taxpayers. Nearly every city department hardened its opposition, and when the City Planning Commission cast a vote of no confidence, the monorail lost momentum.

On August 20, 1959, the City Council voted four-to-three to terminate the project. Fitzmorris performed the coup de grâce, writing with relish "that the aerial rail transportation system . . . is infeasible and contrary to the public interest."

After the monorail derailed, Morrison saw his local political fortunes wane in favor of national service. He went on to become a globe-trotting diplomat until his tragic death in a 1964 plane crash. Fitzmorris, meanwhile, would be frustrated in multiple runs for executive office, and ended up serving twice as lieutenant governor. Schiro succeeded in his quest to be mayor, and although he rode no monorail to his inauguration, he did install an old colleague as chair of the newly formed Regional Planning Commission: the same Thomas J. Lupo who lobbied for the monorail.

Paging through the 1959 study today, one feels a tinge of melancholy, in part for the dazzling dreams dashed, but more so because we now know the rest of the story. The completion of the interstate system, coupled with massive sub-urbanization and auto dependency, likely would have deprived the monorail of its ridership, while its bulky infrastructure might have blighted boulevards and exacerbated divestment. Houston, we now know, would pull far ahead of New Orleans, whose troubles would only multiply.

One might also surmise the monorail was never intended to be efficient mass transit. Rather, it was a speculative pipe dream by an out-of-state firm seeking to exploit New Orleans's pliable government and use the city as a test bed for an unproven technology. But others might offer a more generous assessment: that an initially impractical idea had morphed into a bold vision for a metro-wide light-rail system, which might have staved off later divestment and made New Orleans more of the modern metropolis visionaries had anticipated.

"Sooner or later," cautioned Mayor Morrison in his final arguments to keep the monorail alive, "we are going to have to provide the people of this city with some additional form of transportation. The time is now."

TUNNEL VISION
A Subterranean Relic beneath Canal Street

Under natural conditions, southern Louisiana's deltaic soils do not lend themselves to subterranean features like basements and tunnels. Abundant groundwater promptly inundates excavations, and organic matter makes the finely textured soils prone to slide laterally when a hole is dug. As a result, underground construction was rare in historic New Orleans.

This began to change in the 1900s, as drainage and pumping technology lowered the water table, and sheet piling and precasting of underground walls stabilized adjacent soils. Local architects began to design actual basements, and engineers started to build the area's first true tunnels—beneath the Intracoastal Waterway in Belle Chasse (1954), in Houma (1961), and under the Harvey Canal (1957).

There's another tunnel in town, and it's in an unexpected place: beneath Harrah's Casino in downtown New Orleans. It's closed off to the public today, but it was originally designed to usher six lanes of high-speed interstate traffic between all points east and the West Bank.

The little-known chamber is a relic of an era of transportation modernization advocated by Mayor deLesseps "Chep" Morrison after World War II. A progressive reformer with a global outlook, Morrison led efforts to improve air-travel connectivity, separate railroad and street crossings, streamline tricky intersections, and widen key arteries. Concurrently, the Louisiana Highway Department in 1946 hired the renowned New York planning czar Robert Moses to propose ways of better connecting New Orleans with the nation.

Moses's "Arterial Plan for New Orleans" advocated widening a number of boulevards, enabling the flow of east-west traffic, and building a Pontchartrain Expressway to access a projected Mississippi River bridge. Most significantly, Moses called for an elevated Waterfront Expressway connecting Elysian Fields Avenue with the West Bank via the French Quarter riverfront.

The plan was ahead of its time and funding. But with the launch of the national interstate system in the 1950s, two components of Moses's plan, the Pontchartrain Expressway and the Mississippi River Bridge (1958), came to fruition, and additional proposals were added by the early 1960s.

Planners by that time envisioned inbound traffic on a new highway from the east (future Interstate 10) to bifurcate at North Claiborne and Elysian Fields avenues. There, an elevated Claiborne Expressway would take motorists into the heart of the city and onward to Metairie, while a second elevated Riverfront Expressway (the new name for Moses's Waterfront Expressway) would take them down Elysian Fields, around the French Market, between the Mississippi and the French Quarter right by Jackson Square, and onto the bridge to the West Bank.

Both the Claiborne and the Riverfront expressways would connect with the extant Pontchartrain, forming a triangle. The plan gained traction, and in 1964 it officially became part of the nation's interstate highway strategy.

Resistance fomented immediately—but for only part of the project and from only part of the population. Preservationists and French Quarter residents recoiled at the idea of a noisy, smelly thruway severing the city's showcase neighborhood from its river. With their sizable civic clout, they launched an impassioned and well-organized effort to kill the Riverfront Expressway. Folks along North Claiborne Avenue, who were predominantly African American, brought to bear fewer resources and less political capital to have their say on the Claiborne Expressway slated for their backyard.

The Riverfront Expressway tunnel, a 700-foot-long box culvert intended to connect inter-state traffic from points east with the Mississippi River Bridge and the West Bank, is seen here under construction in 1966. It would become obsolete three years later, when the Riverfront Expressway was canceled. *Graphic by Richard Campanella.*

One day in 1966, workers started cutting down North Claiborne Avenue's famed live oaks to make way for the elevated highway. It barely got any coverage; all the attention went to the debate over the Riverfront Expressway, with preservationists opposing it bitterly, and business interests supporting it enthusiastically, in the name of progress and to keep downtown New Orleans relevant in this era of suburbanization.

Chief among the Riverfront Expressway advocates was City Hall, which, with one eye on the rise of Houston and another on the expansion of the petroleum industry, had embarked on three other massive downtown modernization projects: the building of an International Trade Mart, the widening of Poydras Street, and the construction of a sprawling Rivergate Exhibition Hall.

That's where the tunnel came in.

To evade the congestion of the Central Business District, engineers planned for the Riverfront Expressway to drop below grade between Canal and Poydras streets. That required a tunnel, and the construction of the Rivergate Exhibition Hall on that exact spot required that the two be built jointly, even though the expressway remained officially undecided.

So the city contributed 1.3 million taxpayer dollars to integrate the tunnel into the exhibition hall and construct both together. Ostensibly, building the tunnel prematurely would prevent having to tear up the area twice. But it's probably fair to say the city's ulterior motivation was to create a sense of momentum and inevitability for the Riverfront Expressway. Surely federal officials would be impressed to see a municipality so eager to modernize that it would get the federal roadway started on its own—and if it dispirited the opposition, all the better.

So tasked, architects at the Curtis and Davis firm designed a two-level basement beneath the Rivergate's main exhibition area, with the lower level for storage and the upper for mechanical equipment. Under the Rivergate's breezeway and concourse, the two basements would become one, forming a twenty-foot-high flat-ceiling "box culvert" with three lanes of traffic in each direction and a total combined width of ninety-eight feet.

Roughly seven hundred feet long and perfectly straight, the tunnel looked something like a gigantic men's tie box, built of steel and reinforced concrete and set into the soil between lower Canal and Poydras. Contractors began work in 1964; the International Trade Mart (today's World Trade Center) arose in 1965; the tunnel was completed in 1966; and the Rivergate Exhibition Hall opened in time for the city's 250th birthday in 1968.

One year later, New Orleanians received stunning news from Washington. Citing Section 106 of the National Historic Preservation Act, the U.S. Department of Transportation deemed the Riverfront Expressway would indeed do irreversible damage to the historic French Quarter—exactly as preservationists had argued— and canceled the project. The victory marked the first time citizens defeated an elevated federal waterfront expressway, the likes of which had disfigured so many other cities' downtowns.

By this time, the Claiborne Expressway was all but complete and ready for Interstate 10 traffic. And a perfectly useless interstate tunnel lay below the city's most valuable real estate. What to do with it? Creative citizens in 1969 suggested turning the tunnel into an 820-seat theater performance space. Others envisioned a science museum or "an international food, cultural and entertainment mart" with a high-rise residential complex above. One city official interviewed by the

Times-Picayune in 1987 joked the tunnel could be used for "growing mushrooms or for the world's biggest wine cellar"; others called for an "underground swimming hole[,] giant fish tank [or] tunnel of love."

Circumstances aboveground had changed by this time. The Louisiana Superdome (1975) and the Convention Center (1984) gave conference organizers new options for exhibition space, and both made the Rivergate seem small and outdated by contrast—despite its dazzling freeform Expressionist design, widely admired by architects. With the push to legalize land-based "gaming" in the early 1990s, casino interests entered the picture, and they cast their eyes on the Rivergate.

Despite vocal opposition, the Rivergate was demolished in early 1995 to make way for a sprawling new Harrah's Casino, whose riverside flank would overlay the old tunnel. Facilities Director Patrick Maher explained how engineers shored up the tunnel with new steel girders and columns and split it into two levels connected by ramps, while updating its pump and drainage system.

The Rivergate's old basements, meanwhile, were converted into a maze of offices and work spaces so labyrinthine that managers named hallways after French Quarter streets to aid navigation. (Maher's office is at "335 Royal.") Engineers also dug a new pedestrian tunnel beneath Poydras so patrons could move between Harrah's parking garage and its gambling facilities without having to cross a street.

After lengthy construction delays, the casino finally opened in late 1999. Today, pedestrians walking Convention Center Boulevard would have no way of knowing a half-century-old, city-owned interstate tunnel lies below Harrah's breezeway. A close look, however, betrays clues: slight but conspicuous swells in the asphalt of lower Canal and Poydras perforated by cracks in the pavement, each lining up precisely with the tunnel, the result of its uneven subsidence rates compared to surrounding soils.

A similar phenomenon happened at Louis Armstrong New Orleans International Airport, where a tunnel built in 1991 to connect Veterans Boulevard and Airline Drive, since abandoned, now bulges above the tarmac as adjacent soils have sunk faster than the concrete chamber—nature's way of telling us, perhaps, that these deltaic soils, despite modern technologies, still do not lend themselves to subterranean construction.

AUTHOR'S NOTE: *In late April 2016, two years after I wrote this column, a chunk of lower Canal Street asphalt collapsed into a deep pit, initially mystifying authorities. It soon became apparent that the so-called "Canal Sinkhole" occurred immediately* *adjacent to the fifty-year-old tunnel. While the concrete box-culvert itself was rock-solid, the particular section of Canal Street abutting it was insufficiently supported below and, coupled with the subsidence that created the above-mentioned cracks in the street surface, led to the failure. The "Canal Street Sinkhole" became a cause célèbre in the popular discourse, and even inspired a "Sinkhole de Mayo" street party on May 5, ostensibly to bring attention to the city's deteriorating infrastructure.*

THE WIDENING OF POYDRAS STREET

Few places in our city transformed so suddenly and dramatically as Poydras Street, and it all began fifty years ago. The artery entered the 1960s as a four-lane commercial corridor lined with nineteenth-century storehouses amid the occasional early twentieth-century bank or office. It ended the 1970s as a capacious corporate boulevard shadowed by Internationalist skyscrapers and anchored by two striking Modernist landmarks.

Many New Orleanians equate Poydras's redevelopment with the 1970s oil boom and the city's efforts to capture its share of Texas petroleum wealth. Indeed, much of the Poydras streetscape brings to mind the oil-industry headquarters in and around Houston's Main, Rusk, and Dallas streets, and part of the impetus for building the Louisiana Superdome was to answer Houston's Astrodome.

But the original motivation for Poydras's transformation was not as corporate showcase nor a home for Big Oil, but as a key link in a modernized transportation system. Calls for its widening date to 1927, when St. Louis–based design firm Bartholomew and Associates, consulting for the recently formed City Planning Commission, identified Poydras's "present width of 74' [as] hardly sufficient to meet the demands of trucking" and recommended broadening it to 100 feet along its downtown flank.

Bartholomew's emphasis on trucking indicated that Poydras Street, first laid out in 1788, had long been something of a blue-collar cousin to Canal Street. With its ample width, river access, and circumvention of both the high-density French Quarter and the residential faubourgs, Poydras attracted gritty port-city land uses such as wholesalers, shippers, warehousing, and light industry while repelling the sort of elegant retail trade that made Canal Street famous.

267

To be sure, Poydras had some retail, but hardly was it upscale. The Poydras Market, an open-stall emporium built in 1838, had developed a reputation for being, according to the *Daily Picayune* in 1858, "intolerably filthy" and "so crowded as to be almost impassable," leaving shoppers "disgusted at the uncleanliness." Positioned in Poydras's extra-wide neutral ground from Penn to South Rampart, the marketplace generated lots of foot traffic and helped make intersecting Dryades Street (originally called Phillippa, now O'Keefe) home to saloons and brothels.

All this made proletariat Poydras Street that much more déclassé, and when the municipal market system declined in the 1920s, planners declared the Poydras Market "no longer needed and . . . a serious traffic hazard." After the pavilion was cleared away in 1932, that part of Poydras benefited from widened lanes and ample parking, and it got planners thinking about the street's larger potential.

After World War II, the city embarked on an ambitious transportation improvement program. Consulting for state highway authorities in 1946, New York City planner Robert Moses devised an "Arterial Plan for New Orleans," which called for the streamlining of east-west traffic flow and the construction of a "Pontchartrain Expressway" to access a projected Mississippi River bridge. Moses also recommended connecting Elysian Fields Avenue with the bridge courtesy of a "Waterfront Expressway" fronting the French Quarter.

By the time the Pontchartrain Expressway and bridge opened in 1958, local planners had revised Moses's scheme to include an interstate coming in from the east to split at North Claiborne and Elysian Fields, at which point an elevated "Claiborne Expressway" would take motorists toward Metairie while a "Riverfront Expressway" (the new name for Moses's Waterfront Expressway) would take them down Elysian Fields, along the Mississippi, and over the bridge. That four-sided arterial plan positioned Poydras as a logical grade-level connector. "The widening of Poydras st.," one leader told the City Council in 1960, "is . . . vital to the successful operation of a proposed riverfront expressway, [and] will be a clear and specific demonstration to (federal officials) of city government's real interest in the expressway project."

What sealed the deal for Podyras's widening was a concurrent plan of equal grandiosity. With the city's 250th anniversary (1968) on the horizon and the rivalry with Houston intensifying, leaders sought to enlist New Orleans as a "World Trade Center," an imprimatur that called for member cities to build imposing complexes for global industries to convene and establish local offices. Everyone agreed that the best place for such a project was the city's front door, where Canal and Poydras met the Mississippi River.

Poydras Street is seen here (1973) running from lower left to upper right. Widened in 1965 with the intention of improving traffic flow, the broadened artery would instead serve to host corporate skyscrapers erected during the 1970s oil boom. In the foreground, the Louisiana Superdome is under construction. *Photograph from author's NOPSI/Entergy collection.*

So the city proceeded to acquire properties and, in 1965, completed the International Trade Mart (today's World Trade Center). Next came a lavish exhibition hall—but there was a problem. Federal approval of the Riverfront Expressway, which would pass right through the complex, was delayed on account of fierce resistance from preservationists for its impact on the historic French Quarter.

Because the city ardently desired the Riverfront Expressway to proceed, it paid to install a 700-foot tunnel beneath the exhibition hall and trade mart. Workers then set about erecting the hall above. The optimal way to access all these new improvements was to widen Poydras Street, thus giving, as one *Times-Picayune* reporter put it, "the somewhat bottled-up wholesale district an inlet and outlet."

In March 1964, voters passed a bond issue, and with a budget of $3.4 million, the Department of Streets got to work acquiring forty-seven properties fronting the lower side of Poydras from Penn to Delta (now Convention Center Boulevard)—just as Bartholomew had recommended back in 1927.

On November 23, 1964, Mayor Victor H. "Vic" Schiro swung a ceremonial "crash ball" into old buildings at Poydras and South Peters, officially kicking off the widening. The scene epitomized an era when large-scale demolition of historical structures was almost universally viewed as a sign of progress. But there were some voices of dissent. On a building marked DEMO in big red letters, one proto-urbanist scrawled, "Memo to Vic, One widened avenue makes two more necessary, increases traffic congestion and decreases the life of a city."

In another case, Poydras restaurateur Simon Landry, resigned to losing his property, devised a clever back-up plan. Landry also owned the adjacent edifice on Tchoupitoulas Street, and by moving his enterprise into that space, he thus retained its 401 Poydras address after the widening. That business was Mother's Restaurant, and that maneuver explains why the ever-popular diner today is "on" Poydras Street even though its structure faces Tchoupitoulas. Patrons queuing outside the Poydras door are actually standing in the space of Mother's original building, established in 1938 and razed in March 1965.

Ricca Demolishing Company used a bulldozer rather than a wrecking ball to gently push over old walls, so as to salvage architectural components and not threaten adjoining buildings. Some bricks were destined for an LSU fraternity house, while doors and window frames ended up in Ricca's salvage store. The corridor now cleared, the Sewerage and Water Board proceeded to install drainage while New Orleans Public Service, Inc., connected underground utilities. In November 1965, Boh Brothers began paving the street with concrete and asphalt, followed by sidewalk construction and landscaping.

After an August 16, 1966, dedication ceremony featuring a parade of antique cars, 132-foot-wide Poydras boasted six traffic lanes, two parking lanes, and a 16-foot-wide neutral ground—not for greenery but indentured turning lanes. Traffic, after all, drove the entire project.

During that same ceremony, however, the chairman of the Chamber of Commerce alluded to another emergent reason. "The land on either side of Poydras," he stated, "should be developed [as] a 'promenade,' as a favorite and . . . important site for buildings that need to be 'seen.'" That comment echoed a new conversation over the notion of "air rights." Just a few years earlier, builders of the Plaza Tower on Howard and Loyola (itself a midcentury widening project) designed a subterranean coupling system which allowed concrete pilings to be driven deeper into hardened suballuvial clays. Sturdier foundations enabled the erection of true skyscrapers upon New Orleans's soft alluvial soils (or, rather, below them), which thus converted downtown air space into potentially valuable real estate.

For a while, the expectation was that Loyola Avenue would become the city's new skyscraper boulevard. But after the 1967 decision to erect a world-class domed stadium—the stunning Louisiana Superdome—at one end of Poydras, followed by the 1968 opening of the Expressionist-style Rivergate Exhibition Hall at the river end, the momentum swung in favor of Poydras. This remained the case even after the U.S. Department of Transportation stunned the city in 1969 by canceling the Riverfront Expressway, concurring with preservationists that it would do irreversible damage to the French Quarter.

The reversal of fortune repurposed the already-widened Poydras Street as less of a traffic throughway (complete with an obsolete tunnel) and more of a corporate corridor, a character cinched with the 1972 opening of One Shell Square, the city's tallest building at 697 feet. In subsequent years, sixteen other high-rises arose along Poydras, more so than any other local street, most of them directly or indirectly fueled by the oil boom. Many downtown property owners eagerly cleared their parcels of old buildings to capitalize on the rising land values—for new skyscrapers, for parking lots, or sometimes simply to preempt a demolition moratorium sought by the growing preservationist movement.

The oil bust of the mid-1980s put an end to the Poydras boom, and during the bleak era that followed, New Orleans found itself with a surplus of downtown office space, a deficit of white-collar jobs, and a petrol industry regrouping in Houston. But when the downtown real estate market heated up again in the 2010s, construction resumed on Poydras, this time with hotels, residences, and restaurants, along with a larger number of smaller and more diversified tenants in its office buildings.

And unlike the days of the wholesale district, when 74-foot-wide Poydras ranked as Canal Street's blue-collar cousin, modern Poydras Street—all 132 feet of it—is now decidedly upscale.

NEW ORLEANS EAST'S CORE PROBLEM

Consider eastern New Orleans. Or is it New Orleans East? Or "The East"? Or Plum Orchard, Kenilworth, Eastover, and Versailles? The lack of an agreed-upon name is emblematic of the challenges faced by this vast section of Orleans Parish.

Residents express frustration that they must continually make an argument for their region's existence, let alone for political attention and private investment. Indeed, they struggle just to get on the map. Flung outwardly from the metropolitan heart like the feathers of a shuttlecock, eastern New Orleans often gets clipped from maps of the city proper, depriving it of cartographic attention—and everything that goes with it. That which literally lies on the margins often gets figuratively marginalized.

While its geographical position works against eastern New Orleans's argument, so does its internal geography. It lacks an identifiable core—no central plaza, no historic quarter, no walkable business or entertainment district, no famous landscaped park.

Neighborhoods, I've long held, are defined more by their cores than their peripheries. When you hear the words "Lower Garden District," for example, you probably think of its central focal point, Coliseum Square, before any secondary streets come to mind. Likewise, Jackson Square, Audubon Park, Harrison Avenue, and Oretha Castle Haley Boulevard mark the psychological nuclei or axes of the French Quarter, Uptown, Lakeview, and Central City and impart to those neighborhoods iconography and character.

Eastern New Orleans, on the other hand, comes across as an undifferentiated expanse of subdivisions sans a salient center. As a result, eastern New Orleans lacks a sense of place, and finds itself excluded from the popular perception of classic New Orleans.

It's a geographical problem with historical roots. Whereas historic New Orleans grew outwardly from an original core settlement starting in the 1700s, eastern New Orleans was the exact opposite: it grew inwardly from a peripheral framework of transportation arteries, mostly in the 1900s. Prior, this area comprised two vast basins: Bayou Bienvenue on the south side, and, on the north, an expanse of shrubby marshes (the French called them Petit Bois, or Little Woods) extending to the shores of brackish Lake Pontchartrain. Separating the two basins was a narrow topographic ridge formed by a former channel of the Mississippi River and later by its Bayou Metairie/Bayou Gentilly/Bayou Sauvage distributary.

Historically, this high ground (today's Old Gentilly Road and Chef Menteur Highway) represented the only terrestrial access to the interior. All other ingress and egress required a boat traversing lakes Pontchartrain and St. Catherine, through the Rigolets and Chef Menteur passes, or up Bayou Bienvenue. Thus, most of the swampy, marshy interior of present-day eastern New Orleans remained wild into the late 1800s.

Railroads began to change this in the 1870s, when tracks were laid for the Louisville and Nashville Railroad along the shoulder of the topographic ridge to connect New Orleans with Biloxi and Mobile. In the 1880s, another line was laid for the New Orleans and North Eastern Railroad along the lakeshore to connect with Slidell. For the first time, New Orleanians could now conveniently access the eastern marshes. Tiny communities formed along the tracks, joining the truck farms and dairies that had long lined Old Gentilly Road.

Access brought to light the area's economic potential, which motivated the city to install drainage canals and pumps. By the 1910s, the former marsh and swamp became "reclaimed." Investors followed suit, chief among them the New Orleans Lake Shore Land Company, whose president, cotton merchant Frank B. Hayne, came to own seventy-five hundred acres of the now-drained basin. He proceeded to sell hundreds of five-acre tracts, not for residential development but for citrus groves. Americans by this time had developed a taste for tropical fruits, and Louisiana oranges grown in eastern New Orleans could be readily shipped to regional markets via rail and ship lines. Shell roads were established across the drained basin in the form of a superblock grid that would be recognizable to motorists today. Mature orange trees were sent in from Florida and planted, and thousands of acres of orange groves arose.

The company's plans for industrial-scale orange production were frustrated by bad weather, blight, and world war. What remained by the 1940s were scores of smaller individual orchards and truck farms supplying municipal markets via, on the south, the recently paved State Highway 90, which passed through enclaves named Lee, Micheaud (Michoud), and Chef Menteur (near Fort Macomb), and on the north, by a lakeshore boulevard named after Hayne, which paralleled the tracks to Slidell. A ride on that railroad would have taken passengers past tiny hamlets named Seabrook, Citrus, Edge Lake, Little Woods, and, the farthest out, South Point.

Residents of these coastal outposts lived in raised wooden camps and tended to groves and gardens, fished and hunted, or maintained the railroad and tended the locomotives. Many middle-class New Orleanians owned camps built on the lake, and something of a weekend recreational economy, complete with bathing facilities and hotels, developed here and elsewhere in eastern New Orleans.

By this time, another peripheral transportation artery came into the picture, and it was a big one: the Inner Harbor Navigation Canal, which had been excavated during 1918–23 to connect the Mississippi River with Lake Pontchartrain. A boon to barge traffic, the waterway created so many jobs along Downman Road

273

Paris Road in eastern New Orleans, a "suburb within the city" that comprised swamp and marsh until the 1910s, citrus orchards for the next few decades, and subdivision construction starting in the late 1960s. *Photograph by Richard Campanella.*

and elsewhere that it became known colloquially as the Industrial Canal. But the waterway also severed the east from the heart of the metropolis, while introducing saltwater into the city even as soils began to subside below sea level because of drainage.

Then, during World War II, the Intracoastal Waterway was dug along the area's southern tier, essentially rendering eastern New Orleans an island. By midcentury, the area was ringed with railroads, roads, and canals, each lined with limited industrial or residential development. But it was still largely undeveloped at its core.

The eastern New Orleans we know today is largely a product of five events of the late 1960s: Hurricane Betsy, which flooded parts of the area but also served as an impetus to erect hurricane-protection levees; NASA's Michoud Assembly Plant, which brought hundreds of well-paying jobs to the area; the movement of the white middle class out of the central city; the Mississippi River–Gulf Outlet Canal, which brought oceangoing ships into the area even as it accelerated coastal erosion; and, last but not least, Interstate 10, which, for the first time, brought accessibility to the core of eastern New Orleans.

Each of these transformations, particularly I-10, instigated waves of housing development, and by the 1970s, subdivisions with names like Plum Orchard, Kenilworth, and Versailles were built where stood citrus groves fifty years earlier, and wilderness a century prior. Development would have extended farther eastward—ramps had been built on I-10 to anticipate it—had not the petroleum market crashed in the early 1980s. Lands belonging to New Orleans East Inc., which had been poised to urbanize over twenty thousand acres of wetlands in far eastern Orleans Parish, instead became Bayou Sauvage National Wildlife Refuge. As part of its ambitious project, the company erected along I-10 a massive concrete sign emblazoned with NEW ORLEANS EAST, branding the area with that corporate moniker despite its demise. The name stuck.

At first, New Orleans East drew mostly white middle-class populations fleeing the inner city for what was billed as a "suburb within the city." But when African Americans gained political power in City Hall in the late 1970s, many of those white families departed New Orleans altogether and resettled in adjacent parishes. In their stead came black families, among them substantial numbers of the upwardly mobile middle and upper classes, who later bought into posh subdivisions such as Eastover. Vietnamese refugees, meanwhile, settled in the Versailles area starting in 1975 and, their numbers later supplemented by immigrants, have since prospered and bought into surrounding subdivisions. Multifamily housing and Section 8 vouchers, meanwhile, brought in large numbers of working-class and poor households, and with them came the social problems affiliated with poverty.

By century's end, geophysical problems increasingly came to light. Surrounded by saltwater, bowl-shaped in its elevation, detached from the metropolitan core, adjacent to eroded marshes and ungated surge-prone canals, and ill protected by what proved to be flimsy levees, New Orleans East lay both physically and socially vulnerable to catastrophe. It suffered terribly when Hurricane Katrina struck in 2005, and, to add insult to injury, saw relatively little media and volunteer attention as it struggled to recover, in large part for its lack of a compelling historical narrative and picturesque cityscape.

How might New Orleans East address its geography problem? One obvious suggestion would be to establish some sort of iconic core—a walkable mixed-use district with a distinctive architectural profile, where it's great to work, shop, recreate, and live. But forcing an urban form on a suburban space may be exactly that—forced—and we are all too familiar with the propensity of such grand plans to collapse under their own weight.

Instead, I might suggest we simply accept that New Orleans East is fundamentally nonnucleated, and build upon its historical-geographical strength: peripheral assets. New Orleans East's gorgeous lakeshore and eastern wetlands are among the most underutilized natural resources in the region. The picturesque hamlets and fishing camps that once lined Hayne Boulevard, the citrus groves, bathhouses, and recreational parks such as Lincoln Beach (an integral memory of thousands of African Americans during the last years of segregation) lie unmarked and unremembered today, yet have great potential.

Along its western and southern flanks, New Orleans East boasts the city's premier inventory of industrial sites, all accessible by interstate, rail, and canal. Chief among them is Michoud, which has unmatched opportunities for everything from building fuel tanks to developing drones to making movies. New Orleans East could also improve its interior infrastructure by beautifying below-grade outfall canals with trees and landscaping, as recommended by experts involved in architect David Waggonner's "Dutch Dialogues" project. The region's open drainage system, with its runoff-storing lakes and lakefront pumps, is the envy of other parts of the city, and may be aestheticized into something truly distinctive.

Yes, these are costly undertakings. But they are also scalable, and may be pursued incrementally with minimal disruption to everyday life. Tens of thousands of full-canopy shade trees, meanwhile, would do wonders in giving sun-drenched streets an appealing garden-suburb character.

And that is what New Orleans East needs most—a distinctive character, a sense of place, an embrace of what it is—and an acceptance of what it is not.

REGIONAL GEOGRAPHIES

FOUR CADASTRAL FINGERPRINTS ON THE LOUISIANA LANDSCAPE

Louisianans love to argue how their state deviates from the national norm, and usually invoke gastronomy, musicality, linguistics, or civic fête as evidence. In the years following the Louisiana Purchase, nobody needed to evidence that argument; distinctions were pervasive and profound. Creoles and Americans did just about everything differently, from language and religion to law, architecture, servitude, urban design, even cemeteries.

Another difference that affects the Louisiana landscape to this day involved the seemingly arcane concept of a cadastral system.

The term comes from the Latin *capitastrum*, meaning a register or ledger. A cadastral system is a method of surveying land into parcels (cadasters) and officially recording their locations, dimensions, and ownership.

They sound quotidian, but cadastral systems are important in ways that cannot be overstated. In a free-market economy such as ours, in which agency is availed to the individual, privately owned land is the provenance of wealth, undergirding all subsequent financial commitments and constituting the original valuation to which all future value is added. (Marxism, on the other hand, views labor as the source of wealth and, bent on holding land collectively, impugns the very notion of cadastral systems.)

Cadastral systems, and the gravitas with which they are maintained, thus become critical to the chain of financial agreements and investments that follow. In a system where wealth begets wealth, the begetting begins with land—and all subsequent begetting needs to see the *capitastrum* confirming the particulars.

When Western powers claimed the Americas, they understood that land conceded to private entities would quite literally lay the groundwork for wealth production. They proceeded to survey cadasters over lands previously occupied by indigenous societies with no such concept. What followed was the largest land transfer the world has ever known, and it would create tragic injustices for some while imparting key advantages to others.

Just as English, French, Spanish, and American societies practiced different philosophies of law and government, each also "did" cadastral systems its own way. English settlers brought over their metes-and-bounds method, which documented parcels by the streams, ridges, boulders, trees, or roads which met ("mete") to form the property's boundaries ("bounds"). Metes-and-bounds

This oblique image of the False River area near New Roads and St. Francisville shows the French long-lot surveying system at left, the American township-and-range grid at lower right, and the irregular English metes-and-bounds system at upper right. *Image courtesy Google Earth.*

worked fine at first—until, rather inexorably, streams would migrate, boulders would roll, and trees would die. The result: feuds, lawsuits, and an obstacle in the land-ownership/wealth-creation cycle.

The French, who mostly colonized riverine environments, subdivided land into "long lots" with narrow frontages along the waterway and an elongated slice of the fertile land behind it. This arrangement aided transportation and irrigation as well as animal-drawn field work, in that it minimized the number of turns.

Spanish authorities, with their focus on ranching over cropping, had little need for elongated riparian lots or irregular family farms, so they created expansive *sitios* or *ranchos* (estates) instead.

The Americans, namely Thomas Jefferson, developed something entirely different, and it would be revolutionary. Known today as the Public Land Survey (PLS) or "township-and-range," their system was based not on curvaceous or ephemeral landscape features but on a theoretical grid of cells with unique labels set within a baseline and principal meridian (X and Y axis). Township-and-range's spatial rigidity, plus the fact that it usually preceded rather than followed initial settlement, turned land into a rock-solid foundation for wealth production—at least for those who could lay their hands on it.

It took a while for the French to establish a stable cadastral system in Louisiana, given the colony's weak and distant authority. Instead, vast concessions were made liberally, and too often they were used merely for timber extraction rather than agricultural development. Displeased, the Crown issued an edict in 1716 which provided for land redistribution "in the proportion of two to four *arpents* front by forty to sixty in depth." An *arpent* was the equivalent of an English acre, measuring 192 feet, and the surveyor who laid them out was the *arpenteur*.

Viewed cartographically, the French long-lot (or arpent) system traced a splendid serpentine effect, with parcels converging in concave river bends and diverging on convex sides. Viewed economically, the system made hydrological and geophysical sense and benefited from careful administration. By the 1750s, riparian lands throughout lower Louisiana had the French cadastral imprint.

But by this time, war raged between England and France. Sensing impending defeat, the French ceded all its territories west of the Mississippi plus New Orleans to the Spanish, to keep them out of the hands of the hated English—who got everything else.

Now Spain and England would inscribe their cadasters into the Louisiana landscape.

Spanish authorities, not wanting to rile disgruntled French Creoles and realizing this environment was better suited for agriculture than livestock, respected extant cadasters and allowed French long lots to continue. However, in the Mexican territory near the prairies of southwestern Louisiana, livestock took priority, and Spanish officials laid out cattle-friendly sitios measured by units such as *varas* (rods) and *ligas* (leagues). To this day, southwestern Louisiana is cowboy country, and it exudes a Texan air.

As for the English, their slice of Louisiana was called British West Florida, and to its lands Anglo settlers brought the same metes-and-bounds system of the Eastern Seaboard. With Britain's defeat in the American Revolution, this area became Spanish West Florida—but once again, the Spanish here decided to recognize extant English cadasters.

The new century brought stunning new developments for Louisiana. The English by this time were long gone, though their metes-and-bounds remained in the Feliciana parishes. The Spanish had retroceded their part of Louisiana to the French in 1800, but left behind their sitios in the southwest. The French then sold the colony to the United States, but left their arpents along Louisiana's rivers and bayous. That left millions of other arpents—or rather, acres—for the Americans' township-and-range. They began in 1807, when surveyors extended westward the Thirty-first Parallel (the northern boundary of old Spanish and British West Florida and the "top" of the Florida Panhandle today) to form the baseline. For the principal meridian, 92° 24′ 55″ West longitude was selected because it ran through the middle of the Territory of Orleans. Thus formed the X-Y axis for the townships, ranges, and sections needed to parcel out Louisiana lands west of the Mississippi River. For lands to the east, the circa-1803 Washington Meridian was extended southward (in 1819) along longitude 91° 09′ 36″ to form a secondary Y-axis, called the St. Helena Meridian. The stage was now set to superimpose American order over colonial chaos.

Alas, the Creoles would hear none of it, and the Americans, like the Spanish, wisely did not press the issue. Why make unnecessary trouble? Cadastral systems, after all, have deep cultural resonance, and because of their foundational capacity to generate wealth, it takes little short of a radical revolution to eradicate them.

So instead, Congress passed an act in 1807 confirming most colonial-era land holdings, and a second act in 1811 authorizing surveyors to continue laying out long lots in areas of colonial settlement. Township-and-range would fill in everywhere else.

What resulted was a cadastral map that looks a bit like liquid spilled on graph paper, with the old French system splaying out along finger-like rivers and bayous and the rigid American grid filling in between. And if you peer closer, you can still see old English metes-and-bounds in West Feliciana Parish and relics of old Spanish sitios by Texas.

Louisiana is distinct among the fifty states in that it retains the cadastral imprints of all four powers of the North American stage: French (including French Canadian), Spanish, English, and American. Just as we have a uniquely mixed legal jurisdiction of Roman civil law and English common law, we also have a one-of-a-kind cadastral amalgamation, and it influences literally every space we traverse every day.

So next time you debate Louisiana's distinctiveness, set aside the standard food-and-music arguments and explain instead the state's cadastral story. Better yet, invite people to get a window seat on their next flight and gaze at the landscape below. They'll see patterns in Louisiana unlike any other in the United States.

THE OZONE BELT

New Orleanians today generally think of St. Tammany Parish as the Northshore. Before the Lake Pontchartrain Causeway opened in 1956, city dwellers called it "across the lake." Others described all of Louisiana between the Pearl and Mississippi rivers as "the Florida Parishes," a term traceable to 1763–1810, when these lands pertained to British West Florida, Spanish West Florida, and briefly the West Florida Republic. But throughout the late nineteenth and twentieth centuries, St. Tammany and adjacent parishes were known far and wide by one curious nickname: "the Ozone Belt."

The term reflected an era in medical history, before germ theory, when humans sought explanations for maladies and their remedies in things that they could physically perceive. New Orleans, "the necropolis of the South," with annual death rates ranging from 4 to 7 percent or higher, provided all too many opportunities for both lay people and professionals to speculate why so many suffered.

The main suspect was the backswamp, the alleged source of "miasmas," or noxious vapors, thought to cause yellow fever and other diseases. Remarked one anonymous writer in 1850 on New Orleans's swamplands, "this boiling fountain of death is one of the most dismal, low and horrid places on which the light of the sun ever shone[,] belching up its poison and malaria . . . under the influence of a tropical heat." (The word *malaria,* Italian for "bad air," indicted the marshes for Rome's constant plagues.)

In our ancestors' mental map, the New Orleans backswamp—virtually all the lowlands between the city and the lake—was one big geographical health risk. Its polar opposite was the gently undulating piney woods across breezy Lake Pontchartrain and along the Mississippi Gulf Coast, which were thought to be refuges from malady and havens of remedy.

To bucolic places like Mandeville, Bay St. Louis, and Pass Christian escaped wealthier New Orleanians by the thousands every August and September, and those towns eagerly erected cottages, hotels, and fancy resorts to lodge them.

One particular piney-woods town had another attribute to offer: artesian spring water, a healthy alternative to the filthy river water or rain-filled cisterns of New Orleans. In the early 1850s, two New Orleans investors, Joseph Bossier and William Christy, acquired land by the springs, built cottages, and established an omnibus line to connect with steamers and trains to New Orleans. A *Picayune* journalist who visited "Christy Springs" in 1855 raved not only of "the sparkling liquid that gushes from springs" but also "the bracing air, impregnated with the odor of the pine" and recommended both for "the healthy as well as the invalid."

It is unclear whether Bossier and Christy specifically coined "Ozone Belt" or if the term arose from the vernacular. What is clear is that, by the late 1800s, that nickname was widely used regionally and even nationally to mean today's Northshore, and among its most enthusiastic promoters were hoteliers, real estate developers, and railroad agents. Covington and Abita Springs formed the heart of the Ozone Belt, but advocates of Hammond, Franklinton, Pearl River, and southern Mississippi did not hesitate to include themselves in this salubrious space.

Why ozone? People thought pine trees charged the atmosphere with balsam, a fragrant resin in woody vegetation often used as medicine (hence "balm"). They also sensed that electricity in the atmosphere, as a 1900 *Picayune* article put it, had "intense powers of oxidizing and decomposing organic substances, and purify the air by destroying malignant microscopic organisms." What resulted, they thought, was ozone—cathartic fresh air. St. Tammany had extensive pine forests, artesian springs, the breezy lake, clean rivers, and its fair share of lightning storms. The euphonic word "ozone" worked well in capturing their wholesome interactions—and a brand was born.

Seeking purity each summer, upper-class New Orleanians boarded steamers and trains bound for places like Covington's Claiborne Hotel, the physician-owned Ozonia Rest Cure Inn, or the Southern Hotel, built in 1907 and reopened in 2012. Those seeking remedy for "consumption" convalesced at the Louisiana Tuberculosis Sanitarium. Slidell had Sabrier's Resort right by the railroad station, while the Oaklawn Inn, "A Piney Woods Resort without a Peer," positioned itself along the New Orleans Great Northern Railroad near Lacombe.

As for Christy Springs, it was renamed Abita Springs, and its hospitality business boomed at places like the Ozone Belt Hotel and cottages built within a forest of towering pines. The town's mayor, who had migrated to the region for its healthful properties, was also its premier doctor, president of the town's Board of Health, and owner of its main pharmacy. To the north, Franklinton tapped into its artesian wells and hoped to duplicate Abita Springs's success. To the east, Pearl River aimed to sell both its clean water and air with its Ozone Springs Hotel. At the same time, the Florida parishes were also developing a timber industry—so much so that proto-environmentalists worried, as a 1906 *Picayune* article

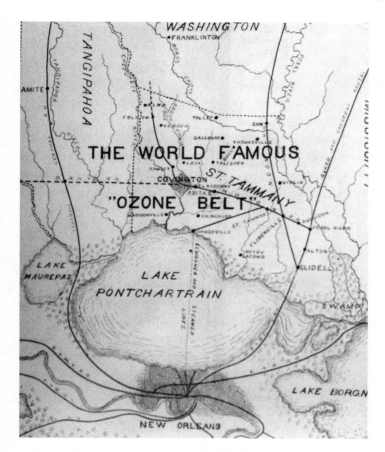

Louisiana eco-tourism, circa-1900 style. *From "The World Famous Ozone Belt," by J. I. and W. Sanford, ca. 1905.*

expressed, whether the "splendidly healthful localities [of] the 'ozone' belt of St. Tammany . . . may lose [their] health-restoring properties if the trees are cut away."

We now know our ancestors were entirely wrong about ozone. In fact, it's dangerous to humans, and, ironically, a pollutant of forests. But they were not entirely wrong about the geo-medical dots they connected. It was not the wetlands and cistern water that killed New Orleanians; it was virus-infected mosquitoes. But those vectors found ideal habitats in the marshes and cisterns, and they conveniently obtained their blood meals from human hosts living adjacently in high density. *Aedes aegypti*, the yellow fever mosquito, had a particular penchant for urban habitats, and to this day, this species is more likely to be found in the inner core of New Orleans than the suburban or rural periphery.

The undulating pine savannas of low-density St. Tammany Parish, on the other hand, had few of these conditions. Its water was purer because there were fewer people to pollute it, and because some of it flowed from artesian wells unavailable in deltaic New Orleans.

And while electricity in the air had nothing to do with malignant microbes, lightning strikes are quite frequent in St. Tammany, because continental cold fronts arrive there without encountering the stabilizing effects of Lake Pontchartrain's warm waters. Sharper temperature clashes produce intense storms and lighting strikes, not to mention occasional tornados. The "lake effect" also explains why the Northshore's temperatures drop lower at night and are the first to freeze each winter—which also cuts down on mosquito populations.

So while our ancestors' medical understanding was way off, their geographical reasoning was not. "A remarkable fact about [Covington]," wrote the *Chicago Clinic and Pure Water Journal* in 1903, is "that when New Orleans . . . quarantines against yellow fever, this locality is never quarantined and the village council invites the refugees from all over the South to come to its healthful climate . . . in the 'Ozone Belt.'" In the parlance of modern bioscience, St. Tammany's environment offered "ecological services," and cities like Covington, Abita Springs, and Mandeville succeeded in turning them into dollars without depleting the resource.

In time, medical advances, the discovery of the yellow-fever virus, and improved municipal services in New Orleans would undermine the rationale for St. Tammany's health-tourism industry. Summertime in the city was no longer dangerous. Highways and later airplanes allowed New Orleanians to vacation farther away and for different reasons. The resorts closed, and the summer cottages became full-time homes.

Yet the myth of the Ozone Belt endured, and it continued to attract medical refugees. Among them was famed writer Walker Percy, who as fellow southern writer Shelby Foote explained in a book by David Horace Harwell, "was allergic to everything on earth," and moved to "healthy" Covington in the "Ozone Belt . . . because of its numerous longleaf pines." Added Foote, "Now we know that ozone is the deadliest thing in the world, so they don't advertise themselves as the Ozone Belt anymore."

Residents continued using the old brand into the late twentieth century. "Tired of pollution?" asked a 1987 classified ad for an Abita Springs property.

"Breathe in the clean air of the ozone belt." But usage has dropped off dramatically in recent decades, likely for two reasons. One was news of a hole in the earth's atmospheric ozone layer, an environmental problem that came to light in the 1980s and became an issue in the 1992 U.S. presidential election. "Ozone" took on an alarming tone, and "ozone belt" sounded more like a warning than a boast. The other factor was suburbanization. As journalist and author Ron Thibodeaux explained in an email, "'Ozone Belt' faded from usage as St. Tammany transitioned from small towns and piney woods to the final suburban frontier of Greater New Orleans. We moved there in 1990, just as that dynamic was gaining momentum, and I only heard the term come up in casual conversation a handful of times in all those years, always from seasoned natives."

A century ago, we disdained wetlands and valued ozone. Now we value wetlands and disdain ozone. And while some folks still say "the Florida parishes" and others continue to think of St. Tammany as being "across the lake," just about everyone else calls it the Northshore—including the Northshore.

As for the Ozone Belt, Thibodeaux said, "it's a term that might best be described today as archaic, if not obscure." Today, we find only a few usages remaining in the landscape: the name of a car wash, a stump-grinding business, a road, a sports field and a few others, most of them in Covington—the "heart," a hundred years ago, of the Ozone Belt.

COASTAL LOUISIANA LUGGER CULTURE

Tourists a century ago admired many of the same features of the New Orleans cityscape enjoyed by visitors today. Some elements, like the French Quarter and the cemeteries, have remained largely intact, while others have transformed markedly, such as the port and the French Market. Still others have disappeared entirely, among them the ubiquitous luggers that once sailed the littoral margins of the deltaic metropolis.

Luggers were small, round-hulled wooden sloops built by hand and used regionally to transport the coastal abundance to the urban marketplace. Their most distinctive characteristic was their "lug rigs," colorful canvas sails mounted on sharply angled spars tethered to a single mast, which gave the vessels phenom-

"Lugger Landing," on the riverfront by the French Market, a key node in the region's vital oyster trade. *Photograph courtesy Library of Congress.*

enal maneuverability—and, to the eyes of visitors, a jaunty and picturesque Old World charm.

One might think the vessel's name comes from their lugging of heavy cargo, but more likely it derived from the old nautical term for its specialized sail, else the Dutch word "logger," meaning trawling. There may also be a French etymology.

Because oysters constituted their principal cargo, the boats were commonly called oyster luggers, and their leatherneck crews formed a sort of coastal-urban subculture. Up to two hundred luggers plied regional waters in the early 1800s, each with crews of three to six men, and the total fleet grew substantially by the early 1900s.

Luggers circulated daily from mid-September through late April from across eighty thousand acres of both natural and cultivated oyster reefs in St. Bernard, Plaquemines, and Lafourche parishes. When the bivalves were not in season, luggers hauled fish, game, citrus, Creole tomatoes, truck-farm produce—whatever sold.

Where did the lugger come from? Researchers debate the extent to which folk boating designs, much like vernacular architecture, may be traced to external influences versus local invention. The original idea might have arrived courtesy of immigration or interaction with native peoples, which individuals then adapted to local conditions as resources and technology permitted.

Some claim the lugger design came to Louisiana from France, the British Isles, or the Low Countries. Others point to Mediterranean and Adriatic influences arriving with Sicilian, Croatian, Greek, and Spanish immigrants, all of whom predominated in the Louisiana fishing industry.

Perhaps a clue can be gleaned from New Orleans's sister city of the West, San Francisco, which also boasted a fleet of lugsail-like fishing vessels, called feluccas. Introduced by Italian fishermen, feluccas shared San Francisco Bay with a comparable lugsail watercraft from yet another distant region, the famous junks brought in by Chinese immigrants from Hong Kong's Victoria Harbor.

One traveler, Catharine Cole, used both "lugger" and "felucca" to describe what she saw along the New Orleans riverfront during her visit in the 1890s. "Just below Canal Street," Cole wrote, "there is a wharf known as lugger landing, [where] you may see the red-sailed, felucca-like boats from the Barataria, and some day even buy redfish, or shrimp, or white pelican . . . from the olive-skinned captain."

A second Lugger Landing at the foot of Ursuline Street specialized in the oyster trade, due to its proximity to the French Market. Also known as Picayune Tier, the landing featured a wooden platform hinged to the wharf such that it floated up and down with the river stage. Luggers would dock perpendicularly to the planked tier and lay down gangplanks for a team of unloaders to carry the sacks to a wooden pavilion.

It might have all looked scenic and charming to outside eyes, but to insiders, this was business. There was money to be made, and interests to be defended. Who got to unload the luggers presented one point of contention. Members of the Oyster Discharging Association, a union described in an 1894 *Picayune* article as comprising "Turks, Russians, Austrians, Italians, and other nationalities, some . . . engaged in the unloading of oysters since 1860," guarded their jobs from off-duty banana unloaders eager for addition work. ("Austrians" connoted Croatians from the Dalmatian Coast, which at the time was part of the Austro-Hungarian Empire.)

Once the harvest was laid out in the pavilion, authorities from the Louisiana Oyster Commission would inspect the oysters for infection and collect taxes due to the state—two additional flashpoints for oystermen, who found themselves at legal loggerheads with regulators constantly in this era.

Yet another controversy involved lugger routes. While lower-coast oysters arrived on the Mississippi, those harvested in the Lake Pontchartrain basin came up either Bayou St. John and the connecting Old Basin Canal in the Fifth Ward, or through the New Basin Canal at the edge of the Third Ward. Those rival waterways, the former private and the latter state-owned, battled each other in court for years for the right to be the sole lake-oyster port.

Acrimony and litigation also flew among oyster harvesters, luggermen, wholesalers, retailers, restaurateurs, and shuckers, each group suspecting one of the others of taking home more than its fair share of the profit, or gaining an unfair advantage from the state.

After disputes were negotiated and the bureaucracy completed, the oysters were iced and sold to wholesalers at $1.25 to $3.00 per barrel. Some were loaded on wagons destined for local markets; others went by rail car to regional buyers. The best catch went directly to the city's storied restaurants and saloons, where they commanded upwards of $4.00 per barrel. "Counter oysters," eaten raw at the bar, topped the list, and tended to come from the saltier waters of Bayou Cook on the west bank of Plaquemines Parish, as well as Barataria Bay and Grand Isle. Lower-quality "cooking oysters," which went straight into the fryer, usually came from the lower-salinity interior waters farther from the Gulf. Competition ensued even at the consumption end of the trade. "The Acme and the Gem, two rival saloons," reported the *Picayune*, "entered into a brisk competition" in the late 1870s, "bringing prices down from 30 to 20 cents per dozen. All the rest of the dealers were compelled to follow suit."

Like today, New Orleanians craved oysters particularly on Christmas Day, most popularly in the form of oyster dressing. In 1915, despite the harrowing hurricane a few months earlier, fifteen vessels deposited at Lugger Landing a record 2,010 barrels of choice counter oysters on Christmas Eve morning.

After the luggermen sold their catch to the wholesalers, they restocked their vessels with supplies needed back in the country and prepared for the long trip home. While reloading, the luggermen would, according to one 1904 account, "loiter idly about, smoking cigarettes or cooking their meals over queer little charcoal furnaces. The [Tier] is a picturesque sight." In fact, the lugger trade was anything but an idling affair. Time was of the essence, and any innovation that sped delivery or maximized profit was adopted without sentimentality.

Three factors ended the lugsail era: the advent of commercially available boat motors starting in the 1910s; the expansion of the riverfront Public Belt Railroad, which needed the lugger landings' dock space; and the mounting popularity of gas-powered trucks, which could deliver delicate delectables to market faster, better, and cheaper. When fitted with refrigeration, truck transportation cut out multiple middlemen, and among them were the luggermen and their loaders.

Picayune Tier became obsolete, the Oyster Discharging Association folded, the Old Basin Canal (now the Lafitte Corridor) was filled in by 1930, and the last stretch of the New Basin Canal was eradicated by 1950 (now a stretch of I-10 and West End Boulevard). Yet despite seemingly endless ecological and economic crises, the regional oyster industry thrives today, though no longer must it contend with sailing its antique wooden sloops onto Lugger Landing.

Modern oyster vessels in Louisiana are still called luggers, and some of them date from the early 1900s, but few if any have sails, much less lugsails. Wrote the *Picayune* in 1925, "The Chinese junk, the Italian felucca, the British barkentine, the American clipper ship or our own Barataria lugger are equally things of loveliness afloat. But . . . they are doomed [by] the chug-chug of the motorboat . . . driving them steadily and surely from the seas."

COUNTIES, PARISHES, AND A LOUISIANA MYSTERY

That Louisiana has parishes and not counties stands as a mark of the state's cultural distinction, one that Americans elsewhere learn in grade-school geography class or courtesy of a polite but firm correction from a proud Louisianan. So embedded is "parish" in the state's spatial parlance that merely saying "counties" and "Louisiana" in the same sentence sounds dissonant, like off-key music.

In fact, for the first forty years of American dominion, the two terms coexisted as separate geographies serving different purposes. The eventual adoption of "parish" may be viewed as a victory of localism over national assimilation, but in truth politics and pragmatism played key roles. There's also something of a mystery here.

In colonial times, French and Spanish authorities felt no pressing need to break their claim into official sub-jurisdictions with rigid borders. Settlers were too few, and the terrain too vast and swampy, to necessitate precise delineation, and because colonials answered to a king, there was no need to draw up firm electoral districts or voting precincts. Instead, people regionalized the colony based loosely on settlement cores and peripheries and the waterways among them. From east to west, beyond present-day Louisiana state borders there was La Mobile, Biloxi, le Détour aux Anglois (English Turn), and Nouvelle Orléans. Continuing upriver, "Chapitoulas" implied the area by today's Jefferson/Orleans parish line; Cannes Brulee was Kenner; La Côte des Allemands was the name given to the German settlements across the river, Manchac was just south of present-day Baton Rouge, and Pointe Coupée covered the confluence of the Mississippi and Red rivers, which led respectively to the Natchez and Natchitoches regions. (Orthography, it should be noted, was as fluid as the geography.) Barataria, Lafourche, Attakapas, and Opelousas referred broadly to the coastal marshes heading westward toward Spanish Mexico, whose border with French Louisiana was so vague that both empires tacitly viewed the area (Los Adaes) as "neutral ground." Throughout Louisiana, there simply weren't enough settlers nor hands-on government to call for hardened jurisdictional boundaries through unchartered swamps and piney woods.

The Catholic Church had different spatial exigencies, as it tended to its flock on a regular and more intimate basis. Houses of worship had to be built; masses were celebrated weekly if not daily; and there were sacraments to administer, children to educate, tithings to collect, and cemeteries to maintain. These services required a more congealed sense of community geography, although here too, ecclesiastic borders tended to be loosely drawn around churches. In French, these units were called *paroisses*, in Spanish *parroquias*, and in English *parishes*, and there were twenty-one of them throughout Louisiana by late colonial times. Because Catholicism predominated among the populace, parishes gained credibility and expediency as a way to organize Louisiana human geography—something that would eventually prove useful to government.

After the Louisiana Purchase, representatives of the United States installed a governing apparatus they had honed elsewhere, and jurisdictional divisions topped the list. In a section titled "Counties," the Legislative Council in 1805 broke the Territory of Orleans "into twelve counties, to be called the counties of Orleans, German Coast, Acadia, Lafourche, Iberville, Pointe Coupée, Attakapas, Opelousas, Natchitoches, Rapides, Ouchitta and Concordia," and stipulated that many boundaries would follow the ecclesiastic "parishes of St. Charles . . . the parishes of St. Bernard and St. Louis [present-day St. Louis Cathedral,] . . . the parishes of St. Charles and St. John," etc. The resulting twelve counties thus reflected Catholic parish lines or aggregations thereof, as well as colonial-era settlement concentrations. They also entailed some completely invented straight lines.

Despite their widely disparate sizes and populations, these twelve circa-1805 counties found their way into the State Constitution of 1812, which lumped them into districts for the election of senators, the apportionment of House members, and the creation of court districts. In other words, these were not units of civil governance, as other states understood "counties," but rather electoral and judicial districts. Nor were they purely ministerial: because they influenced who got elected where, counties were politically controversial, and the Creole population—who were relative newcomers to the machinations of democracy—tended to view them suspiciously, as a maneuver by which the incoming Americans might tilt representation in their favor. One Louisiana historian would later call the counties "pernicious."

For the purposes of civil governance, the Americans in 1807 realized that the twenty-one extant ecclesiastic units from late colonial times did a better job of regionalizing the settled landscape than their own twelve sprawling counties, and, after some adjustments, adapted them into nineteen official "parishes." More were added as former Spanish West Florida and the old "neutral ground" by the Mexican border joined the state, and as larger parishes in the prairie and piney woods regions were broken into smaller ones. For decades to come, both counties and parishes coexisted, the former for electoral and judicial purposes, the latter for civil governance as well as religious congregational purposes. The dual systems were as confusing as many of their lines, which in this era of parochialism and weak central government, remained ambiguous—as did many of the parish seats, which changed when populations shifted or courthouses burned.

What made the county/parish terminology additionally problematic was its dual misalignment with other American states, which used "districts" to mean what "counties" meant in Louisiana, and "counties" to mean what "parishes" meant here. Both units kept popping up in state legislation and constitutions from the 1810s to the early 1840s, giving them continued life in both legal lexicon and the vernacular. But this being a mostly French-speaking Catholic state, at least in the south where the majority of the population lived, parishes were more familiar in every way, religiously, politically, spatially, and linguistically. Counties, on the other hand, felt alien—the word does not translate smoothly into French or Spanish—and they never caught on.

What killed counties in Louisiana was the Constitution of 1845. When delegates convened in Jackson and New Orleans to craft the document from August 1844 to May 1845, they used the word "county" or "counties" nineteen times in the published *Proceedings of the Constitutional Convention*. But the context of some usages—for example, "county or district," and "county or parish"—suggests delegates grappled with the term's ambiguity. When the final constitution was ratified on November 5, 1845, the word "parish" could be found roughly a hundred times, but "county" and "counties" had disappeared entirely. Electoral representation would now be apportioned by parish units and their populations, as well as by new senatorial districts. The Constitution of 1845 ended all talk of counties and permanently entrenched parishes in the map and political culture of Louisiana.

Why, after forty years, was a nationally standardized concept abandoned in favor of something sui generis? No explanation was provided by delegates for the omission, and it's tempting today to view this story as a triumph of localism and traditionalism over external agents of change. This era saw the peak of the political wrangling between the older, locally born Catholic francophones (Creoles, including in this context Cajuns) and the more recently arrived English-speaking, mostly Protestant Anglo-Americans. Debates arose constantly over matters such as the French versus English language, Roman Civil Law versus English Common Law, Creole versus Anglo voter apportionments, and other cultural-political flashpoints. Counties were an American import, and they symbolized American political power, whereas *paroisses, parroquias,* and *parishes* spoke of all things Creole: Catholicism, the *ancien régime,* the Creole sense of place, the Gallic dialect. The excising of counties may have represented an Anglo concession, or Creole pushback, to finally silence an unloved term already eschewed by the populace.

Pragmatism also played a role. To this point, Vidalia historian Robert Dabney Calhoun, interviewed by the *New Orleans Times-Picayune* in 1937, explained the last time "county" came up in state law. An act of December 16, 1824, stipulated that "the sheriff of the Parish of St. John the Baptist shall be ex-officio sheriff of the county of German Coast, and that in the future only one sheriff shall be appointed for said county." The act illustrated how redundant jurisdictions could lead to waste and confusion. When in 1843 that same sheriff attempted to pay his state taxes using his $290 compensation, which had been issued as notes by a now-defunct bank and was therefore worthless, the state had to pass a bill to authorize the transfer "from the sheriff of the German Coast county." That was the last time "county" appeared in state law, and the uncertainty of the sheriff's vague parish/county double-duty may have set off a conversation among legislators and led to the pointed exclusion of "county" from the 1845 Constitution.

"There never was a legislative act formally abolishing the old counties; nor was there such abolition by the new constitution," explained Calhoun. "The old counties had died years before from a pernicious political anemia," he said, in reference to how the original counties swayed electoral representation. "The old counties," he concluded, "may be likened to a row of old picture frames which were allowed to hang on the wall for many years after the portraits had been removed."

But what precisely changed over the course of 1844–45, when "county" came up repeatedly at the convention but then utterly disappeared in the final constitution, never to resurface?

So far as I can determine, it's a mystery.

"FORWARD THRUST" AND THE RESHAPING OF SOUTHERN GEOGRAPHY

In 2014, Argentine President Cristina Fernández de Kirchner broached the idea of shifting her country's capital from Buenos Aires, by far the nation's largest city and a key port in the global economy, to Santiago de Estero, a provincial city one-twelfth the size and a thousand kilometers inland.

The seemingly illogical idea aimed, rather rationally, to spread out national development by relocating into the interior the seat of government—the one economic sector largely detached from the geographical exigencies that drive most urban locations, such as navigable rivers and natural resources, and thus fairly portable. They're called "forward-thrust" capitals, and they've been tried a number of times worldwide.

Forward-thrust projects usually arise in relatively young and large countries whose primate cities, usually on coasts, monopolize most economic, cultural, and political power, and leave interiors relatively undeveloped and backward. The world's best example of rebalancing such a spatial mismatch is Brasília, a once little-known tropical forest in the hinterlands of Brazil to which, in 1960, the national government moved from its previous home in the world-famous coastal metropolis of Rio de Janeiro. There are other examples: in 1908 Australia created a planned inland capital named Canberra to counterbalance coastal Sydney and Melbourne. Pakistan thrust its capital from coastal Karachi to interior Islamabad in 1960; Belize moved its government from coastal Belize City to interior Belmopan in 1970; Nigeria moved its capital inland in 1991, as did Kazakhstan in 1997 and Myanmar in 2005. In some cases, the moves benefit the greater good of the country; in others, they benefit only some. Harvard researcher Filipe R. Campante points out that forward-thrust capitals spatially separate civil servants and the citizens they're supposed to serve, and can make government "less effective, less responsive, more corrupt and less able or willing to sustain the rule of law."

Postcolonial North America presented good habitat for forward-thrust undertakings. While neither Washington, D.C., nor Ottawa represents a pure example of the strategy, it's worth pointing out that both cities were established courtesy of top-down geopolitical decisions rather than bottom-up economic geographies, and, as capitals, both effectively shifted power away from big, old ports (New York and Philadelphia in the United States, Montreal and Quebec City in Canada) and toward less-developed areas.

The South presented even better habitat for forward thrust. Most southern states developed predominantly from the outside in, starting with coastal or riverine settlements such as Charleston, Savannah, Pensacola, Mobile, Natchez, New Orleans, and Galveston. These communities all became primate cities as well as capitals of their respective realms (states, colonies, or in the case of Galveston, a republic). Today, only one retains the rank as largest city in the state—New Orleans, and barely—and all have since relinquished their capital status to interior locales: Columbia, Atlanta, Tallahassee, Montgomery, Jackson, Baton Rouge, and Austin, respectively. To be sure, other factors were involved in these shifts, and none is so pure a specimen of forward-thrust as Brasília. But all of them ended up spatially reshuffling political power—and the attendant jobs, houses, roads, commerce, and culture—in the same coastal-to-interior, larger-to-smaller, urban-to-rural, and richer-to-poorer direction.

Louisiana offers a case study. New Orleans in the early 1800s grew from a colonial orphan with a population of only 8,000 to, by 1840, the largest city in the South and third largest in the nation. It formed Louisiana's unquestioned economic, cultural, and political epicenter, even though it was tucked deep down in the southeastern corner of an overwhelmingly rural state. In just about every way except the literal, New Orleans lay closer to New York than to Natchitoches.

Those incongruences laid the groundwork for discontent, and when the time came in 1845 for state representatives to rewrite the state constitution, their differing country-versus-city interests came into relief. One way to rebalance power, delegates decided, was to decrease New Orleans's number of seats in the state senate. Another way was to relocate its state legislature and governor to somewhere farther inland, into the country.

The "country argument" held that the very nature of a large metropolis unfairly advantaged its denizens to convene and lobby for their city's interests, and to shunt to state coffers any improvement projects they desired but did not wish to fund. The "city argument" countered that all the resources needed for governing, from adequate meeting spaces to printing presses to support expertise in the form of lawyers, advisers, and clerks, could be more readily found in a booming city of over 100,000 than in outlying hamlets.

Those on the country side, who like many rural Louisianans today tended to reprove notoriously libertine New Orleans, responded by pointing out how the many insalubrious temptations of "the Great Southern Babylon" might distract elected officials from tending to the solemn business of government.

What won the country argument was a powerful lobby on its side: affluent, urbane planters of sugarcane, cotton, rice, and the other agricultural commodities on which the wealth of New Orleans depended—far more than it needed the mundane apparatus of state government. In essence, city delegates realized they had more of a stake in their country cousins' argument than in a handful of government jobs.

Delegates thus agreed to move the state capital out of New Orleans by at least sixty miles, enough to keep the urban influences to a minimum. In 1848, the Louisiana Legislature officially relocated itself and the home of the governor to Baton Rouge, a city that, in 1840, was 2 percent the size of New Orleans.

Today, greater Baton Rouge is 62 percent the size of metro New Orleans, and its parish population exceeds that of Orleans by 20 percent. That change has many explanations, of course, but a major one, from Baton Rouge's perspective, is the stabilizing presence of state government—the essence of forward thrust.

Variations of forward thrust may be found in municipal history as well. When Mayor deLesseps "Chep" Morrison relocated City Hall from its cramped confines at Lafayette Square to a spacious modern Civic Center in the late 1950s, he did so in part to spread downtown development into a previously poor "back-of-town" neighborhood (which happened to be Louis Armstrong's birthplace). Not coincidentally, Morrison's new City Hall complex reflected the same bold architectural Modernism under construction at the same time in Brasília.

As for adjacent jurisdictions, Jefferson Parish keeps its seat of government in the West Bank city of Gretna in large part to counterbalance the economic and demographic preponderance of East Jefferson. Farther downriver, Plaquemines Parish government seated itself in tiny Pointe à la Hache to help keep its sparsely populated East Bank relevant to the larger West Plaquemines population. But after the courthouse was torched by arsonists in 2002 and parish government moved across the river to Belle Chasse, neither Pointe à la Hache nor East Plaquemines was ever quite the same.

St. Bernard Parish, meanwhile, evidences what happens when forward thrust goes in the opposite direction. The parish courthouse, once located in the rural eastern flanks of the parish, moved in the 1930s to Chalmette, where industry and urbanization from nearby New Orleans had been spreading. The country-to-city shift has left rural eastern St. Bernard nearly as depleted of resources as East Plaquemines, while the urbanized western part of the parish claims the lion's share of demographic, economic, and political activity.

Looking over our region and state, it is striking how much of the cultural conversation we engage in today has been influenced by these political-geographical decisions. Much has been written about the cultural chasm, for example, between southern and northern Louisiana, coast and interior, city and country; between lively New Orleans and livable Baton Rouge, rowdy Natchez and staid Jackson, gracious Charleston and Savannah and modern Columbia and Atlanta.

President Fernández de Kirchner left office in 2015 without having convinced Argentines to thrust their capital inland. But if the plan ever resurfaces, and it may well, expect a comparably interesting case study of the intersection of political and cultural geography.

LOUISIANA RADIO STATIONS AND THE (INCONVENIENT) LOCAL MUSIC LACUNA

Music ranks as a premier jewel in Louisiana's crown of cultural distinction, and sundry forums are devoted to documenting its production, performance, and personalities. But what music are Louisianans *consuming*? That is, what genres and artists are actually listened to by the 4.4 million of us, and not just the critics and connoisseurs who do most of the music discoursing? Is our aggregate consumption as heavily Cajun and zydeco, or jazz-blues-funk, as the production side of the scene might suggest?

Music consumption may be estimated in a variety of ways, including online activity, purchases, playlists, and live-performance attendance. Here I use radio station formats as a gauge of listenership.

First, a preemptive rebuttal: As in any quantification of a complex phenomenon, airplay is an imperfect measure of musical tastes. For one, not everyone listens to the radio, and certainly not all day. Many stations play a wider variety than their branded format ("Classic Rock," "Oldies," "Adult Contemporary") might suggest, and those with seemingly nationwide formats ("Urban," which usually implies hip-hop and rap) may in fact air locally produced material such as bounce, brass band, or second-line music. Others, particularly public and college stations, play eclectic musical segments in pointed defiance of single-genre programming, while the conglomerates behind many commercial stations generally drive musical tastes as much as they reflect them. So while I acknowledge that radio station formats shine only so much light on overall music consumption, the patterns they illuminate are nonetheless informative and revealing because ultimately it is we listeners who control the dial. Stations constantly reposition themselves so that we select them and their musical offerings. Since the advent of the medium, radio stations have both created and reflected our collective tastes, and I would posit they generally do the same among Louisianans—thus they're a reasonable data set for this analysis.

To understand patterns of music consumption on the airwaves, I gathered Federal Communications Commission licensing records, tagged each station by its broadcast locations and signal strengths, determined its primary format courtesy of its branding and airplay, and binned the varying descriptions into thirty main format categories. Then I mapped out the results.

What we see might surprise those Americans who, inculcated by relentless media representations, imagine a Cajun soundtrack accompanying every Louisiana landscape. But it would not surprise anyone who has ever driven across the state with their finger on the scan button. Louisianans are much more likely to listen to—or at least hear—musical genres with global appeal than those rooted locally.

Consider, for example, the accompanying map, in which the numerous white circles and gray triangles representing stations playing global, national, or regional (that is, southern but not particularly Louisianan) music are evenly distributed throughout the state, and occur both north and south of the "Boudin Curtain" separating the Anglo-dominant Protestant north from the Acadian Triangle and the mostly Catholic south. The pattern (or lack thereof) grows stronger

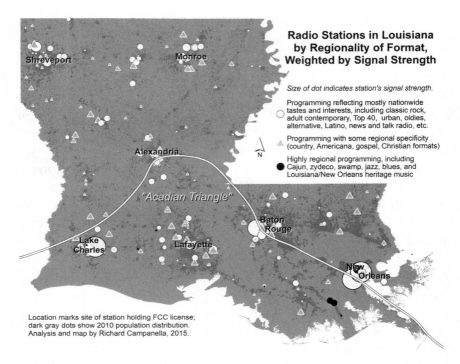

Louisiana radio stations, mapped by the regionality of their musical format. *Analysis and map by Richard Campanella.*

when we weight the stations by the power of their broadcast signals. According to this map, Louisianans are consuming more or less the same music as Americans elsewhere.

Spots of localism do occur, and for good reasons. If we might expect the state's only jazz, blues, and Louisiana/New Orleans music station to be in the putative Birthplace of Jazz, we would be correct: it's New Orleans's listener-supported WWOZ. Likewise, if we would predict Cajun, zydeco, and swamp-pop stations to predominate in the Cajun region south of the Boudin Curtain, we'd be right again: all seven are within the Acadian Triangle.

But for every confirmation of an expected local pattern (black dots), we see much more evidence that mainstream genres prevail broadly. Poring over the distribution of Christian programming, adult contemporary, classic rock, Latino, and urban, which are numerically overwhelming and scattered evenly across the state, one suspects there is greater variation of musical preference *within* Louisiana communities than among them. The only exceptions are precisely those genres for which the state is famous—Cajun music, zydeco, and jazz—which really do form a distinct, albeit highly confined, geography.

Phrased another way, relatively few Louisianans are consuming the famous local genres that get all the attention on the production side—and the little local music that does get airplay tends to occur in very limited geographies. Louisianans who consume global material, meanwhile, do so in larger numbers, in broader spaces, and with little fanfare from Louisiana music writers.

Other non-radio measures corroborate that we're not listening to the music we're "supposed to." The data-mining platform Echo Nest (the.echonest.com), which analyzes musical trends through billions of online data points, determined the top artist listened to in Louisiana was not BeauSoleil, Dr. John, the Neville Brothers, or Rosie Ledet—but the Canadian-born rapper Drake. Indeed, most of Louisianans' favorite performers according to Echo Nest's metrics were out-of-state artists known mostly for hip-hop and rap. Only when its analysis aimed to identify the "most distinctive artist by state"—that is, "the artist . . . listened to proportionally more frequently in [Louisiana] than they are in all of the United States"—did a local talent top the list: Baton Rouge–born rapper Kevin Gates.

Returning to our radio data, the top three most common station formats in Louisiana, regardless of signal strength, are Christian (54 stations, many including talk programming), country (both modern and classic, 45 stations), and Adult Contemporary (including urban adult contemporary, 31 stations). We have to go fairly far down the list before getting to gospel (13), Cajun, zydeco, and swamp (7), and jazz, blues, funk (1).

This inconvenient lacuna of localism has not been lost on local music aficionados, and at least one prominent voice seemed perplexed by it. "Why aren't local radio stations playing more local music?" asked Jan Ramsey, longtime editor of New Orleans's *Offbeat Magazine* in an October 2014 editorial. Relatedly, she puzzled over the proclivity of Louisianans planning krewe balls and festivals—folks who ought to personify what we mean when we say "locals"—to hire ordinary pop bands covering national standards. "I just think it's a real shame," Ramsey sighed, "that with the rich musical tradition that we have[,] most of the population doesn't respond all that well to local musicians." The paradox begs the question of what exactly "local music" means, to which side of the production/consumption dualism it applies, and to what extent Louisiana society is musically distinctive.

Being a geographer rather than a musicologist or music critic, I will refrain from making any sweeping conclusions from this cursory analysis. But I would point out that, to the degree that a society's musicality implies consumption as well as production, an empirical look at radio station formats reveals a wide gap between (1) the perception of localism in all things musical in Louisiana, and (2) the reality that national mainstream music wins over many, many Louisiana ears.

LOUISIANA TOPOGRAPHY
Third Lowest, Third Flattest—and Most Interesting

Unless you live in the piney hills of northern Louisiana or the loess bluffs of West Feliciana Parish, the word "rugged" probably rarely arises in your Louisiana lexicon. Likewise, it's safe to say that whoever coined the slogan "Sportsman's Paradise"—which has been circulating since the 1860s and appearing on state license plates since the late 1950s—was not referring to hiking or mountain climbing.

Yet despite its subtlety, topographic elevation has been extraordinarily consequential in Louisiana's human geography, because of its effects on soil fertility and habitability, and more broadly because anything weak in supply but strong in demand attains great value. Our state is, after all, largely alluvial and deltaic in its physical geography, a product of sediment-laden water transported by gravity and guided by topography. Thus it is of interest to put some numbers on our gentle terrain and see how it compares nationwide.

In terms of elevation—that is, vertical distance from mean sea level—Louisiana's lowest spots fall entirely within metro New Orleans. Drainage of the backswamp and encirclement by manmade levees have caused roughly half of the metropolis, namely those areas farthest from the Mississippi River, to drop below the level of the sea, a circumstance unique in the region. The contiguous urbanized portions of Orleans, Jefferson, St. Bernard, and Plaquemines parishes thus rank as Louisiana's (and the South's) lowest terrain, with an average elevation of 0.5 feet below sea level. The lowest human-inhabited area within that bowl is the Eastover neighborhood in eastern New Orleans, of which roughly half is 10 to 14 feet below sea level. Parts of Lakeview and Gentilly are not much higher, at 6 to 8 feet, while certain dry canal beds throughout the metropolis are 18 to 20 feet below sea level.

Two hundred miles to the northwest, in rural Bienville Parish, lie the quartz sands of the Cockfield Formation, a series of pine-covered hills peaking at Louisiana's summit, 535-foot-high Mount Driskill. This high point measures one-tenth of a vertical mile above the state's lowest point in eastern New Orleans. Contrast Louisiana's elevational range to that of California, whose apex (14,505-foot-high Mount Whitney) and nadir (Death Valley, -282 feet) are separated by 2.8 vertical miles. Alaska, meanwhile, rises 3.85 vertical miles from the sea to the summit of Denali, which also happens to have the world's highest base-to-peak elevation. In Mount Driskill, Louisiana has the third-lowest state high point in the nation, after Delaware (450 feet) and Florida (345 feet). It's also one of the few states whose tallest building—New Orleans's One Shell Square, 697 feet—towers over its natural zenith.

As it happens, Louisiana also has the third-lowest mean elevation of American states: 98 feet above sea level on average, a third more than Florida's 63-foot average and over double Delaware's 44-foot mean. (Interestingly, Alaska is nowhere near the nation's highest state, despite Denali; every one of our western states is substantially higher on average, with Colorado the loftiest at 6,855 feet. That's seventy Louisianas stacked on top of each other. Picture that.)

Elevation is but one metric of terrain. To capture more robustly the lay and shape of the land, the notion of topography is better suited. The word "topography" once had a broader and more literal meaning, implying the description (-graphy) of place (topo-). Usages in the nineteenth century, such as in John Howard Hinton's *History and Topography of the United States of North America* (1846), roughly matched how we currently use the word "geography," touching upon everything from geology and flora to demographics and local history. What altered topography's meaning was the inclusion of elevation contours on previously planimetric maps produced by the U.S. Army Corps of Topographical Engineers and (later) the U.S. Geological Survey (USGS). Because elevation contours were the most salient features on these popular new "topographic maps," Americans began to associate "topography" with the shape and height of land surfaces—what technically is called hypsography ("description of height"). This was not necessarily the case in other anglophone countries, where "topography" tends to retain its original meaning.

Today, in American English, topography implies the lay, shape, and form of land features as measured by elevation as well as slope, aspect, curvature, and water flow (hydrology). Of these metrics, slope—that is, the degree that a landform rises vertically for every distance it runs horizontally—best captures a landscape's overall ruggedness (or flatness). A 90-degree slope is a sheer cliff; a 45-degree slope rises as high as it runs laterally; and a 0-degree slope is a flat plane.

How does Louisiana stack up in terms of slope? To calculate this and other measurements for this essay, I acquired USGS GTOPO30 digital elevation models, which plot global elevations for every 1,000-by-1,000-meter cell (pixel). I then computed the slope for each pixel and averaged the results by state and by each of Louisiana's sixty-four parishes.

Just as Louisiana has the third-lowest state summit and average elevation, it also turns out to be the third-flattest state, with an average slope of only 0.152 degrees. This means the landscape undulates 1 vertical foot for every 373 horizontal feet traversed. In rural terms, that's roughly the equivalent of walking up a single river levee during a one-mile walk; in urban terms, it's like stepping up one curb per city block. Pretty darn flat, but not the flattest: once again, Florida (0.115 degrees) and Delaware have us beat, with the First State gauging a nearly pancake-flat 0.103-degree average slope.

There's a wide numerical gap between these three average slopes and the next cohort of mostly midwestern states, demonstrating that Delaware on the Atlantic Coast, Louisiana on the Gulf Coast, and Florida on both coasts together form the nation's tide-washed littoral doormats.

For the record, the most rugged state in the Union is not in the Mountain West nor Alaska, but Hawaii—and for good reason: small as that volcanic archipelago is, the Hawaiian Islands are rugged throughout. The same cannot be said of states like Colorado, Wyoming, or Montana, where vast eastern prairies tamp down the average slopes of their rugged western halves.

Within Louisiana, our most rugged parishes are Lincoln (0.46 degrees average slope) and Claiborne (0.43 degrees—also our highest parish, averaging 267 feet above sea level), both of which are within 150 miles of Arkansas's Ouachita Mountains. If all of Louisiana were as undulating as Lincoln Parish, we'd have the surface roughness of Nebraska. Still pretty darn flat.

Yet despite Louisiana's lack of topographic elevation—indeed, perhaps because of it—our slight variations have proven highly consequential in the historical and cultural geography of our state. Just a few feet of elevation in deltaic New Orleans, for example, can spell the difference between a faubourg founded in the Napoleonic Age and a subdivision laid out in the Jazz Age—or Space Age. Just a few dozen feet separating the alluvial bottomlands of the Mississippi River and its tributaries from the abutting terraces and bluffs also distinguish eighteenth-

and nineteenth-century plantation landscapes from adjacent twentieth-century lumber-and-railroads areas. To a remarkable degree, maps of such diverse phenomena as shotgun-house distributions, French long lots, rice-and-crawfish intercropping, sugarcane cultivation, tree farming, and the state's livestock industry all reflect underlying patterns of topographic elevation.

"The cultural landscape is fashioned out of a natural landscape by a cultural group," wrote geographer Carl O. Sauer. "Culture is the agent, the natural area is the medium, [and] the cultural landscape is the result." Topographical elevation adds a third dimension to that medium, and paradoxically, nearly flat Louisiana may the best place to evidence its importance.

THE SEDUCTION OF EXCEPTIONALISM

"New Orleans is like most other American cities."

"Louisiana is a typical southern state."

"New Orleanians generally eat the same food and enjoy the same music as most other Americans."

How often do you hear statements like those? Rarely, I suspect. On the contrary, we usually hear—or hold—that this city and this state deviate from the norm, in numerous and fundamental ways. We're different. Unique. Sui generis.

Call it exceptionalism: the view that Louisiana society emerged through different channels and finds itself today a place apart from the American mainstream. "Exceptionalists" see this society's enduring uniqueness as traceable to our colonial origins, and maintain, explicitly or implicitly, that its ethos remains in the Franco-Hispanic-Afro-Caribbean world from which it spawned. They see evidence in everything from music and food to attitudes, race relations, linguistics, architecture, and politics. Exceptionalism is practically an article of faith in Louisiana; it seems to be strongest in the New Orleans and Acadian regions, and emanates across the Catholic south and up to Natchitoches before petering out in the Protestant north. It even spills over into coastal Texas and Mississippi, and Mobile claims its share.

Exceptionalism is invoked proudly, often axiomatically and sometimes defensively, across a remarkably wide social spectrum, regardless of race, class, education, gender, and age. Transplants, paradoxically, adhere to exceptionalism more stridently than native Louisianans, probably because most of them (including myself) were originally drawn to this place for its mystique of the exotic. Exceptionalism forms the bedrock of local civic pride, and merely questioning it can earn rebuke. Even when the points of distinction are problematic, such as political corruption, they still seem to generate a certain rustic swagger, perhaps because exceptionalism ascertains authenticity, and in a world that seems increasingly affected, authenticity comes across as, well, exceptional.

All well and good. The sense that things are different "down here" does, after all, have a fair amount of empirical support. What other city has dropped by half below the level of the sea, surrounded threateningly by the very water bodies that created and sustain it? What other American state counts hundreds of thousands of francophones in its citizenry? What other region has so fine an example of a mixed legal jurisdiction, of multiple surveying systems, of diverse architectural traditions? Where else can you find such a natural resource–based economy, such a culinary canon, such a calendar anchored by civic festivity? If exceptionalism boosts local pride and draws tourists as *lagniappe* (where else can you say that?), what's the problem?

The problem is this: researchers—that is, the documenters and interpreters of historical and cultural information—all too often *start out* with the assumption that all is different here, before they analyze the data. So positioned, they usually end up confirming what they suspected all along. *Uniqueness in, uniqueness out:* the presumption of exceptionalism can become a self-fulfilling hypothesis. Rather than resulting from critical thinking, exceptionalist interpretations all too often derive from not thinking critically. This is particularly unfortunate because it undermines the value of careful research that *does* validate exceptionalism.

The phenomenon is a common one in epistemology; it's called confirmation bias. Sometimes it's intentional, such as when an "independent" consultant hired by special interests invariably determines that the client was right all along. Historiography—that is, the ever-changing processes of producing historical information—is replete with examples of players, ranging from the unaware and the naive to the scheming and the pernicious, arriving at the archives with narratives already set in their heads.

Exceptionalism began to form in the Louisiana narrative starting in the colonial and early American years, and gained momentum during the "local color" literary genre of the late 1800s, which, driven by a market that craved nostalgia and exoticism, delivered both *ad nauseam*. Teachers have since passed exceptionalism on to students, tourism operators inculcate it in visitors, and storytellers relate it to mass audiences. When was the last time you read a novel about New Orleans or saw a film about Louisiana that did not depict its subjects as different in some flattering, intriguing, or patronizing way? Even as I caution my students all semester long against presupposing exceptionalism, I nonetheless see it inscribed in their final research papers, oftentimes cheerfully declared in the opening sentence.

What get lost in the exceptionalism argument are some realities that are anything but exceptional, yet nonetheless are important parts of the modern-day Louisiana story. For all the singing of the uniqueness mantra in New Orleans, who can argue that most modern-day New Orleanians don't speak English, indulge in national popular culture, shop at big-box chains, and interact socially and economically with other Americans and the world on a daily basis? Most Louisianans are networked into the global economy, wired into the Internet, connected to cable television, and linked into social media in numbers that are perfectly comparable with peer states.

Unique foodways?—then who's buying all that Stouffer's in the frozen-food aisle at Walmart?

Unique music?—then why do most commercial radio stations (which usually have the most listeners) play mainstream pop music, and those featuring local and regional music have so few listeners they must rely on donations to operate?

Unique society?—greater social differentiation can probably be found between the Garden District and Central City than between New Orleans and other American cities.

For better or worse, Louisianans overwhelmingly lead lives that, save for some major vestiges of dissimilarity such as Mardi Gras, would be immediately recognizable, if not identical, to other Americans. Distinctions *do* exist, and they do go deep, but not, I suspect, as deep or as often as we oftentimes presume. (Need evidence? Look around your everyday life.)

Exceptionalism can be seductively deceptive: it privileges the picturesque; it over-tells that which is intriguing, scandalous, and charming and under-tells that which seems banal, quotidian, and monotonous. Thus its appeal to writers, filmmakers, and tourism marketers—and its danger to serious researchers. In fact, *not* all is picturesque and outrageous, nor was it ever. Much of ordinary life in Louisiana is just that: ordinary. Whatever the nature of the region's Franco-Hispanic-Afro-Caribbean inheritance, it is fair to say that assimilation and modernization have subsumed the lion's share of it into the modern American norm.

Researchers would be remiss to ignore this, and fiction writers would be courageous to acknowledge it.

By no means do I suggest that we instead lunge toward assimilationist explanations and roll our eyes at exceptionalism. Rather, I suggest that researchers, myself included, arrive at the archives, or the interview, or the archaeological dig, minimally burdened by either preconception. We might benefit from the careful and judicious wisdom of the scientific method: start out presuming all is neutral (null hypothesis), gather the data in a thorough and representative fashion, analyze it fairly, and let the chips fall where they may.

More often than not, the results will fall somewhere in the murky middle, and that is a perfectly legitimate—and refreshing—finding to report.

DISASTER AND RECOVERY

NEW ORLEANS WAS ONCE ABOVE SEA LEVEL

Early one morning in September 1975, in a quiet Metairie subdivision west of Transcontinental Drive, a ranch house suddenly exploded in a fireball so powerful it damaged twenty neighboring buildings and broke windows a mile away. The structure itself plus four adjacent houses were reduced to rubble, and eleven people were seriously injured.

It had happened before, and it would happen again. At least eight times between 1972 and 1977, well-maintained homes in modern subdivisions, all within a mile, exploded without warning. "Scores of Metairie residents," reported the *Times-Picayune,* "wondered whether they are living in what amounts to time bombs." Unnerved, Jefferson Parish authorities and Louisiana Gas Service Company technicians investigated the smoldering ruins and determined the proximate cause to be a broken gas line. But the number and density of the explosions suggested an ultimate cause, one that went beyond shoddy workmanship or tragic happenstance.

The culprit, it turned out, was soil subsidence. Buried gas lines had twisted as Metairie's recently drained former swampland settled unevenly, causing concrete slab foundations to tilt and buckle. In extreme cases, the lines ruptured and leaked gas accumulated in cavities beneath the slab or wafted up into attics. All that was needed to ignite an inferno was an electrical spark or a lit cigarette. After a flurry of finger-pointing and lawsuits, parish officials eventually required slab foundations to be set upon a grid of pilings driven into sturdier, deeper earth, below the superficial level most prone to sinkage, and by requiring "goose neck" hook-ups designed to bend with shifting.

The pilings stabilized the foundations, and the flexible connections put an end to the gas-line fissures. But gardens, driveways, and streets continued to sink, particularly in this central-western section of Metairie, which had an especially thick layer of subterranean peat—ancient marsh grass and swamp tree leaves and stumps integrated into the mud like coffee grinds, material prone to severe consolidation when dried. At least one researcher contended it was not broken gas lines but the rotting of this organic matter, following the removal of water and the introduction of air pockets (oxidation), that produced the deadly gas.

Exploding houses represent an extreme example of how soil subsidence can be a public health hazard, and we should be thankful the new building codes effectively treated this frightening symptom. But the larger problem remains, and it represents a geophysical hazard shared by all areas, to greater and lesser extents, within the levee-protected artificially drained metropolis south of Lake Pontchartrain.

Understanding the process and dangers of soil subsidence requires a grasp of our local geology. Formed almost entirely by a channel-jumping, seasonally overtopping Mississippi River during a period of 5,000 to 7,200 years, our underlying land comprises five components: sand, silt, and clay particles; water; and organic matter. The river and its distributaries deposited the largest quantities of the coarsest sediments (sand and silt) immediately, making the areas closest to its channels the highest, while dispersing smaller quantities of finer sediments (finer silts and clay particles) farther back, making the backswamp and marshes lower in elevation. All areas were above sea level, albeit barely in some reaches, and the lowest areas—today's Metairie, Lakeview, Gentilly, Broadmoor, New Orleans East, and the fringes of the West Bank—accumulated the most runoff and thus preserved the most organic matter in their waterlogged soils.

Subsidence first started to occur when the river no longer spread new dosages of fresh water and sediment onto its deltaic landscape. In prehistoric times, this would occur when the Mississippi jumped channels, leaving the old deltaic "lobe" to subside while building a new one elsewhere. During the 1700s–1900s, the diminished deposition came as a result of the artificial levees erected along the lower Mississippi to prevent springtime flooding. Those historical deluges, of course, represented disasters for humans, but they were naturally beneficial to deltaic soils, and without them, they gradually settled.

The vast majority of our modern soil subsidence, however, is attributable not to the erection of levees along the Mississippi but to the installation of drainage apparatus within metro New Orleans. Starting in the 1890s, New Orleans developed a sophisticated system to direct runoff through gutters and underground pipes to a series of pumping stations, which would push the water through "outfall canals" and into surrounding water bodies, principally Lake Pontchartrain. Engineer Albert Baldwin Wood made the new system that much more efficient when he developed his patented Wood "screw pumps," which dramatically increased outflow speed and capacity while removing debris. The basic design, with key modifications such as pumping station locations, was extended into eastern New Orleans in the 1910s and 1920s and replicated in adjacent parishes in subsequent decades.

The effect of municipal drainage on urban geography was nothing short of revolutionary. Wrote George Washington Cable in 1909, "there is a salubrity that

Shading indicates areas in metro New Orleans which have sunk below sea level since the turn of the twentieth century. The lowest significantly sized areas, shown in darker shades of gray, lie ten to twelve feet below sea level. *Map by Richard Campanella, based on FEMA LIDAR elevation data.*

could not be when the . . . level of supersaturation in the soil was but two and half feet from the surface, where now it is ten feet or more. . . . The curtains of swamp forest are totally gone[,] drained dry and covered with miles of gardened homes." New Orleanians moved *en masse* off the high ground by the river and into new auto-friendly subdivisions on former swamps to the north, west, and east. We no longer had to worry about topography. There was one big problem. In removing unwanted swamp water and urbanizing wetlands, artificial drainage opened up cavities in the soil body, which oxidized the organic matter, which in turn opened up more cavities. Finely textured particles settled into those air pockets, and the soil sunk.

Architects were among the first to notice the impact upon the cityscape. "Was the drainage of the city responsible for the settling of the old [St. Louis] cathedral wall a few days ago?" pondered a 1913 article in the *Times-Picayune*. "Will similar breaks in the walls of all of the old downtown buildings occur, and will it force them to be rebuilt? These are two questions which are worrying New Orleans architects and engineers."

By the 1930s, a metropolis that originally lay above sea level had seen one-third of its land surface sink below that level. By the 2000s, roughly half of the metropolis lay below sea level, by three to six feet in parts of Broadmoor, five to eight feet in parts of Lakeview and Gentilly, and six to twelve feet in parts of Metairie and New Orleans East. Why those spots? Because they were the lowest to begin with, and thus had the most water to lose closest to the surface and the most peat to oxidize.

The good news is that 50 percent of our metropolis remains above sea level. The bad news is that it used to be nearly 100 percent above sea level, and it was we humans who managed to sink it. The worst news is that, because the world's seas are rising, we're sinking relative to those bloating seawaters at a pace roughly double the absolute rate at which the land alone is lowering. And of course it's the sea that makes this matter potentially deadly.

When Hurricane Katrina's surge ruptured the levees, it poured so swiftly and accumulated so deeply in so many areas because they had become bowl-shaped. Had a similar surge come upon an unsubsided landscape, say two hundred years ago, it would have generally washed off the next day, as surges do in coastal Mississippi and elsewhere. And of course those landscapes would not have been populated. Instead, the Katrina deluge sat for weeks, impounded, on top of fully developed neighborhoods. People drowned in part because of the unforeseen effects of swamp drainage and soil subsidence.

In urban areas, there is no true solution for soil subsidence; it is not feasible to "reinflate" soils with water while urban life continues above. It is beneficial, however, to restore a certain level of water content to the soil body in the interest of abating future sinkage. This may be done by slowing the movement of runoff as it moves across the cityscape and absorbing or retaining as much of it as possible, through porous surfaces, retention ponds, bioswales, and widened and landscaped grade-level outfall canals. As for undeveloped and undrained areas along the lower Mississippi, it is possible, indeed imperative, to reverse further subsidence and erosion through coastal restoration techniques such as river diversions, sediment siphons, and the beneficial use of dredged sediments.

While we can't truly solve the problem of urban soil subsidence, we can effectively treat the symptoms—by building on piers and pilings above the grade, such that water in our yard does not become water in our house. An entire local industry exists to counter the effects of subsidence on structures, including sand-pit operators supplying fill and shoring specialists who jack up houses. One such outfit has been in business consistently since 1840, the same year Antoine's Restaurant opened. Apparently house leveling and fine dining make for job security in this town.

We can also acknowledge that topography matters, and that our higher ground is a valuable resource which ought to host larger populations.

Finally, we can learn the lessons of history—and geography, and of the tragic explosions in Metairie in the 1970s—by thinking long and hard before leveeing, draining, and urbanizing any additional wetlands on this deltaic plain.

A BRIEF HISTORY OF FRENCH QUARTER FLOODING

After nearly ten years, a certain detail of the Hurricane Katrina–induced deluge of 2005 has found its way back into the national news. At issue is this: were there, in fact, floodwaters, not to mention dead bodies, "in the French Quarter," as embattled NBC anchor Brian Williams had stated in recollections of that terrible week? Or were these reports exaggerated, especially in light of revelations that Williams had embellished a 2003 incident in Iraq?

Initial reaction to the Katrina statements did not flatter Williams. New Orleanians know well that the "sliver by the river" in general, and the French Quarter in particular, remained dry, and that its higher terrain explains why city founder Bienville established New Orleans here in 1718.

But then photographic evidence to the contrary began to circulate, and it had the effect of quelling at least some of the doubt. While most of the French Quarter did indeed remain dry, the streets surrounding Williams's hotel, the Ritz-Carlton, did not. By my measurement, they were part of the 9 percent of the 260 acres bounded by Canal, North Rampart, Esplanade, and North Peters—that is, the French Quarter as most people perceive it—which were inundated by shallow saltwater in the days immediately after Katrina.

That 9 percent was entirely in the neighborhood's upriver/lakeside (western) corner, four or so blocks that are surprisingly low-lying for a neighborhood that is otherwise relatively elevated. And it wasn't the first time they flooded; by my count, this section of the French Quarter has seen its streets inundated by outside water (that is, from river, lake, or sea, not including heavy rainfalls) at least four times in the past 200 years.

To understand French Quarter topography, we have to go back to 4,300 years ago, when the Mississippi River began wending eastward along what is now Metairie Road, Gentilly Boulevard, and Chef Menteur Highway, disembaguing into the sea in present-day eastern St. Bernard Parish. The river's main channel forked around present-day City Park and sent a secondary channel, or distributary, down what is now Bayou Road and Esplanade Avenue.

Over the next 3,000 years, wherever the water flowed, sediment got deposited and banks rose in elevation. This created today's Metairie/Gentilly Ridge as well as the Esplanade Ridge, the latter of which would shore up what would later become the downriver/lakeside (northern) quadrant of the French Quarter. Then, around 1,100 years ago, the Mississippi lunged in a new direction, and, through its springtime flooding cycles, deposited sediment and created new land along its current channel. These processes raised the elevations of immediate riverside areas throughout present-day New Orleans, to eight to twelve feet above sea level, including in the French Quarter—even as the river, which of course flows above the level of the sea until it joins it, would occasionally overtop and inundate its banks with alluvium-rich water, further raising their elevations.

This happened in 1719, just one year after the founding of New Orleans, when the bloated Mississippi sent a thin sheet of excess water across the nascent outpost. The incident worked against Bienville's argument that his site ought to become the colony's headquarters and capital rather than Mobile, a designation which officials instead transferred to Biloxi. But shortly after the 1719 flood, engineers began erecting artificial levees along the city's riverfront. In time, overtop flooding directly from the river would gradually recede as a source of flood threat. By 1723, New Orleans was declared the capital, and Bienville's project gained momentum.

But while that threat diminished over the 1700s and early 1800s, it remained high from river levee failures (crevasses) occurring elsewhere in the crescent, which could fill the lowlands and inundate the city via its lower-lying rear. This happened in May 1816, when a crevasse on a plantation in present-day Carrollton filled the backswamp and swelled into the rear flanks of the city five miles downriver. "One could travel in a skiff from the corner of Chartres and Canal streets to Dauphin," read one account written in 1887, "down Dauphin to Bienville, down Bienville to Burgundy, thus to St. Louis Street, from St. Louis to Rampart, and so throughout the rear suburbs."

Why those streets? Because they comprise the one section of the original city, today's French Quarter, which had received the least amount of sediment deposition from either the Esplanade Ridge formation starting 4,300 years ago, or the formation of the present-day "sliver by the river" starting 1,100 years ago. Today, it stands two feet lower than the North Rampart/Esplanade corner of the neighborhood, and seven to eight feet lower than Decatur and North Peter streets.

Flooding happened there again starting May 3, 1849, when a crevasse on Pierre Sauvé's plantation in present-day River Ridge began filling the backswamp, reaching Rampart on May 15 and peaking on May 30–June 1 at the intersection of Bourbon and Canal Street. (Not coincidentally, this was precisely where the uppermost floodwaters stood in a photograph I captured at 8:04 a.m. on August 30, 2005, the morning after Katrina.)

It happened once again in June 1871, when a crevasse at Bonnet Carré sent excess river water into Lake Pontchartrain, much like the spillway does today—except that easterly winds prevented the lake's normal outflow to the Gulf of Mexico. The high lake water thus backed up into the New Basin Canal, toward downtown, and on June 3, caused a breach in the canal's guide levee at Hagan Avenue. Once again, floodwaters crept into the French Quarter's low rear edge. Illustrations of the day show adjacent sections of Canal Street strewn with floating boats and people in waist-deep water.

On the morning of Monday, August 29, 2005, failures in federal floodwalls and levees on the western side of the Industrial Canal in the Upper Ninth Ward, in two spots on the London Avenue Outfall Canal in Gentilly, and in one section of the Seventeenth Street Outfall Canal in Lakeview allowed Katrina's surge to inundate the heart of New Orleans's East Bank. Even after the storm passed, floodwaters continued to rise, into Wednesday, under clear blue skies. Why? Because a surge as vast as Katrina's does not immediately flow back to the sea once the hurricane passes; rather, it slowly works its way back, and continues to spill through deep ruptures in floodwalls and levees, stopping only when outside and inside water levels equalize.

By the morning of August 30, the flood reached as far uphill as Canal at Bourbon Street, on terrain two feet above normal sea level. By the afternoon of Wednesday, August 31, the deluge crested at Royal/St. Charles Avenue, three feet above sea level. I captured a photograph at 1:17 p.m. that afternoon showing a large inflatable raft floating right in front of Rubenstein's.

As for the French Quarter, during those two days and probably into Thursday, up to two feet of saltwater covered 100–400 North Rampart, 100–300 Burgundy,

Photograph of Canal Street taken by the author at 1:17 p.m. on August 31, 2005, shows the Katrina deluge cresting beyond the St. Charles Avenue intersection (note inflatable boat), over three feet above sea level. These same floodwaters would have inundated a low-lying corner of the French Quarter in the distant right. *Photograph by Richard Campanella.*

100–200 Dauphine, and the 100 block of Bourbon, not to mention all of Iberville Street lakeside of the 800 block and all of Canal lakeside of the 700 block. Williams, who had stayed at the Ritz-Carlton, would have found himself surrounded by the uppermost edge of the flood footprint, and it was deep enough all around to float small boats.

New Orleanians will make what they wish of Brian Williams's statements, including the separate question of the dead bodies. But as for understanding the geography of our city and the catastrophe of ten years ago, perhaps it is time to add an important caveat to the popular talking point that the French Quarter unconditionally "did not flood." While indeed positioned on higher ground, the original city, like all other neighborhoods, has its low spots, and though they stand above sea level, they are not immune to flood risk.

We've known this for over two hundred years.

THE KATRINA OF THE 1800S
Sauvé's Crevasse

Prior to 2005, a disaster known as Sauvé's Crevasse had been described as the largest flood in New Orleans history, at least in terms of spatial extent. It's worth remembering today for a number of reasons, starting with the fact that, like Katrina and most other major deluges here, it began with a levee break.

Locals called them "crevasses" back then—"the name given to a fissure or breaking of the Levée," as one journalist explained in 1823, "almost uniformly produced by neglect." Crevasses happened regularly along the lower Mississippi, and the worst ones tended to get named for the nearest plantation or settlement, such as the Macarty or Carrollton Crevasse of 1816, which flooded parts of the French Quarter.

In the spring of 1849, rising waters began to undermine the levee fronting Pierre Sauvé's sugarcane plantation in what is now River Ridge in Jefferson Parish. Sauvé was not alone in this predicament; other planters eyed their softening levees worriedly as the river gained height and strength. The embankments lining the Fortier parcel in present-day Waggaman on the West Bank ("Right Bank" in those days) were the first to fail, on April 17, unleashing a "rush of water [of the] most awful destructive appearance" with a "noise . . . heard from a long distance." Luckily, it inundated mostly uninhabited lands and flowed harmlessly out Bayou Verret and into Lake Cataouatche.

Sauvé's levee on the East ("Left") Bank had long been tenuous, even under natural conditions, because it lay on the river's cutbank side. There, powerful currents leaned leftward as they muscled their way around a sharp meander, scouring bankside sediments and sometimes sending a chute of water onto the land. For this reason a natural distributary—bayous Metairie, Gentilly, and Sauvage, the last of which still exists—had for centuries flowed out of the river in this vicinity and wended eastward, forming the Metairie-Gentilly Ridge.

On May 3, Sauvé's levee finally gave way. Lunging river water quickly widened the crevasse to 150 feet long and 6 feet deep. The torrent destroyed everything in its path and accumulated in the swampy lowlands known today as Hoey's Basin, around today's Earhart Expressway and Jefferson Highway in Elmwood and Jefferson. The flood that would become known as Sauvé's Crevasse had begun.

Because the Metairie Ridge (today's Metairie Road) restrained the floodwaters from flowing northward toward Lake Pontchartrain, they instead spread eastward

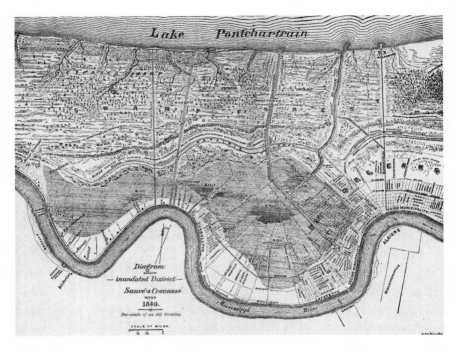

The 1849 crevasse in the levee at Pierre Sauvé's plantation is marked at far left, and the resulting inundation is mapped in the shaded area. Downtown New Orleans appears at lower center right. *Map from* Report on the Social Statistics of Cities *(1886), courtesy Perry-Castañeda Library, University of Texas at Austin.*

into present-day Hollygrove, Fontainebleau, Broadmoor, and Mid-City, most of which were within Jefferson Parish and undeveloped at the time. On May 8 waters reached a level high enough to subsume the New Basin Canal and its guide levees (now the I-10 corridor near Xavier). Unlike those of the Fortier Crevasse, Sauvé's waters crept into urbanized areas, past Broad, Claiborne, Dryades, and into New Orleans's city limits, at the time at Felicity Street. The track bed of the present-day St. Charles Streetcar Line helped block the water from rising too far into uptown, although some did make it past St. Charles (aptly called Nyades at the time, the water nymphs of Greek mythology) between Washington and Upperline, cresting nearly at Magazine Street.

Downtown, floodwaters from Sauvé's Crevasse, which lay fully fifteen miles away, flooded upper North Rampart, Burgundy, Dauphine, and Bourbon streets. But they went no farther east than present-day Lafitte Street, because, unlike those of the New Basin Canal, the guide levees of the Old Basin (Carondelet) Canal, now the Lafitte Corridor, successfully blocked them.

On June 4, a *Daily Picayune* journalist climbed up the St. Charles Hotel and described the view from the 185-foot-high cupola. "Far away [to] Carrollton . . . to the lands in the vicinity of the Sauvé crevasse, the surface of the country on the left bank of the Mississippi is one sheet of water, dotted in innumerable spots with houses. . . . The streets in the Second Municipality [above Canal Street] are now so many vast water courses [issued] from the bosom of the swamp. . . . New Orleans [looks like] the city of Venice." Had he looked further, he might have seen additional flooding from another crevasse at English Turn, from the still-open Fortier Crevasse, from a break in the Kenner levee, and from weak spots at Bonnet Carré which would later rupture. The year 1849 was to nineteenth-century Louisianans what the year 2005 was to us.

Volunteers heroically plugged Sauvé's Crevasse on June 20, but not before 220 city blocks, two thousand structures, and twelve thousand residents were flooded. Within a few days, water receded out the two canals and Bayou St. John, or percolated into the soil body. Displaced citizens returned home to clean up, and the city began repairing damaged infrastructure with funds raised by a special tax. The deluge also left behind a "deposit of alluvion [with] vegetable and animal matter," worrying officials that an epidemic would follow. The crevasse threatened to reopen repeatedly for many months, keeping everyone on edge.

"May Heaven avert from us another such catastrophe!" implored the *Picayune* journalist at the end of his report. "May our citizens, in their foresight and their intelligence, devise some means of raising an insuperable barrier to another inundation from [the Mississippi River]!"

It's informative, 165 years later, to view the responses to that call for help through the lens of Katrina.

Bad as it was, the 1849 deluge mostly affected cane fields and woods. Although planters took a hit with crop losses, only one-tenth of the flood footprint actually inundated populated areas. Likewise, only around 10 percent of the New Orleans population found water in their abodes, and rarely was it deeper than a couple of feet. The very deepest inundations measured six feet, and only in two small spots.

Readers know all too well these figures were much, much worse during Katrina.

And whereas roughly fifteen hundred people died in 2005, I know of no deaths directly attributable to Sauvé's Crevasse. Contrary to officials' concerns, the deluge may have actually saved lives. Only months earlier, cholera plagued the populace, but floodwaters and heavy rains had washed away filthy stagnant pools, and as had happened in 1816 after the Carrollton Crevasse, death rates actually declined. The environment also benefited, as the flood replenished the soil body with fresh water and sediment, two resources needed by a delta to sustain itself against subsidence and the encroaching sea.

But, to Louisianans at the time, a levee had failed and people suffered deprivations. Understandably, they wanted improvements, as did other Americans settling along the Mississippi River. Much like Katrina, Sauvé's Crevasse became a rallying cry for better levees, and its high water line would serve as a local benchmark for subsequent protection. A state law a few years later mandated that the levees along the New Basin Canal "shall be raised to the level of the high water from Sauvé Crevasse of 1849, so as to protect the city from inundation from any future crevasse."

Regionally, Sauvé's Crevasse added momentum to a congressional act passed a few months earlier in 1849, itself having been motivated by valley-wide floods in 1844. The Act to Aid the State of Louisiana in Draining the Swamp Lands ceded federally owned swamps to the state to encourage their reclamation and economic exploitation, thus generating revenue for levee enhancements along the Mississippi. On the heels of the 1849 floods, the so-called "Swampbuster Act" was expanded in 1850 to twelve additional states in the Mississippi Valley, plus two more elsewhere in 1860.

Over the next century, this law would lead to the reclamation of 65 million acres of wetlands, producing wealth and opportunity but also luring people into floodplains and setting up for inevitable flood losses. In Louisiana, the act helped pave the way for extractive and developmental activity in wetlands and marshes, which created jobs and revenue but also environmental losses through canal excavation and swamp drainage.

Sauvé's Crevasse and similar incidents also informed the federal government's ongoing effort to master control of western waterways. Research conducted in the 1850s primarily for navigation improvements eventually led to the creation of the Mississippi River Commission in 1879 and federally sponsored levee improvements in later decades. After the searing lessons of the Great Mississippi River Flood of 1927, the Flood Control Act of 1928 cemented the federal government's commitment to a massively augmented river management system complete with spillways and reservoirs—but without liability should they fail.

The system was a success, and today, New Orleanians no longer fear the sort of riverfront crevasses that threatened their ancestors. But, as a result of the wet-lands damage and leveeing of the Mississippi attributable in part to post-Sauvé responses, plus later oil, gas, and navigation-canal excavation, swamps and coastal wetlands have deteriorated while seawater creeps upward and inward. In essence, over the past two centuries, we have transferred the source of New Orleans's flood threat from high springtime rain and snowmelt flowing out the Mississippi River, to late-summer hurricanes blowing in from the Gulf of Mexico.

Whereas our ancestors would have eyed tensely the extraordinarily high river stages of May 2011 and January 2016, we rested assured our river control sys-tem would work, and it did. But whereas our ancestors generally did not worry about surges from Gulf storms, we nearly lost our city to them in 2005, when our hurricane-protection system failed. In silent testimony to this irony, the site of Sauvé's Crevasse, where rapids tore through 165 years ago, is today a pleasant residential subdivision, situated well above sea level and completely unflooded by the 2005 deluge.

THE GREAT ALGIERS FIRE OF 1895

A hundred and twenty years ago, the heart of Algiers burned to ashes. The 1895 conflagration ranks as the third worst in New Orleans history, after the 1788 and 1794 French Quarter fires, and sheds light on turn-of-the-century society as well as its response to crises—mostly for the better, some for the worse. The footprint of the disaster also helps decipher the cityscape of the modern-day neighborhood of Algiers Point.

At 12:45 a.m. in the windy darkness of Sunday, October 21, 1895, a fire ignited within a crowded Morgan Street tenement known disparagingly as "The Rookery." Northeasterly winds fanned the flames throughout the two-story common-wall apartments, sending a dozen poor, mostly Italian immigrant families fleeing for their lives. Among them were the wife and children of Paul Bouffia, who operated a fruit stand at 307 Morgan, where the fire seemed to have originated.

An alarm was sounded, and three horse-drawn fire trucks arrived promptly from the Engine 17 House on Pelican Avenue. Firemen operating the largest steam pump set its hose into the river, while the other two pump crews tapped into ground wells within a block of the fire. Streams of water arched into the orange glow, and spectators breathed a sigh of relief. But because it had been a dry autumn, the wells "were emptied of water [within] half an hour," wrote local historian William H. Seymour in 1896, leaving only the river pump to douse the rooftop flames. They ignited adjacent houses beyond the pump's reach, and by 2:00 a.m., the 300 block of Morgan and both sides of 200 Bermuda were one gigantic bonfire visible for miles.

Chief Daly of the Algiers Fire Station called for help, but it took a solid hour for larger pumps to arrive via ferry from downtown. By that time, the fire had consumed the Eighth Precinct Police Station and the Algiers Courthouse, located in the century-old Duverjé Plantation House, along with most of 200 Morgan. Reams of official records dating to colonial times added fuel to the fire, and "when the old roof fell in," wrote Seymour, "it sent up a shower of sparks . . . windward" into still more doomed houses. Realizing the blaze was now beyond control, Algierians frantically removed valuables from their homes and carted furniture down to the batture, even as tank trucks and their skittish horses struggled to run relays from the river to the pumper trucks. Mayor John Fitzpatrick and his police and fire chiefs saw firsthand the sheer inadequacy of their resources: wells too dry, pumps too weak, hoses too short, firemen too few, and fuel too plentiful, in the form of wooden houses and yards stocked with coal and firewood—all in the face of that unrelenting wind.

Some would later blame the disaster on Algiers's low prioritization from City Hall (the community, part of unincorporated Orleans Parish, had been annexed into the City of New Orleans in 1870, but remained village-like and isolated from the urban core), a complaint still heard today. Others blamed the firefighters. "The principal causes of the rapid spread of the flames were not only the scarcity of water and a furious wind," wrote the *Picayune*, "but the poor work of the fire department. When they lost control of the fire they became demoralized."

The blaze next consumed both sides of 300 Delaronde, then 300 Bermuda, followed by 200 and 400 Delaronde, most of 100–400 Pelican Avenue (including the fire station), and 100–300 Alix—plus all the intervening streets of Bermuda, Seguin, and Bouny down to Powder. Viewed from downtown, the conflagration must have formed a frightful sight, spanning a quarter-mile at its widest point with hundred-foot-high flames licking the night sky.

Three factors explain why the fire did not destroy all of Algiers. For one, alert operators of the Hotard & Lawton Saw Mill activated their steam pumps and, with 1,300-foot hoses tapping into unlimited river water, were able to soak rooftops

Lavergne Street served as a firebreak for the Great Algiers Fire of 1895 because powerful steam pumps from a nearby sawmill were able to draw water from the Mississippi River and control the flames. For this reason, this circa-1850s townhouse survived the disaster. *Photograph by Richard Campanella.*

and save everything downriver from Lavergne Street. Tugboat crews, meanwhile, sprayed water into the coal barges moored along the river, preventing them from igniting. Most importantly, the wind shifted direction and blew the flames into depleted areas. The fire burned itself out.

By dawn, ten blocks were charred utterly, leaving "a forest of chimneys" amid lingering smoke and glowing embers. At least 193 houses were destroyed and dozens more damaged, not to mention commercial assets and infrastructure. Roughly twelve hundred people found themselves homeless, and while no one was killed, some suffered minor burns and smoke inhalation. Losses were estimated at $400,000, or $11.4 million in today's dollars. There was no Red Cross nor FEMA at the time, nor any government disaster-relief programs to mitigate the losses for those who did not have fire insurance.

How did the fire start? Raising suspicions among neighbors was the rumor that Paul Bouffia, of 307 Morgan, had recently acquired insurance. Bouffia was not a popular man; the *Picayune* cited a source describing him as "heartily disliked," with "a very bad reputation," particularly among his own people, one of whom he had "nearly killed." Neighbors spoke of his suspicious behavior the day prior, and reports circulated "that he had [started] two fires in the place before, which narrowly escaped being disastrous."

Police located Bouffia and carted him to a provisional police station. Enraged survivors gathered outside, "and some were bold enough to openly cry out to lynch him." Others, according to Seymour, spoke of "a contemplated expulsion of the Italian element of the population." Only four years earlier, in 1891, eleven Italians accused of murdering the city's police chief had been cornered and shot by a mob at the Orleans Parish Prison, precipitating an international crisis between the United States and Italy. Bouffia might have met the same fate had not the police safeguarded him until the mob dispersed.

Meanwhile, a mob of a different sort gathered on the ferry, this one of curious gawkers from across the river. So many spectators mounted the iron bridge to the Algiers Ferry House that it collapsed, sending a hundred people into the water. Twenty people were injured, two girls disappeared into the current, and a woman was later found drowned. The initial response of some New Orleanians to the disaster was, in sum, more disastrous than the fire, and both the lynch mob and the bridge collapse gave the city some highly unflattering national news coverage.

What got less coverage was the charitable response of so many New Orleanians. Leaders and citizens alike formed a Relief Committee that Sunday afternoon and secured food and shelter for the homeless at churches, meeting halls, and schools (though all were racially segregated). In the ensuing weeks, nearly $16,000 in donations was raised, or $457,000 in today's dollars—enough, along with insurance claims ($300,000, or $8.5 million today) and social support networks, to get victims back on their feet, if not whole again. The episode serves as a reminder that disaster response in this era came mostly from social support networks, religious institutions, civil society, and charity.

The neighborhood recovered speedily, as the fire had occurred during prosperous times and in the midst of promethean Progressive Era infrastructural improvements. Streets were paved; electrification arrived; a waterworks plant was built to resolve pressure problems; a viaduct was installed to decongest riverfront activity; and a new Moorish-style courthouse with asymmetrical crenellated towers was built, a distinctive landmark to this day. New Victorian townhouses and exuberant gingerbread shotgun houses were erected in such numbers that, by late 1896, according to Seymour, "a walk along those attractive streets makes it difficult to realize that this was the same so lately in ashes and ruins." A similar stroll today is a living lesson in 1896-style urbanism, and it is quite beautiful. One might be tempted to say that, if Algiers had to burn, it did so at a good time.

As for Paul Bouffia, the target of the lynch mob's vengeance, overwhelming evidence arose at a November court hearing that he was on the East Bank when the fire started, and that the accusations against him were entirely traceable to personal animus. "Opinion in Algiers has changed altogether in favor of the suspected man," reported an out-of-state newspaper, and Bouffia was set free.

WHEN BUBONIC PLAGUE CAME TO TOWN

One night in June 1914, a forty-nine-year-old Swedish sailor recently arrived at New Orleans agonized feverishly in a downtown boardinghouse. Rushed to Charity Hospital, he would soon die the loneliest of deaths—in an isolation ward, far from home, surrounded by solemn doctors consulting furtively.

An autopsy confirmed their suspicions: cause of death was bubonic plague, the dreaded lymphatic disease spread by infected fleas on rats. "Black Death," which had nearly wiped out parts of Europe and Asia in the 1300s, had arrived at New Orleans—at the Volunteers of America Home at 713 St. Joseph Street, to be exact.

Previously, bubonic plague had been considered an Old World disease. It had been in recession during most of the era of European contact with the New World, 1500s–1800s, and the long journey across the Atlantic further kept at bay the bacteria and its vectors. This started to change in the late 1800s, by which time invasive rat populations had established themselves throughout the Americas and larger ships crossed the oceans faster and more frequently. It was just a matter of time before infected fleas would find suitable hosts in this vast new habitat.

The first bubonic case in the Western Hemisphere appeared in Brazil in 1899. San Francisco was next in 1900, followed by Puerto Rico and Cuba in 1912. All were trading partners with New Orleans.

Concerned, city and state health officials launched a preemptive rat-trapping campaign in July 1912. Within days, they caught an infected rat on the Stuyvesant Docks between Louisiana and Napoleon avenues. No other specimens were found in 1912 or 1913, and authorities breathed a sigh of relief.

Then, on June 28, 1914, the Swede died.

A second human case came to light the next day, and additional people fell victim at a pace of one every three days for the rest of the summer. August 1914 saw the peak of the outbreak, and it's safe to say that the average New Orleanian that summer worried more about bubonic plague than the war erupting in Europe, a conflict that would eventually involve the United States.

What could have been an epidemiological disaster at the most inopportune moment, however, instead became a resounding public-health success. Key to the control of the epidemic was that federal, state, and city authorities took the earliest signs of the plague with utmost seriousness. Working cooperatively and with broad public support, officials pounced on every suspicious situation with overwhelming force—to levels that might almost seem heavy-handed today. Residents of that Volunteers of America Home, for example, were marched out to be quarantined in an old plantation outside the city, and all furnishings inside were burned in a bonfire on St. Joseph Street while the surrounding neighborhood was put under armed guard.

Infected patients, meanwhile, were sent to a special contagion ward and treated with a newly devised anti-plague serum so powerful that, in one case, it turned a 108-degree fever into a 96-degree chill and required the ice packs around the man's body to be replaced by hot water bags. "The patient was literally hauled back from the edge of the grave," recounted C. L. Williams, who participated in the response and lectured on it years later.

For the other 350,000 residents of the city, a three-pronged prevention strategy was enacted. It entailed reducing the rat population through a massive trapping campaign, finding and destroying nesting and breeding "foci," and, finally, transforming the cityscape to separate rats and humans as much as possible. An army of 380 workers swept across the city to carry out the campaign. In a single week, they inspected 6,500 railcars and 4,200 buildings, fumigated 101 ships, trapped 20,000 rodents, laid nearly 300,000 poison baits, and discovered seventeen infected rats. Using sound scientific protocols, workers recorded data for each trapped rat, and when a laboratory analysis identified an infected specimen, its point of origin was subjected to a scorched-earth campaign of fumigation, burning, and in some cases, complete leveling. A building right next door to the campaign's headquarters was demolished for this reason. Tactics like these went on daily, citywide, for months.

Ground zero in the geography of rats proved to be the Stuyvesant Docks, where that first infected specimen had been found two years earlier. Here, mechanical conveyors transferred midwestern grain among railroad cars, ships, and elevators. Coupled with the warm fresh river water and ample nesting opportunities, the Stuyvesant elevators were a veritable rat nirvana. The campaign made them into a rat graveyard.

Cases abated by year's end, but the campaign carried into 1915, when the city passed ordinances calling for the "rat-proofing" of buildings. Codes were put in place to get human living spaces raised above the land surface—an architectural tradition long practiced anyway for flooding reasons—while mandating floorboards be layered with concrete and barriers installed around crawl spaces.

While the degree to which rat-proofing materially affected the city's architecture is unclear, it's worth noting that this same era also witnessed the decline of traditional vernacular buildings such as shotgun houses in favor of subdivision-based bungalows and, in time, tract housing set on concrete slabs. Although rat-proofing ordinances did not cause these transformations, they may have abetted them. Other codes passed in 1915 regulated the raising of animals within city limits and required the use of closed garbage cans.

Bubonic plague did not end decisively in New Orleans; rather, it petered out. A human death in 1919 led to a redeployment of the 1914 strategy, only this time targeted at black rats—"roof rats," which live at higher levels than ground-dwelling Norway rats—as well as ships, the primary rodent pathway into the city. It was equally successful, and by the late 1920s New Orleans was declared free of bubonic plague.

Because of the rigor of the New Orleans campaign, the 1914 outbreak was limited to around thirty human cases and ten deaths, sparing possibly thousands from disfiguring illness and death. From a purely pragmatic standpoint, the campaign also had an immeasurable economic impact, in that it allowed the city to play a key role in the American involvement in World War I. Local authorities had successfully lobbied the military for a naval facility and quartermaster depot as well as port modernization, all of which created jobs and valuable new infrastructure. Troops in transit pumped money into the local economy, and Mississippi River traffic boomed as vast quantities of matériel heading for the front had overwhelmed the nation's rail system and forced the federal government to reinvigorate the inland waterways system, additionally benefiting New Orleans.

War, of course, is a terrible thing, but life in New Orleans would have been that much worse had the conflict coincided with epidemic and quarantine.

The 1914 campaign would serve as a model to control similar outbreaks elsewhere. "New York May Be Next [in] War on Rodents, Following Example of New Orleans," read a 1915 *New York Times* headline, which went on to detail "Boston, Philadelphia, and other important seaports" emulating the Crescent City's approach. When the plague appeared in Los Angeles in the 1920s, New Orleans quarantine station chief Dr. T. J. Liddell was dispatched to California as an expert adviser.

The success exemplifies how locally devised solutions to adversity can lay the groundwork for future economic strength. Consider, for example, how much of New Orleans's medical sector today may be traced back to the city's nineteenth-century battles with yellow fever. Or how the Dutch parlayed flood control and water management into national wealth-creation industries. Or how the Poles turned the destruction of World War II into a national proficiency in historical restoration.

New Orleans has all too many opportunities to convert liabilities to assets, in everything from public education and poverty to urban drainage, subsidence, hypoxia, and coastal erosion. This much is clear: New Orleans's war on bubonic plague would not have been won if public and private sectors as well as citizens had not been coordinated and united against a common enemy.

THE GREAT STORM OF 1915

August 2015 marks the anniversaries of four major New Orleans hurricanes: ten years since Katrina and Rita, fifty since Betsy, and one hundred since the Great Storm of 1915. Most New Orleanians recall all too well some or all of the first three, but the 1915 hurricane, with hardly any living witnesses, has been largely forgotten. That World War I–era tempest is worth remembering because it struck at a time when the modernizing metropolis had not yet suffered the sort of geophysical deterioration that would exacerbate our more recent disasters.

Summer 1915 had already proven tragic for the Gulf Coast. An August hurricane had killed four hundred people in Galveston, despite the new seawall erected by the Texas city in the aftermath of its horrific catastrophe of 1900, the deadliest natural disaster in American history. Just six years earlier, in 1909, a major hurricane destroyed Grand Isle and flooded the lowlands in New Orleans as well.

Now, on September 22, 1915, sailors reported a new system brewing in the Lesser Antilles. Over the next week, it wended between the Yucatan Peninsula and Cuba, evading cooler land surfaces while drawing energy from the warm sea. The vortex strengthened.

Tracking the reports in New Orleans was famed meteorologist Isaac M. Cline, the tragic figure of the Galveston Hurricane of 1900 and, by 1915, probably the most qualified storm forecaster in the nation. Stationed in the Weather Bureau office in the recently opened U.S. Post Office (today's Fifth Circuit Court of Appeals Building), Cline analyzed incoming data and realized that a direct hit on New Orleans was imminent. On Tuesday morning, September 28, he noted an ominous "cirrus veil" clouding city skies, following a "faint brick-dust" sunset. The outermost feeder bands arrived that night, each one accompanied by sporadic gusty rain. New Orleanians took shelter at home or in sturdy neighborhood buildings; evacuation was neither a possibility nor a recommendation. If anything, coastal denizens fled into the city to join their urban compatriots in the relative safety of the metropolis. Cline sent out messages to outlying communities to do exactly that, pronto.

The eye struck Grand Isle around midnight and veered to position New Orleans in the system's dangerous northeastern quadrant. At dawn on September 29, what would become known as the Great Storm of 1915 arrived at the city, and, just like Katrina ninety years later, it would take one full excruciating day to wreak its havoc.

Low barometric pressure plus hundred-mile-per-hour winds swelled Gulf waters by fifteen to twenty feet, while Lake Pontchartrain rose by five feet, the highest recorded to date. That was enough to overtop the meager lakefront levees and, as during Katrina, penetrate the adjoining London Avenue, Orleans, and Seventeenth Street outfall canals. More seawater entered city limits via the circa-1830s New Basin Canal (now the West End Boulevard–Interstate 10 corridor) and the circa-1790s Old Basin Canal (now the Lafitte Greenway), which connected with Bayou St. John and the lake. "The overflow from these sources, [plus] about 7¼ inches of rainfall, was a most discouraging feature of this day's development," understated a Sewerage and Water Board engineer.

Saltwater began to impound in low spots in present-day Lakeview and Broadmoor, which were still largely uninhabited at the time. "Over that portion of the city lying between the Old Basin Canal and Broadway and from Claiborne Avenue out to Lake Pontchartrain," wrote Cline, "the water depth driven in by the storm ranged from 1 to 8 feet."

Next came the levee failures, or "crevasses," as francophone New Orleanians called them. The Florida Avenue rear-protection levee breached in a number of spots, allowing Bayou Bienvenue to pour into the lightly populated rears of the Seventh, Eighth, and Ninth wards. (The Industrial Canal was not yet dug, so there was no distinguishing an upper and lower Ninth Ward.) Flooding was worse in St. Bernard and Plaquemines parishes, in part because, as during Katrina, the swollen Mississippi spilled laterally over the riverfront levees and swept across the low country.

Back in New Orleans, gales gusted until 6:35 p.m., when they abated and reversed directions as the eye of the three-hundred-mile-wide system passed twelve miles west of downtown. That evening, a *Times-Picayune* reporter described "a peculiar lightening . . . flaring up in sheets not unlike the fire coming out of the mouths of serpents," as the storm proceeded into Tangipahoa and St. Tammany parishes. At dusk, New Orleanians peered out their windows and surveyed their circumstances. "CITY CUT OFF FROM REST OF WORLD," read a worried headline in that evening's *Item*.

By the next morning, sun shone over the Crescent City. Residents were stunned by the effects of the wind: over twenty-five thousand structures suffered serious structural damage, among them eleven major churches which lost their steeples. French Market pavilions were leveled; the Old French Opera House was damaged; and the famous St. Louis Hotel, Horticultural Hall in Audubon Park, and Leland University on St. Charles Avenue were all so battered they were subsequently demolished.

As for the floodwaters, they receded everywhere except within levee-encircled areas, where the pumps from the recently installed municipal drainage system took four days to eject them into adjacent water bodies. Damages exceeded $13 million, with roughly half in New Orleans proper. At least 275 Louisianans perished, including at least 43 in the Rigolets and Lake Catherine. Isaac Cline described the storm as "the most intense hurricane of which we have record in the history of the Mexican Gulf coast and probably in the United States."

In retrospect, the marvel of the Great Storm of 1915 was the ferocity of its wind damage—yet also the limit of its water damage. "'STORM PROOF!' *The Record Shows New Orleans*," crowed the *Item* the day after. That was gross overstatement, but compared to Betsy, Katrina, Rita, Gustav, and other hurricanes, the 1915 storm arrived stronger and better positioned to devastate New Orleans utterly. Four reasons explain why it did not.

First, nearly nineteen hundred additional square miles of marsh and swamp surrounded the city and region, acting as terrestrial friction against Gulf surges. Second, no major navigation canals allowed Gulf waters to penetrate into the city's eastern flanks. Third, the newly installed municipal drainage system had not yet had enough time to dry out the lakeside lowlands and allow them to sub-side—but nonetheless served to pump out the water that did become impounded. Finally, urbanization and population of lakeside and outlying environs had barely begun by 1915, and most New Orleanians remained on the higher ground closer to the Mississippi River.

Since the Great Storm of 1915, we've lost those nineteen hundred square miles of wetlands; we dug two big funnel-forming navigation canals in the eastern marshes, not to mention thousands of miles of oil and gas canals; we allowed our topography to sink into below-sea-level bowls; and we encouraged development to sprawl out broadly as if none of these things mattered.

The rest, as they say, is history.

But it was no coincidence.

ONE STORM, ONE DILEMMA; TWO DECISIONS, TWO CONSEQUENCES

Ten years ago this month, thousands of displaced New Orleanians found them-selves in the throes of a major life decision. Should they return and rebuild de-spite great uncertainty, or cast their lot elsewhere?

In the foreseeable future, residents of coastal Louisiana will grapple with a comparable choice, as planners increasingly speak of radically reconfiguring the mouth of the Mississippi River in the interest of forestalling further land loss. Should coastal communities remain in eroding marshes, or end their way of life and move inland so that aggressive restoration may commence? Should we en-deavor to save all communities, even if doing so puts everyone at greater risk? Or should we sacrifice some so that a greater number can have a greater good?

A hundred years ago this week, two unnamed individuals were confronted

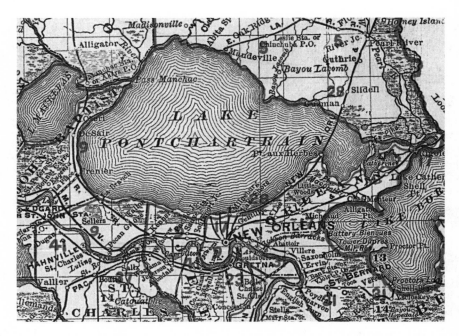

This 1895 map shows the rail lines passing through Manchac to the west of Lake Pontchartrain (left), and through the Rigolets to the east (right), both of which would play roles in a terrible drama during the Great Storm of 1915. *Map (detail) courtesy Library of Congress.*

with a microcosm of this same essential dilemma. The circumstances involved one massive hurricane as it inundated two similar places on either side of the same lake, presenting the same excruciating choice. While their decisions shine faint light on our path ahead, together they testify that decent people and decent arguments can be found on either side of the "save-all-risk-all" versus "sacrifice-some-save-many" dilemma.

The Great Storm of 1915

It was on September 22, 1915, that authorities began receiving reports of a tropical system in the West Indies. It gained power through the Caribbean, entered the Gulf of Mexico, and bore northwestwardly across fueling warm seas. At the Weather Bureau office by Lafayette Square, meteorologist Isaac Cline realized the storm track positioned New Orleans for a direct hit. Word got out to city dwellers, who on Tuesday, September 28, took shelter at home or in public buildings.

Residents of outlying marshes were delayed in receiving warning. Two particular regions were at maximum risk: St. John the Baptist Parish's Manchac isthmus to the west of Lake Pontchartrain, and Orleans Parish's narrow Rigolets land bridge to the lake's east. Both were home to fishing and hunting communities, with loggers predominating in Manchac and sportsmen's camps in the Rigolets, and both had railroads running through them.

At dawn on September 29, the hurricane made landfall at Grand Isle with at least Category 4 force. Tens of thousands of structures would be damaged by wind or water, yet ample coastal wetlands absorbed much of the surge in the town proper, and the population remained generally safe. That was not the case in Manchac or the Rigolets, which had only open water to their east—and that's where the surge was coming from.

In Manchac, a fourteen-year-old girl by the name of Helen Schlosser Burg described what happened to her once-idyllic village of Wagram. "Water was all around . . . risen about 10 feet," she told local historian and author Wayne Norwood in a 1990 interview. "Waves were hitting against the house[;] all of us kids were crying and scared to death."

Helen's parents realized the family was doomed if they stayed put, so they took flight in a pirogue for a nearby schoolhouse partly protected by the railroad tracks. But when the water "had risen to 20 feet, [it came] over the track [and] the building was starting to move." They reboarded the pirogue and paddled for the dubious refuge of the swamp.

Then they heard the whistle.

It was Train No. 99, making its way from Hammond to Harahan, pulling cars full of evacuees from the nearby enclaves of Manchac, Ruddock, and Napton. With ever-rising seawater covering the rails and splashing against the hot boiler, time was of the essence. One could only imagine the split-second decision confronting the engineer. Stopping the train would save Wagram's residents. But the lost time would heighten the risk facing passengers already on board.

The Rigolets

Forty miles straight east, a similar drama played out in the Rigolets, home to hunting and fishing camps. The meteorologist Cline made a point of telephoning the Anglers' Club on the morning of the storm to urge a last-minute evacuation. Incredibly, the call went through, and Cline urged the club's caretaker, Manuel Marquez, to flag down the last inbound train. He later recorded the conversation:

"[T]he train [will] not stop for [us]," Marquez countered.

"[Then] put a cross tie on the track" and force them to stop, Cline replied.

"They will put me in jail," Marquez groused.

"You would be better off in jail than where you are now and for God's sake stop that train at all hazards and come to New Orleans[!]"

Moments later, the Mobile Limited steamed through the turbid waves hauling cars loaded with anxious passengers. As Marquez frantically flagged it down, the engineer found himself in the same moral quandary as his counterpart in Manchac. Keep rolling, or brake?

He braked.

But he did so with pointed ambivalence, and while Marquez rushed off to gather the others, the engineer changed his mind. "The rising tide was jeopardizing the passengers on the train," Cline later explained, "which could not wait until the people could be collected from the houses."

Manchac

The train in Manchac, meanwhile, plowed through tempestuous surf near the wrecked Wagram schoolhouse. "Everyone started waving their arms and screaming," recalled Helen Schlosser, "hoping the engineer would see us." Like his counterpart in the Rigolets, the Manchac engineer also braked. But in this case, he granted time for people to round up their kin. "We loaded onto the train and then headed south," said Helen, "stopping at each house and picking up people." Each stop rescued additional victims. But it also expended precious time. The surge heightened. Water entered the cars.

Finally, time ran out. The track had washed away, stranding Train No. 99 with waves "about 15 feet high . . . 20 or 25 feet now. . . . hitting against the train." The *Times-Picayune* reported a train "mysteriously dropped out of sight between Manchac and New Orleans."

Consequences

After the storm, rescuers surveyed the damage. What they saw was tragic.

In Manchac, Helen recounted twenty-eight dead, including family members and neighbors stranded in or near the train. In the Rigolets, Marquez's "lifeless body, with 23 others . . . were found strewn over the marshes," wrote Cline, among them the caretaker's wife, sister, nine children, and grandchildren plus eleven club patrons.

As for the engineer who left the Rigolets people behind, "the last train in," reported the *Times-Picayune*, "was the Mobile Limited, which reached the city at 11:50 o'clock a.m., [having gone] some distance . . . through water." All on board survived. The Anglers' Club, meanwhile, had been "literally splintered into kindling wood."

The dual tragedies of the West Indian Hurricane of 1915—or what Cline called the Great Storm of 1915, "the most intense hurricane of which we have record"— are unique to their circumstances. But the ethical dilemmas involved are timeless, and they have parallels to our situation today.

Should coastal inhabitants advocate for heightened levees? Or should they read the tea leaves of limited federal wherewithal and rising flood insurance rates and move "inside the wall"?

Should we focus on barrier-island restoration rather than freshwater diversions so that fishing economies may be preserved? Or do we need all restoration strategies deployed maximally as soon as possible?

Should we try to sustain all communities? Or should we expropriate the riskiest so that larger numbers in less-risky areas may gain greater sustainability?

Put succinctly, is an exodus from paradise necessary for its redemption?

Two ethical philosophies are at play here. Those who find themselves sympathizing with the Manchac engineer's decision hold a deontological stance. Deontology (literally, "binding duty") maintains that certain actions are intrinsically right or wrong, regardless of consequences. This was the philosophy held by those who argued ten years ago that all New Orleans neighborhoods had a right to return, or who feel today that the nation is morally obligated to save all vulnerable enclaves.

Those who find themselves resigned to the Rigolets engineer's choice are "utilitarians" who sense the best decision is that which produces the greatest good for the greatest number. That is, while some actions might seem more righteous than others, in the end it's their consequences that matter. This philosophy is known as consequentialism or utilitarianism.

The Manchac engineer might have been morally principled in stopping at each town, bound by duty to save everyone. But that deontological inclination ended up costing the lives of those on the train.

The Rigolets engineer might have seemed coldly utilitarian in his decision to abandon people. But that consequentialist philosophy ended up saving lives.

If you're like me, your heart is with the Manchac engineer. But your intellect probably understands the Rigolets engineer.

Likewise, in a world of limited resources and a Louisiana coast sinking amid rising seas—Wagram itself, notes local historian Wayne Norwood, "no longer exists, [its] farm land now in the lake because of erosion"—the intellect understands that some communities may have to be ceded so that coastal restoration may be fast-tracked to protect the many.

But the heart begs otherwise—especially if it's beating within the body of a coastal resident.

WHAT THE NATION'S BEST-EDUCATED AMATEUR PLANNERS LEARNED FROM HURRICANE ISAAC. AND GUSTAV. AND RITA AND KATRINA. AND CINDY, IVAN, LILI, ISIDORE, AND GEORGES . . .

AUTHOR'S NOTE: *This essay, published in* Places Journal, *was written for nationwide readers in the weeks after Hurricane Isaac in 2012.*

Few regional societies have gained a more rigorous place-based education in recent years than the inhabitants of greater New Orleans and coastal Louisiana. The past two decades have imparted, to nearly two million people, college-level lessons in geography, hydrology, climatology, engineering, civics, disaster recovery, sociology, and urban planning. The "curriculum" was tough, the "tuition" high, and the "classes" time-consuming, and all the while the "students" worked full-time jobs, maintained households, and raised families—in a poor region and during difficult economic times.

By some measures the schooling began with a "professor" named Andrew twenty years ago. But Hurricane Andrew, which wrecked southern Florida and disheveled south-central Louisiana on August 24–26, 1992, was a Category 5 exception to an otherwise placid year during a relatively quiet period of tropical activity. That ended in 1995, when the pace of storm development upticked markedly and has remained high ever since.

1998

The education began in earnest with Hurricane Georges on September 28, 1998. By that time, scientists had become convinced, and word had gotten out to policy-makers and citizens, that a century's worth of soil subsidence, coastal erosion, and sea-level rise would bring storm surges dangerously close to levee-rimmed, bowl-shaped New Orleans. That meant that officials increasingly discouraged coastal denizens from seeking refuge in the metropolis, as well as New Orleanians sheltering themselves in sturdy civic buildings, as they had done for Betsy in 1965, the Hurricane of 1947, and prior. A last-minute meteorological twitch pushed Georges toward Biloxi and mostly spared New Orleans, but not before tens of thousands of families fled in the city's first large-scale evacuation—only to find themselves mired in horrendous and potentially dangerous traffic jams with no place to go. Thus began residents' high-school education in geography and disaster planning: coastal wetlands buffer storm surges. If they erode, the waves come right up to the levees, and if they overtop them, Gulf waters flood our bowl-shaped city. Ergo, evacuation would become the new order. And that was easier said than done.

2002–2004

Sophomore-, junior-, and senior-year lessons on these same themes came from Isidore (2002), Lili (2002), and Ivan (2004), the last of which triggered a full-scale metropolitan evacuation. By then authorities were deploying a new "contraflow" system which allowed outbound traffic to drive on inbound lanes, an unsettling experience requiring careful planning and inter-agency coordination. This lesson would take time to learn, and the Ivan evacuation proved to be even more tortuous than Georges. Ivan, too, spared the city, and in retrospect it may have taught a bad lesson to citizens, in that it made officials seem too cautious and prone to crying wolf. It also made "hunkering down" at home, or utilizing civic shelters-of-last-resort, seem like wise recourse, especially for those without cars or cash for many days evacuated.

The year 2004 also saw authorities themselves taking remedial lessons from an instructor named Hurricane Pam, a federal-state exercise designed to understand the impact of a hypothetical Category 3 storm that overtopped the levees. It was not pretty.

2005

Summer 2005 opened with a pop quiz. A sloppy early-July tropical storm named Cindy came ashore, the likes of which happen annually and barely raise an eyebrow. Cindy, however, nearly raised the roof. Under-predicted and under-reported, the storm caused a startling amount of wind damage, blackened the electrical grid, left local broadcast meteorologists red-faced, and later matriculated in the record books as a Category 1 hurricane. Lesson: hurricanes are complex, multivariate phenomena defined by uncertainty, and the way we categorize them often underreports hidden dangers and misleads the public. And this being early July, we may be in for quite a summer.

Indeed it was—the busiest on record. The late summer of 2005 awarded residents of this region interdisciplinary Bachelor of Science degrees courtesy of professors named Katrina and Rita. The twosome taught crash courses on August 29 and September 23 so tough that many students did not survive. Those who did learned more than they ever wanted to. We learned

—that we had been worrying too much about the tolerable problem of levee overtopping, and too little about the unthinkable catastrophe of multiple levee failures.

—that our federal flood protection was a system in name only—piecemeal, disjointed, shoddily engineered, poorly maintained, sloppily inspected, underfunded, and oversold.

—that the Army Corps of Engineers, FEMA, and other agencies at the federal, state, and local levels bore responsibility for various elements of the fiasco.

—that the deltaic terrain had subsided deeper, and the sea had risen higher, than engineers had foreseen, yet no adjustments were made to the defense system.

—that a century of navigation, oil, gas, and drainage-canal excavation, plus the leveeing of the Mississippi River, had turned nearly two thousand square miles of coastal marshes into scored and scarred watery surfaces offering minimal friction against storm-pushed waters gliding and funneling inland.

—that the absence of closeable gates at the mouths of outfall canals, a result of interagency disputes, meant outside water could penetrate the heart of the metropolis but for the floodwalls—which failed.

—that it was a mistake to locate (circa 1895) the lift pumps of the municipal drainage system in the interior of the basins they drained, because subsequent subsidence meant the pumps would be lifting water above people's homes via elevated outfall canals lined with floodwalls—which collapsed.

—that a deluge respects no jurisdictional boundaries, and a breach on one side of the parish line may well flood folks on the other.

—that topographic elevation matters, and that while living on higher ground may not guarantee against flooding, it will ensure shallower flood depths, usually substantially.

—that the Army Corps of Engineers is not liable for flooding caused by the failure of federal flood-control devices, but rather only when navigation projects lead to flooding.

—that evacuation only works if you have a car—and even then, it's costly, difficult, and potentially dangerous.

—that municipally approved shelters of last resort are a good idea only if the municipality has every intention of keeping said places safe and fit for human occupancy.

—that nursing homes, hospitals, and any place with elders or the infirm need their own power and provisions, else will turn into death traps.

—that emergency responders need to be on-site and on the offensive before the storm, not arriving afterwards playing defense. And they need to be on the same wavelengths—literally: radio frequencies.

—that a calamity of this nature brings out the best in most people, but the worst in some.

—that a metropolitan-scale deluge wrecks *all* urban systems: electricity, gas, water, and sewerage treatment and distribution, telephony and communications, transportation ingresses and egresses, refuse collection and disposal, all forms of health care, schooling, policing, incarceration, and most ominously, fire suppression. It also stews together the gasoline and oil of hundreds of thousands of vehicles, and the toxins of local industries and hundreds of thousands of households. It damages asphalt, taints soils, deposits sediment, kills animals, and poisons vegetation. And did we mention the mold?

Professors Katrina and Rita were not without a sense of humor. They also taught us that an evacuated metropolis leaves behind, oh, two hundred thousand refrigerators loaded with putrid pot-pies and rancid raviolis. Who would have guessed. Each toxic box had to be duct-taped, wobbled out to the curb, hauled off by specialized HAZ-MAT units, drained of fluorocarbons, and discarded along with a roughly equal number of destroyed cars and millions of tons of household interiors.

2006–2007

For the next couple of years, residents of greater New Orleans and southern Louisiana did graduate work in disaster recovery and urban planning. In marathon civic sessions and innumerable neighborhood meetings, we learned how to rebuild a city: houses, neighborhoods, businesses, schools, cultural events—everything. We came to understand that cultural memory and economic inequality informs people's interpretations of why the floodwaters and recovery resources were not evenly distributed, spawning suspicions, conspiracy theories, and race-, class-, and place-based resentment and competition. We also learned that people tend to resist proposals for change after a disaster, and crave instead normalcy—and the more radical the change, the greater the resistance. We learned it's easier and less controversial to let people resettle wherever they were and wherever they wanted, rather than redraw the urban footprint in light of the geographical lessons learned. Indeed, some students *unlearned* lessons, while others became bona fide amateur experts in everything from citizen participation in planning, to public health, to running a nonprofit, to starting a business, to dealing with FEMA, the Road Home program, the Army Corps of Engineers, law, policy, and city government. Having lectured and interacted with members of the public on a wide range of geographical topics before, during, and after Katrina, I can personally attest to the dramatically heightened level of knowledge and understanding among average citizens on these topics. Hurricanes, like wars, are great geography teachers.

2008

Hurricane Gustav provided an opportunity for us to earn continuing education units. Coming within a few days of the third anniversary of Katrina—school usually begins around September 1—Professor Gustav began with a test of what we learned during our undergrad years. We did well. The storm was powerful, though certainly no Katrina, yet the levees and floodwalls (undergoing upgrades at the time) prevented a repeat of 2005. The contraflow evacuation passed too, in part because authorities had been inculcating the public about preparing for such a scenario. A new system of public buses ensured that those without cars did not get left behind, and it too worked well. There were no more centers of last resort; nearly everyone evacuated—and this time, everyone knew to empty their refrigerator. Officials scored high in securing the city *before* the strike and guarding against looting during and afterwards. They allowed people to take their pets on evacuation buses, a wise and humane new policy which prevented a repeat of heart-wrenching dramas in 2005, often involving children. And they let evacuees return as soon as possible so they could bring their stilled city back to life.

On that note, we also gained insights in thinking back on the past ten years. While evacuations can save thousands of lives if a catastrophe like Katrina happens, they can also be terribly expensive, disruptive, and even fatal for some. I myself began to wonder: can a modern metropolis survive living one-fifth of every year under the threat of massive interruption to all forms of human life? Or would this major competitive disadvantage drive away families and investors and eventually winnow the population down to that of a Venetian-like boutique city?

2010–2011

Additional continuing education units were earned from a 2010 guest lecturer from England, who gave the entire world a lesson in the risks of deep-sea drilling and what happens when a blowout preventer fails in its eponymous task. From the BP Deepwater Horizon disaster, we learned firsthand lessons on topics such as surface slicks, tar balls, containment booms, dispersants, oil-eating microbes, and the relationships among ecology, culture, and economics. A year later, we learned a very different lesson, this time a comforting one: that while the Army Corps of Engineers is relatively new to handling hurricane storm surges, it has two hundred years of experience in managing the Mississippi River, and rates tops in the world in this herculean task. Exceedingly high water came down the Mississippi River system from April through July 2011, and the intricate system of spillways, floodways, easements, levees, weirs, control structures, and armoring installed after the Great Flood of 1927 worked flawlessly in keeping the number of flood victims to an absolute minimum.

2012

The 2012 school year opened precisely seven years after Katrina and nearly four years after Gustav, when Hurricane Isaac imparted our latest batch of tests and classes. Some we flubbed; others we aced. As Cindy (should have) taught us in July 2005, we relearned from Isaac that storm categorizations can be deceptively simplistic, especially after the 2009 elimination of storm-surge estimations from the Saffir-Simpson scale. We made the mistake of poo-pooing Isaac's Category 1 status and were startled at its strong surge driven in on a 45-degree-angle track, with metro New Orleans positioned in the dreaded northeastern quadrant. We also came to appreciate the relevance of a storm's forward momentum. Isaac slowed to nary a jog as it approached the mouth of the Mississippi and meandered erratically westward of New Orleans for the better part of two days. A slowed system means more time for surge, wind, and rain (totaling twenty inches for the duration of the event, more than Katrina and Gustav combined) to do their damage. Mercifully, the rain was fairly well distributed spatially and temporally, but the winds pulled down thousands of poles and wires and left nearly the entire region without power for three to six days. The same happened in earlier storms, but because most people had evacuated for them, few suffered the full extent of the outages. This time was different. Enraged customers shook their fists at Entergy for the interminable wait night after sweltering night. Their discomfort was undeniable and their frustration inevitable, but their accusations of incompetence and foot-dragging were faulty and unreasonable on technical grounds. A task of this nature is enormous, dangerous, and logistically complex, and by most qualified assessments, Entergy exceeded expectations. The Department of Energy, which grades utilities on power restoration and is more than eager to flunk a laggard, gave Entergy an "A+" for their Isaac work. Nevertheless, we learned that the burying of electrical utilities, which protects lines from winds and falling trees, deserves a thorough cost/benefit analysis. Nearly ten times in the past fifteen years this region has suffered widespread storm-related blackouts; at what point do these burdensome interruptions and repeat variable costs become more expensive than the fixed cost of burying utilities once and for all?

We also learned some good news. The Army Corps of Engineers' $14.5 billion levee-upgrading project worked perfectly. No longer called a flood-protection system but rather the Risk Reduction System (now there's a lesson), the effort fast-tracked thirty years of work—heightened levees; strengthened floodwalls; built Dutch-style surge barriers, closeable canal gates with bypass pumps, and the world's largest pumping station—in six years. The new system promised protection against a storm that has a 1 percent chance of occurring in any given year. The metropolis needs and deserves a higher level of protection; Katrina was measured as a 0.25 percent storm and therefore would have partially penetrated the upgraded defenses. Nevertheless, on the heels of the Army Corps' perfectly executed control of the Mississippi River Flood of 2011, I would offer that New Orleanians should start relearning how to respect and trust these talented engineers, and recognize how vastly improved the department has become since the shocking lessons of Katrina.

The completed Risk Reduction System persuaded authorities in New Orleans not to declare a mandatory evacuation ahead of Hurricane Isaac. This, to me, deserves another leadership kudo. Whereas Katrina and Gustav warranted mandatory evacuations, Isaac did not, and I am buoyed by the fact that authorities resisted the litigiously tempting instinct to "err on the side of caution" and pull the get-out trigger. For all the discomfort and damage of Isaac, it would have been much worse if a million people had been forced out onto the road needlessly. The billions of taxpayer dollars spent on risk reduction ought to pay more dividends than just keeping water out of the city. Too many unnecessary evacuations may hobble this metropolis even if another Katrina does not.

But non-evacuation also changes place-based planning. It means people sheltering at home will likely lose their power and suffer in subtropical heat—no trivial matter for elders—and may need cooling centers and other sanctioned spaces with provisions, medicine, communications, and climate control. It means hospitals and nursing homes must have their own generators. It means homeless people need shelters. And it means that, while authorities may discourage people from circulating beyond their homes during non-evacuations, they cannot arrest them for so doing, as during a mandatory evacuation.

Similarly, the Risk Reduction System changed the physics of where the storm surge went. By how much, we do not yet know, but this much is clear: surge flooding during Isaac occurred in places that never flooded before, such as Braithwaite, located on the relatively high natural levee of the Mississippi River in Plaquemines Parish, and in LaPlace in St. John Parish, relatively far from open Gulf waters. Did the successful protection of areas inside the improved federal levees send waves reverberating into adjacent areas that were weakly guarded by inadequate parish levees? Or did Isaac's wicked 45-degree track and maddeningly slow shuffle account for the difference? If and when these questions are answered empirically, I ponder what might be the lesson. Surely no one is suggesting that the Risk Reduction System, which protects over a million people inside, ought to be compromised for the sake of a few thousand outside. And extending that federal system—in this nation of limited resources—would only pass the reverberations onto the subsequent perimeter of communities.

Finally, Isaac iterated a lesson delivered repeatedly since the 1990s: that while structurally engineering our way out of this problem may extend the life of this metropolis for another few generations, long-term sustainability will come only when we figure out how to rebuild sinking, eroding coastal wetlands at a pace faster than the level of the sea is rising. Given the low supply of sediment in the

Mississippi and the costly and complex nature of diverting sediment and fresh-water onto the coastal marshes, our time window in which we can reverse the course of this battle is narrowing. If we take home one additional lesson from the graduate school of the past two decades, may it be that the Army Corps' success in fast-tracking massive structural engineering projects during 2006–12 must be replicated for nonstructural coastal restoration during the 2010s and 2020s.

Else we might not survive our PhD.

THE GREAT FOOTPRINT DEBATE, UPDATED

AUTHOR'S NOTE: *This essay was originally published as a guest editorial in the* Times-Picayune *as the tenth anniversary of Hurricane Katrina neared in the summer of 2015.*

In the heady aftermath of the Katrina deluge, New Orleanians grappled with the possibility that certain neighborhoods would be expropriated for green space and their city's urban footprint "shrunk." As a participant-observer in that debate, I penned in April 2006 a guest editorial that aimed to capture the range of arguments.

At one end, I wrote, were the "abandonists," who contended greater New Orleans was geophysically unsustainable and, as one geologist put it, we best "cut our losses now and move . . . to higher ground." This side usually argued from a purely scientific stance, and put little thought into the implications or alternatives to abandoning a city.

At the opposite end were those who advocated for maintaining the entire urban footprint at all costs. Seeing this debate as primarily a social question, "maintainers" held that everyone had a right to return, and that adequate levees could and should be built around everyone.

In between fell the "concessionists," who tried to justify those social values against the troubling scientific data. Their answer: concede certain low-lying, hard-hit areas to nature and shrink the urban footprint to its higher historic urban core.

By late 2006, it was clear that the "maintainers" had prevailed. No neighborhoods were closed, and people resettled in existing patterns. The 2011 completion of the Army Corps of Engineers' $14.5 billion improved levee system seemed to validate their position that the whole footprint could come back—even though coastal conditions have only deteriorated beyond levee walls.

What has emerged in the past decade is a fourth stance—that of the "mitigators." Mitigators seek to reduce the costs of life, damage, and disruption *before* disasters strike. In New Orleans, mitigation means building above the grade and raising existing homes. It involves strengthening building codes, installing shutters, and getting key infrastructure out of the basement. It means improving local drainage, zoning new development out of flood zones, and rebuilding natural defenses. Mitigation also entails streamlining evacuation and training first responders.

We may think of the mitigation argument as the logical outcome of the maintainers' victory to keep the full urban footprint vis-à-vis the dire coastal erosion and sea-level rise pointed out (softly) by the concessionists and (loudly) by the abandonists.

Probably the most effective way to understand what risk and mitigation mean to the average metro-area homeowner is to look at federal flood insurance. Congress created the National Flood Insurance Program (NFIP) in 1968 largely because private companies had stopped writing flood policies. They were too risky to make a profit. NFIP aimed to reduce the costs of disaster recovery by pooling and managing risk beforehand, and to protect federally backed mortgages in flood zones. But NFIP also lured development into flood-prone areas. When catastrophes struck—namely Katrina, Ike, and Sandy—claims surged, and NFIP fell into debt, to the tune of more than $20 billion.

The Biggert-Waters Flood Insurance Reform Act of 2012 sought to make NFIP solvent by realigning premiums with actual risk. But, incredibly, no one in Washington seemed to have calculated what impact this would have on affordability. Else they would have foreseen what many stunned homeowners learned in 2013: their flood insurance rates had skyrocketed by 1,000 to 3,000 percent. Protests ensued, and Biggert-Waters was itself "reformed" with the Homeowner Flood Insurance Affordability Act of 2014, which essentially implemented gradual rate increases rather than sudden jumps.

But the writing is on the wall: Rates are going up because risk is going up. Since 1980, the nation has suffered more than $260 billion in flood damages, and floods have accounted for 85 percent of all declared disasters. Flood "costs borne by the Federal government are more than any other hazard," stated FEMA, and "with climate change, we anticipate that flooding risks will increase."

The optimal response, wrote University of New Orleans professor emerita of sociology and disaster expert Dr. Shirley Laska in an email communication, is to

Extent of Hurricane Katrina–induced flooding is shown in a shaded tone in this obliquely viewed satellite image. *Graphic by Richard Campanella using LandSat Thematic Mapper imagery.*

mitigate. "Mitigation, primarily elevating houses, is the way to achieve affordable flood insurance. . . . It is possible to remain in moderately at-risk areas using engineered mitigation efforts, combined with land use planning that restricts development in high-risk areas."

Without these interventions, folks outside of metro New Orleans's improved levee system will bear the brunt of mounting risk. Those inside will also see effects. Roughly half of metro-area residents live within lower-lying, higher-risk "A" flood zones, where houses must be certified to be raised above base flood elevation (BFE) before flood insurance may be acquired and a mortgage secured. Houses in "B" zones, which have a lower 0.2 percent chance of flooding, do not need elevation certificates to qualify for flood insurance, which adds not only to their safety but to their value. Thus the importance of natural topography—one of the premier "concessionist" arguments a decade ago.

Historians in the future will probably understand why we ended up reopening the full urban footprint after Katrina; it would have been legally complex, fiscally exorbitant, socially divisive, and politically contentious to shrink it. And doing so probably would have increased housing costs, squeezed out the poor, and exacerbated neighborhood gentrification.

But geographers may be less forgiving. As our land sinks further, as sea level rises, and as unknowns such as levee maintenance and certification will affect

FEMA's flood-zone and BFE calculations, risk reduction and mitigation will be-come more critical—and more costly.

The nation's willingness to pay for it, meanwhile, may grow tenuous. Indeed, it's not even a safe bet locally: witness how voters in St. Bernard, the single most thoroughly Katrina-damaged parish, defeated not once but twice a tax mill-age needed to pay for levee upkeep. That move may well increase their flood insurance.

If and when the next one hits, I hope we will revisit "the Great Footprint Debate" of a decade ago and realize that, while mitigation will improve our re-silience now and in the near future, the "maintainer" argument itself cannot be maintained forever—at which point the "concessionist" argument may be the best hedge against the "abandonists."

At least one local leader, looking back to 2005, seemed to acknowledge this. Said St. Bernard Parish President David Peralta in a 2014 interview with the *Times-Picayune*, "we probably should have shrunk the footprint of the parish at the very beginning."

KATRINA
An Alternative History—or Rather, Geography

AUTHOR'S NOTE: *This essay was written on the occasion of the tenth anniversary of Hurricane Katrina in 2015.*

When hurricanes approached New Orleans in times past, city dwellers generally did not worry about Katrina-like surge flooding; wind was their major concern. Nor did they evacuate the city; indeed, coastal denizens would flock *to* New Orleans, not away from it, and locals took shelter in sturdy buildings if they left home at all. New Orleanians in the 1800s saved their deepest fears for far deadlier and more destructive disasters of epidemics, fires, and Mississippi River floods, in that order.

Today it's the exact opposite. We no longer worry about river floods, and fret no more or less about fire and disease than Americans elsewhere. But as for hur-ricanes, we now dread their fatal surges much more so than their winds, and join our coastal neighbors in fleeing the entire region when a big one approaches.

What changed was our environment, courtesy of our actions. We scored and scoured the coastal wetlands with oil, gas, and navigation canals, allowing saltwater to intrude and marshes to erode. We drained the backswamp, which caused it to sink below sea level, and encouraged its urbanization without ensuring sturdy flood protection. We put the Mississippi River in a straitjacket of artificial levees, and inadvertently starved the deltaic plain of its two most critical resources, fresh water and sediment. We viewed every drop of rainwater falling within the metropolis as an enemy, and strove (less than successfully) to pump every drop out, rather than storing as much as possible on the landscape and letting it recharge the groundwater. We abandoned our architectural tradition of building houses raised on piers in favor of poured concrete slabs flush with the ground, such that water accumulation in the street became water in our homes.

In sum, we imposed engineering and architectural rigidity on a deltaic environment that is fundamentally fluid, and convinced ourselves we had mastered it even as it collapsed.

Make no mistake: the catastrophe of ten years ago can be blamed, proximately at least, on the failure of under-funded, under-engineered federal levees and floodwalls in the face of a very powerful storm surge. But ultimately, the Katrina deluge happened because a century of environmental degradation made the task of preventing that deluge more and more difficult.

I offer here an "alternative history"—that is, a geography of New Orleans that might have been, had we made different decisions over the past century.

Imagine, for example, if we had never drained the backswamp in the early 1900s, and places like Metairie, Lakeview, Gentilly, New Orleans East, and the fringes of the West Bank remained swamp and marsh. One might argue we'd have missed the growth opportunities enjoyed by rival American cities and ended up a smaller metropolis, perhaps the size of Mobile or Pensacola. All the great family stories and local culture of those neighborhoods would not have played out in those spaces, and we might be the lesser for it today.

But one could also argue that, undrained, metro New Orleans would still be above sea level and buffered by expansive wetlands. If any of Katrina's surge made it upon the landscape, it would have flooded uninhabited wetlands—and barely, because they would not have been bowl-shaped in their topography and able to impound water. Katrina would have been a windy day, not a lethal catastrophe. We'd be living on a sinuous urban footprint, following the shape of the Mississippi, at higher population densities and entirely on higher ground.

What if we never dug those canals across thousands of linear miles of coastal Louisiana? The region would have been deprived of much of the wealth and jobs produced by two of its largest industries, petroleum and port commerce. But it would also have benefited from well over a thousand additional square miles of coastal wetlands which have otherwise eroded. There would have been no Mississippi River–Gulf Outlet Canal (MR-GO) to allow saltwater to intrude, no "funnel" at the juncture of the Intracoastal Waterway and the MR-GO, and no Industrial Canal to bring seawater along adjacent neighborhoods. Katrina's surge would have had no eastern ingress, and instead would have encountered friction as it moved across healthier marshes. Cypress swamps which never would have died would have thwarted the surge's advance.

What if we placed our circa-1900 drainage pumps at the lakefront perimeter, rather than in the interior? The Seventeenth Street, Orleans Avenue, and London Avenue outfall canals would have been designed to flow below grade level; there would have been no flood walls to rupture, and thus no floodwaters in Metairie and Gentilly.

What if we had developed an "open" drainage system a hundred years ago, one which stored runoff on the landscape, like those in Rotterdam and Amsterdam? We would have had less subsidence and a whole lot fewer nuisance floods from heavy downpours.

What if we had built all houses above the grade, as we did historically? There would have been substantially less damage from Katrina's flood, and we'd all be enjoying lower flood insurance rates today.

And what if the U.S. Army Corps of Engineers had built suitable levees, if Congress had adequately funded them, and if local authorities had properly inspected them? You wouldn't be reading this essay right now.

"Alternative history" gets us nowhere in remaking the decisions of times past. But it does encourage us to think long and hard before repeating past decisions that have since yielded more costs than benefits.

May we drain, levee, and urbanize no more wetlands on this deltaic plain.

May we dig no more canals except for those needed for coastal restoration.

May we mitigate the impact of future disasters by building above the grade, raising existing houses, strengthening architectural codes, and ensuring evacuation is available for everyone.

May we prioritize for radical coastal restoration, using all tactics available as soon as possible.

May we recognize that difficult decisions lay ahead, and that there is no way we can sustain this region into the twenty-second century without returning parts of it to nature in the twenty-first.

WHEN DISASTERS "WIPE THE SLATE CLEAN"— AND WHEN THEY DON'T

It was a metaphor invoked repeatedly in late 2005, by well-meaning citizen-activists as well as professional planners: while the Katrina flood destroyed so much of what was good, it also "wiped the slate clean" of entrenched problems and offered a valuable opportunity to get things right. Now we could finally rebuild sustainably, diversify the economy, and rectify old social wrongs.

Mostly, that did not happen. The grandest recovery plans all flopped, and the boldest visions never got past the envisioning stage. The region's pre-storm shape, form, and infrastructure largely returned, and we've generally resettled in the same patterns, albeit in varying densities.

To be sure, much has changed. There are thousands of new faces amongst our smaller population; neighborhoods like Bywater and Freret Street feel markedly different; and reforms have been enacted in everything from levee standards and building codes to tax assessments and public schools. But the larger metropolitan cityscape—the very element most damaged by the deluge—has endured, so much so that one must inspect closely a satellite image of the city before being able to tell if was captured in 2004 versus 2014.

To explain why no fundamental urban reconfigurations occurred, it helps to revisit a historical disaster that really did precipitate a radical transformation. Comparing its circumstances to that of the Katrina aftermath sheds light on when disasters wipe the slate clean—and when they do not.

The year was 1722, and the four-year-old city of New Orleans, in the words of one eyewitness, "made a very contemptible figure[:] about a hundred forty barracks [and] a few inconsiderable houses, scattered up and down, without any order or regularity." This was not Governor Bienville's original vision; after establishing the city in 1718, he had attempted to guide early development by surveying a baseline about seven hundred feet from the river, between and parallel to today's

Chartres and Royal streets. Angled southwest-to-northeast, the 37-degree line fronted a sharp river bend and faced approaching ship traffic, behind which the city would be laid out.

That rudimentary baseline, however, failed to prevent early urbanization from occurring in a rather desultory fashion, the result of economic and political uncertainty in both France and Louisiana as well as tough local environmental conditions. These and other factors persuaded authorities in Paris in 1719 to designate Biloxi and not New Orleans as company headquarters and colony capital. Dutifully, chief engineer Louis-Pierre Le Blond de la Tour proceeded to design plans for the new coastal capital, and later dispatched his assistant Adrien de Pauger to draw up secondary plans for New Orleans.

Pauger arrived at New Orleans in March 1721 and proceeded to study the terrain. He soon came to realize that Bienville's baseline, set so far back from the river, needlessly squandered valuable high ground and proposed to move it to today's Decatur Street. Inspired by Le Blond de la Tour's plan for Biloxi, Pauger next proceeded to sketch a beautiful six-by-eleven-block orthogonal grid with a centerpiece *place d'armes* fronted by institutions of church and state. He then, in words he penned in a 1721 letter, "brought the town site . . . closer to [the river], being higher on the river bank, [and] to profit from the proximity of the landing place as well as to have more air from the [river] breezes." It was an enlightened design all around, and it gained official momentum when authorities in France changed their minds in December 1721 and shifted the capital from Biloxi to New Orleans.

Yet Pauger met with resistance from residents who, for the prior four years, had been erecting houses willy-nilly, many of which obstructed his projected grid. He huffed at the insolence of one man who "wanted to build as he saw fit, without regularity and without plan," and nearly came to blows with an enraged housewife—and narrowly escaped a duel with her husband—when his straight streets intersected her irregular lot. Pauger went so far as to produce a map illustrating the conflicts to his superiors.

Then, on the morning of September 11, 1722, nature resolved Pauger's problem. "A great wind" swept the settlement, Pauger wrote in documents found by architectural historian Samuel Wilson, "followed an hour later by the most terrible tempest and hurricane that could ever be seen." "With this impetuous wind came such torrents of rain," wrote a colonist named Dumont, "that you could not step out a moment without risk of being drowned[;] it rooted up the largest trees, and the birds, unable to keep up, fell in the streets."

New Orleans's first hurricane destroyed or damaged thirty-four houses plus all ships, cargo, and most infrastructure—a disaster by anyone's definition. But it also represented a golden opportunity for Pauger. "All these buildings were old and provisionally built, and not a single one in the alignment of the new city," he wrote, "and thus would have had to be demolished [without] any great misfortune . . . except that we must act to put all the people in shelter."

Pauger got to work executing his vision. Dumont later recalled how, over the next few months, the engineers "cleared a pretty long and wide strip [now Decatur Street] along the river, to put in execution the plan, [tracing] on the ground the streets and quarters which were to form the new town." The original city of New Orleans—today's French Quarter—was born, and it was after 1722, according to Dumont, that "New Orleans began to assume the appearance of a city."

What can we learn from the disasters of 1722 and 2005 and our relationship to this place we call home? The 1722 storm really did wipe the slate clean, figuratively speaking, because the four preceding years of place-making proved too brief a period of time for residents to inscribe substantial economic or psychological value into these swampy soils. A few dozen damaged or destroyed hovels were hardly worth fighting to rebuild identically, and any loss of economic value would have been likely offset by that which a better-designed city would generate. The promise of a better future, in short, trumped reversion to a brief and mediocre past.

Contrast this with the experience after Hurricane Katrina, by which time nearly three hundred years of prior investment had created a vast wellspring of place-based value. That value took fiscal and economic forms—real estate, home equity, jobs, institutions, infrastructure, priceless art and architecture—but it also took the form of culture, social relationships, historical memory, and, perhaps most importantly, the sort of emotional attachments that geographer Yi-Fu Tuan described as "topophilia": love of place.

In a rustic outpost only four years old, a single morning of gusting rain proved enough to wipe all this away and pave the way for a major urban overhaul. But in 2005, in a metropolis 287 years old, even ten feet of fast-moving seawater could not wash away this repository of civic wealth. Once those fatal waters were pumped out, centuries' worth of inscribed values blossomed back to life.

The parallels, of course, are imperfect. Early French colonial New Orleans was a project of a private company backed by an imperial monarchy, not to mention a slave society, and while citizen resistance could be outspoken at times, authority generally prevailed. After Pauger had a house demolished because it "was not in alignment of the street," for example, the angry owner sought indemnification.

Instead, "Mr. Pauger sent to find him and, after having regaled him with a volley of blows with a stick, had him put in prison, with irons on his feet."

That's not the sort of public engagement we aspire to today, as officials are compelled to hear the citizens who elect them. In the momentous autumn and winter of 2005–6, those citizens voiced their views and stated their values—and, easily withstanding Katrina's surging waters, those place-based values filled slate, after slate, after slate.

NEW ORLEANS AS METAPHOR

AUTHOR'S NOTE: *This essay was penned as a guest editorial in January 2010, during that exciting fortnight after the New Orleans Saints won the National Football Conference championship game but before winning the Super Bowl. This turn-of-the-decade era, only five years after the Hurricane Katrina catastrophe, proved to be a turning point in postdiluvian history, before which the civic mood was gloomy, and after which confidence prevailed.*

Metaphors relate unfamiliar or abstract concepts to things that are known and concrete. The local lexicon abounds in them: New Orleanians have adopted various metaphors to describe the adventures of the post-Katrina era, while outside observers have adopted New Orleans itself as a metaphor for troubling worldwide trends. Only recently have these "place metaphors" become positive and inspiring— and that's where the Saints come marching in.

Think of the vocabulary of the past five years. We used the metaphor "wiped the slate clean" to describe (erroneously, as it turned out) the effect of the floodwaters on the cityscape. We spoke of "the green dot map," "shrinking the footprint," and the "jack-o-lantern effect" to grapple rhetorically with the bitterly controversial proposal to close down certain neighborhoods (which didn't happen), and the problematic pattern of piecemeal recovery (which did). "Sliver by the river" and "the bowl" became geographical and topographical metaphors. "Chocolate city" and "brain gain" became demographic metaphors. "The chicken-and-egg problem" described the dilemma of whether businesses should reopen in depopulated neighborhoods. Postdiluvian New Orleans became, well, awash in metaphors.

A similar tendency occurred worldwide. Countless politicians, activists, and keynote speakers have, since 2005, invoked the name of our city as a metaphor for everything from federal neglect, urban decay, environmental deterioration, and American decline to poverty, bigotry, disparity, and iniquity. Do a Google search *on* the metaphor ("New Orleans is a poster child for . . ."), and you will see New Orleans invoked *as* a metaphor for global warming, economic insecurity, urban vulnerability, "the harm done by blanket government social programs," "human arrogance in the face of nature and disregard for the environment"—and that's just the first five hits.

Pretty grim stuff.

But recently New Orleanians have metaphorically turned the tables on this rhetorical trend. Consider, for example, the poignantly enigmatic slogan, "Be a New Orleanian Wherever You Are." How interesting: here we are ascribing certain positive characteristics to the people and culture of this place, and advocating that they be recognized, appreciated, and adopted in other places. Exactly what those characteristics are goes cleverly unexplained. For some it may be love of place; for others it's festivity, creativity, musicality, *carpe diem,* or simply greeting a stranger on the street—an act, incidentally, viewed as threatening in many cities. New Orleanians as metaphors for something positive, something good, something from which the rest of the nation can benefit: now we're on the right track.

And speaking of nations, consider the "Who Dat Nation." Here we have a metaphorical nationality in which citizenship depends not on borders or birthplace, but passionate love of the Saints—and, right behind that, of New Orleans. It's no coincidence that, while the chant "Who Dat" dates back decades, the phrase "Who Dat Nation" appears to be mostly a post-Katrina phenomenon. Why? Because the cheerful defiance of adversity has universal human appeal. The Who Dat Nation defies four decades of franchise frustration, four decades of municipal decline, and, most significantly, four recent years of bad memories. "Who Dat Nation" offers an alternative to the use of New Orleans as a metaphor for despair. To those who dismiss sports as a trivial and illusionary distraction, consider the civic narratives at work here: Unity. Resilience. Optimism.

Pretty powerful stuff.

The appeal of these themes has expanded the Who Dat Nation beyond national borders. A colleague of mine in Paris informed me of the street celebrations erupting near Notre Dame "when the game finished around 4:30 a.m., which is the deadest time of night in Paris (especially on Sundays): no cars, no sounds. . . .

We biked back from the Left Bank and heard people cheering and Who-Dat-ing at the top of their lungs."

She added thoughtfully, "The interesting thing was that a lot of people were rooting for the Saints but very few actually had any ties to New Orleans."

They were being New Orleanians wherever they were—metaphorically.

SOURCE NOTES

PEOPLE, PATTERNS, AND PLACE

"A Glorious Mess: A Perceptual History of New Orleans Neighborhoods" was drawn from the author's previous research in *Bienville's Dilemma* and *Geographies of New Orleans* (University of Louisiana Press, 2006 and 2008), and appeared in the June 2014 issue of *New Orleans Magazine*.

"'A War of Races': New Orleans's Messy Municipality Era, 1836–1852" originally appeared in the author's "Cityscapes" column in NOLA.com/*The Times-Picayune*, InsideOut section, March 2016.

"'Neutral Ground': From the Political Geography of Imperialism to the Streets of New Orleans" originally appeared in the author's "Geographer's Space" column in *Louisiana Cultural Vistas*, Autumn 2015.

"Cityscapes of the New Orleans Slave Trade," which appeared in *Preservation in Print*, March–April 2013, was drawn from the author's book *Lincoln in New Orleans* (University of Louisiana Press, 2010). Readers are invited to consult this book for sources and references.

"Before Storyville: Vice Districts in Antebellum New Orleans" originally appeared in *Preservation in Print*, September–October 2015. It is drawn from the author's research published in his book *Bourbon Street: A History* (Louisiana State University Press, 2014), where readers may find sources and references.

"Uptown Serendipity: How Inaction Created Space for Eden" originally appeared in the author's "Cityscapes" column in NOLA.com/*The Times-Picayune*, InsideOut section, November 2013.

A version of "Before Tulane, Before Loyola, There Was Leland University" originally appeared in the author's "Cityscapes" column in NOLA.com/*The Times-Picayune*, InsideOut section, May 2015.

"Newspaper Row: The Formation and Dispersion of a Media District" originally appeared in *Preservation in Print*, September 2012.

"Chinatown, New Orleans" originally appeared in the author's "Cityscapes" column in NOLA.com/*The Times-Picayune*, InsideOut section, March 2015, and was based on research published in his book *Geographies of New Orleans* (University of Louisiana Press, 2006).

"Dance Halls, Supper Clubs, and 'Niteries': A Night Out in 1930s New Orleans" originally appeared in *Preservation in Print*, May 2013.

"Origins of the Go-Cup: A Historical Geography of Public Drinking" first appeared in the author's "Cityscapes" column in NOLA.com/*The Times-Picayune*, InsideOut section, July 2014.

"Gentrification and Its Discontents: Notes from New Orleans" was originally published in *New Geography*, March 2013.

"Mapping the Geography of Cool" first appeared in the author's "Cityscapes" column in NOLA.com/*The Times-Picayune*, InsideOut section, 2014.

A version of "Monkey Hill and the Geography of Childhood" originally appeared in the author's "Cityscapes" column in NOLA.com/*The Times-Picayune,* InsideOut section, July 2014.

ARCHITECTURAL GEOGRAPHIES AND THE BUILT ENVIRONMENT

"On Importation and Adaptation: Creole Architecture in New Orleans" originally appeared in the author's "Cityscapes" column in NOLA.com/*The Times-Picayune,* April 2016, and is based on the research and analysis presented in the author's 2006 book, *Geographies of New Orleans* (University of Louisiana Press).

"Shotgun Geography: Theories on a Distinctive Domicile" originally appeared in the author's "Cityscapes" column in NOLA.com/*The Times-Picayune,* 2013, and derives in part from research presented in the author's 2006 book, *Geographies of New Orleans* (University of Louisiana Press), where readers may find sources and references.

"Neoclassicism Comes to the Creole City: Greek Revival Architecture in New Orleans" originally appeared in the author's "Cityscapes" column in NOLA.com/*The Times-Picayune,* May 2016.

"Between Beautiful and Sublime: Italianate Architecture in New Orleans" originally appeared in the author's "Cityscapes" column in NOLA.com/*The Times-Picayune,* June 2016.

"The Reimportation of Richardson Romanesque" originally appeared in the author's "Cityscapes" column in NOLA.com/*The Times-Picayune,* July 2016.

"Touro's Will: The Unexpected Life and Fiery Death of a Gothic Landmark" originally appeared in the author's "Cityscapes" column in NOLA.com/*The Times-Picayune,* August 2016.

"Ornaments to the City": Late-Victorian Architecture in New Orleans" originally appeared in the author's "Cityscapes" column in NOLA.com/*The Times-Picayune,* September 2016.

"California, Here It Came: Golden State Architecture in the Crescent City" originally appeared in the author's "Cityscapes" column in NOLA.com/*The Times-Picayune,* October 2016.

"When New Orleans Embraced Modernism—and Why It Stopped" originally appeared in the author's "Cityscapes" column in NOLA.com/*The Times-Picayune,* November 2016.

"The Ursuline Nuns' Lost Landmark on the Mississippi, 1824–1912" originally appeared in *Preservation in Print,* December 2015.

"Lessons Learned from the Delord-Sarpy House, 1814–1957" originally appeared in *Preservation in Print,* November 2015.

"If the Saints Lose, Don't Blame the Girod Street Cemetery" originally appeared in the author's "Cityscapes" column in NOLA.com/*The Times-Picayune,* InsideOut section, December 2014.

"The St. Louis and the St. Charles: New Orleans's Legacy of Showcase Exchange Hotels" originally appeared in *Preservation in Print,* April 2015.

"The Poydras and Pilié Markets, 1838–1932" originally appeared in *Preservation in Print,* December 2016.

"A Storied Gem Lost to Pyromania: Gallier and Dakin's Merchants' Exchange" originally appeared in *Preservation in Print,* September 2016.

"King Cotton's Crescent City Throne: The New Orleans Cotton Exchange, 1871–1964" is drawn in part from the author's research appearing in *Time and Place in New Orleans: Past Geographies in the Present Day* (Pelican Publishing Co., 2002), where readers may find sources and references.

"If Walls Could Talk, This Starbucks Would Speak of Lincoln," drawn from the author's research for his 2010 book, *Lincoln in New Orleans: The 1828–1831 Flatboat Journeys and Their Place in History* (University of Louisiana Press), appeared in *Preservation in Print*, March 2014.

"The Rise and Fall of the Old Shot Tower, 1883–1905" originally appeared in the author's "Cityscapes" column in NOLA.com/*The Times-Picayune*, InsideOut section, April 2014.

"'Ominous': The Old Criminal Courts Building and a Brief History of Penal Architecture" originally appeared in *Preservation in Print*, April 2016.

"Court Decisions: The Neighborhood Rivalry behind Two Massive Government Buildings" appeared in the author's "Cityscapes" column in NOLA.com/*The Times-Picayune*, June 2015.

"A Legacy of Luxury Lodging: The Original Cosmopolitan Hotel" originally appeared in *Preservation in Print*, February 2016.

"On the Cultural Power of Preservation: The Old French Opera House" originally appeared in *Preservation in Print*, February 2013.

"150 Years after a Great Military Victory, Two Cultural Defeats" originally appeared in the author's "Cityscapes" column in NOLA.com/*The Times-Picayune*, InsideOut section, January 2015.

"Three Exhibition Halls, Three Fates" originally appeared in *Preservation in Print*, November 2014.

"Arnaud Cazenave and the Reinvention of Bourbon Street," which originally appeared in the "Cityscapes" column in NOLA.com/*The Times-Picayune*, January 2016, is drawn from research published in the author's 2014 book, *Bourbon Street: A History* (Louisiana State University Press).

"Motor City in the Crescent City: Arabi's Ford Assembly Plant" originally appeared in the author's "Cityscapes" column in NOLA.com/*The Times-Picayune*, InsideOut section, November 2014.

"In the Ashes of the LeBeau Plantation House, a Lesson in *Carpe Diem*" originally appeared in the author's "Cityscapes" column in NOLA.com/*The Times-Picayune*, InsideOut section, November 2013.

URBAN GEOGRAPHIES

"Beneath New Orleans, a Coastal Barrier Island" originally appeared in the author's "Geographer's Space" column in *Louisiana Cultural Vistas*, Winter 2016.

"Pauger's Savvy Move: How an Assistant Engineer Repositioned New Orleans on Higher Ground" originally appeared in *Preservation in Print*, May 2014.

"Why Prytania Jogs at Joseph: The Colonial Surveying System Undergirding Local Streets" originally appeared in *Preservation in Print*, October 2013.

"Things at Odd Angles Tell Interesting Tales: Explaining a Seventh Ward Urban Artifact" originally appeared in the author's "Cityscapes" column in NOLA.com/*The Times-Picayune*, InsideOut section, April 2015.

"'Fort-Prints' of the French Quarter" will appear in the author's "Cityscapes" column in NOLA.com/*The Times-Picayune* in 2017.

"The Accidental Forest" originally appeared in the author's "Cityscapes" column in NOLA.com/*The Times-Picayune*, InsideOut section, October 2015.

A version of "'So Unsavory a Smell': Managing Streets and City Services in Historic New Orleans" first appeared in *Preservation in Print*, November–December 2012.

"'A Forest of Masts': The Port of New Orleans in Antebellum Times," drawn from research first published by the author in his book *Lincoln in New Orleans* (University of Louisiana Press, 2010), first appeared in *Preservation in Print*, June 2014. Readers are directed to this book for sources and references.

"Addressing Urban Order: A History of House Numbers" originally appeared in the author's "Cityscapes" column in NOLA.com/*The Times-Picayune*, InsideOut section, January 2014.

"A 'Weird and Ghostly Appearance': The Great Light Tower Experiment" originally appeared in the author's "Cityscapes" column in NOLA.com/*The Times-Picayune*, February 2017.

"Early Aerial Perspectives of New Orleans" originally appeared in *Preservation in Print*, December 2013.

"Polymnia Street Goes to War" originally appeared in the author's "Cityscapes" column in NOLA.com/*The Times-Picayune*, InsideOut section, September 2014.

"Monorail Derailed" originally appeared in the author's "Cityscapes" column in NOLA.com /*The Times-Picayune*, InsideOut section, February 2016.

"Tunnel Vision: A Subterranean Relic beneath Canal Street" originally appeared in the author's "Cityscapes" column in NOLA.com/*The Times-Picayune*, InsideOut section, October 2014.

"The Widening of Poydras Street" originally appeared in the author's "Cityscapes" column in NOLA.com/*The Times-Picayune*, InsideOut section, December 2015.

"New Orleans East's Core Problem" originally appeared in the author's "Cityscapes" column in NOLA.com/*The Times-Picayune*, InsideOut section, December 2013.

REGIONAL GEOGRAPHIES

"Four Cadastral Fingerprints on the Louisiana Landscape" originally appeared in the author's "Geographer's Space" column in *Louisiana Cultural Vistas*, Spring 2016.

"The Ozone Belt" originally appeared in the author's "Cityscapes" column in NOLA.com/*The Times-Picayune*, July 2015.

"Coastal Louisiana Lugger Culture" originally appeared in the author's "Geographer's Space" column in *Louisiana Cultural Vistas*, Fall 2016.

"Counties, Parishes, and a Louisiana Mystery" will appear in the author's "Geographer's Space" column in *Louisiana Cultural Vistas* in 2017.

"'Forward Thrust' and the Reshaping of Southern Geography" originally appeared in the author's "Geographer's Space" column in *Louisiana Cultural Vistas*, Winter 2015.

"Louisiana Radio Stations and the (Inconvenient) Local Music Lacuna" originally appeared in the author's "Geographer's Space" column in *Louisiana Cultural Vistas*, Winter 2016.

"Louisiana Topography: Third Lowest, Third Flattest—and Most Interesting" originally appeared in the author's "Geographer's Space" column in *Louisiana Cultural Vistas*, Summer 2016.

"The Seduction of Exceptionalism" originally appeared in the author's "Past Is Prologue" column in *Louisiana Cultural Vistas*, Summer 2014.

DISASTER AND RECOVERY

"New Orleans Was Once above Sea Level" originally appeared in the author's "Cityscapes" column in NOLA.com/*The Times-Picayune*, InsideOut section, February 2015.

"A Brief History of French Quarter Flooding" originally appeared in NOLA.com/*The Times-Picayune* in February 2015.

"The Katrina of the 1800s: Sauvé's Crevasse" originally appeared in the author's "Cityscapes" column in NOLA.com/*The Times-Picayune*, InsideOut section, June 2014.

"The Great Algiers Fire of 1895" originally appeared in the author's "Cityscapes" column in NOLA.com/*The Times-Picayune*, InsideOut section, November 2015.

"When Bubonic Plague Came to Town" originally appeared in the author's "Cityscapes" column in NOLA.com/*The Times-Picayune*, InsideOut section, August 2014.

"The Great Storm of 1915" originally appeared in the author's "Cityscapes" column in NOLA.com/*The Times-Picayune*, InsideOut section, September 2015.

"One Storm, One Dilemma; Two Decisions, Two Consequences" first appeared as a guest editorial in NOLA.com/*The Times-Picayune*, September 27, 2015.

"What the Nation's Best-Educated Amateur Planners Learned from Hurricane Isaac. And Gustav. And Rita and Katrina . . ." originally appeared in *Places Journal*, 2012, placesjournal.org /article/the-nations-best-educated-amateur-planners/

"The Great Footprint Debate, Updated" first appeared as a guest editorial in NOLA.com/*The Times-Picayune* on May 31, 2015.

"Katrina: An Alternative History—or Rather, Geography" originally appeared in *Tulane: The Magazine of Tulane University*, September 2015.

"When Disasters 'Wipe the Slate Clean'—and When They Don't" first appeared in the author's "Cityscapes" column in NOLA.com/*The Times-Picayune*, InsideOut section, August 2015.

"New Orleans as Metaphor" originally appeared as a guest editorial in NOLA.com/*The Times-Picayune*, January 28, 2010.

INDEX

20 - syncretizing

23 - NOLA
    vernacular

      banquette
      red gravy
      making groceries

67 - coterminous

70 - sui generis